hapter 5

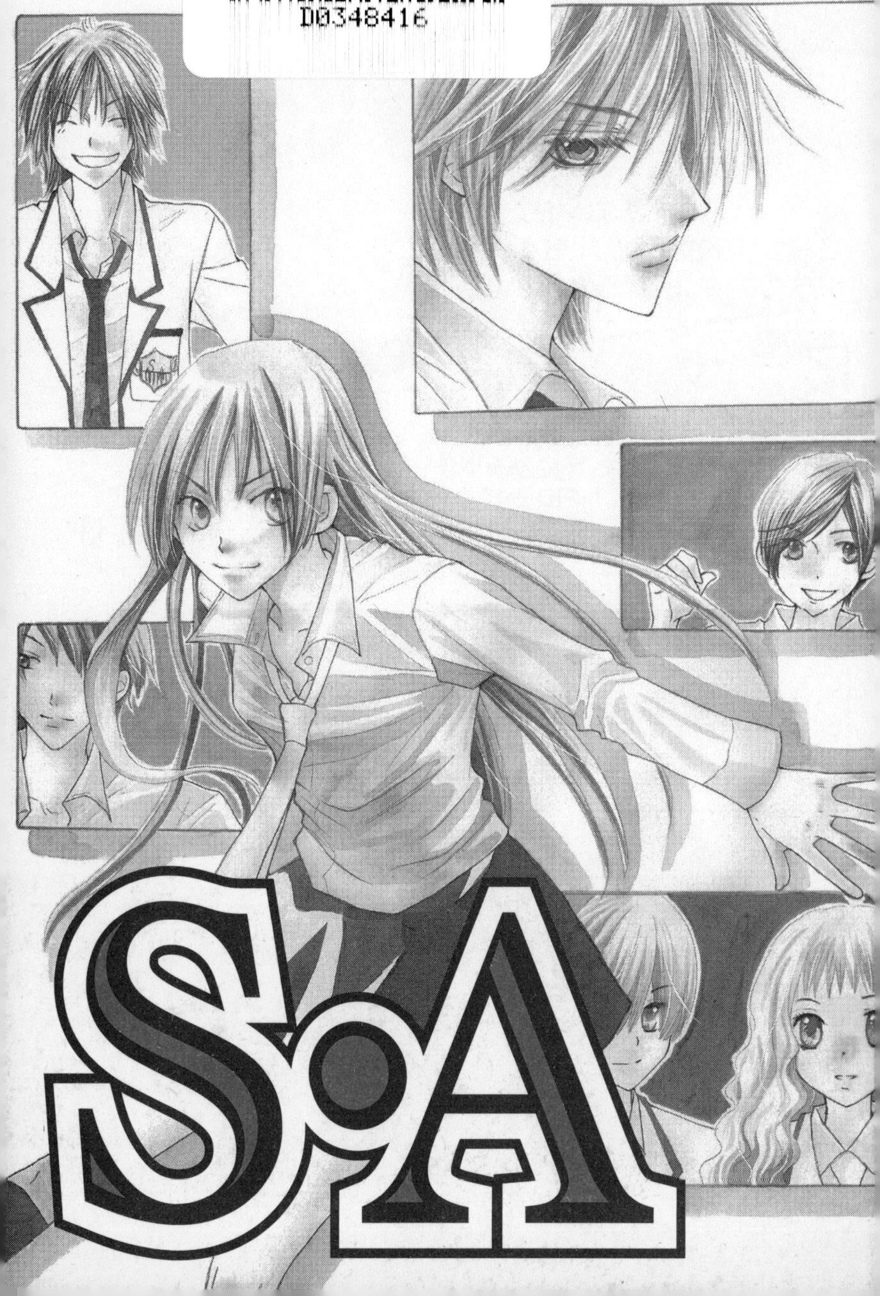
S·A

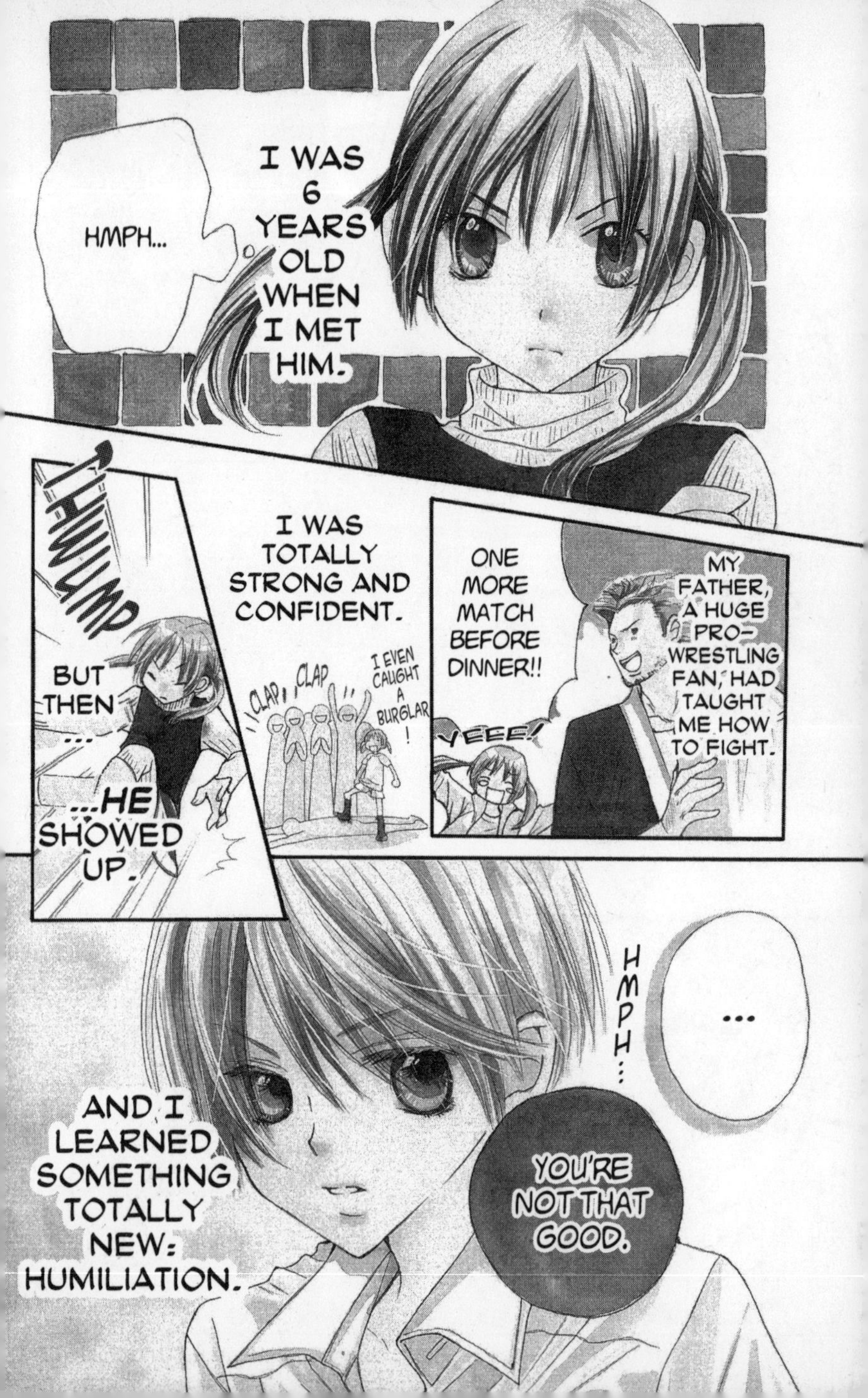
I WAS 6 YEARS OLD WHEN I MET HIM.
HMPH...
MY FATHER, A HUGE PRO-WRESTLING FAN, HAD TAUGHT ME HOW TO FIGHT.
ONE MORE MATCH BEFORE DINNER!!
YEEE!
I WAS TOTALLY STRONG AND CONFIDENT.
I EVEN CAUGHT A BURGLAR!
CLAP, CLAP
THWUMP
BUT THEN...
...HE SHOWED UP.
...
HMPH...
YOU'RE NOT THAT GOOD.
AND I LEARNED SOMETHING TOTALLY NEW: HUMILIATION.

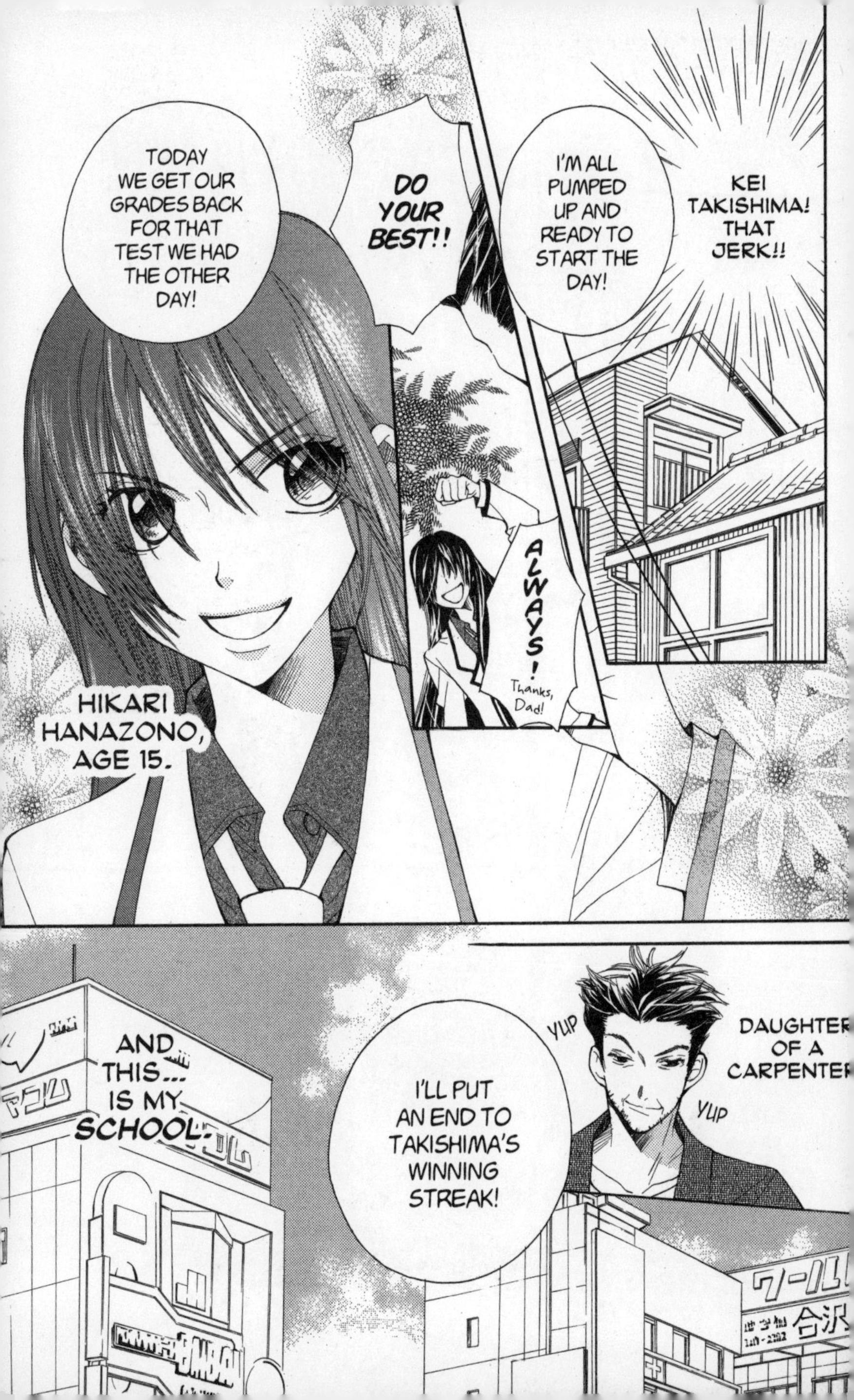
KEI TAKISHIMA! THAT JERK!!
I'M ALL PUMPED UP AND READY TO START THE DAY!
DO YOUR BEST!!
ALWAYS!
Thanks, Dad!
TODAY WE GET OUR GRADES BACK FOR THAT TEST WE HAD THE OTHER DAY!
HIKARI HANAZONO, AGE 15.
DAUGHTER OF A CARPENTER
YUP
YUP
I'LL PUT AN END TO TAKISHIMA'S WINNING STREAK!
AND THIS... IS MY SCHOOL.

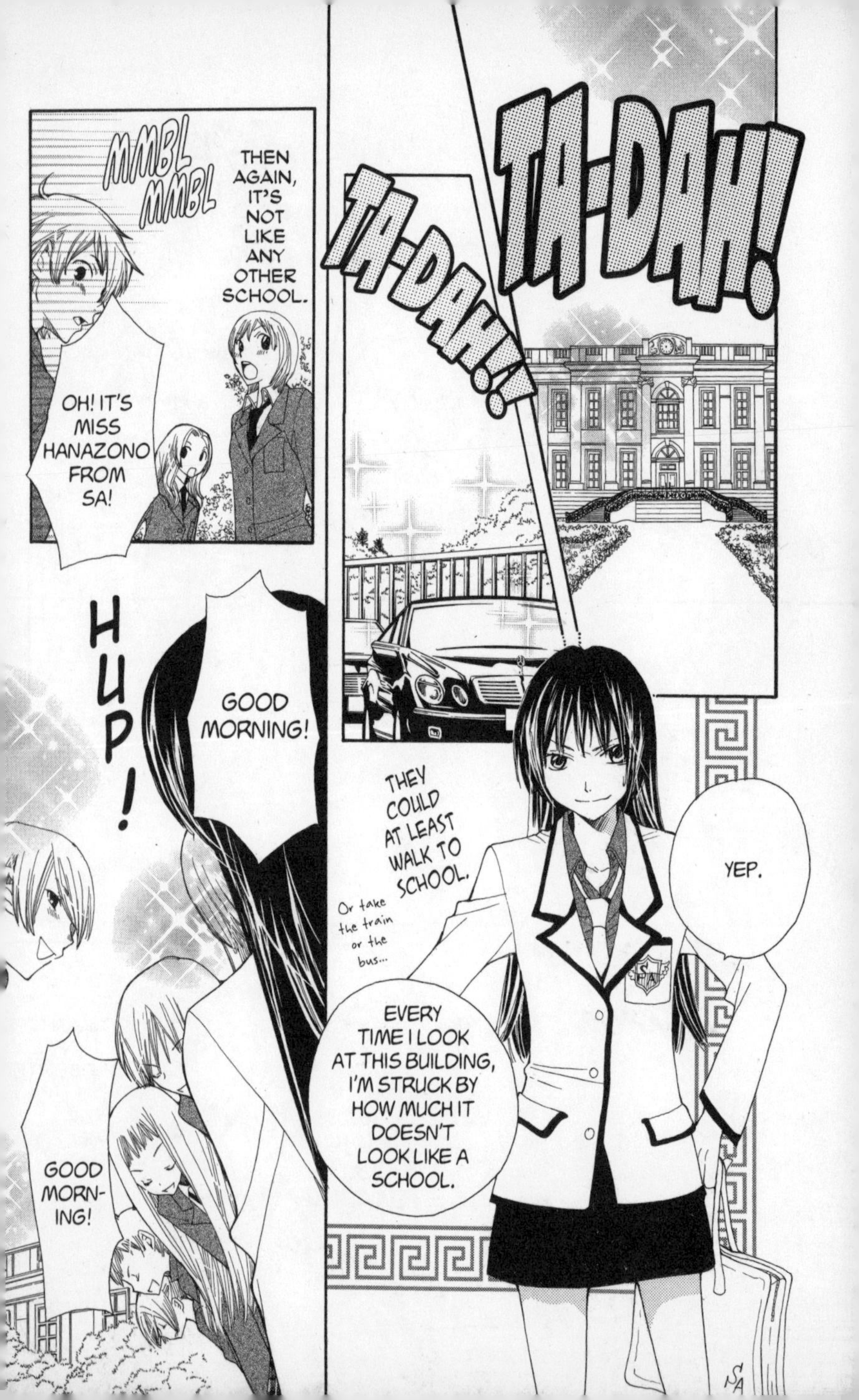
TA-DAH!
TA-DAH!!
YEP.
EVERY TIME I LOOK AT THIS BUILDING, I'M STRUCK BY HOW MUCH IT DOESN'T LOOK LIKE A SCHOOL.
THEY COULD AT LEAST WALK TO SCHOOL.
Or take the train or the bus...
MMBL MMBL
THEN AGAIN, IT'S NOT LIKE ANY OTHER SCHOOL.
OH! IT'S MISS HANAZONO FROM SA!
GOOD MORNING!
HUP!
GOOD MORN-ING!

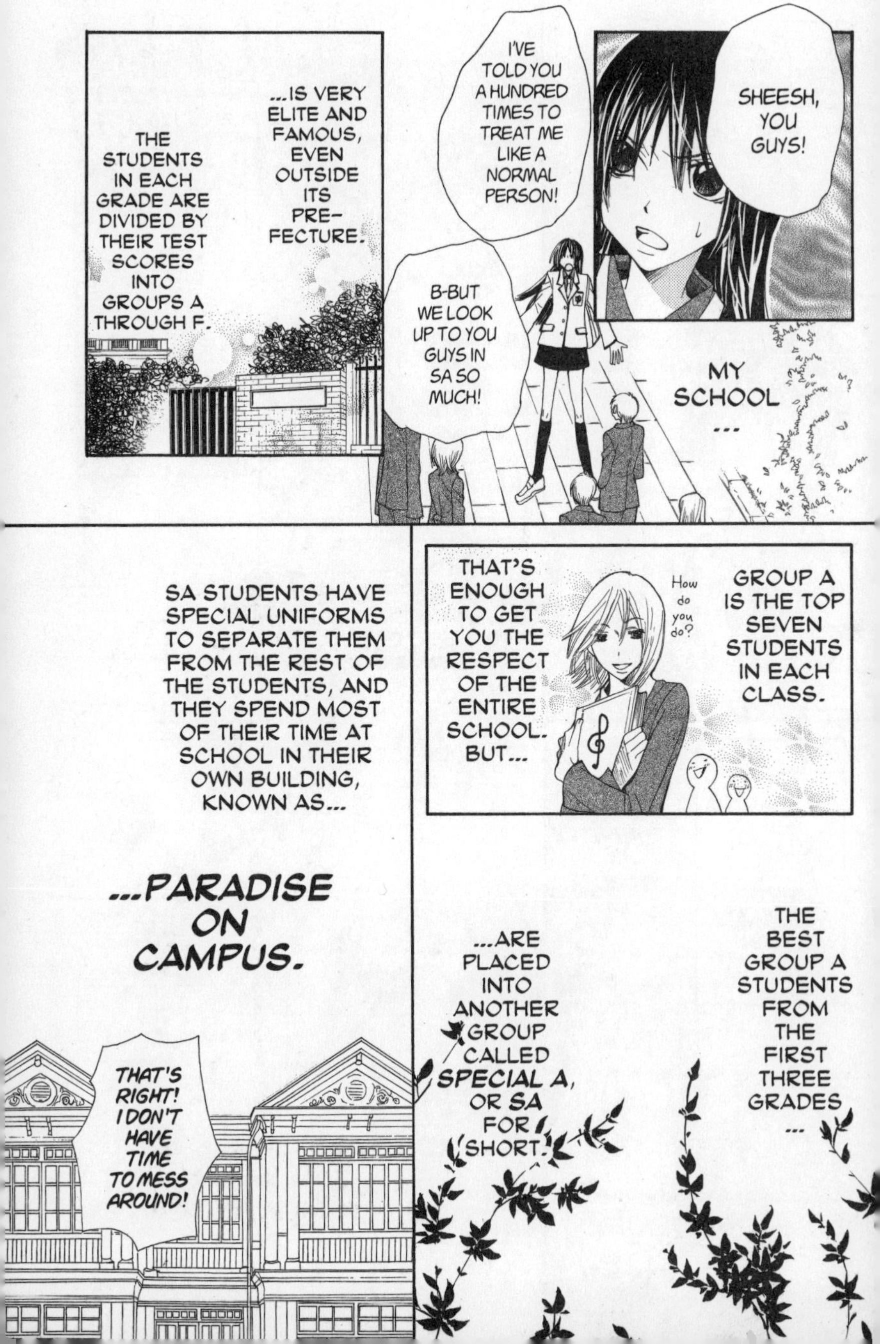
SHEESH, YOU GUYS!
I'VE TOLD YOU A HUNDRED TIMES TO TREAT ME LIKE A NORMAL PERSON!
B-BUT WE LOOK UP TO YOU GUYS IN SA SO MUCH!
MY SCHOOL ...
...IS VERY ELITE AND FAMOUS, EVEN OUTSIDE ITS PRE-FECTURE.
THE STUDENTS IN EACH GRADE ARE DIVIDED BY THEIR TEST SCORES INTO GROUPS A THROUGH F.
GROUP A IS THE TOP SEVEN STUDENTS IN EACH CLASS.
How do you do?
THAT'S ENOUGH TO GET YOU THE RESPECT OF THE ENTIRE SCHOOL. BUT...
THE BEST GROUP A STUDENTS FROM THE FIRST THREE GRADES ...
...ARE PLACED INTO ANOTHER GROUP CALLED SPECIAL A, OR SA FOR SHORT.
SA STUDENTS HAVE SPECIAL UNIFORMS TO SEPARATE THEM FROM THE REST OF THE STUDENTS, AND THEY SPEND MOST OF THEIR TIME AT SCHOOL IN THEIR OWN BUILDING, KNOWN AS...
...PARADISE ON CAMPUS.
THAT'S RIGHT! I DON'T HAVE TIME TO MESS AROUND!

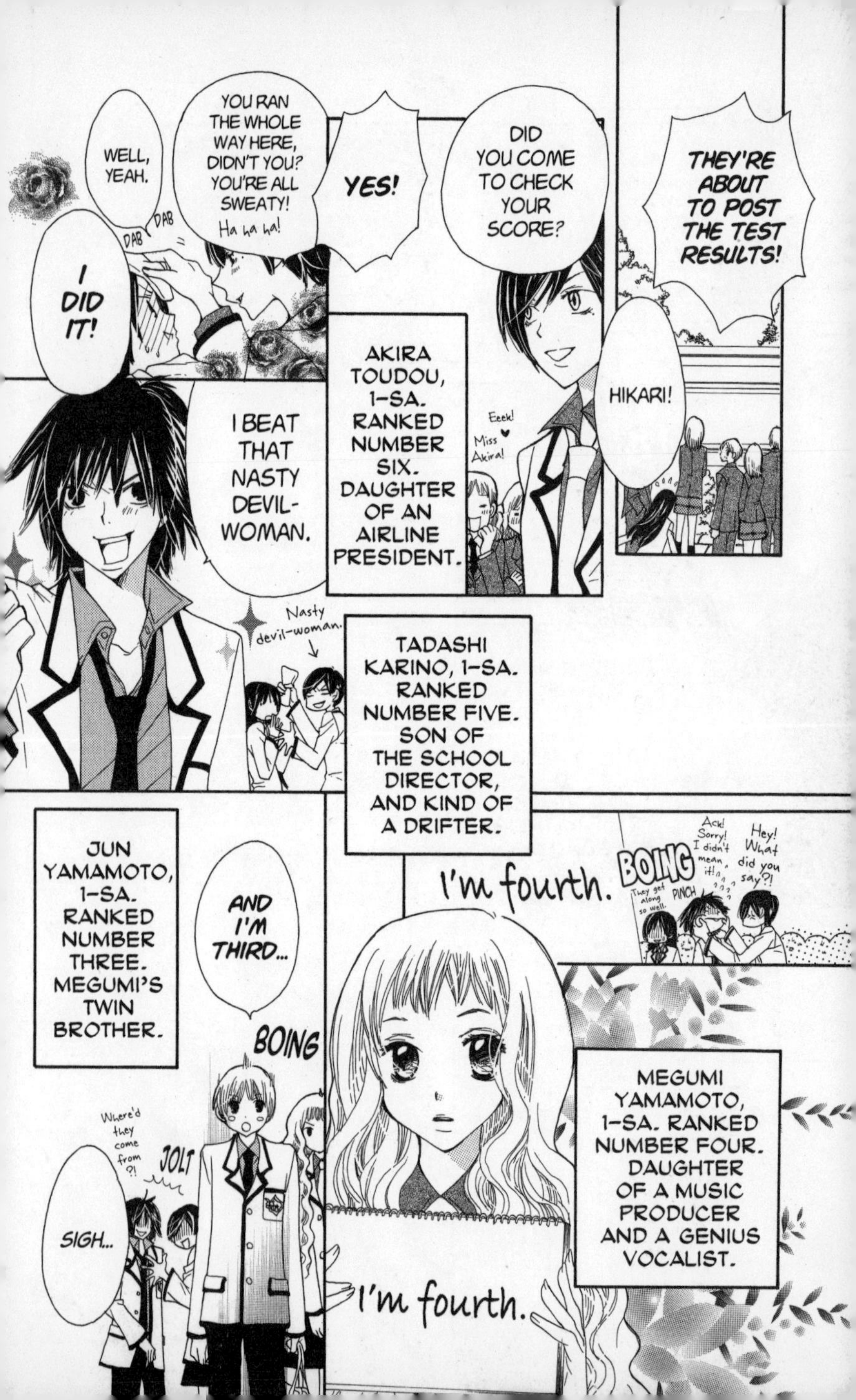
THEY'RE ABOUT TO POST THE TEST RESULTS!
HIKARI!
DID YOU COME TO CHECK YOUR SCORE?
YES!
AKIRA TOUDOU, 1-SA. RANKED NUMBER SIX. DAUGHTER OF AN AIRLINE PRESIDENT.
Eeek! Miss Akira! ♥
YOU RAN THE WHOLE WAY HERE, DIDN'T YOU? YOU'RE ALL SWEATY!
Ha ha ha!
WELL, YEAH.
DAB DAB
I DID IT!
I BEAT THAT NASTY DEVIL-WOMAN.
TADASHI KARINO, 1-SA. RANKED NUMBER FIVE. SON OF THE SCHOOL DIRECTOR, AND KIND OF A DRIFTER.
Nasty devil-woman.
Hey! What did you say?!
Ack! Sorry! I didn't mean it!
BOING
I'm fourth.
PINCH
They get along so well.
MEGUMI YAMAMOTO, 1-SA. RANKED NUMBER FOUR. DAUGHTER OF A MUSIC PRODUCER AND A GENIUS VOCALIST.
I'm fourth.
JUN YAMAMOTO, 1-SA. RANKED NUMBER THREE. MEGUMI'S TWIN BROTHER.
AND I'M THIRD...
BOING
JOLT
Where'd they come from?!
SIGH...

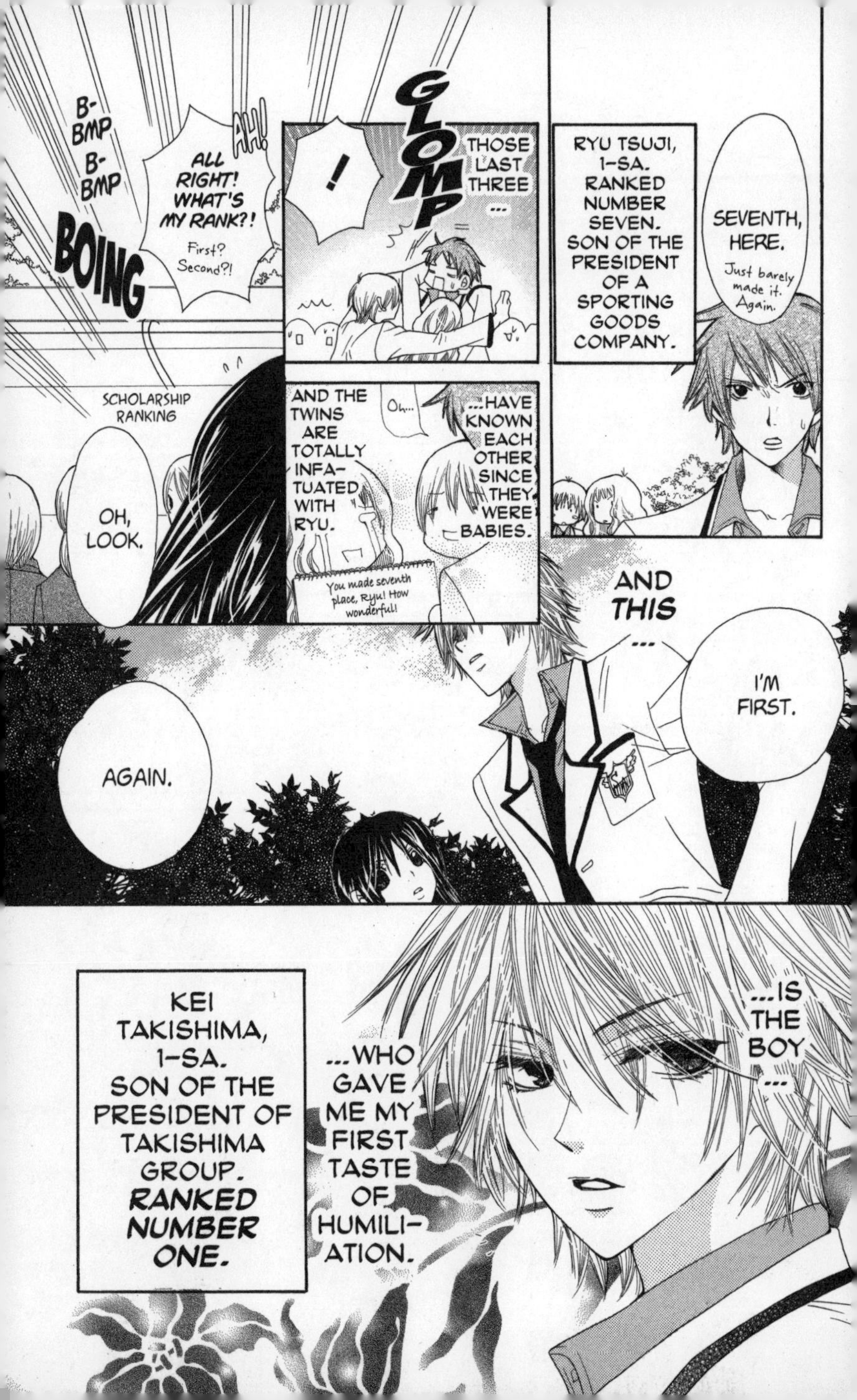
SEVENTH, HERE.
Just barely made it. Again.
RYU TSUJI, 1-SA. RANKED NUMBER SEVEN. SON OF THE PRESIDENT OF A SPORTING GOODS COMPANY.
THOSE LAST THREE ...
GLOMP
!
...HAVE KNOWN EACH OTHER SINCE THEY WERE BABIES.
Oh...
AND THE TWINS ARE TOTALLY INFATUATED WITH RYU.
You made seventh place, Ryu! How wonderful!
AH!
ALL RIGHT! WHAT'S MY RANK?!
First? Second?!
B-BMP B-BMP
BOING
SCHOLARSHIP RANKING
OH, LOOK.
AND THIS ...
I'M FIRST.
AGAIN.
...IS THE BOY ...
...WHO GAVE ME MY FIRST TASTE OF HUMILIATION.
KEI TAKISHIMA, 1-SA. SON OF THE PRESIDENT OF TAKISHIMA GROUP. RANKED NUMBER ONE.

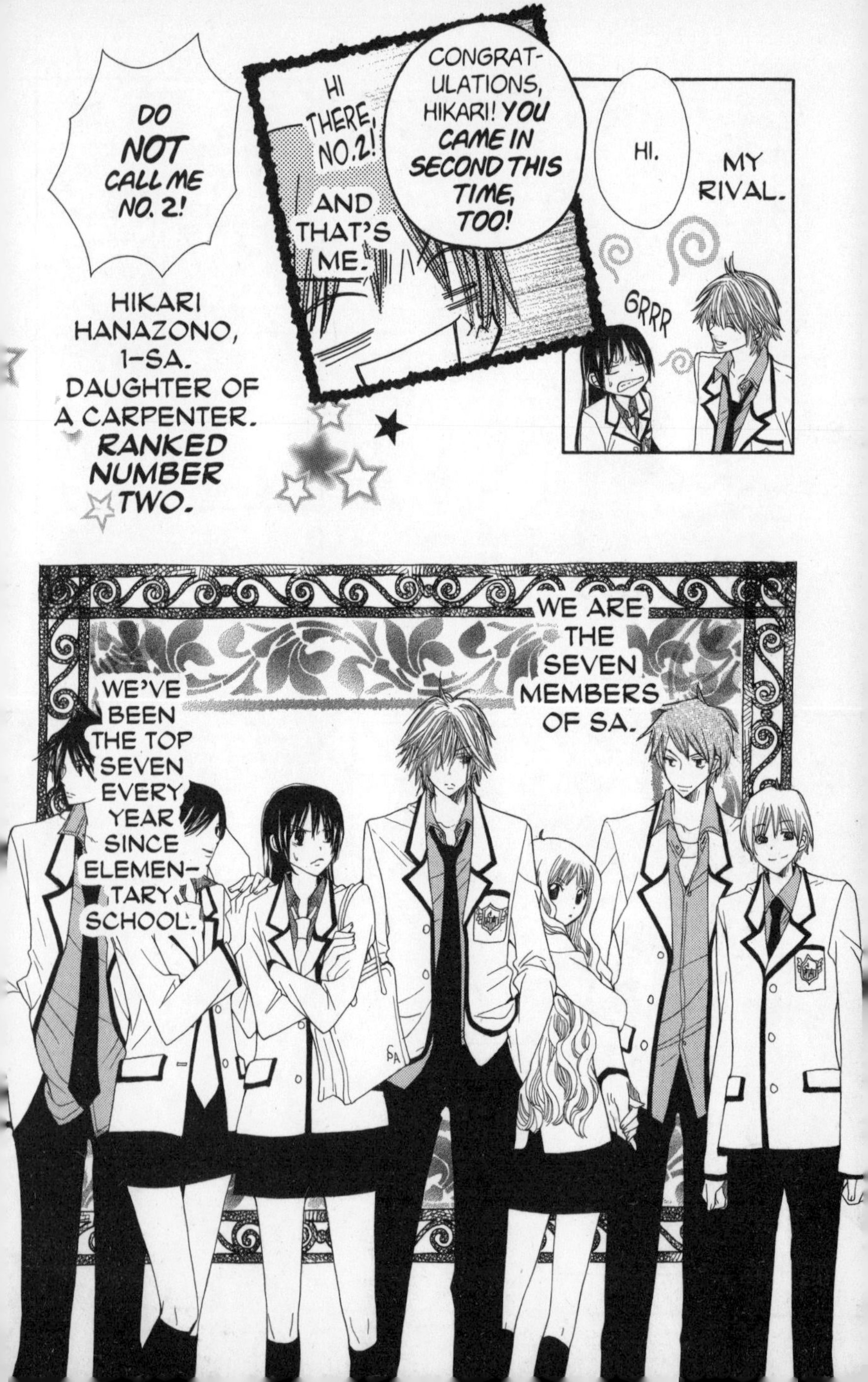
MY RIVAL.
HI.
GRRR
CONGRATULATIONS, HIKARI! YOU CAME IN SECOND THIS TIME, TOO!
HI THERE, NO.2!
AND THAT'S ME.
DO NOT CALL ME NO. 2!
HIKARI HANAZONO, 1-SA. DAUGHTER OF A CARPENTER. RANKED NUMBER TWO.
WE ARE THE SEVEN MEMBERS OF SA.
WE'VE BEEN THE TOP SEVEN EVERY YEAR SINCE ELEMENTARY SCHOOL.

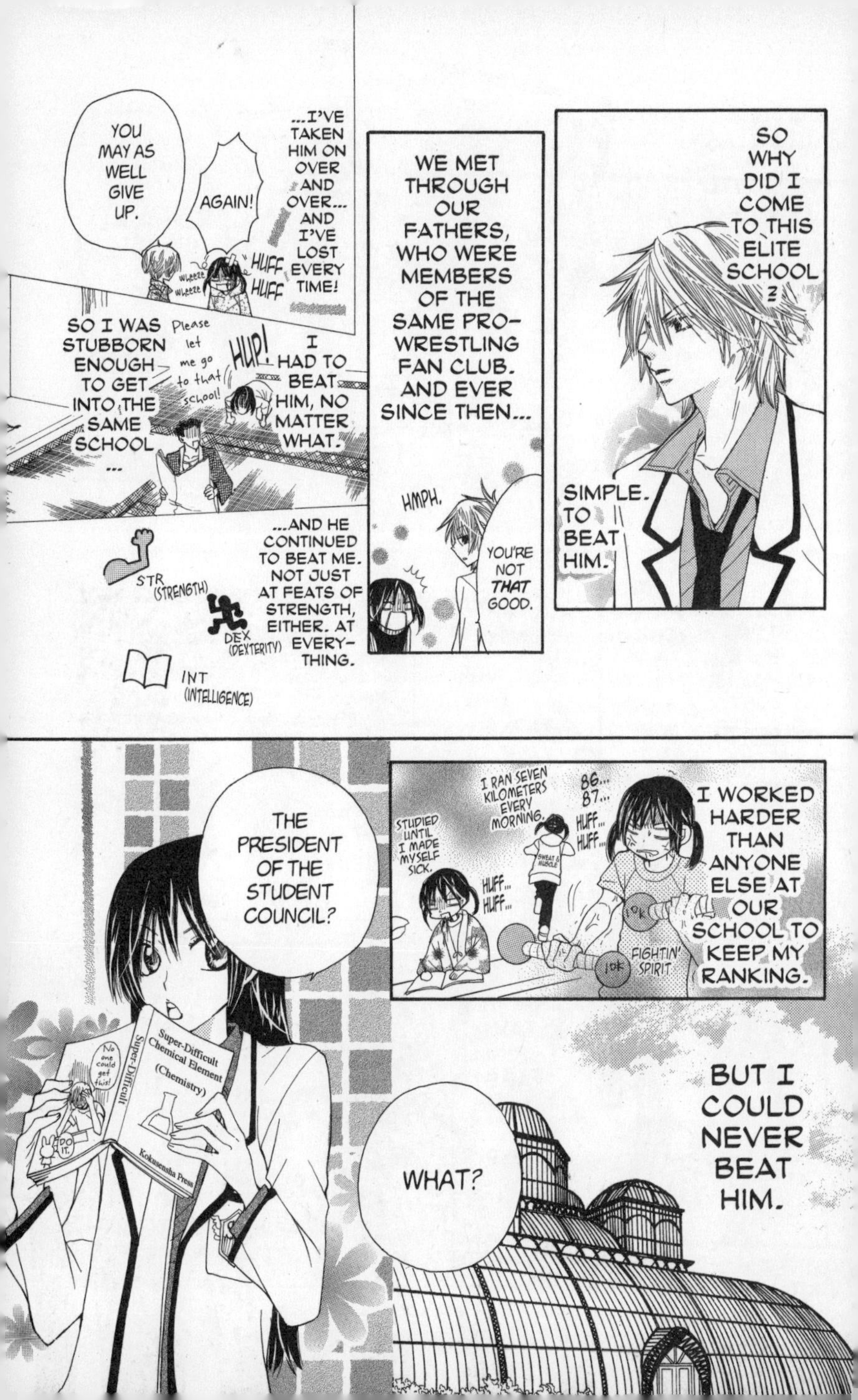
SO WHY DID I COME TO THIS ELITE SCHOOL?
SIMPLE. TO BEAT HIM.
WE MET THROUGH OUR FATHERS, WHO WERE MEMBERS OF THE SAME PRO-WRESTLING FAN CLUB. AND EVER SINCE THEN...
HMPH.
YOU'RE NOT THAT GOOD.
...I'VE TAKEN HIM ON OVER AND OVER... AND I'VE LOST EVERY TIME!
AGAIN!
YOU MAY AS WELL GIVE UP.
HUFF HUFF
wheeze wheeze
I HAD TO BEAT HIM, NO MATTER WHAT.
HUP!
Please let me go to that school!
SO I WAS STUBBORN ENOUGH TO GET INTO THE SAME SCHOOL...
...AND HE CONTINUED TO BEAT ME. NOT JUST AT FEATS OF STRENGTH, EITHER. AT EVERYTHING.
STR (STRENGTH)
DEX (DEXTERITY)
INT (INTELLIGENCE)
I WORKED HARDER THAN ANYONE ELSE AT OUR SCHOOL TO KEEP MY RANKING.
86... 87...
HUFF... HUFF...
I RAN SEVEN KILOMETERS EVERY MORNING.
SWEAT & MUSCLE
10K
FIGHTIN' SPIRIT
10K
STUDIED UNTIL I MADE MYSELF SICK.
HUFF... HUFF...
BUT I COULD NEVER BEAT HIM.
WHAT?
THE PRESIDENT OF THE STUDENT COUNCIL?
Super-Difficult Chemical Element (Chemistry)
Super-Difficult
Kokusensha Press
No one could get this!
DO IT.

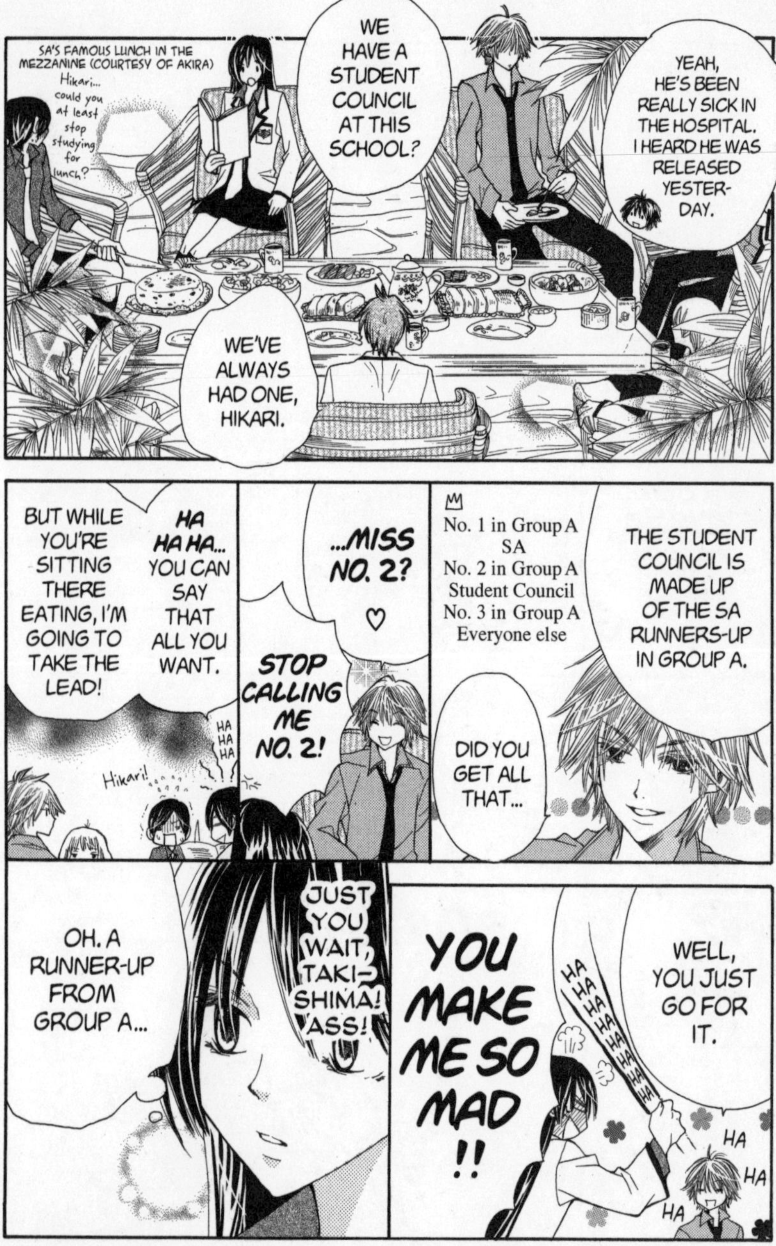
WE HAVE A STUDENT COUNCIL AT THIS SCHOOL?
YEAH, HE'S BEEN REALLY SICK IN THE HOSPITAL. I HEARD HE WAS RELEASED YESTER-DAY.
SA'S FAMOUS LUNCH IN THE MEZZANINE (COURTESY OF AKIRA)
Hikari... could you at least stop studying for lunch?
WE'VE ALWAYS HAD ONE, HIKARI.
THE STUDENT COUNCIL IS MADE UP OF THE SA RUNNERS-UP IN GROUP A.
No. 1 in Group A SA
No. 2 in Group A Student Council
No. 3 in Group A Everyone else
DID YOU GET ALL THAT...
...MISS NO. 2? ♡
STOP CALLING ME NO. 2!
HA HA HA... YOU CAN SAY THAT ALL YOU WANT.
BUT WHILE YOU'RE SITTING THERE EATING, I'M GOING TO TAKE THE LEAD!
HA HA HA
Hikari!
WELL, YOU JUST GO FOR IT.
HA HA HA HA HA HA HA HA HA
HA HA HA
YOU MAKE ME SO MAD!!
JUST YOU WAIT, TAKI-SHIMA! ASS!
OH. A RUNNER-UP FROM GROUP A...

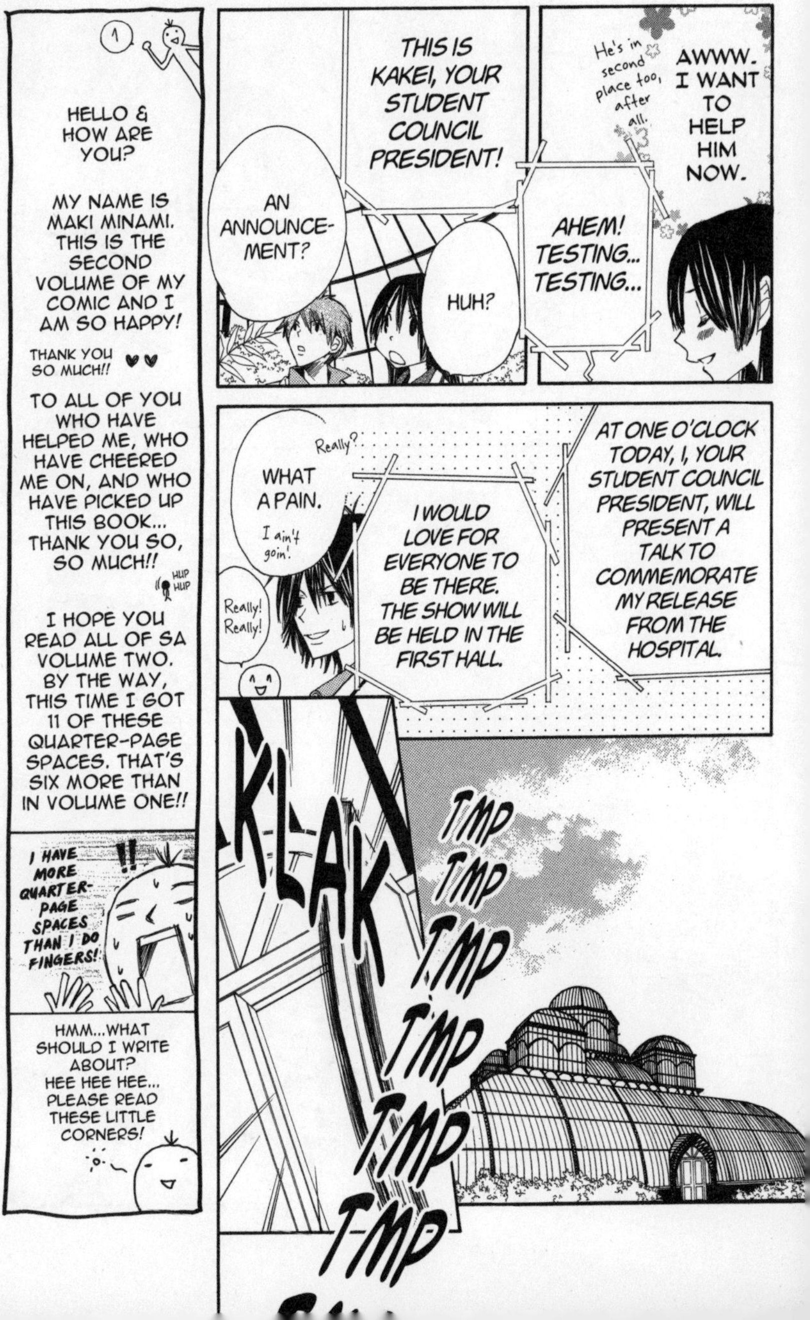
AWWW. I WANT TO HELP HIM NOW.
He's in second place too, after all.
AHEM! TESTING... TESTING...
THIS IS KAKEI, YOUR STUDENT COUNCIL PRESIDENT!
AN ANNOUNCE-MENT?
HUH?
AT ONE O'CLOCK TODAY, I, YOUR STUDENT COUNCIL PRESIDENT, WILL PRESENT A TALK TO COMMEMORATE MY RELEASE FROM THE HOSPITAL.
I WOULD LOVE FOR EVERYONE TO BE THERE. THE SHOW WILL BE HELD IN THE FIRST HALL.
WHAT A PAIN.
Really?
I ain't goin'.
Really! Really!
TMP TMP TMP TMP TMP TMP TMP
KLAK
1
HELLO & HOW ARE YOU?
MY NAME IS MAKI MINAMI. THIS IS THE SECOND VOLUME OF MY COMIC AND I AM SO HAPPY!
THANK YOU SO MUCH!!
TO ALL OF YOU WHO HAVE HELPED ME, WHO HAVE CHEERED ME ON, AND WHO HAVE PICKED UP THIS BOOK... THANK YOU SO, SO MUCH!!
HUP HUP
I HOPE YOU READ ALL OF SA VOLUME TWO. BY THE WAY, THIS TIME I GOT 11 OF THESE QUARTER-PAGE SPACES. THAT'S SIX MORE THAN IN VOLUME ONE!!
I HAVE MORE QUARTER-PAGE SPACES THAN I DO FINGERS!
!!
HMM...WHAT SHOULD I WRITE ABOUT? HEE HEE HEE... PLEASE READ THESE LITTLE CORNERS!

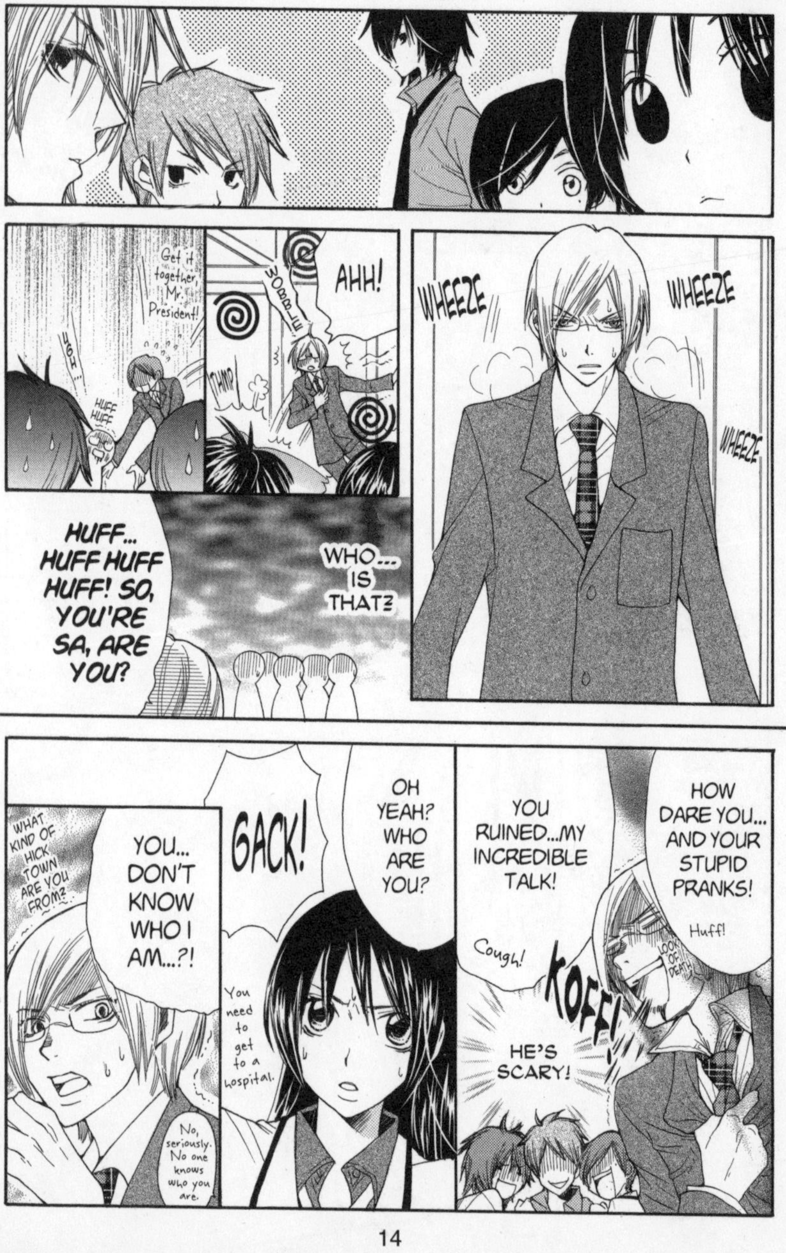
WHEEZE
WHEEZE
WHEEZE
AHH!
WOBBLE
THMP
Get it together, Mr. President!
UGH...
HUFF HUFF
WHO... IS THAT?
HUFF... HUFF HUFF HUFF! SO, YOU'RE SA, ARE YOU?
HOW DARE YOU... AND YOUR STUPID PRANKS!
Huff!
LOOK OF DEATH
YOU RUINED...MY INCREDIBLE TALK!
KOFF!
Cough!
HE'S SCARY!
OH YEAH? WHO ARE YOU?
GACK!
You need to get to a hospital.
YOU... DON'T KNOW WHO I AM...?!
WHAT KIND OF HICK TOWN ARE YOU FROM?
No, seriously. No one knows who you are.

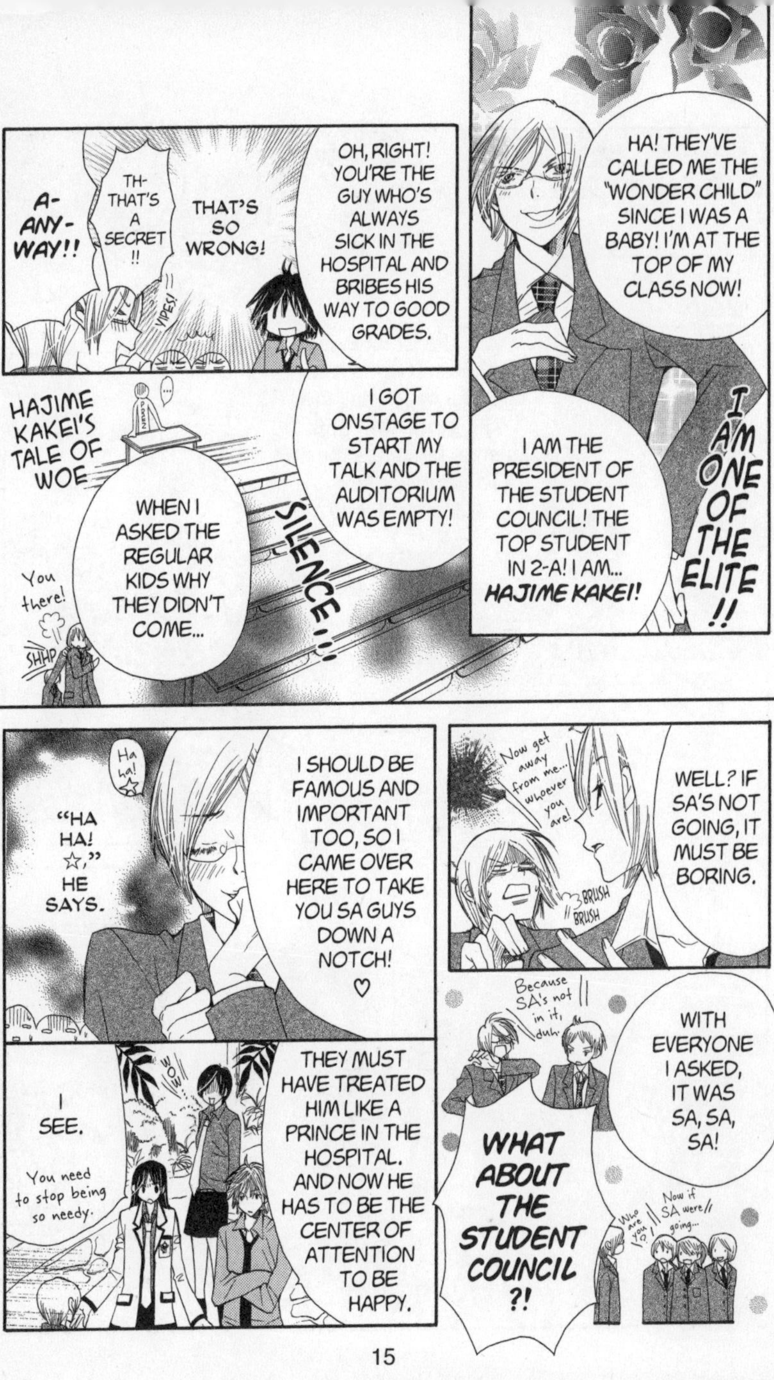
HA! THEY'VE CALLED ME THE "WONDER CHILD" SINCE I WAS A BABY! I'M AT THE TOP OF MY CLASS NOW!
I AM THE PRESIDENT OF THE STUDENT COUNCIL! THE TOP STUDENT IN 2-A! I AM... HAJIME KAKEI!
I AM ONE OF THE ELITE!!
OH, RIGHT! YOU'RE THE GUY WHO'S ALWAYS SICK IN THE HOSPITAL AND BRIBES HIS WAY TO GOOD GRADES.
THAT'S SO WRONG!
TH- THAT'S A SECRET!!
YIPES!
A- ANY- WAY!!
I GOT ONSTAGE TO START MY TALK AND THE AUDITORIUM WAS EMPTY!
SILENCE!!
HAJIME KAKEI'S TALE OF WOE
WHEN I ASKED THE REGULAR KIDS WHY THEY DIDN'T COME...
You there!
SHHP
WELL? IF SA'S NOT GOING, IT MUST BE BORING.
Now get away from me... whoever you are!
BRUSH BRUSH
I SHOULD BE FAMOUS AND IMPORTANT TOO, SO I CAME OVER HERE TO TAKE YOU SA GUYS DOWN A NOTCH! ♡
Ha ha! ☆
"HA HA! ☆," HE SAYS.
WITH EVERYONE I ASKED, IT WAS SA, SA, SA!
Because SA's not in it, duh.
Now if SA were going...
Who are you?
WHAT ABOUT THE STUDENT COUNCIL?!
THEY MUST HAVE TREATED HIM LIKE A PRINCE IN THE HOSPITAL. AND NOW HE HAS TO BE THE CENTER OF ATTENTION TO BE HAPPY.
WOW
I SEE.
You need to stop being so needy.

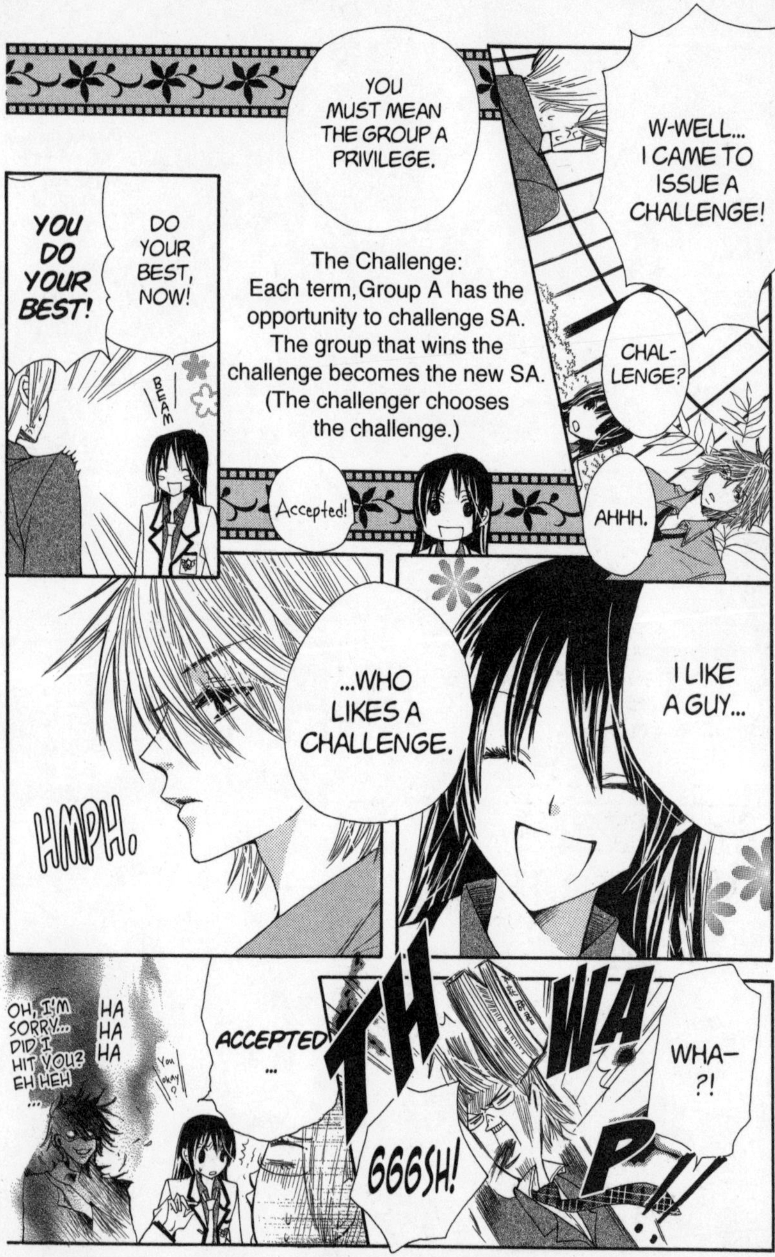
W-WELL... I CAME TO ISSUE A CHALLENGE!
CHAL-LENGE?
AHHH.
YOU MUST MEAN THE GROUP A PRIVILEGE.
The Challenge:
Each term, Group A has the opportunity to challenge SA. The group that wins the challenge becomes the new SA. (The challenger chooses the challenge.)
Accepted!
DO YOUR BEST, NOW!
BEAM
YOU DO YOUR BEST!
I LIKE A GUY...
...WHO LIKES A CHALLENGE.
HMPH.
WHA-?!
THWAP!!
GGGSH!
ACCEPTED...
You okay?
HA HA HA
OH, I'M SORRY... DID I HIT YOU? EH HEH...

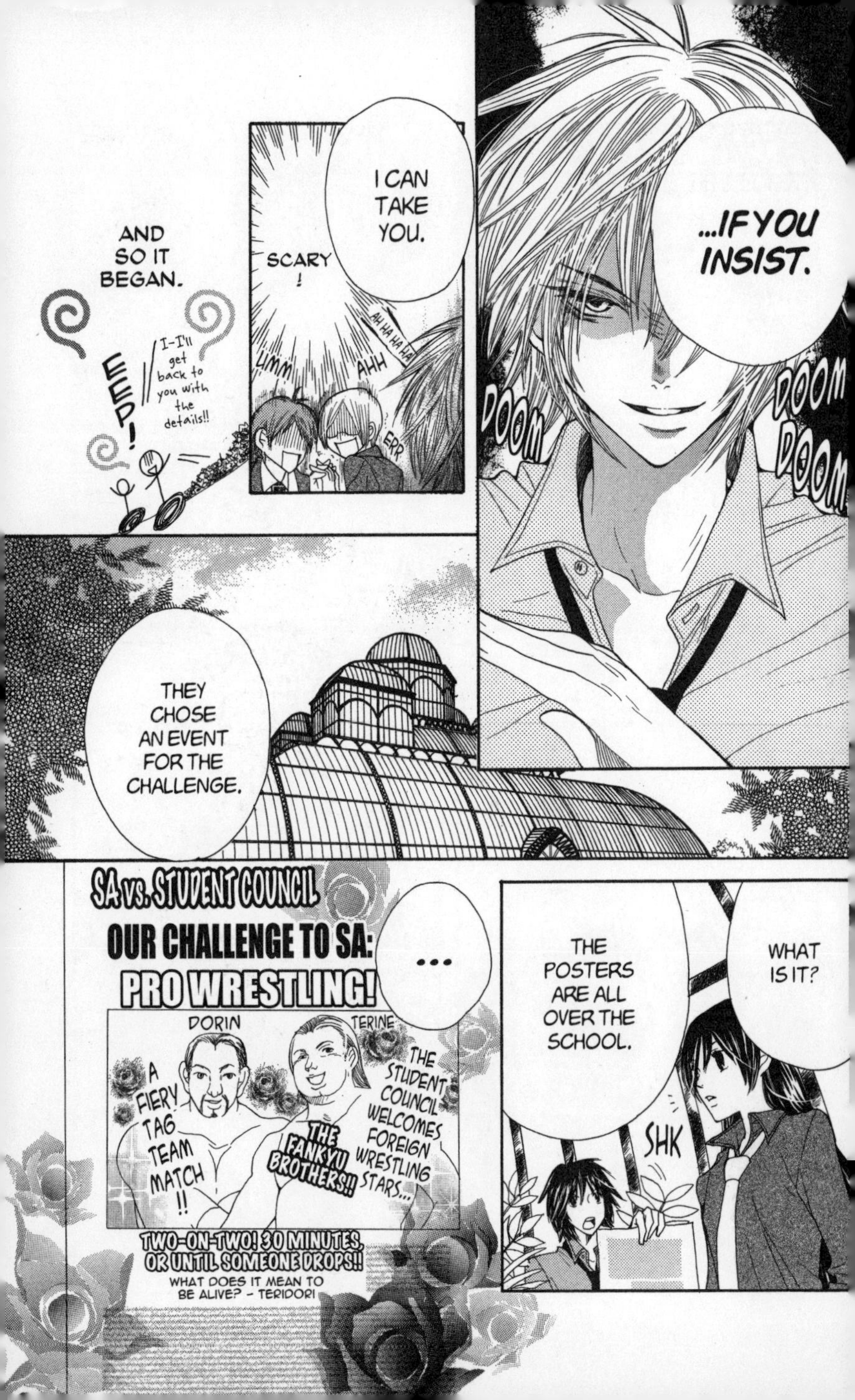
...IF YOU INSIST.
DOOM
DOOM
DOOM
DOOM
I CAN TAKE YOU.
SCARY!
AH HA HA HA
AHH
UMM
ERR
AND SO IT BEGAN.
EEP!
I-I'll get back to you with the details!!
THEY CHOSE AN EVENT FOR THE CHALLENGE.
WHAT IS IT?
THE POSTERS ARE ALL OVER THE SCHOOL.
SHK
...
SA vs. STUDENT COUNCIL
OUR CHALLENGE TO SA:
PRO WRESTLING!
DORIN
TERINE
A FIERY TAG TEAM MATCH!!
THE FANKYU BROTHERS!!
THE STUDENT COUNCIL WELCOMES FOREIGN WRESTLING STARS...
TWO-ON-TWO! 30 MINUTES, OR UNTIL SOMEONE DROPS!!
WHAT DOES IT MEAN TO BE ALIVE? - TERIDORI

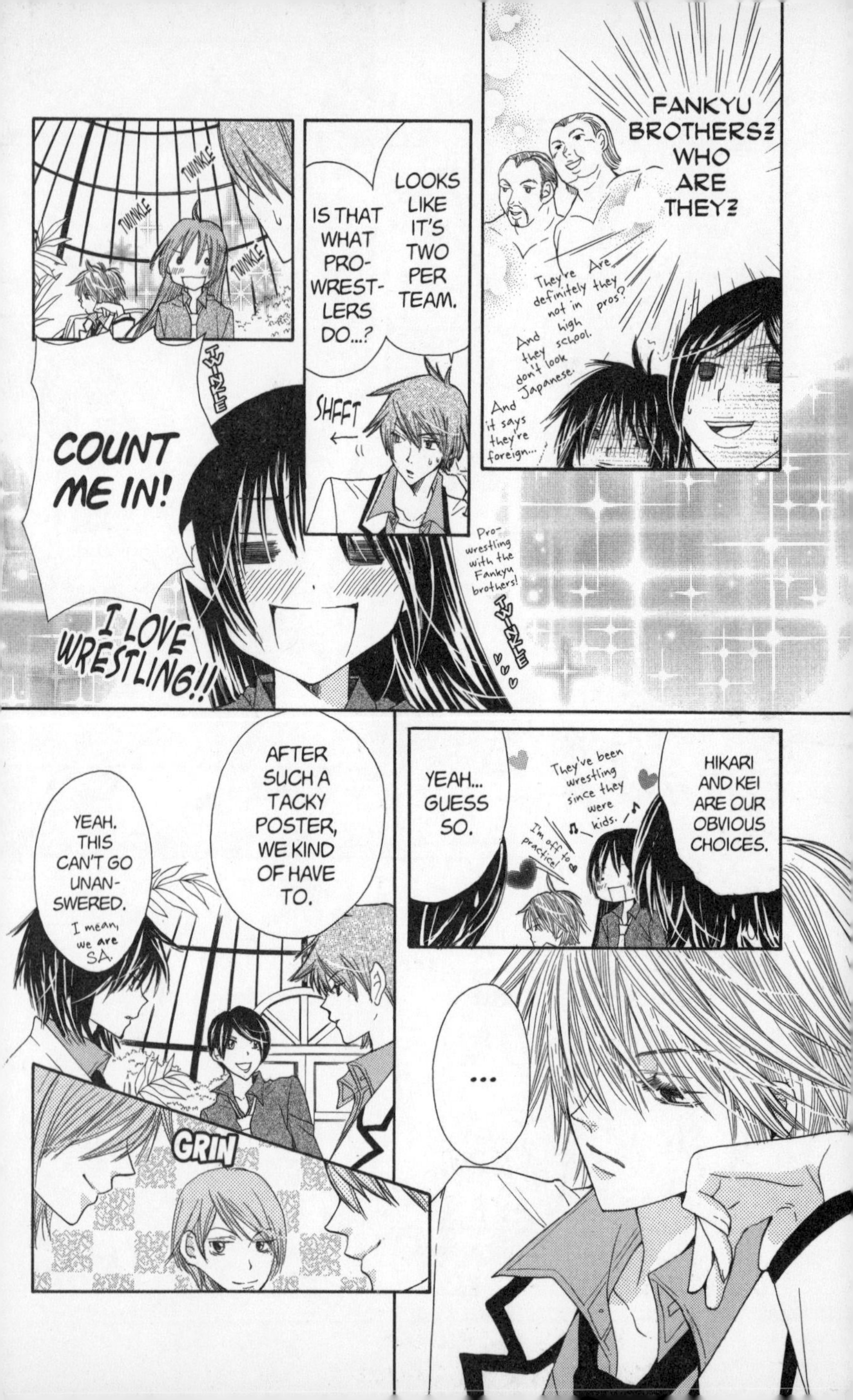
FANKYU BROTHERS? WHO ARE THEY?
They're definitely not in high school.
Are they pros?
And they don't look Japanese.
And it says they're foreign...
LOOKS LIKE IT'S TWO PER TEAM.
IS THAT WHAT PRO-WRESTLERS DO...?
SHFFT
TWINKLE
TWINKLE
TWINKLE
TWINKLE
COUNT ME IN!
I LOVE WRESTLING!!
Pro-wrestling with the Fankyu brothers!
TWINKLE
HIKARI AND KEI ARE OUR OBVIOUS CHOICES.
YEAH... GUESS SO.
They've been wrestling since they were kids.
I'm off to practice!
AFTER SUCH A TACKY POSTER, WE KIND OF HAVE TO.
YEAH. THIS CAN'T GO UNANSWERED.
I mean, we are SA.
...
GRIN

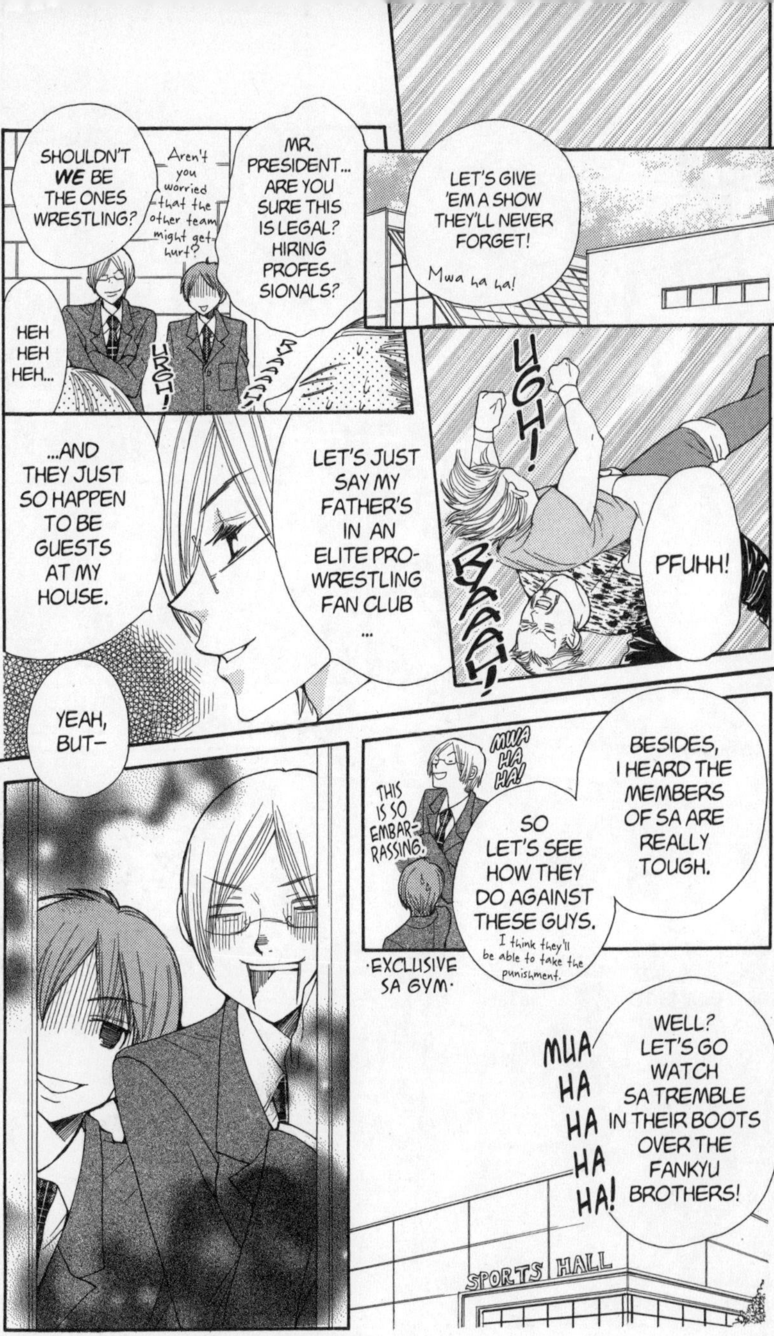
LET'S GIVE 'EM A SHOW THEY'LL NEVER FORGET!
Mwa ha ha!
MR. PRESIDENT... ARE YOU SURE THIS IS LEGAL? HIRING PROFESSIONALS?
Aren't you worried that the other team might get hurt?
SHOULDN'T **WE** BE THE ONES WRESTLING?
BAAAAH!
URGH!
HEH HEH HEH...
UGH!
PFUHH!
BAAAAH!
LET'S JUST SAY MY FATHER'S IN AN ELITE PRO-WRESTLING FAN CLUB ...
...AND THEY JUST SO HAPPEN TO BE GUESTS AT MY HOUSE.
YEAH, BUT—
BESIDES, I HEARD THE MEMBERS OF SA ARE REALLY TOUGH.
SO LET'S SEE HOW THEY DO AGAINST THESE GUYS.
I think they'll be able to take the punishment.
MUWA HA HA!
THIS IS SO EMBARRASSING.
·EXCLUSIVE SA GYM·
WELL? LET'S GO WATCH SA TREMBLE IN THEIR BOOTS OVER THE FANKYU BROTHERS!
MUA HA HA HA HA HA!
SPORTS HALL

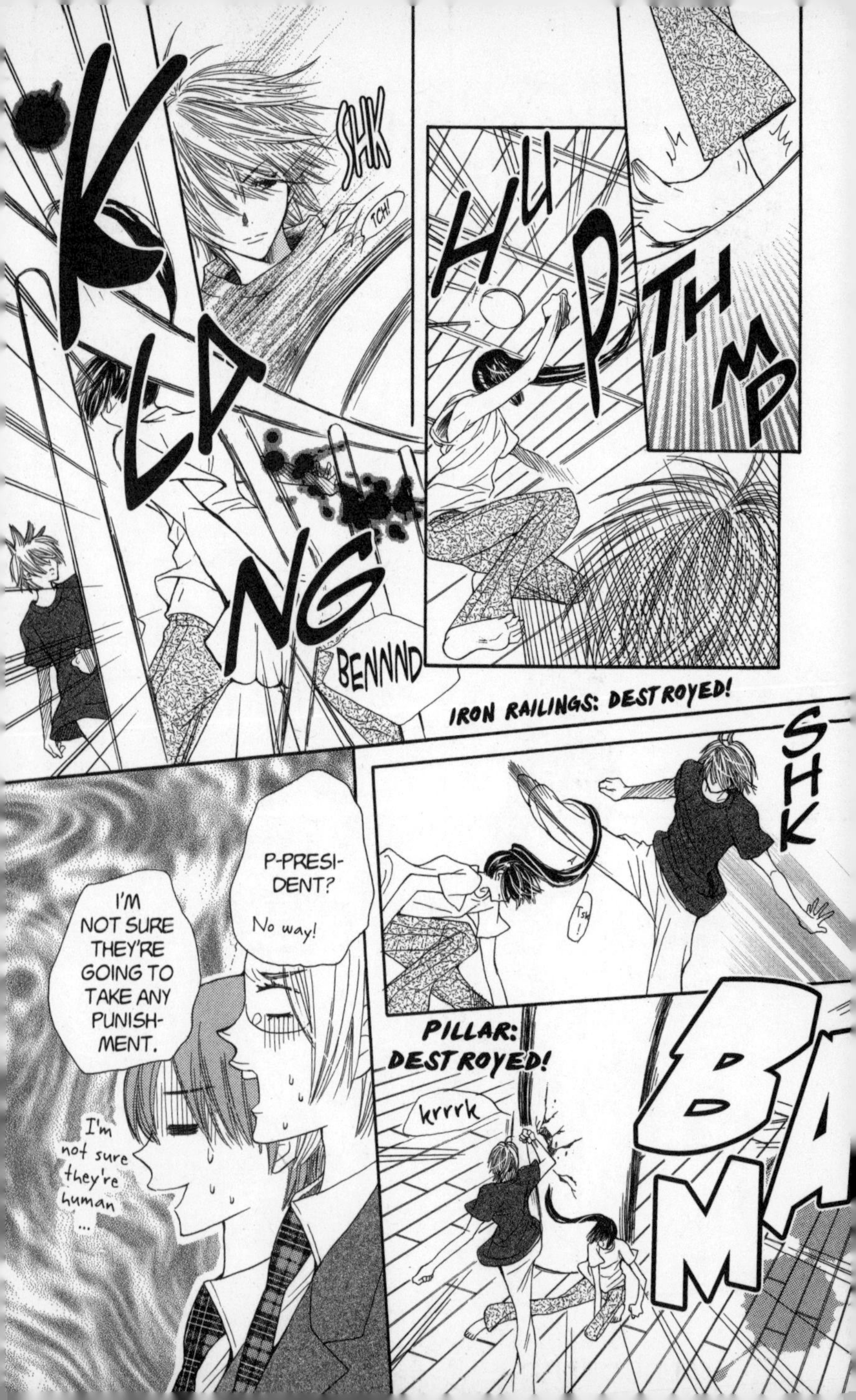
THMP
HUP
SHK
TCH!
KLANG
BENNND
IRON RAILINGS: DESTROYED!
SHK
Tsk!
PILLAR: DESTROYED!
krrrk
BAM
P-PRESIDENT?
No way!
I'M NOT SURE THEY'RE GOING TO TAKE ANY PUNISHMENT.
I'm not sure they're human...

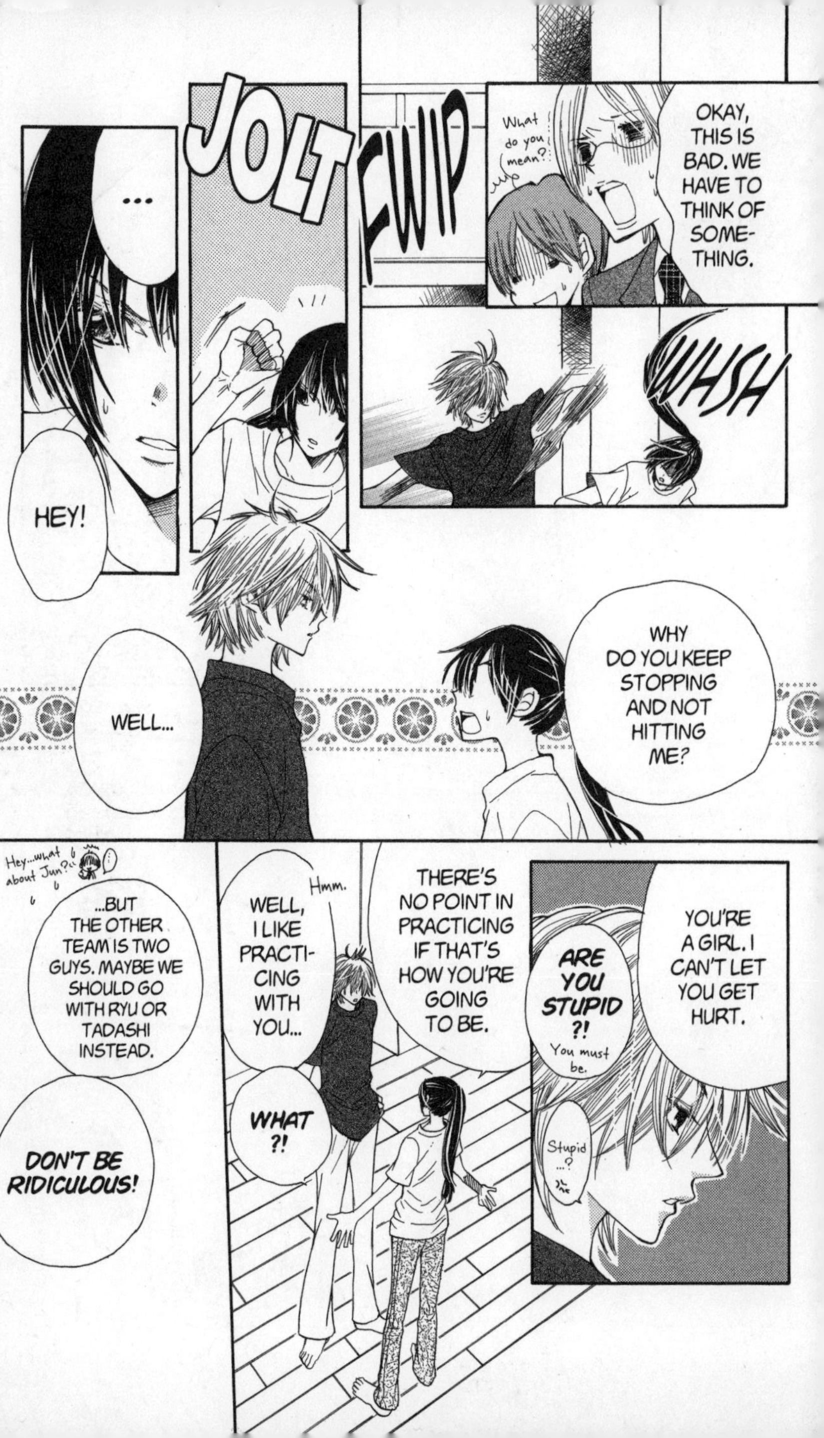
OKAY, THIS IS BAD. WE HAVE TO THINK OF SOME-THING.
What do you mean?
WHSH
FWIP
JOLT
...
HEY!
WHY DO YOU KEEP STOPPING AND NOT HITTING ME?
WELL...
YOU'RE A GIRL. I CAN'T LET YOU GET HURT.
ARE YOU STUPID?!
You must be.
Stupid...?
THERE'S NO POINT IN PRACTICING IF THAT'S HOW YOU'RE GOING TO BE.
WELL, I LIKE PRACTI-CING WITH YOU...
Hmm.
WHAT?!
Hey...what about Jun?
...BUT THE OTHER TEAM IS TWO GUYS. MAYBE WE SHOULD GO WITH RYU OR TADASHI INSTEAD.
DON'T BE RIDICULOUS!

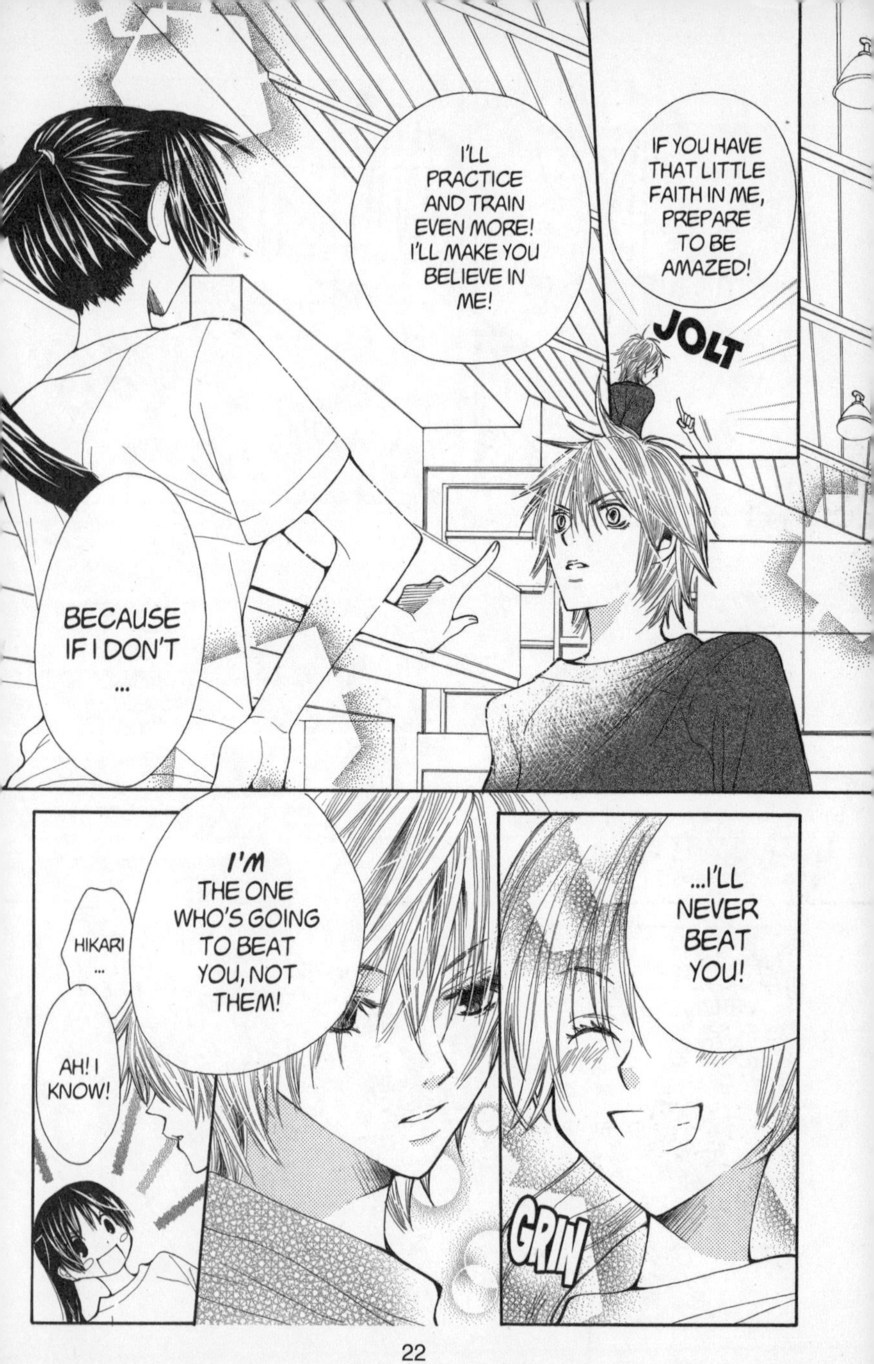
IF YOU HAVE THAT LITTLE FAITH IN ME, PREPARE TO BE AMAZED!
JOLT
I'LL PRACTICE AND TRAIN EVEN MORE! I'LL MAKE YOU BELIEVE IN ME!
BECAUSE IF I DON'T ...
...I'LL NEVER BEAT YOU!
GRIN
I'M THE ONE WHO'S GOING TO BEAT YOU, NOT THEM!
HIKARI ...
AH! I KNOW!

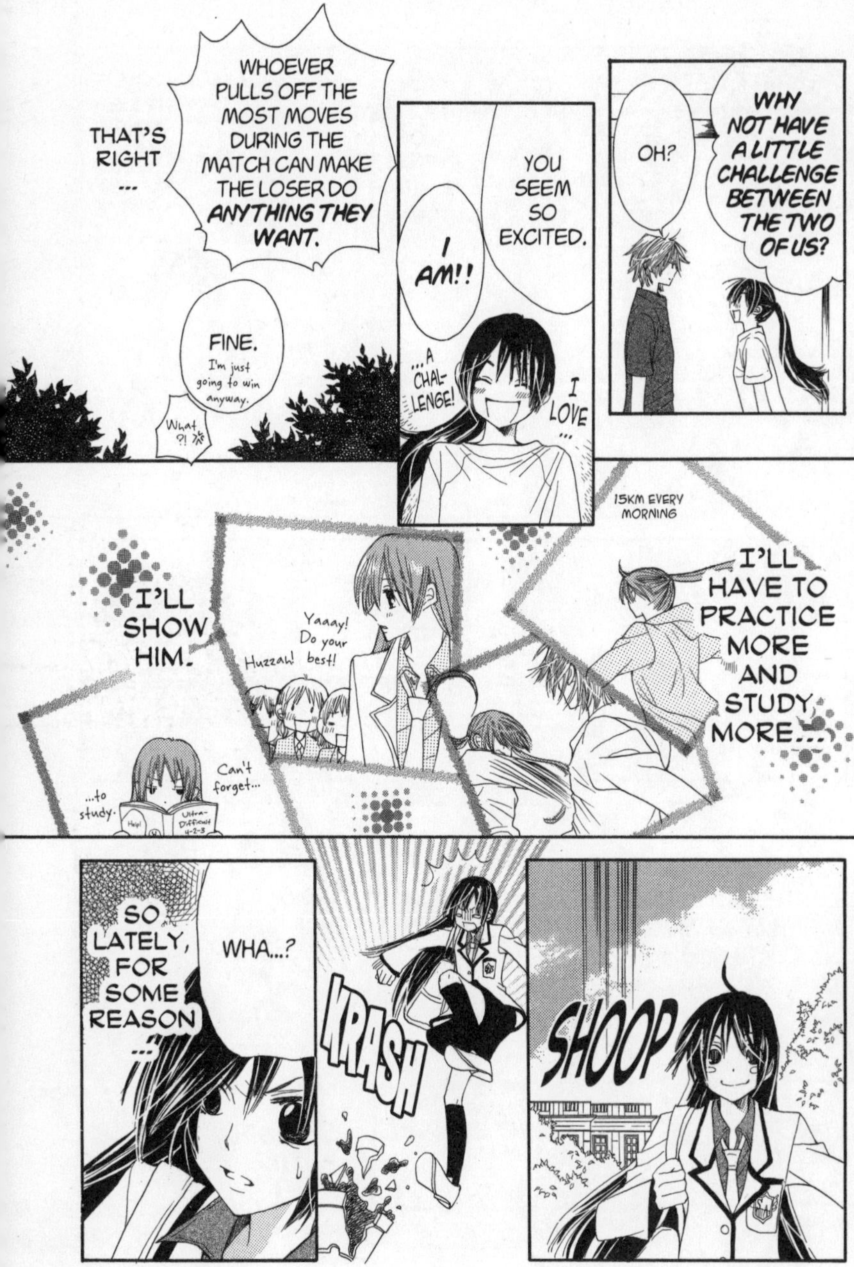
WHY NOT HAVE A LITTLE CHALLENGE BETWEEN THE TWO OF US?
OH?
YOU SEEM SO EXCITED.
I AM!!
I LOVE...
...A CHALLENGE!
THAT'S RIGHT...
WHOEVER PULLS OFF THE MOST MOVES DURING THE MATCH CAN MAKE THE LOSER DO ANYTHING THEY WANT.
FINE.
I'm just going to win anyway.
What?!
15KM EVERY MORNING
I'LL HAVE TO PRACTICE MORE AND STUDY MORE...
Yaaay! Do your best!
Huzzah!
I'LL SHOW HIM.
Can't forget...
...to study.
Help!
Ultra-Difficult 4-2-3
SHOOP
KRASH
WHA...?
SO LATELY, FOR SOME REASON...

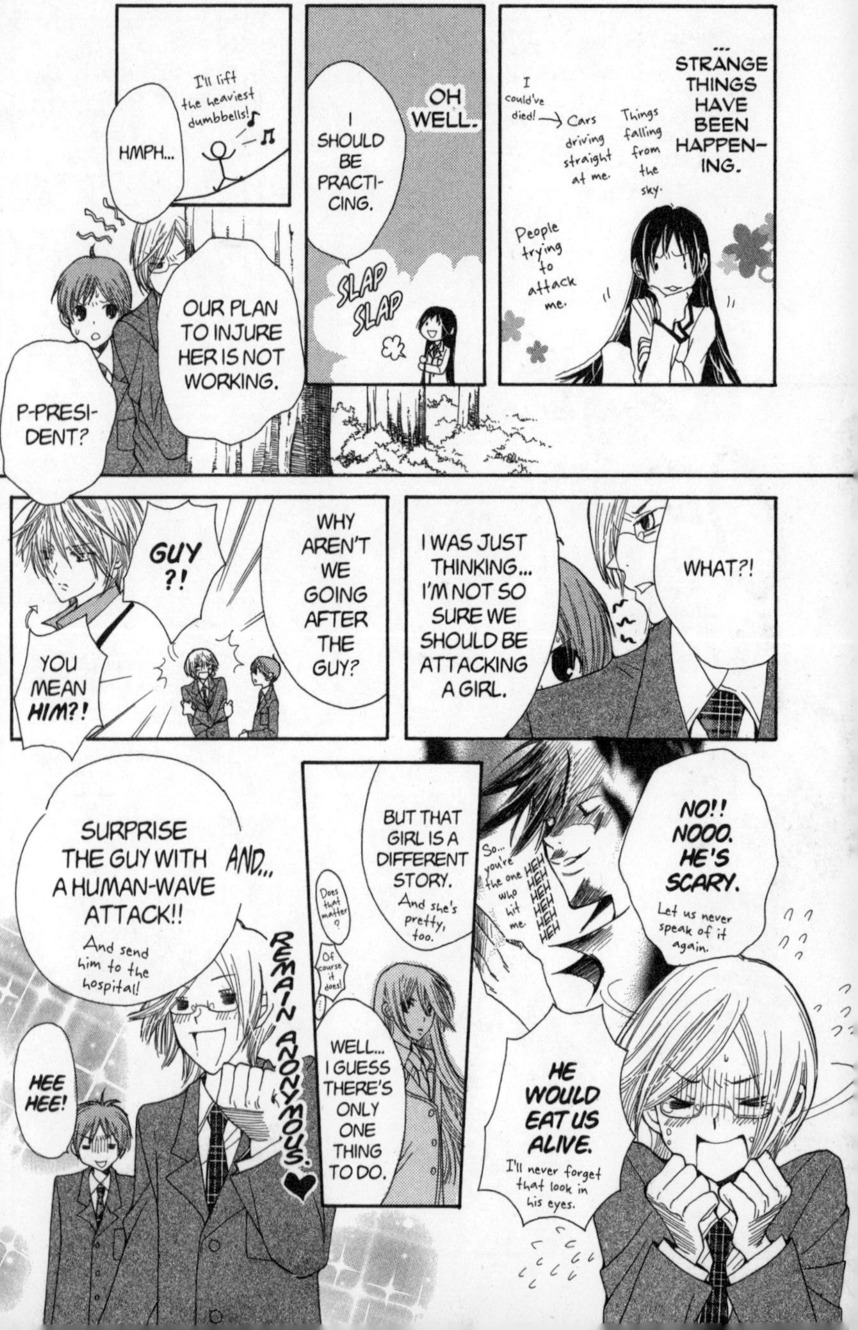
...STRANGE THINGS HAVE BEEN HAPPENING.
Things falling from the sky.
I could've died! → Cars driving straight at me.
People trying to attack me.
OH WELL.
I SHOULD BE PRACTICING.
SLAP SLAP
I'll lift the heaviest dumbbells!
HMPH...
OUR PLAN TO INJURE HER IS NOT WORKING.
P-PRESIDENT?
WHAT?!
I WAS JUST THINKING... I'M NOT SO SURE WE SHOULD BE ATTACKING A GIRL.
WHY AREN'T WE GOING AFTER THE GUY?
GUY?!
YOU MEAN HIM?!
NO!! NOOO. HE'S SCARY.
Let us never speak of it again.
So... you're the one who hit me.
HEH HEH HEH HEH HEH HEH
HE WOULD EAT US ALIVE.
I'll never forget that look in his eyes.
BUT THAT GIRL IS A DIFFERENT STORY.
And she's pretty, too.
Does that matter?
Of course it does!
WELL... I GUESS THERE'S ONLY ONE THING TO DO.
SURPRISE THE GUY WITH A HUMAN-WAVE ATTACK!!
AND...
And send him to the hospital!
REMAIN ANONYMOUS.
HEE HEE!

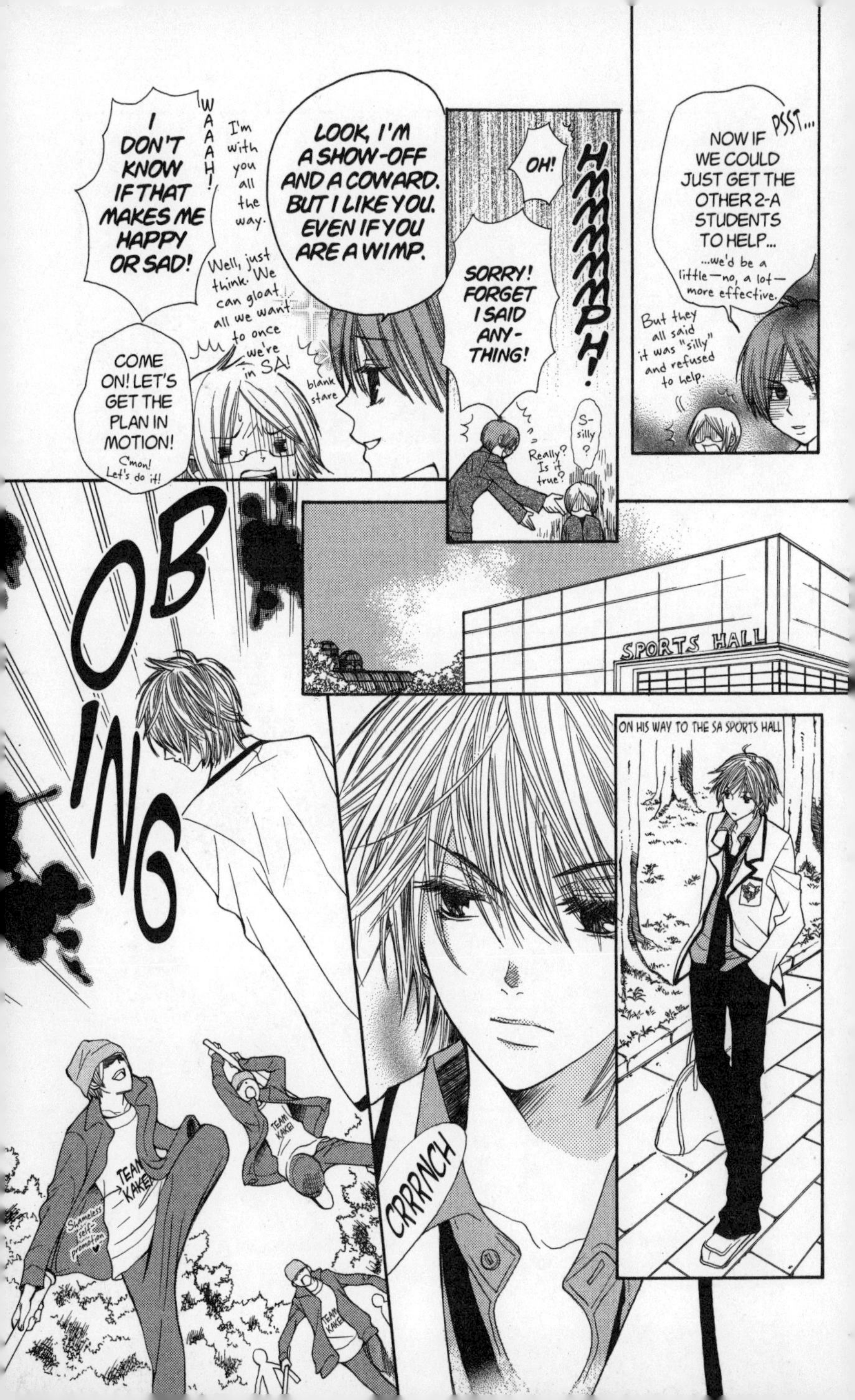
PSST...
NOW IF WE COULD JUST GET THE OTHER 2-A STUDENTS TO HELP...
...we'd be a little—no, a lot—more effective.
But they all said it was "silly" and refused to help.
OH!
HMMMMMPH!
SORRY! FORGET I SAID ANY-THING!
S-silly?
Really? Is it true?
LOOK, I'M A SHOW-OFF AND A COWARD. BUT I LIKE YOU. EVEN IF YOU ARE A WIMP.
I'm with you all the way.
WAAAAH!
I DON'T KNOW IF THAT MAKES ME HAPPY OR SAD!
Well, just think. We can gloat all we want to once we're in SA!
blank stare
COME ON! LET'S GET THE PLAN IN MOTION!
C'mon! Let's do it!
SPORTS HALL
ON HIS WAY TO THE SA SPORTS HALL
CRRRNCH
OBOING
TEAM KAKEI
TEAM KAKEI
TEAM KAKEI
Shameless self-promotion

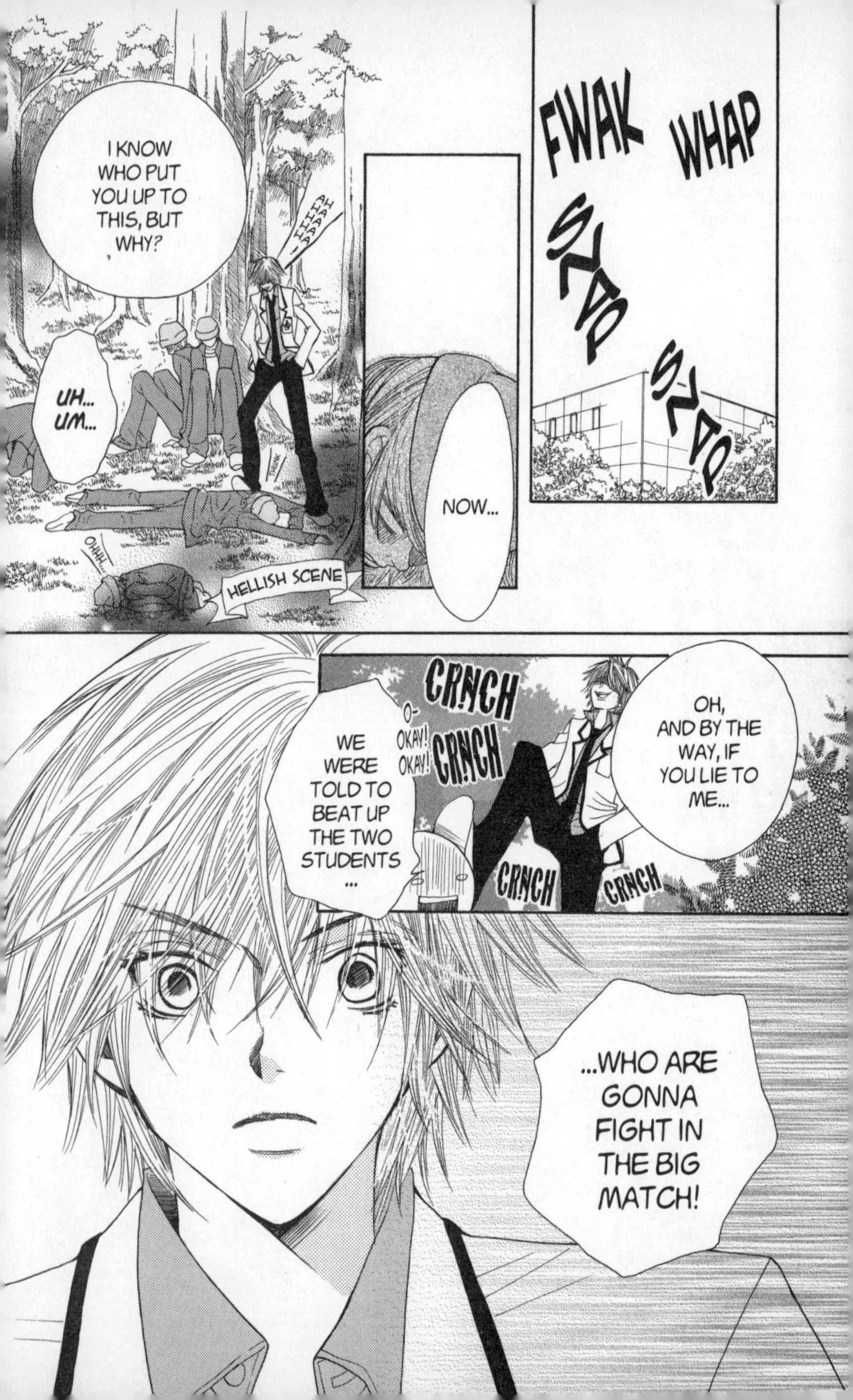
FWAK
WHAP
SLAP
SLAP
NOW...
I KNOW WHO PUT YOU UP TO THIS, BUT WHY?
AH HA HA HA!
UH... UM...
THUNK
OHHH...
HELLISH SCENE
OH, AND BY THE WAY, IF YOU LIE TO ME...
CRNCH
CRNCH
CRNCH
CRNCH
O- OKAY! OKAY!
WE WERE TOLD TO BEAT UP THE TWO STUDENTS...
...WHO ARE GONNA FIGHT IN THE BIG MATCH!

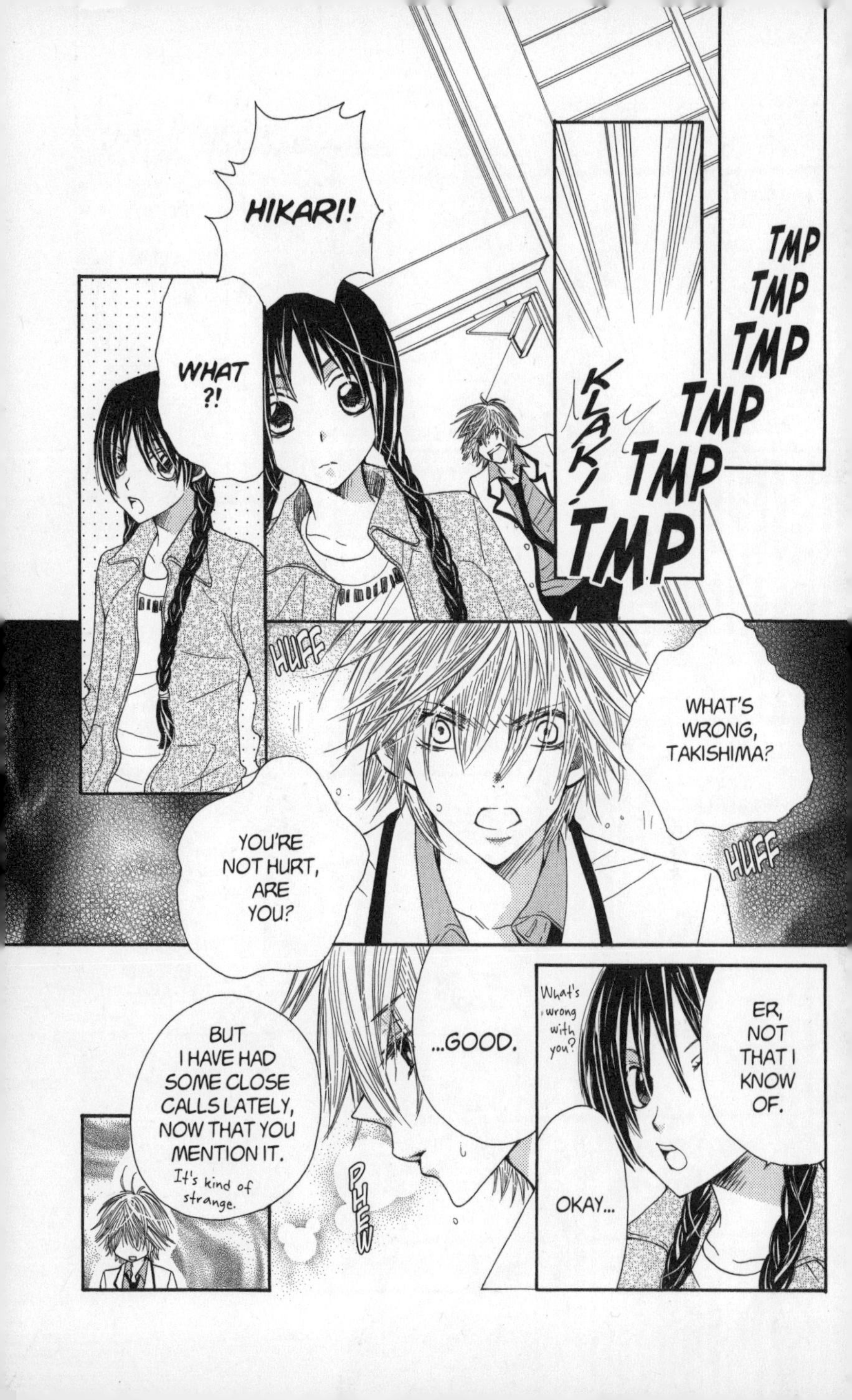
TMP TMP TMP TMP TMP TMP
KLAK!
HIKARI!
WHAT ?!
HUFF
WHAT'S WRONG, TAKISHIMA?
YOU'RE NOT HURT, ARE YOU?
HUFF
ER, NOT THAT I KNOW OF.
What's wrong with you?
OKAY...
...GOOD.
PHEW
BUT I HAVE HAD SOME CLOSE CALLS LATELY, NOW THAT YOU MENTION IT.
It's kind of strange.

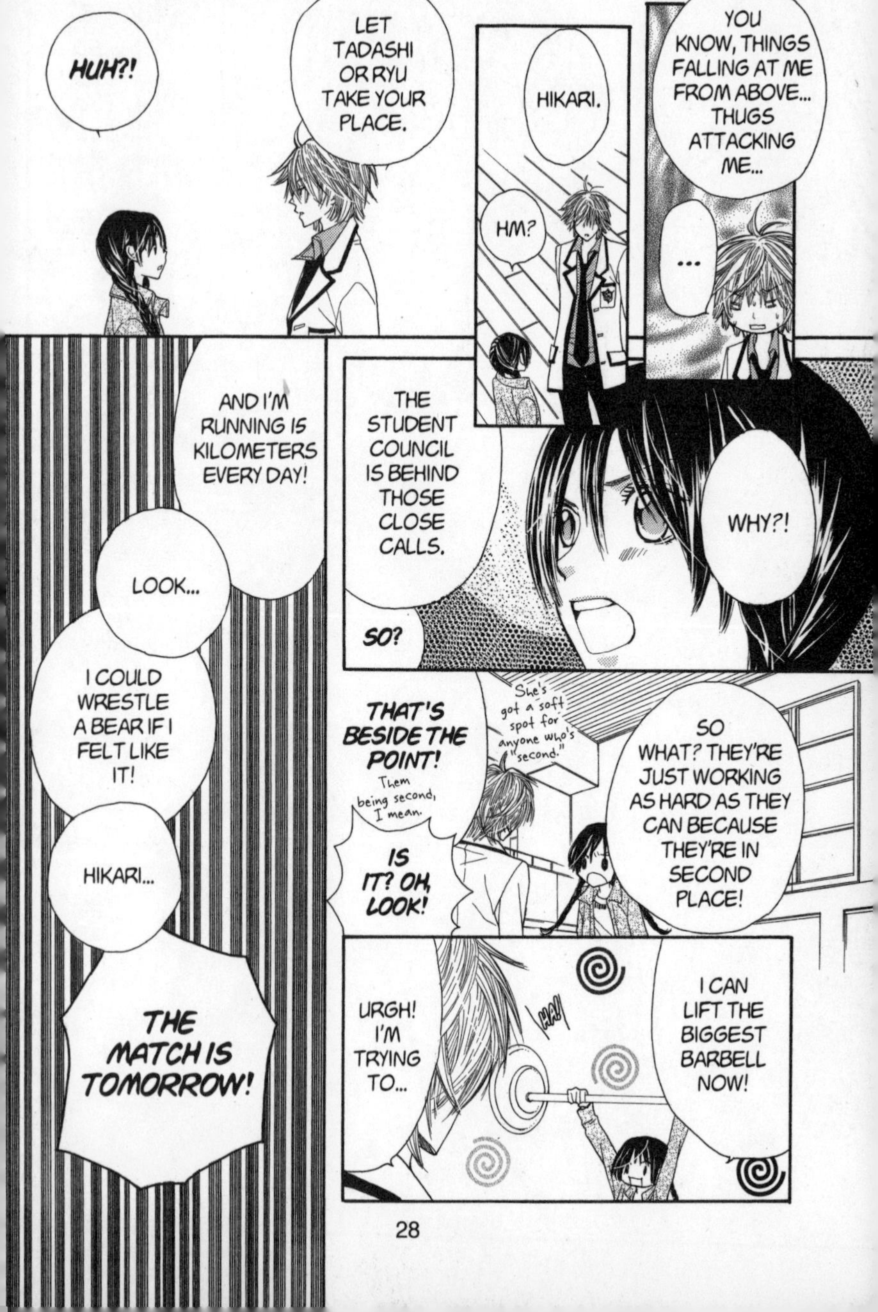
YOU KNOW, THINGS FALLING AT ME FROM ABOVE... THUGS ATTACKING ME...
...
HIKARI.
HM?
LET TADASHI OR RYU TAKE YOUR PLACE.
HUH?!
WHY?!
THE STUDENT COUNCIL IS BEHIND THOSE CLOSE CALLS.
SO?
SO WHAT? THEY'RE JUST WORKING AS HARD AS THEY CAN BECAUSE THEY'RE IN SECOND PLACE!
She's got a soft spot for anyone who's "second."
THAT'S BESIDE THE POINT!
Them being second, I mean.
IS IT? OH, LOOK!
I CAN LIFT THE BIGGEST BARBELL NOW!
HA!
URGH! I'M TRYING TO...
AND I'M RUNNING 15 KILOMETERS EVERY DAY!
LOOK...
I COULD WRESTLE A BEAR IF I FELT LIKE IT!
HIKARI...
THE MATCH IS TOMORROW!

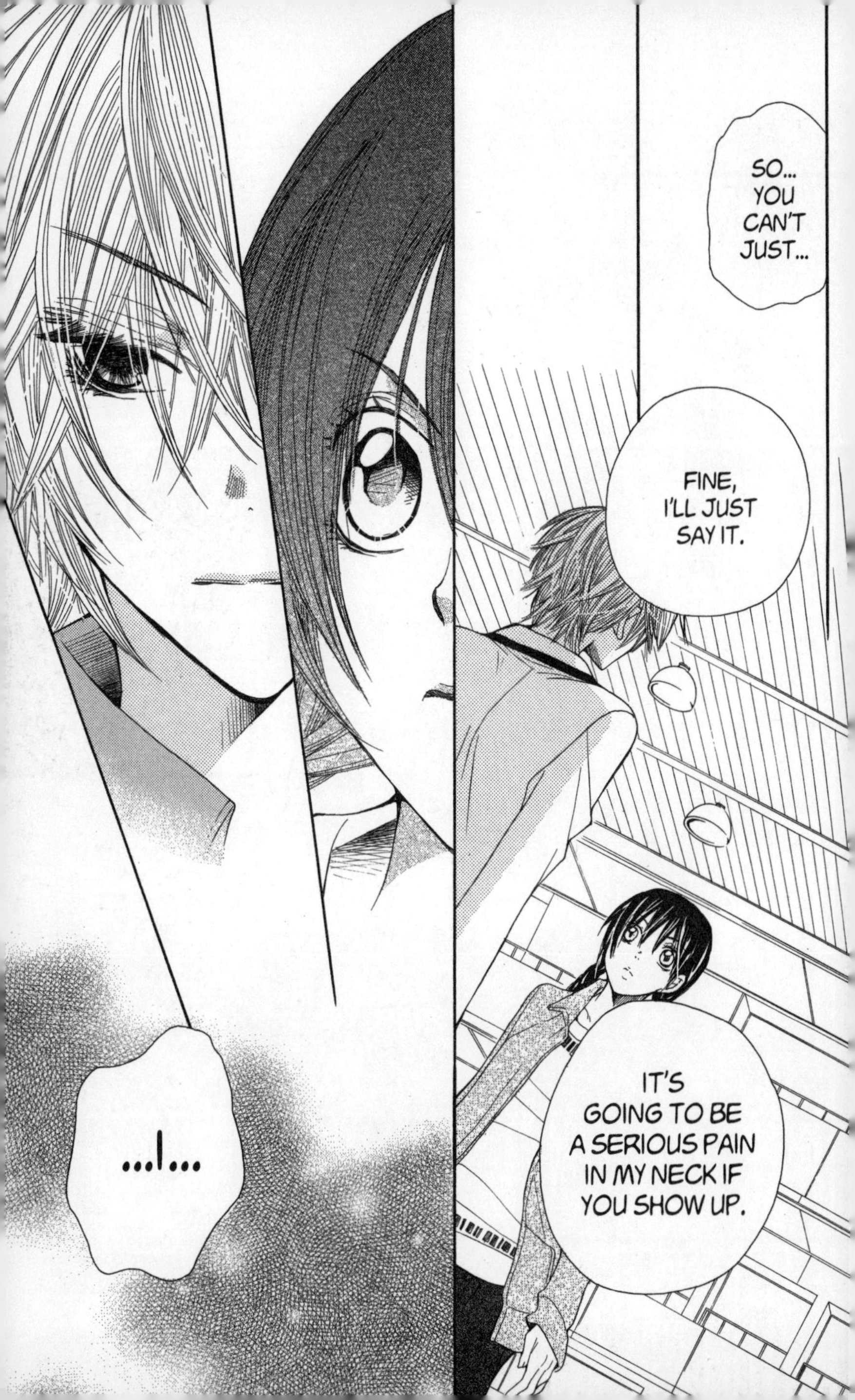
SO... YOU CAN'T JUST...
FINE, I'LL JUST SAY IT.
IT'S GOING TO BE A SERIOUS PAIN IN MY NECK IF YOU SHOW UP.
...I...

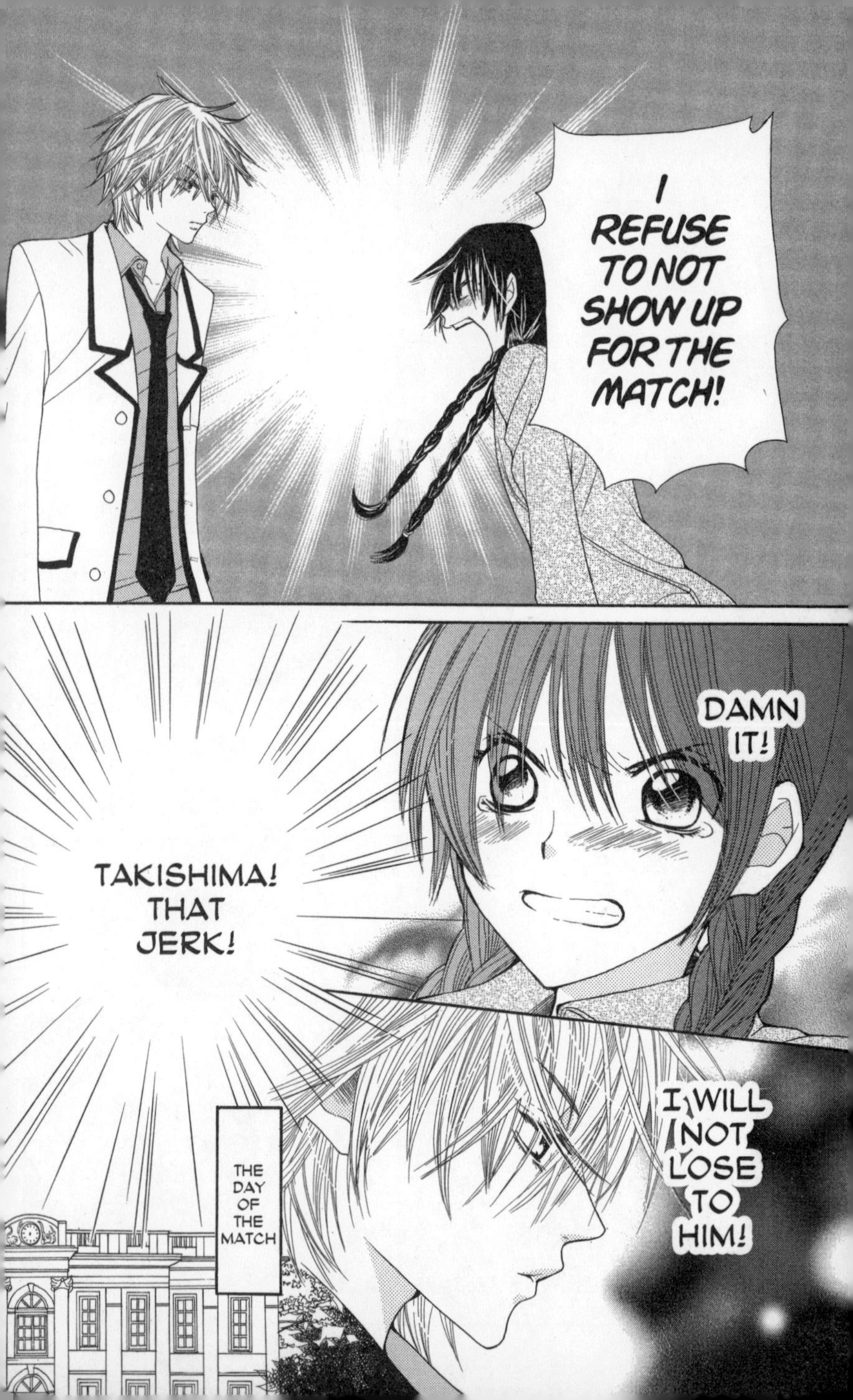
I REFUSE TO NOT SHOW UP FOR THE MATCH!
DAMN IT!
TAKISHIMA! THAT JERK!
I WILL NOT LOSE TO HIM!
THE DAY OF THE MATCH

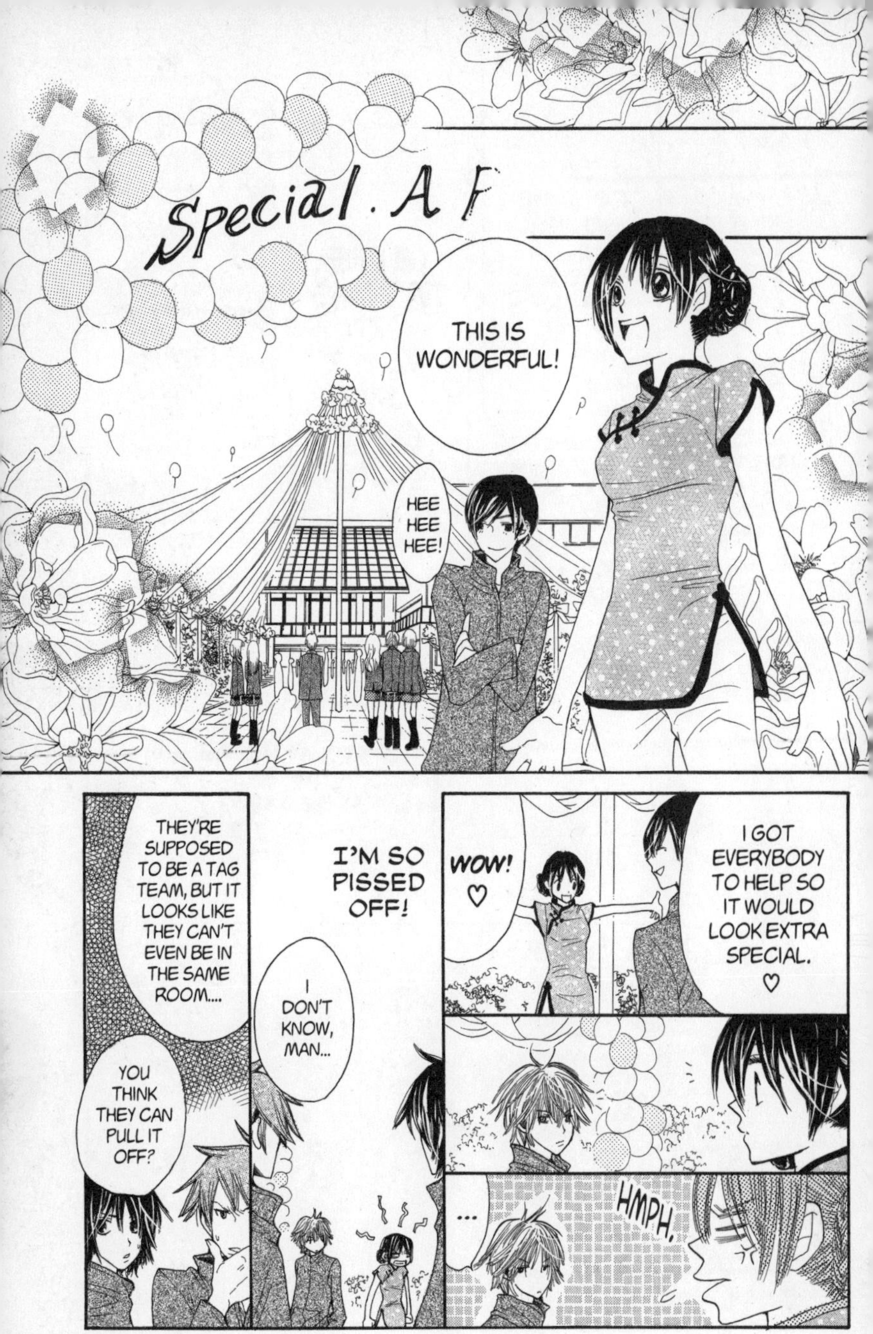
Special.A F
THIS IS WONDERFUL!
HEE HEE HEE!
I GOT EVERYBODY TO HELP SO IT WOULD LOOK EXTRA SPECIAL. ♡
WOW! ♡
HMPH.
...
I'M SO PISSED OFF!
THEY'RE SUPPOSED TO BE A TAG TEAM, BUT IT LOOKS LIKE THEY CAN'T EVEN BE IN THE SAME ROOM....
YOU THINK THEY CAN PULL IT OFF?
I DON'T KNOW, MAN...

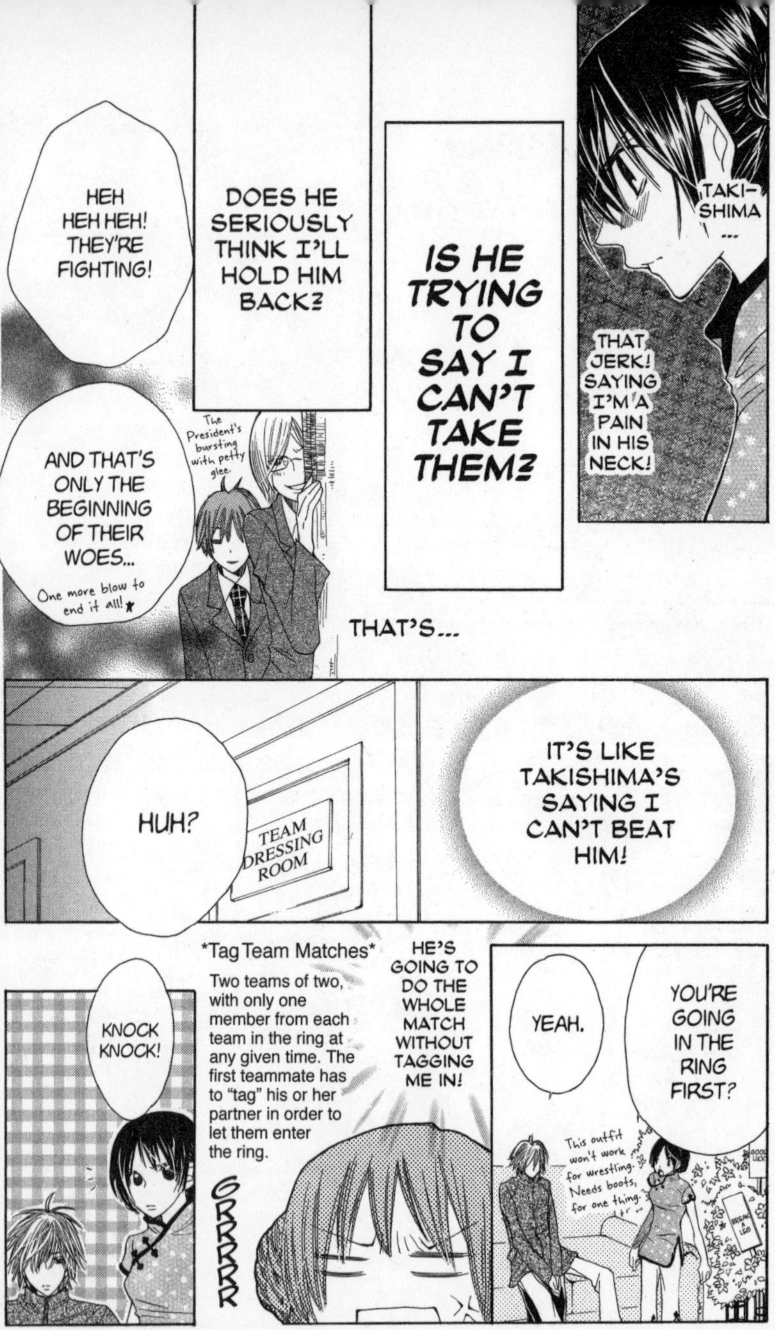
TAKI-SHIMA ...
THAT JERK! SAYING I'M A PAIN IN HIS NECK!
IS HE TRYING TO SAY I CAN'T TAKE THEM?
DOES HE SERIOUSLY THINK I'LL HOLD HIM BACK?
HEH HEH HEH! THEY'RE FIGHTING!
The President's bursting with petty glee.
AND THAT'S ONLY THE BEGINNING OF THEIR WOES...
One more blow to end it all!★
THAT'S...
IT'S LIKE TAKISHIMA'S SAYING I CAN'T BEAT HIM!
HUH?
TEAM DRESSING ROOM
YOU'RE GOING IN THE RING FIRST?
YEAH.
This outfit won't work for wrestling. Needs boots, for one thing.
HE'S GOING TO DO THE WHOLE MATCH WITHOUT TAGGING ME IN!
GRRRRR
Tag Team Matches
Two teams of two, with only one member from each team in the ring at any given time. The first teammate has to "tag" his or her partner in order to let them enter the ring.
KNOCK KNOCK!

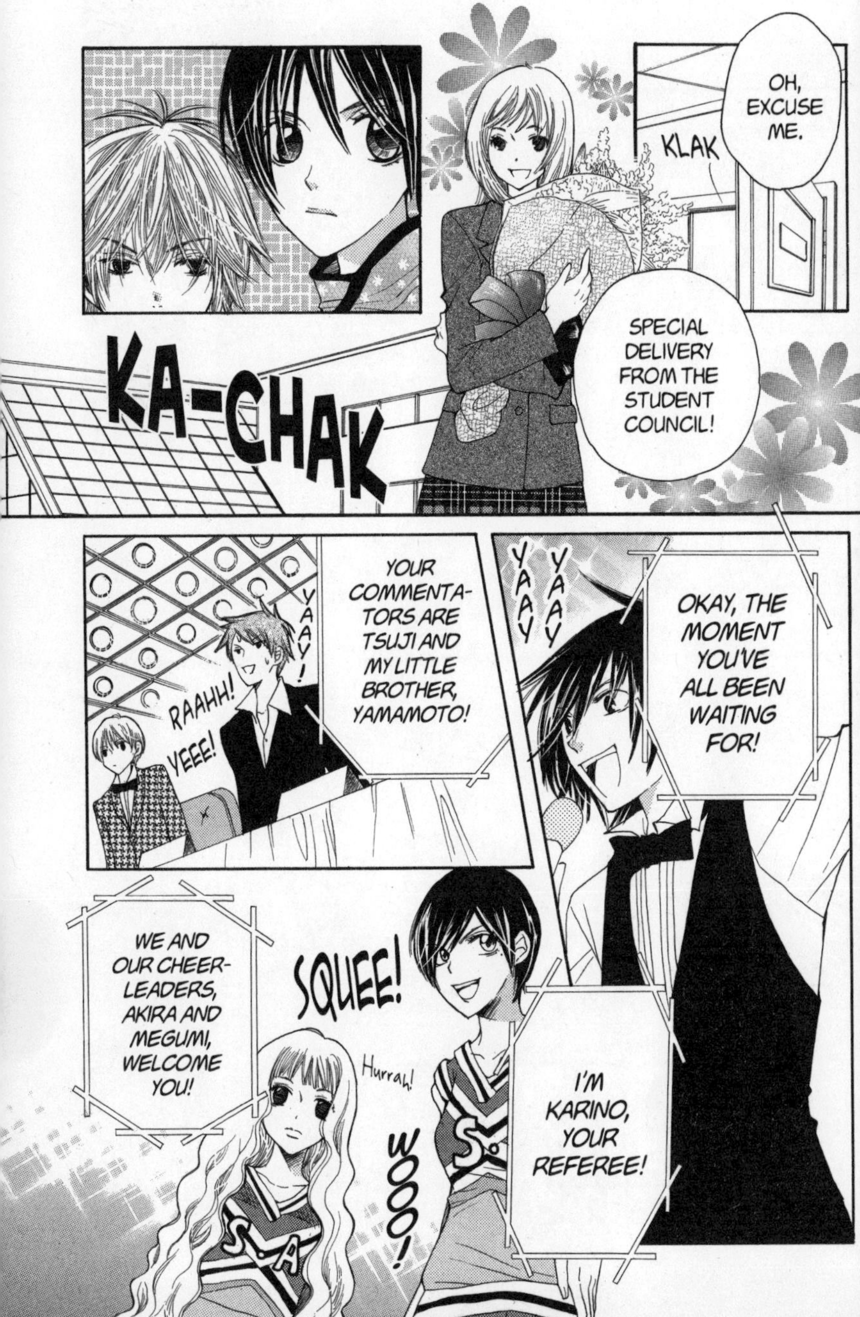
OH, EXCUSE ME.
KLAK
SPECIAL DELIVERY FROM THE STUDENT COUNCIL!
KA-CHAK
YAAY
YAAY
OKAY, THE MOMENT YOU'VE ALL BEEN WAITING FOR!
YOUR COMMENTA-TORS ARE TSUJI AND MY LITTLE BROTHER, YAMAMOTO!
YAAAY!
RAAHH!
YEEE!
I'M KARINO, YOUR REFEREE!
WOOO!
SQUEE!
Hurrah!
WE AND OUR CHEER-LEADERS, AKIRA AND MEGUMI, WELCOME YOU!

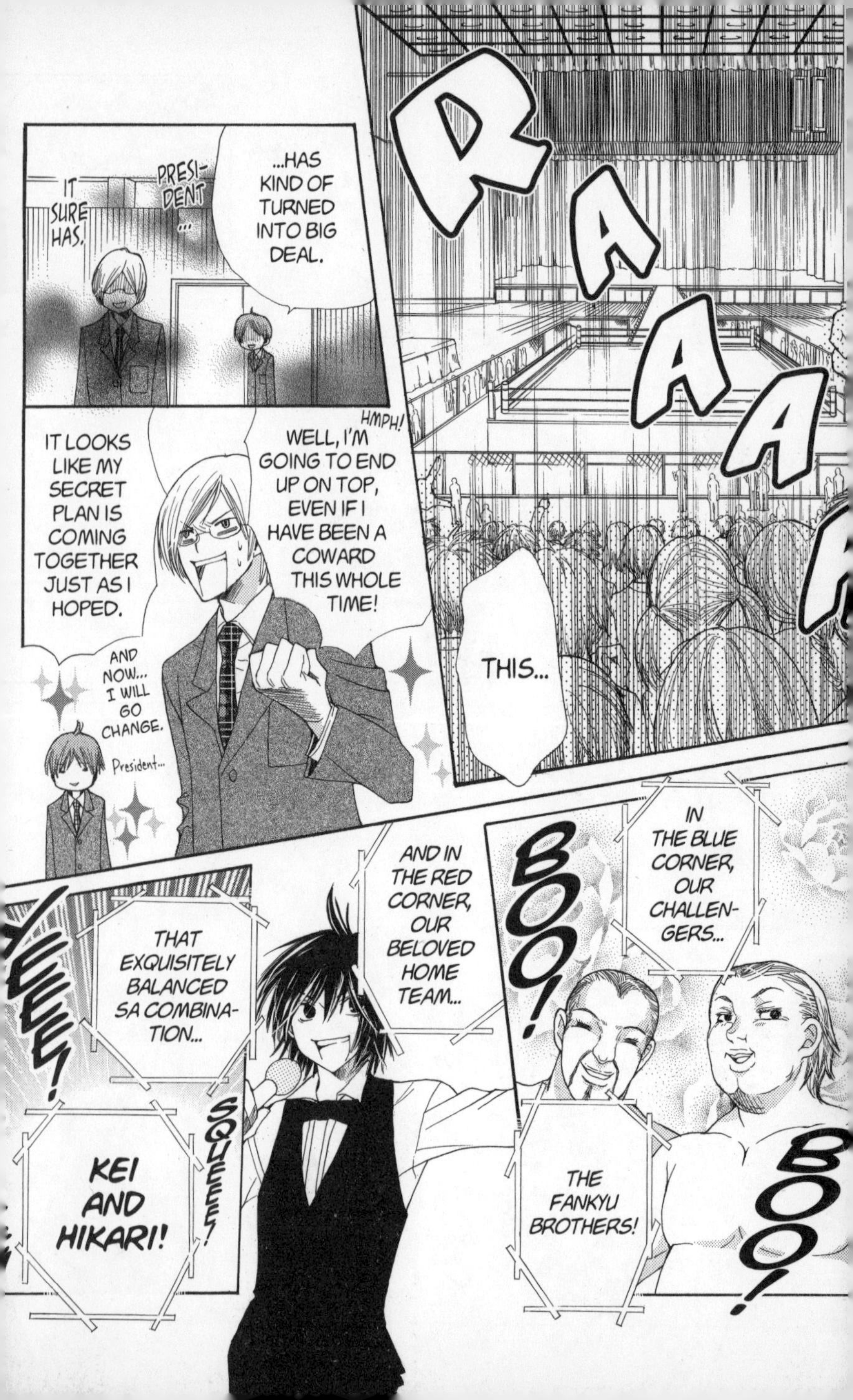

RAAAA
THIS...
PRESIDENT...
...HAS KIND OF TURNED INTO BIG DEAL.
IT SURE HAS.
HMPH!
WELL, I'M GOING TO END UP ON TOP, EVEN IF I HAVE BEEN A COWARD THIS WHOLE TIME!
IT LOOKS LIKE MY SECRET PLAN IS COMING TOGETHER JUST AS I HOPED.
AND NOW... I WILL GO CHANGE.
President...
IN THE BLUE CORNER, OUR CHALLENGERS...
BOO!
THE FANKYU BROTHERS!
BOO!
AND IN THE RED CORNER, OUR BELOVED HOME TEAM...
THAT EXQUISITELY BALANCED SA COMBINATION...
YEEEE!
SQUEEE!
KEI AND HIKARI!

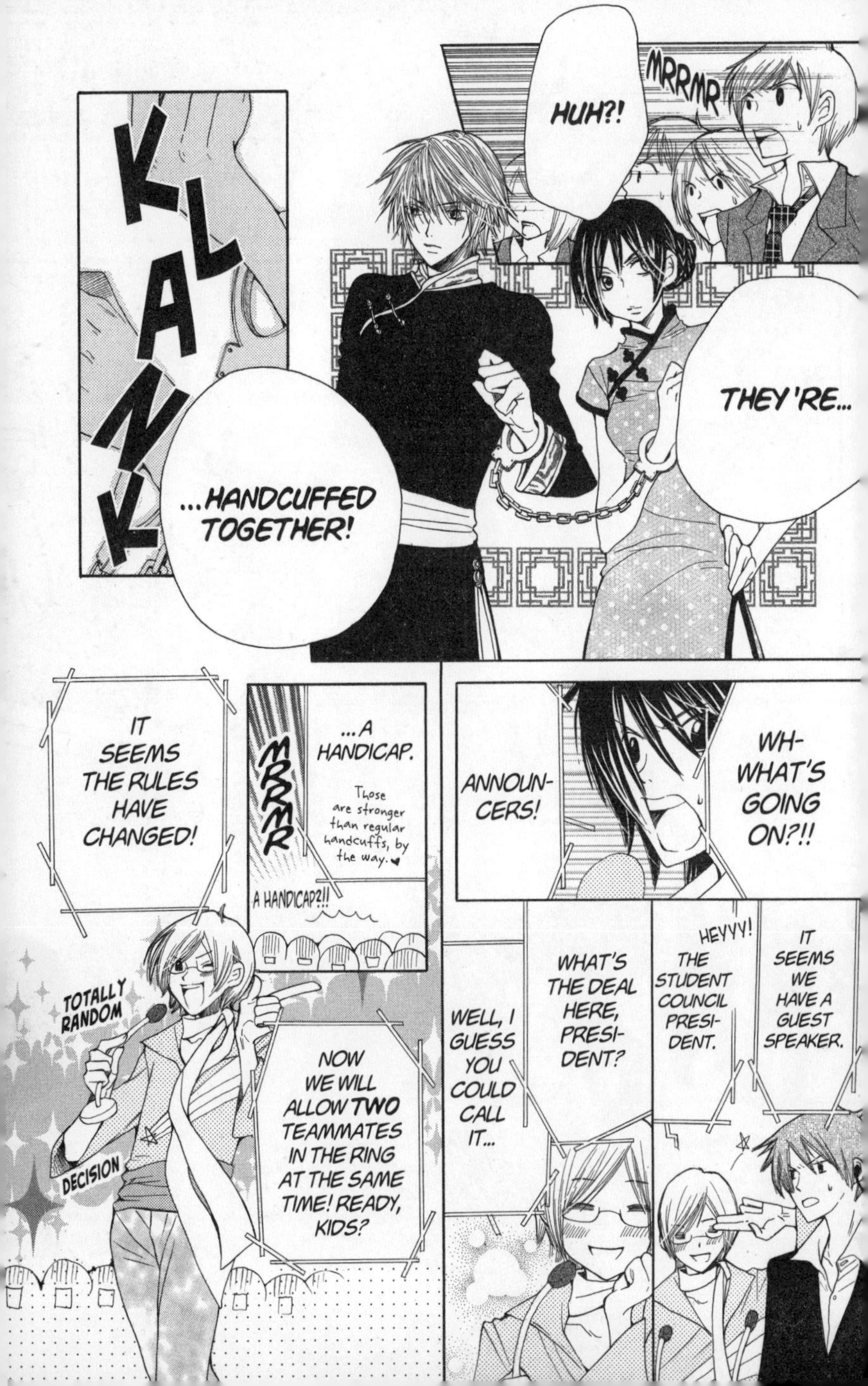
MRRMR
HUH?!
THEY'RE...
...HANDCUFFED TOGETHER!
KLANK
WH- WHAT'S GOING ON?!!
ANNOUNCERS!
...A HANDICAP.
Those are stronger than regular handcuffs, by the way.
MRRMR
A HANDICAP?!!
IT SEEMS THE RULES HAVE CHANGED!
IT SEEMS WE HAVE A GUEST SPEAKER.
HEYYY! THE STUDENT COUNCIL PRESIDENT.
WHAT'S THE DEAL HERE, PRESIDENT?
WELL, I GUESS YOU COULD CALL IT...
NOW WE WILL ALLOW TWO TEAMMATES IN THE RING AT THE SAME TIME! READY, KIDS?
TOTALLY RANDOM DECISION

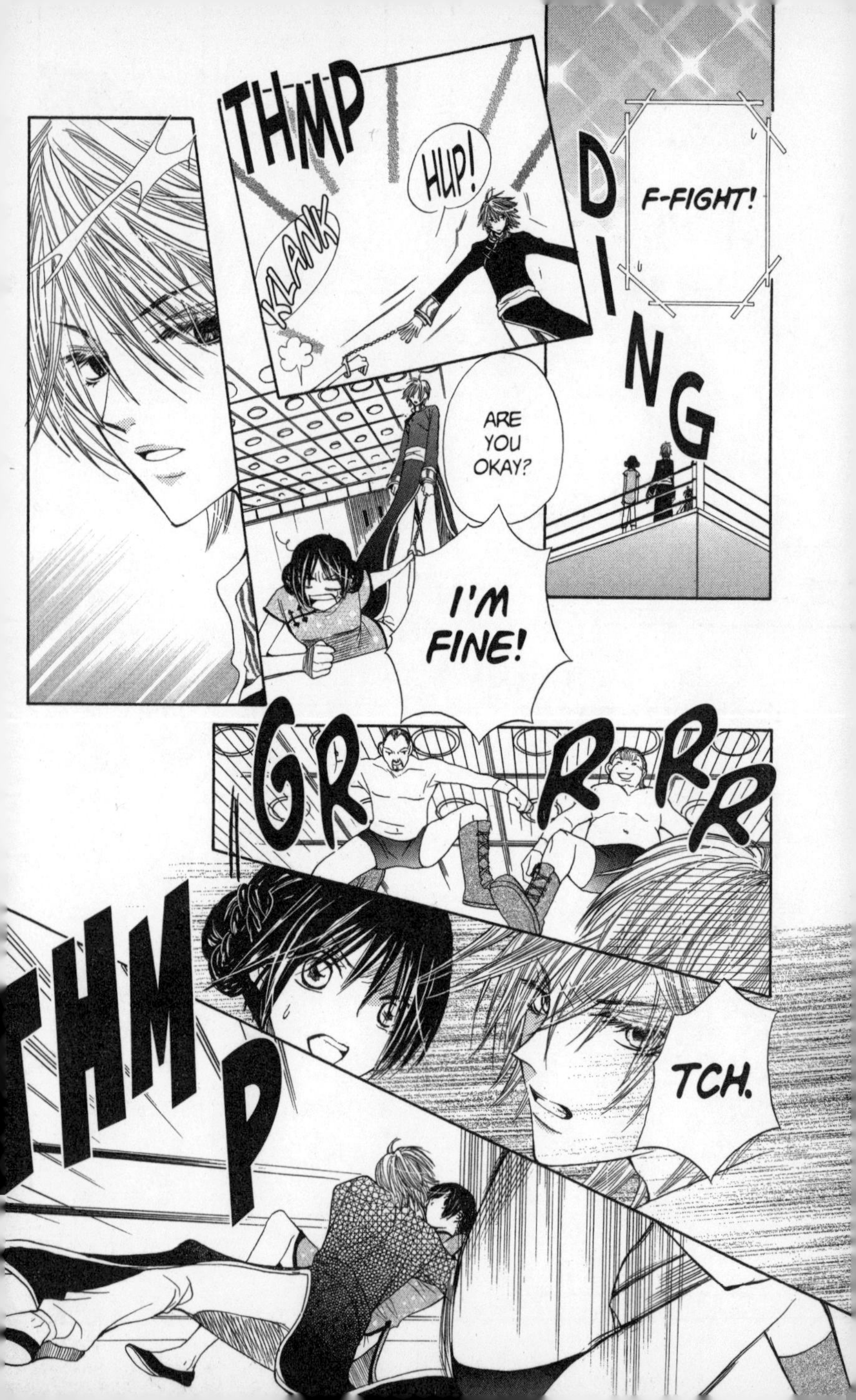
F-FIGHT!
DING
THMP
HUP!
KLANK
ARE YOU OKAY?
I'M FINE!
GRRRR
TCH.
THMP

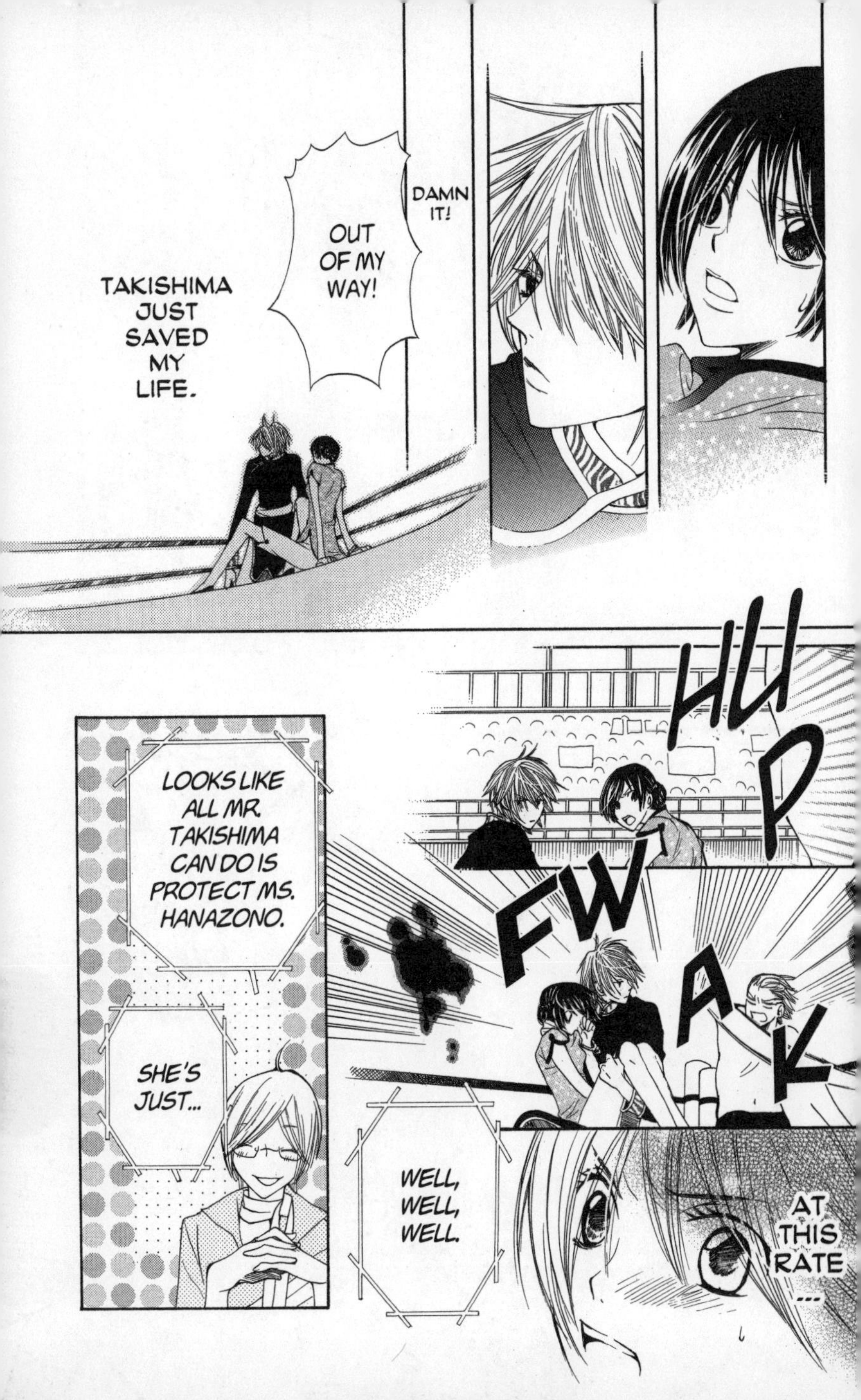
DAMN IT!
OUT OF MY WAY!
TAKISHIMA JUST SAVED MY LIFE.
HUP
FWAK
AT THIS RATE...
WELL, WELL, WELL.
LOOKS LIKE ALL MR. TAKISHIMA CAN DO IS PROTECT MS. HANAZONO.
SHE'S JUST...

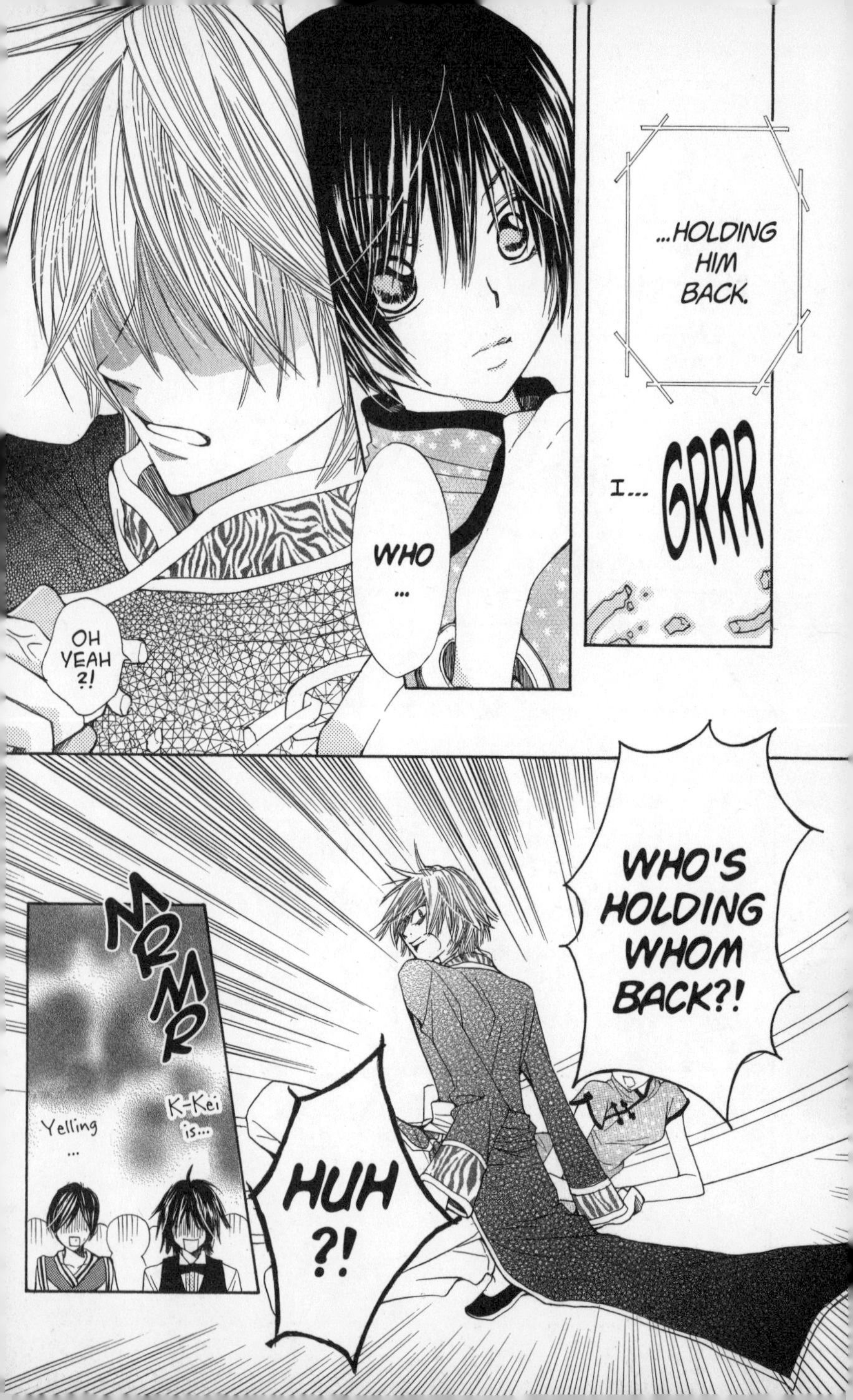
...HOLDING HIM BACK.
I...
GRRR
WHO ...
OH YEAH ?!
WHO'S HOLDING WHOM BACK?!
HUH ?!
MRMR
K-Kei is...
Yelling ...

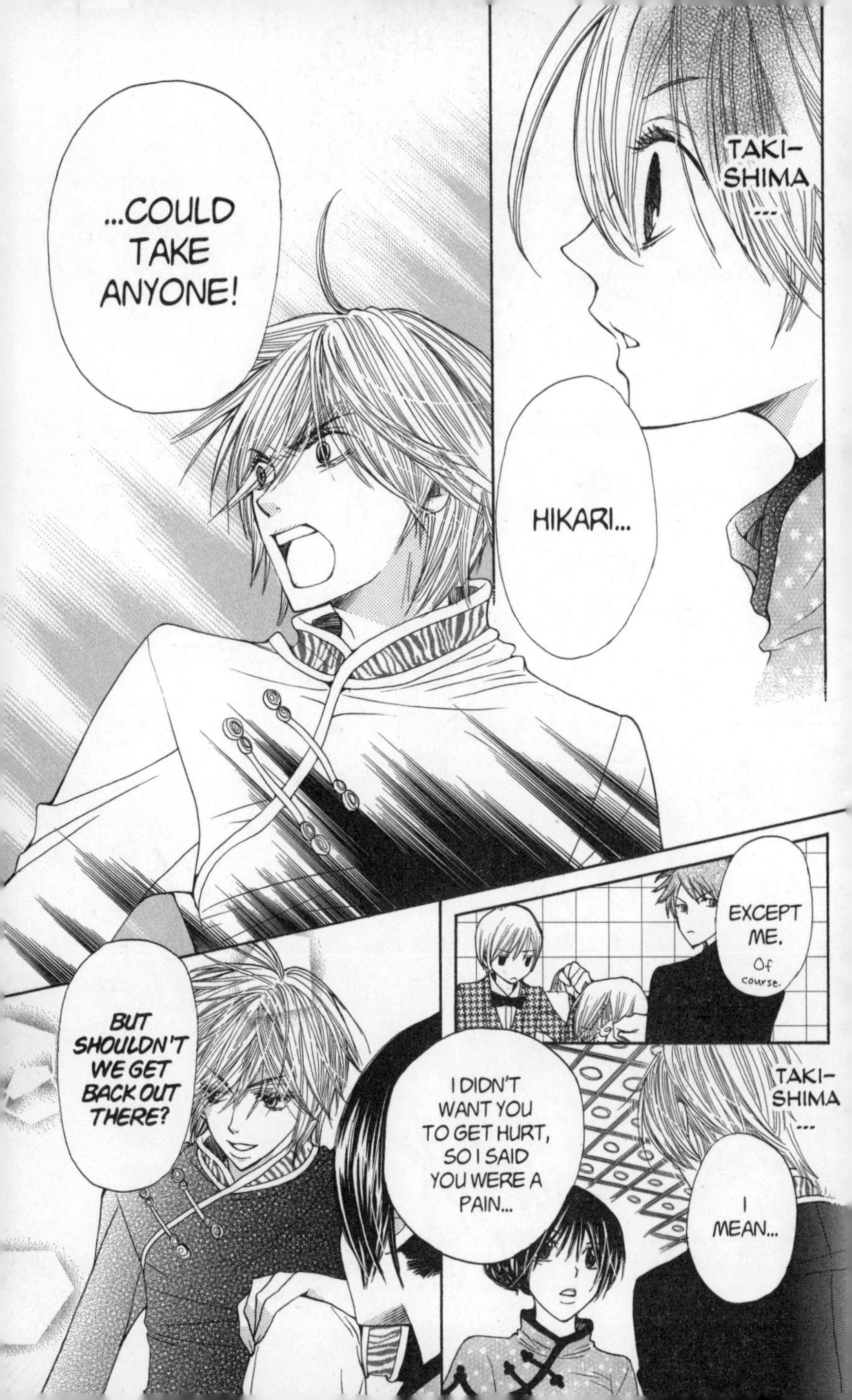
TAKI-SHIMA ...
HIKARI...
...COULD TAKE ANYONE!
EXCEPT ME.
Of course.
TAKI-SHIMA ...
I MEAN...
I DIDN'T WANT YOU TO GET HURT, SO I SAID YOU WERE A PAIN...
BUT SHOULDN'T WE GET BACK OUT THERE?

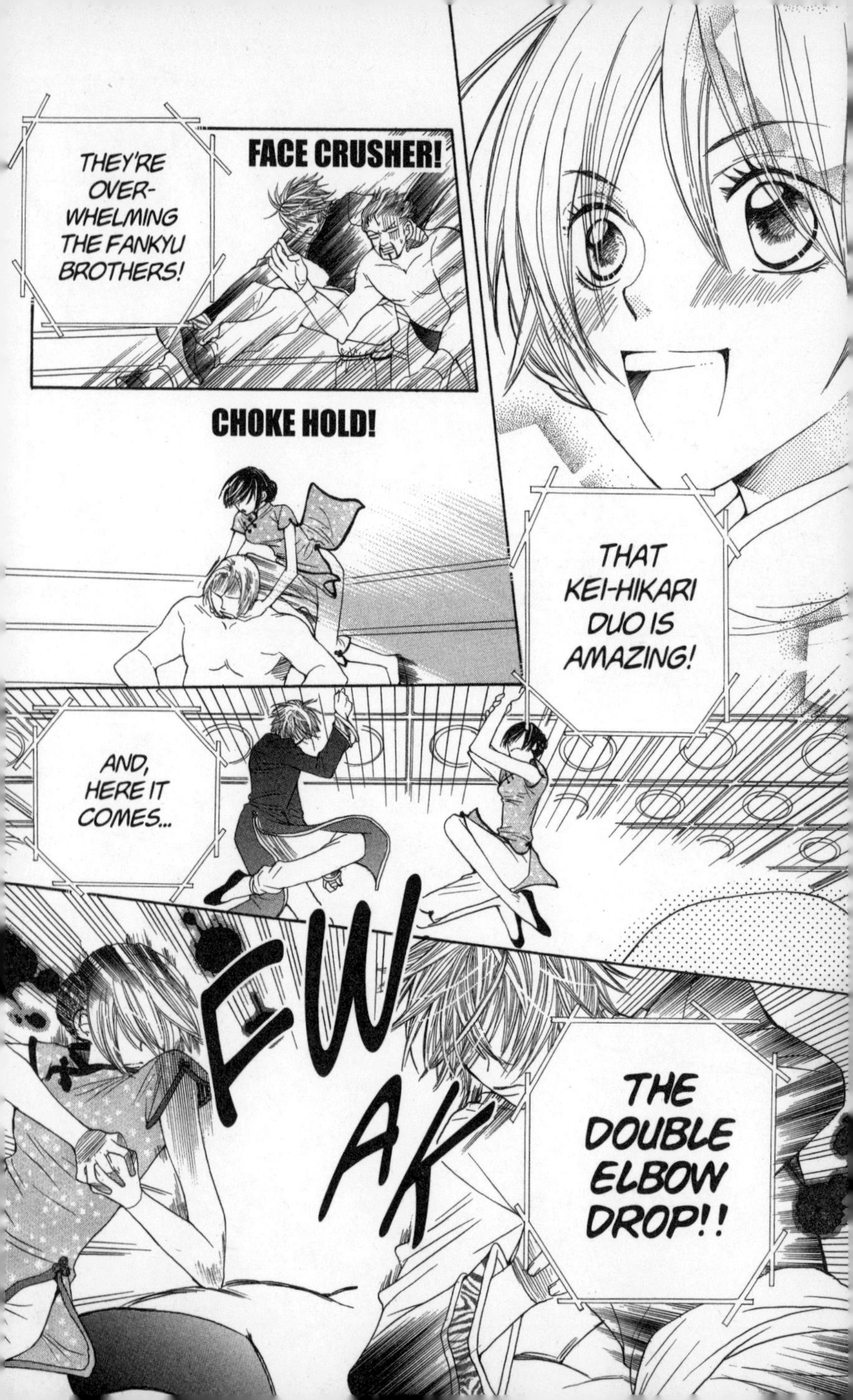
THAT KEI-HIKARI DUO IS AMAZING!
FACE CRUSHER!
THEY'RE OVER-WHELMING THE FANKYU BROTHERS!
CHOKE HOLD!
AND, HERE IT COMES...
THE DOUBLE ELBOW DROP!!
FWAK

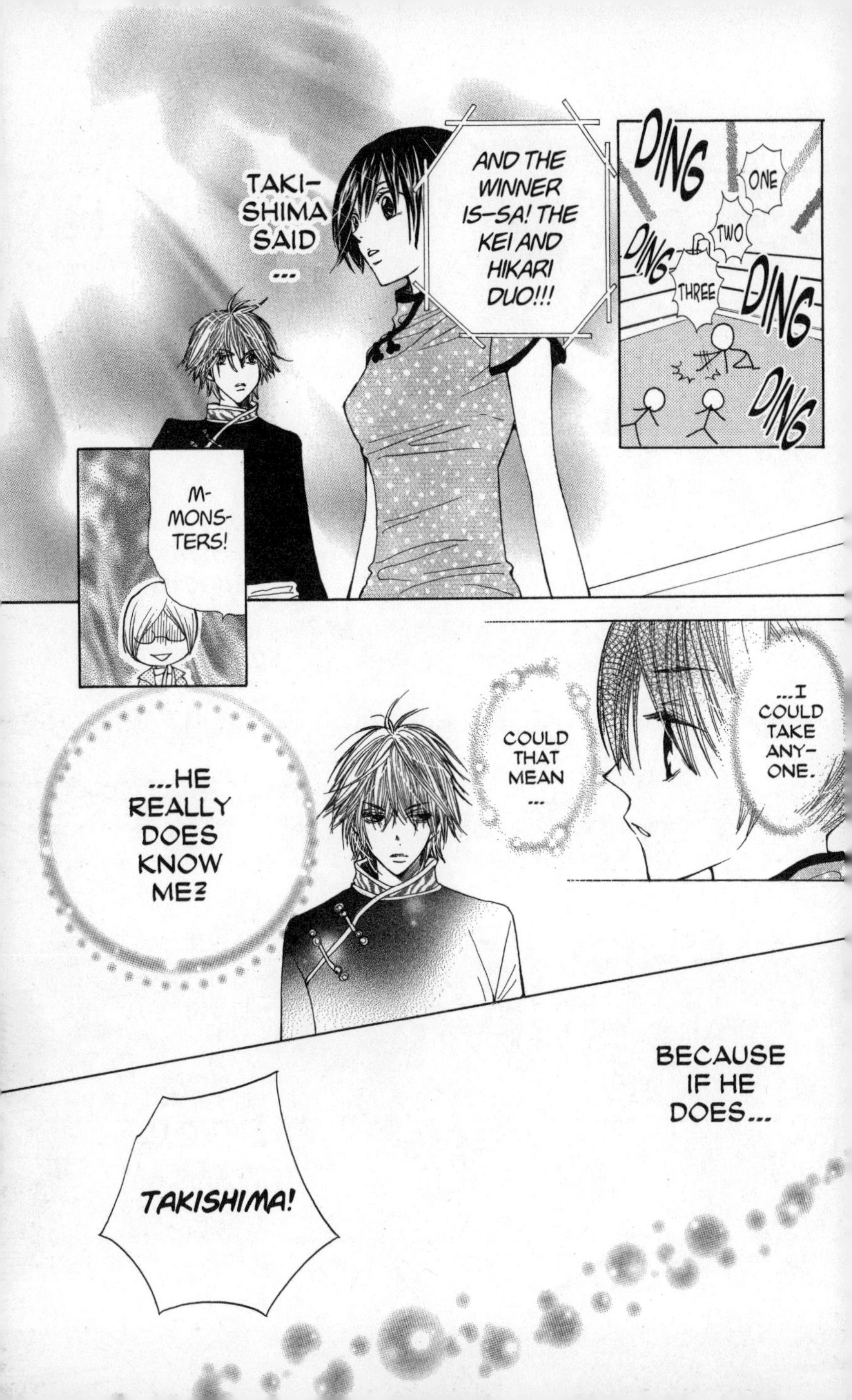
DING
ONE
DING
TWO
THREE
DING
DING
AND THE WINNER IS—SA! THE KEI AND HIKARI DUO!!!
TAKI-SHIMA SAID ...
M-MONSTERS!
...I COULD TAKE ANY-ONE.
COULD THAT MEAN ...
...HE REALLY DOES KNOW ME?
BECAUSE IF HE DOES...
TAKISHIMA!

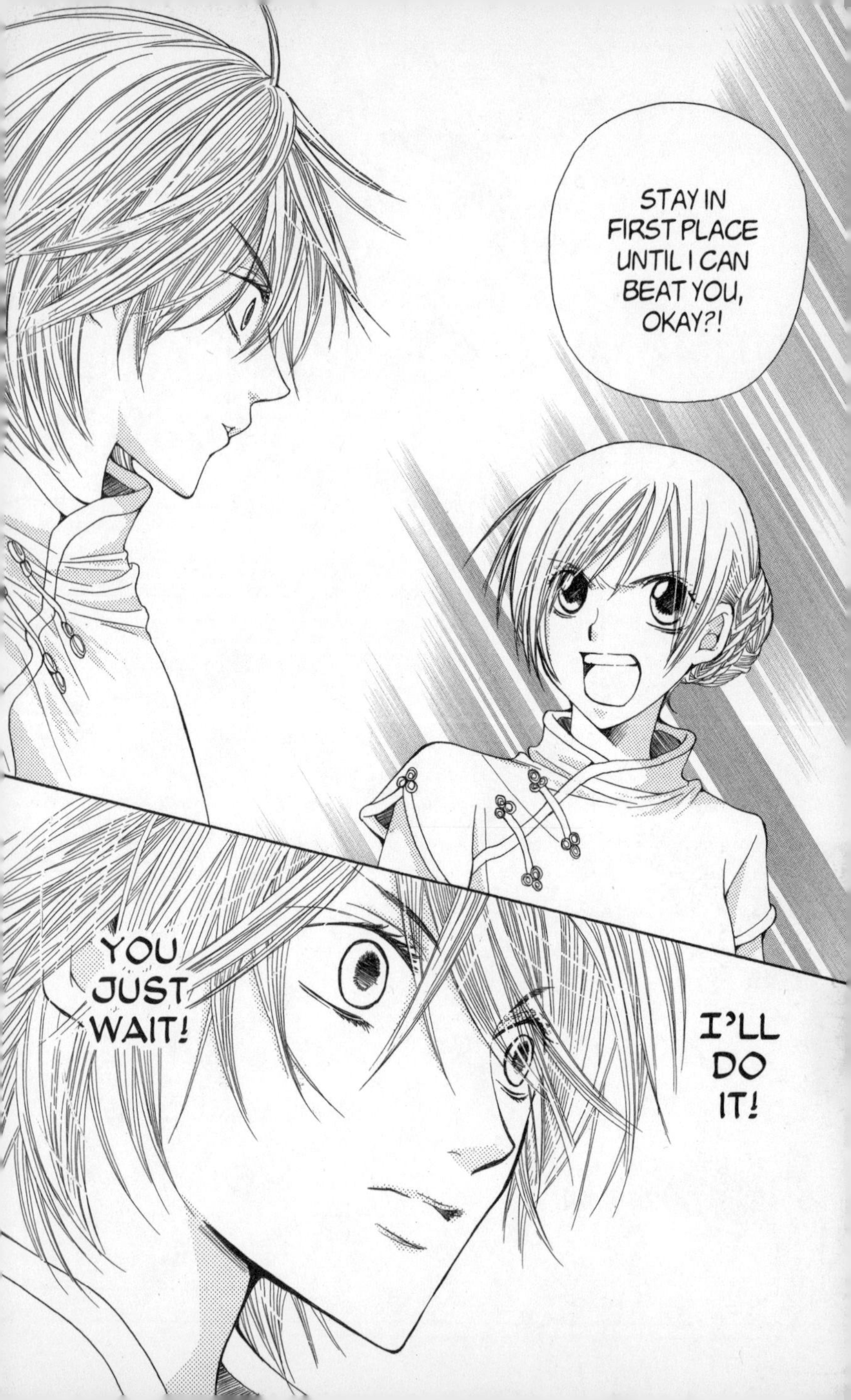
STAY IN FIRST PLACE UNTIL I CAN BEAT YOU, OKAY?!
I'LL DO IT!
YOU JUST WAIT!

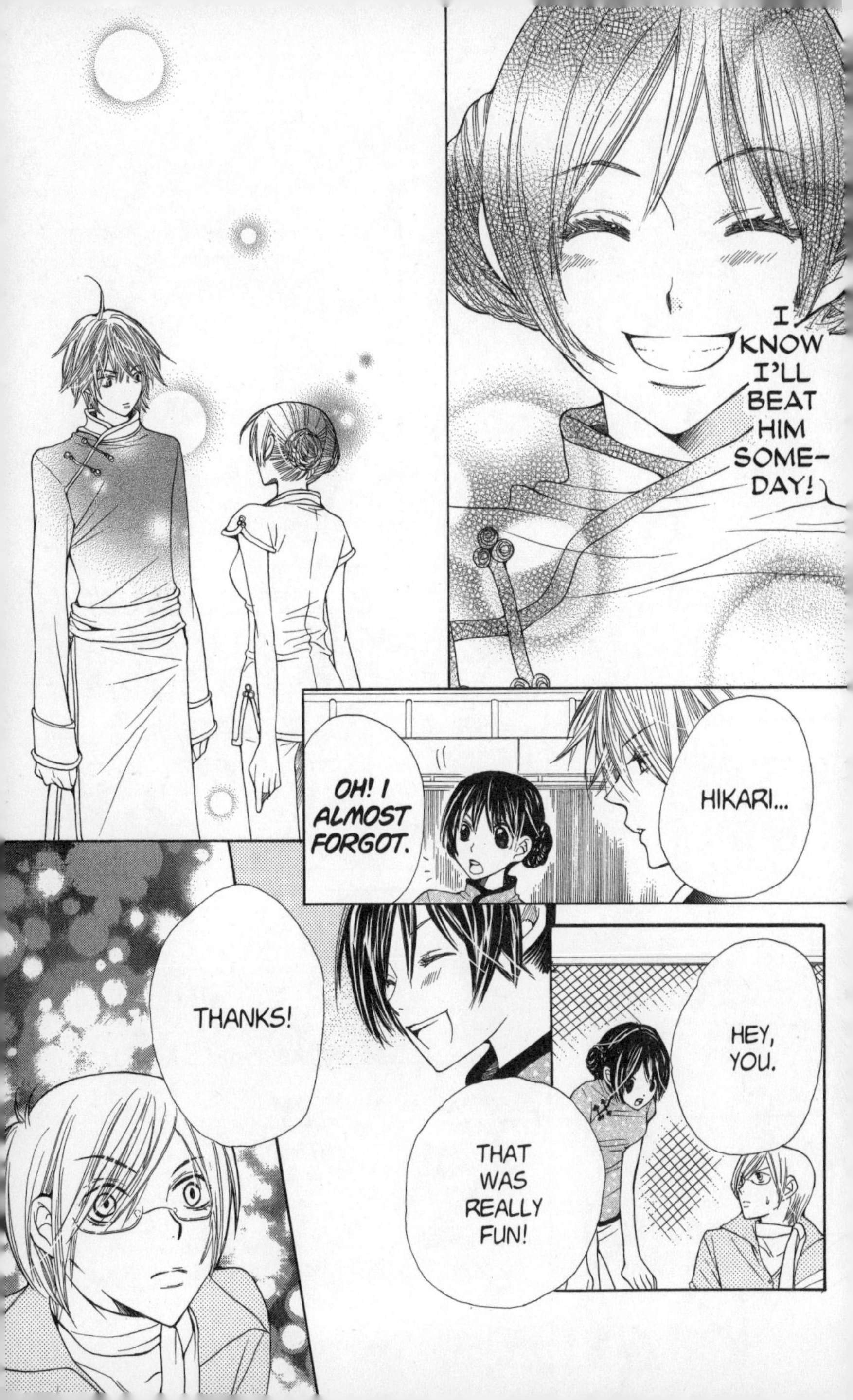
I KNOW I'LL BEAT HIM SOME-DAY!
HIKARI...
OH! I ALMOST FORGOT.
HEY, YOU.
THAT WAS REALLY FUN!
THANKS!

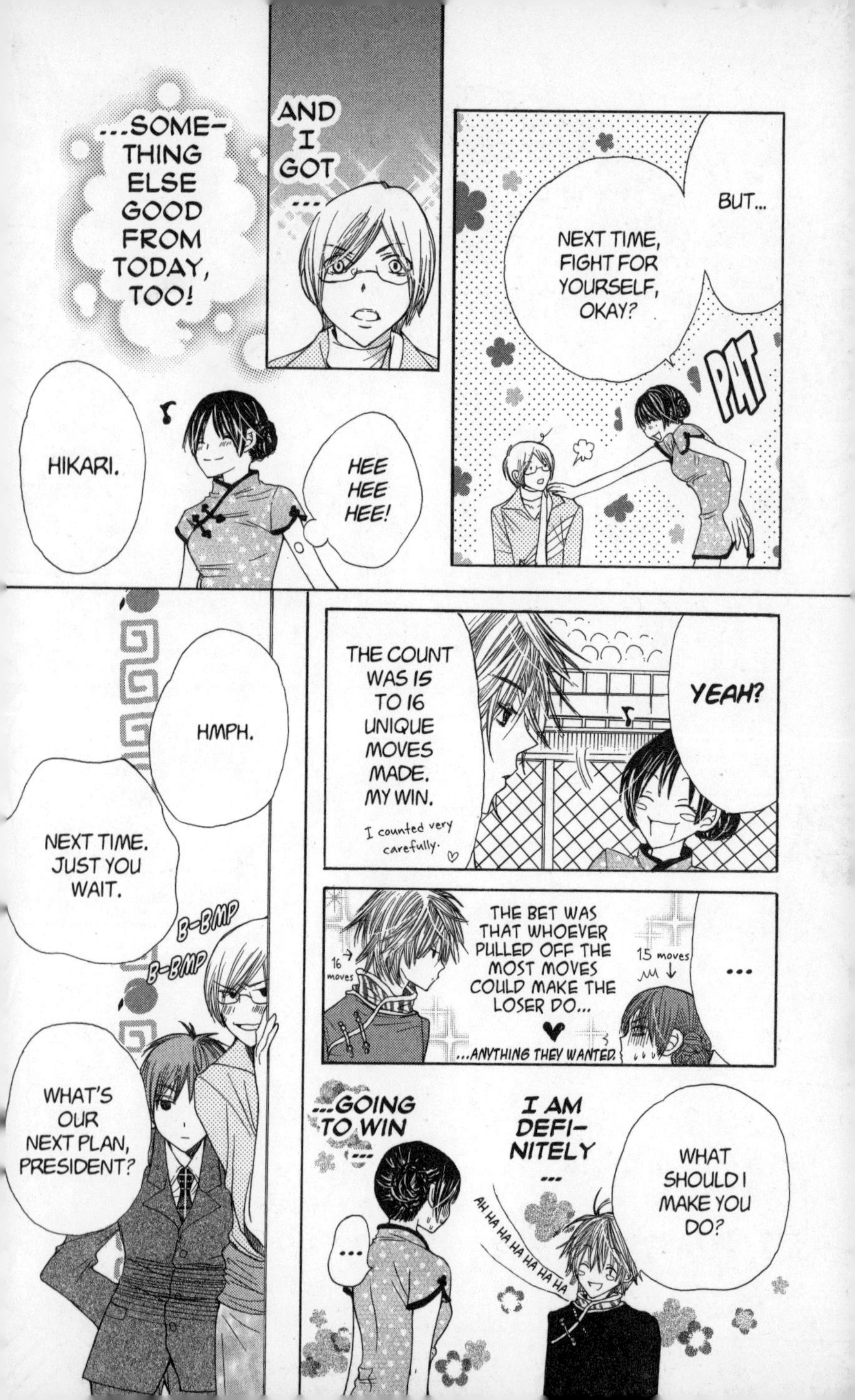
BUT...
NEXT TIME, FIGHT FOR YOURSELF, OKAY?
PAT
AND I GOT...
...SOME-THING ELSE GOOD FROM TODAY, TOO!
HEE HEE HEE!
HIKARI.
YEAH?
THE COUNT WAS 15 TO 16 UNIQUE MOVES MADE. MY WIN.
I counted very carefully.
...
THE BET WAS THAT WHOEVER PULLED OFF THE MOST MOVES COULD MAKE THE LOSER DO...
15 moves
16 moves
...ANYTHING THEY WANTED.
WHAT SHOULD I MAKE YOU DO?
AH HA HA HA HA HA HA
I AM DEFI-NITELY...
...GOING TO WIN...
...
HMPH.
NEXT TIME. JUST YOU WAIT.
B-BMP
B-BMP
WHAT'S OUR NEXT PLAN, PRESIDENT?

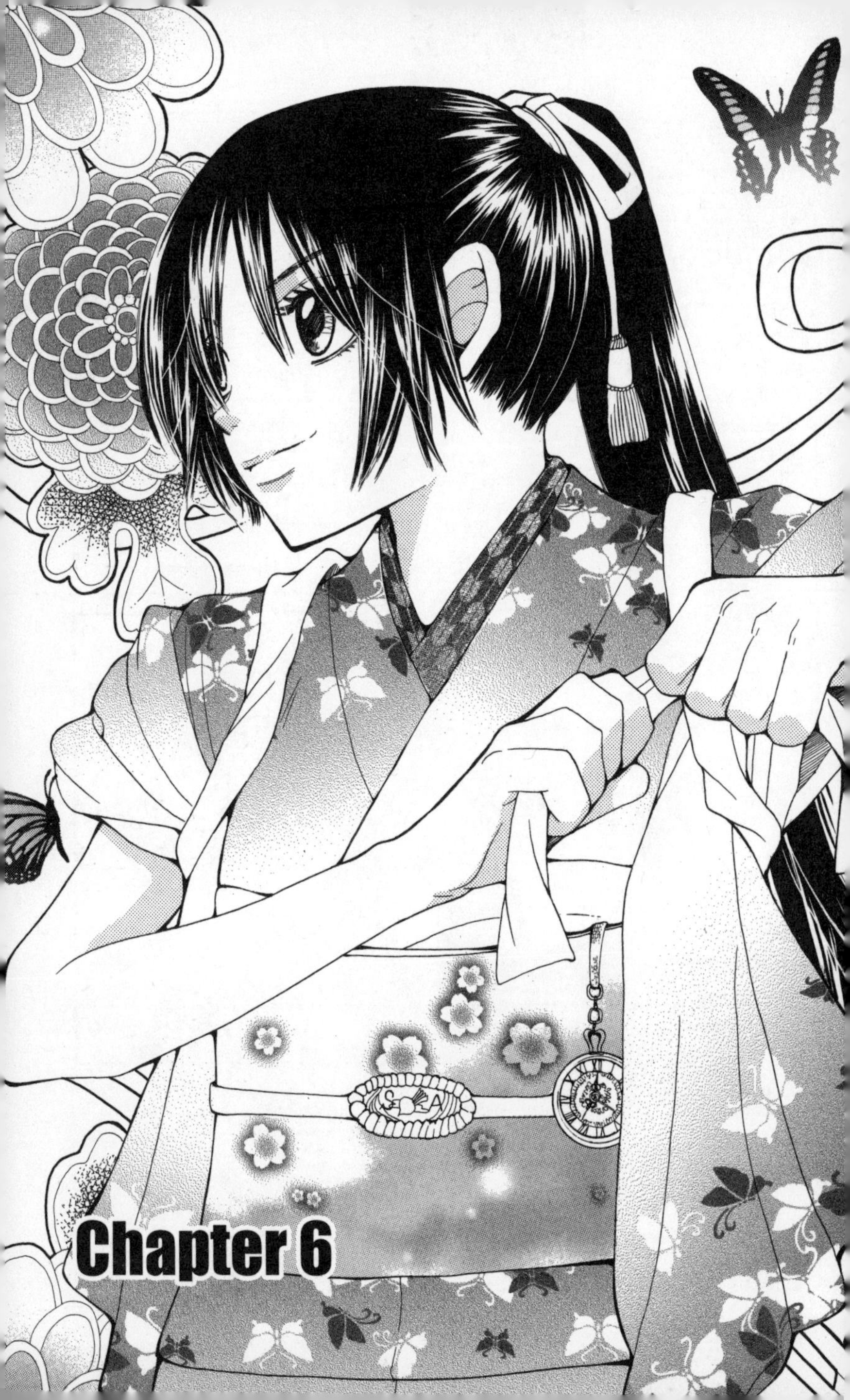
Chapter 6

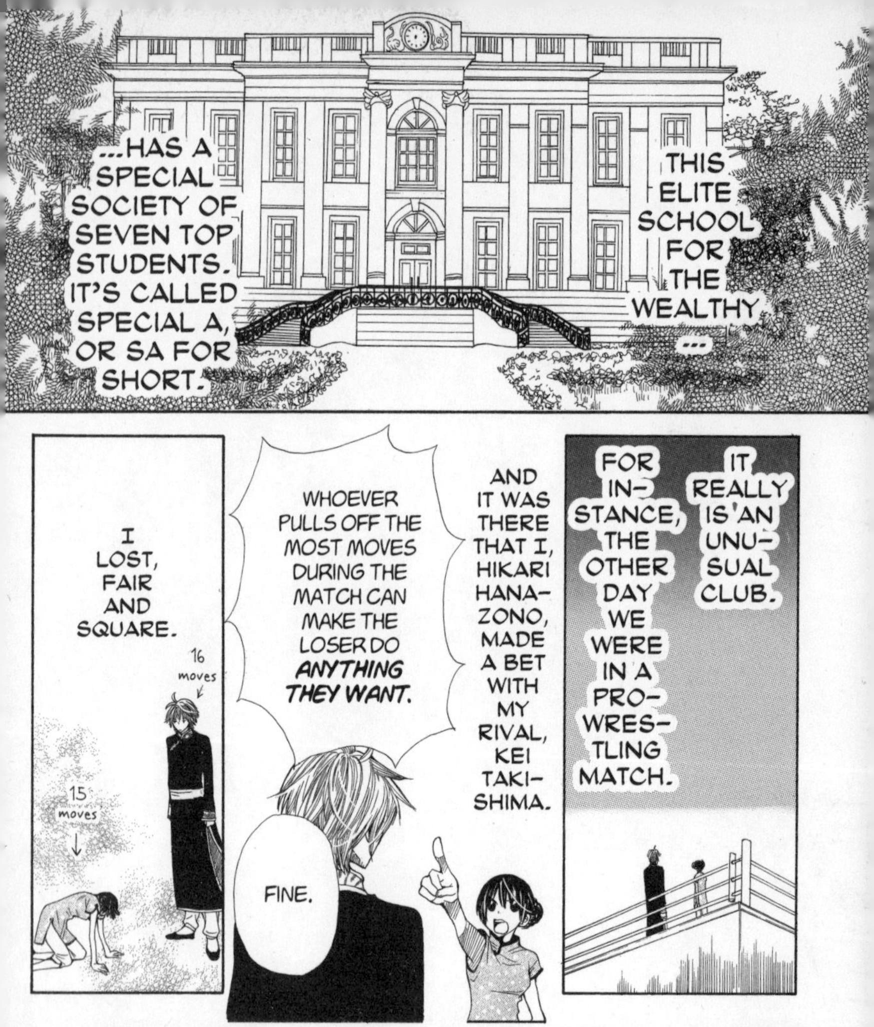
THIS ELITE SCHOOL FOR THE WEALTHY...
...HAS A SPECIAL SOCIETY OF SEVEN TOP STUDENTS. IT'S CALLED SPECIAL A, OR SA FOR SHORT.
IT REALLY IS AN UNUSUAL CLUB.
FOR INSTANCE, THE OTHER DAY WE WERE IN A PRO-WRESTLING MATCH.
AND IT WAS THERE THAT I, HIKARI HANAZONO, MADE A BET WITH MY RIVAL, KEI TAKISHIMA.
WHOEVER PULLS OFF THE MOST MOVES DURING THE MATCH CAN MAKE THE LOSER DO ANYTHING THEY WANT.
FINE.
I LOST, FAIR AND SQUARE.
16 moves
15 moves

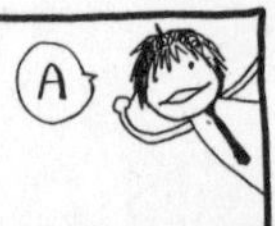
A

•MY FIRST SERIES•

NOW THAT THERE'S A SECOND VOLUME, SA IS OFFICIALLY A ***SERIES!*** REALLY, IT IS ALL THANKS TO YOU. I AM VERY INEXPERIENCED, BUT I WILL WORK HARD TO GET BETTER. PLEASE STAY WITH ME, IF YOU DON'T MIND! "Hup!

BY THE WAY...IN THIS STORY...WE SEEM TO HAVE GONE BACK IN TIME. THEY'RE DOING THEIR SOPHOMORE YEAR AGAIN... THEY'RE REPEATING THE WHOLE GRADE. EVEN THOUGH THEY'RE ELITE STUDENTS. TAKISHIMA TURNED 16 IN VOLUME ONE, BUT HE'S ONLY 15 IN VOLUME TWO. BUT APPARENTLY HE'S STILL OLD ENOUGH TO RIDE OFF ON A STOLEN MOTORCYCLE.♥

Begs for your forgiveness!

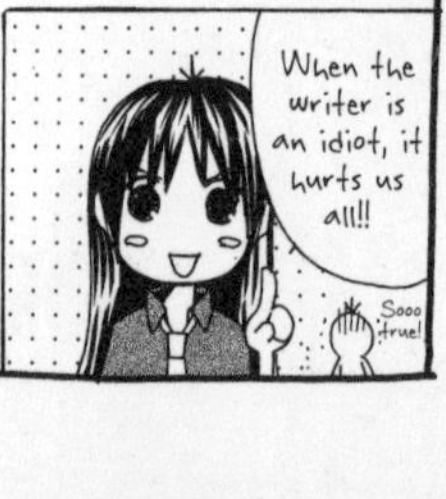
When the writer is an idiot, it hurts us all!!
Sooo true!

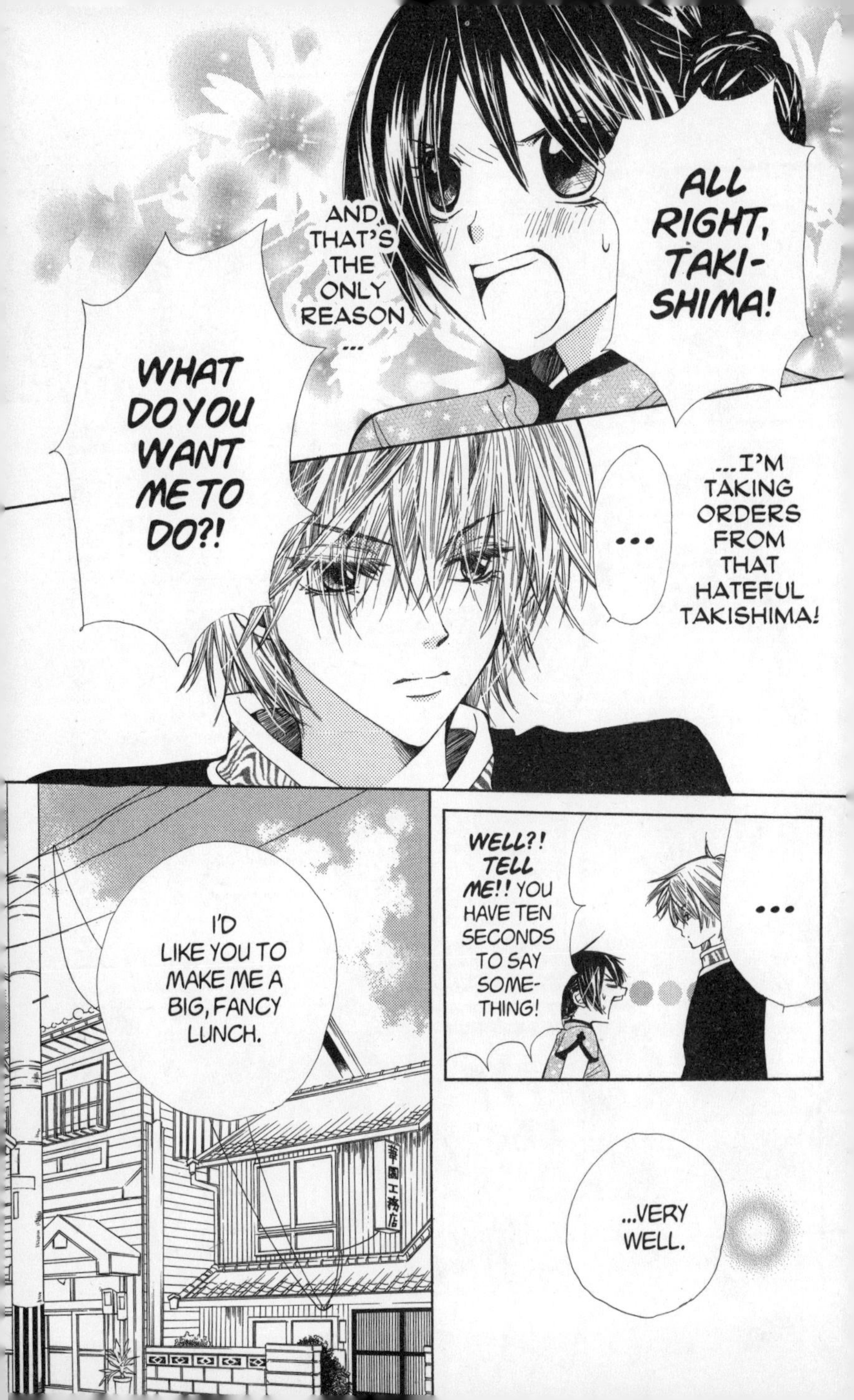
ALL RIGHT, TAKI-SHIMA!
AND THAT'S THE ONLY REASON...
...I'M TAKING ORDERS FROM THAT HATEFUL TAKISHIMA!
...
WHAT DO YOU WANT ME TO DO?!
WELL?! TELL ME!! YOU HAVE TEN SECONDS TO SAY SOME-THING!
...
...VERY WELL.
I'D LIKE YOU TO MAKE ME A BIG, FANCY LUNCH.

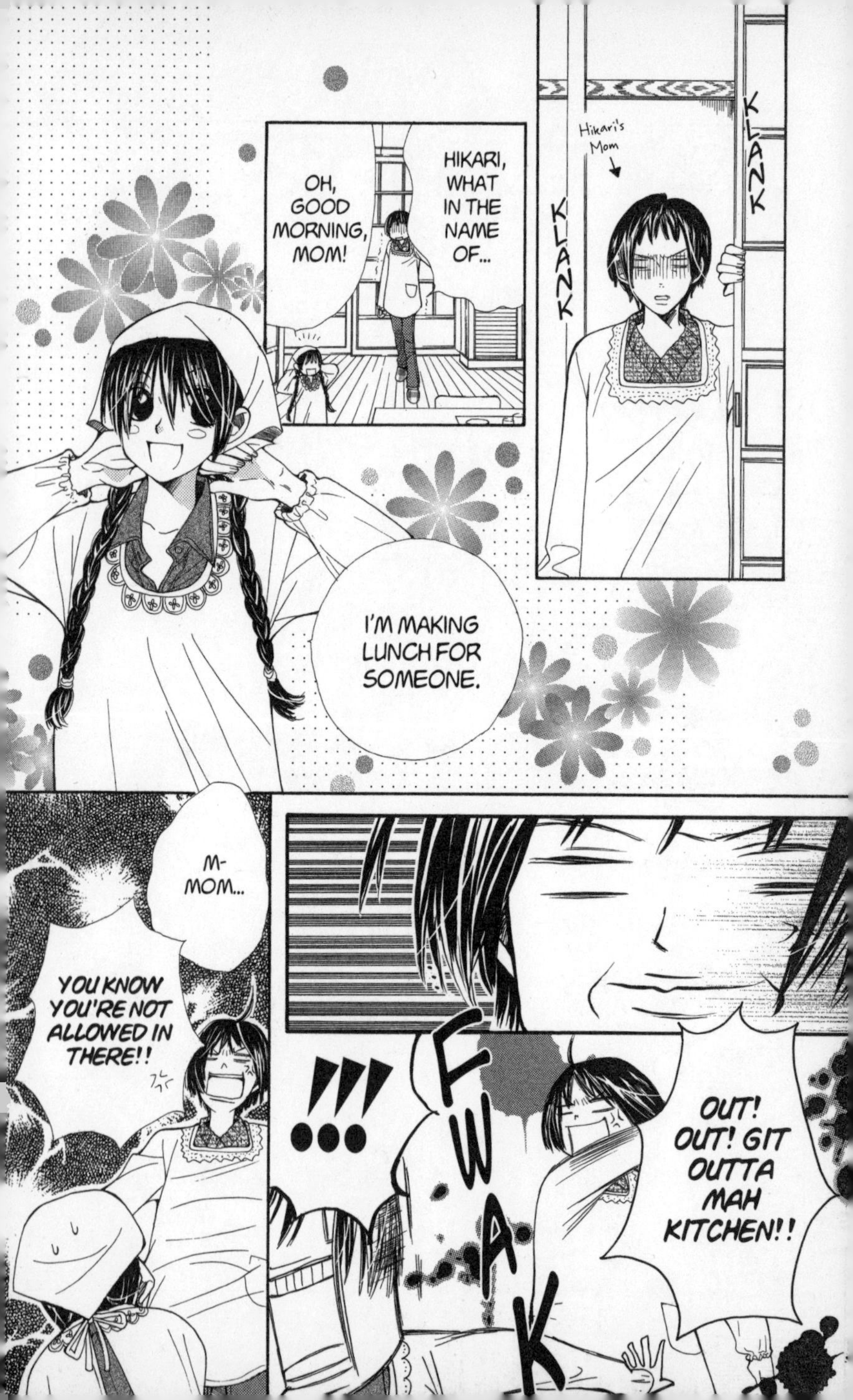
KLANK
KLANK
Hikari's Mom
HIKARI, WHAT IN THE NAME OF...
OH, GOOD MORNING, MOM!
I'M MAKING LUNCH FOR SOMEONE.
OUT! OUT! GIT OUTTA MAH KITCHEN!!
FWAK
!!!
M-MOM...
YOU KNOW YOU'RE NOT ALLOWED IN THERE!!

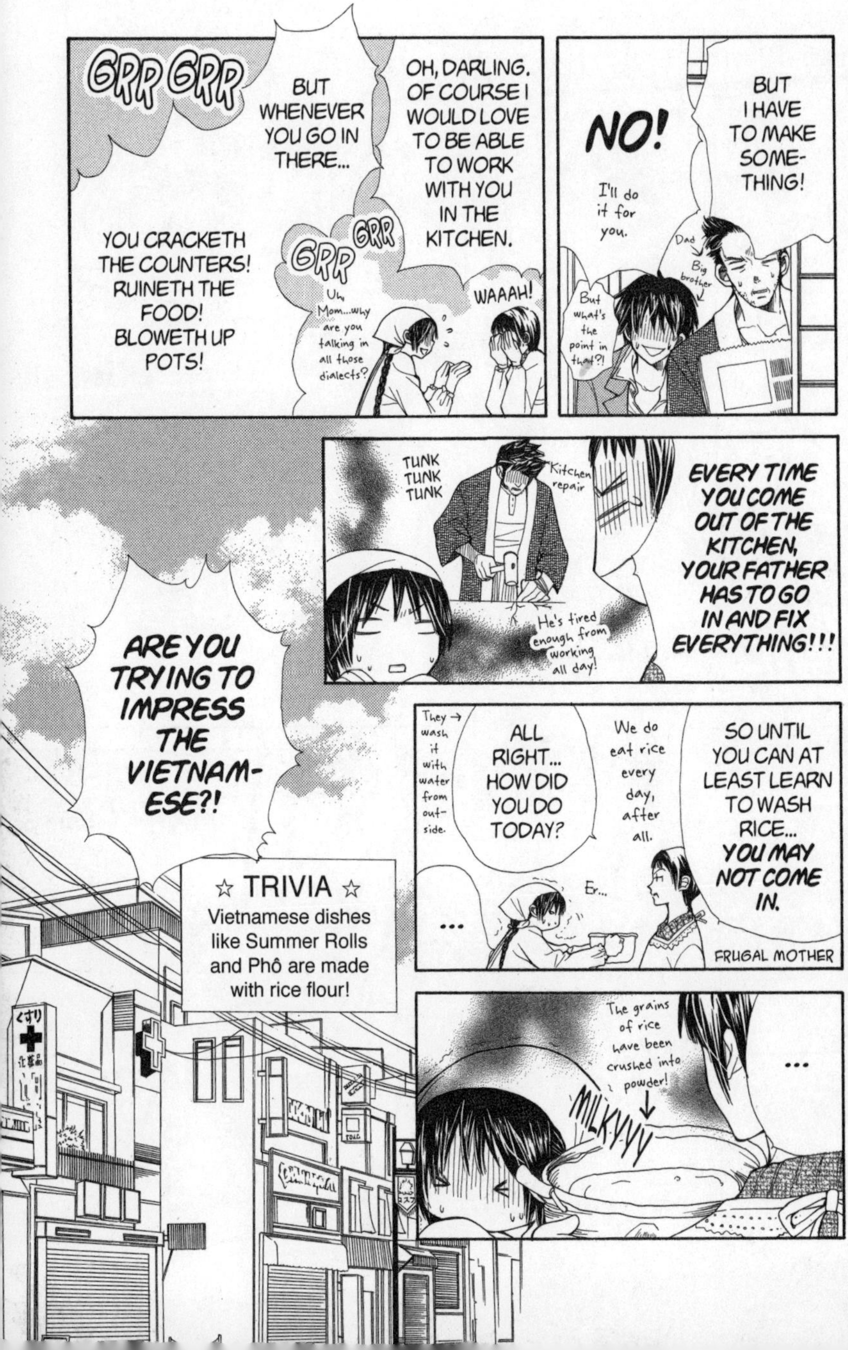
BUT I HAVE TO MAKE SOME-THING!
NO!
I'll do it for you.
Dad
Big brother
But what's the point in that?!
OH, DARLING. OF COURSE I WOULD LOVE TO BE ABLE TO WORK WITH YOU IN THE KITCHEN.
BUT WHENEVER YOU GO IN THERE...
GRR GRR
YOU CRACKETH THE COUNTERS! RUINETH THE FOOD! BLOWETH UP POTS!
GRR GRR
WAAAH!
Uh, Mom...why are you talking in all those dialects?
EVERY TIME YOU COME OUT OF THE KITCHEN, YOUR FATHER HAS TO GO IN AND FIX EVERYTHING!!!
Kitchen repair
TUNK TUNK TUNK
He's tired enough from working all day!
SO UNTIL YOU CAN AT LEAST LEARN TO WASH RICE... YOU MAY NOT COME IN.
We do eat rice every day, after all.
ALL RIGHT... HOW DID YOU DO TODAY?
They → wash it with water from out-side.
Er...
...
FRUGAL MOTHER
...
The grains of rice have been crushed into powder!
MILKYYYY
ARE YOU TRYING TO IMPRESS THE VIETNAM-ESE?!
☆ TRIVIA ☆
Vietnamese dishes like Summer Rolls and Phô are made with rice flour!

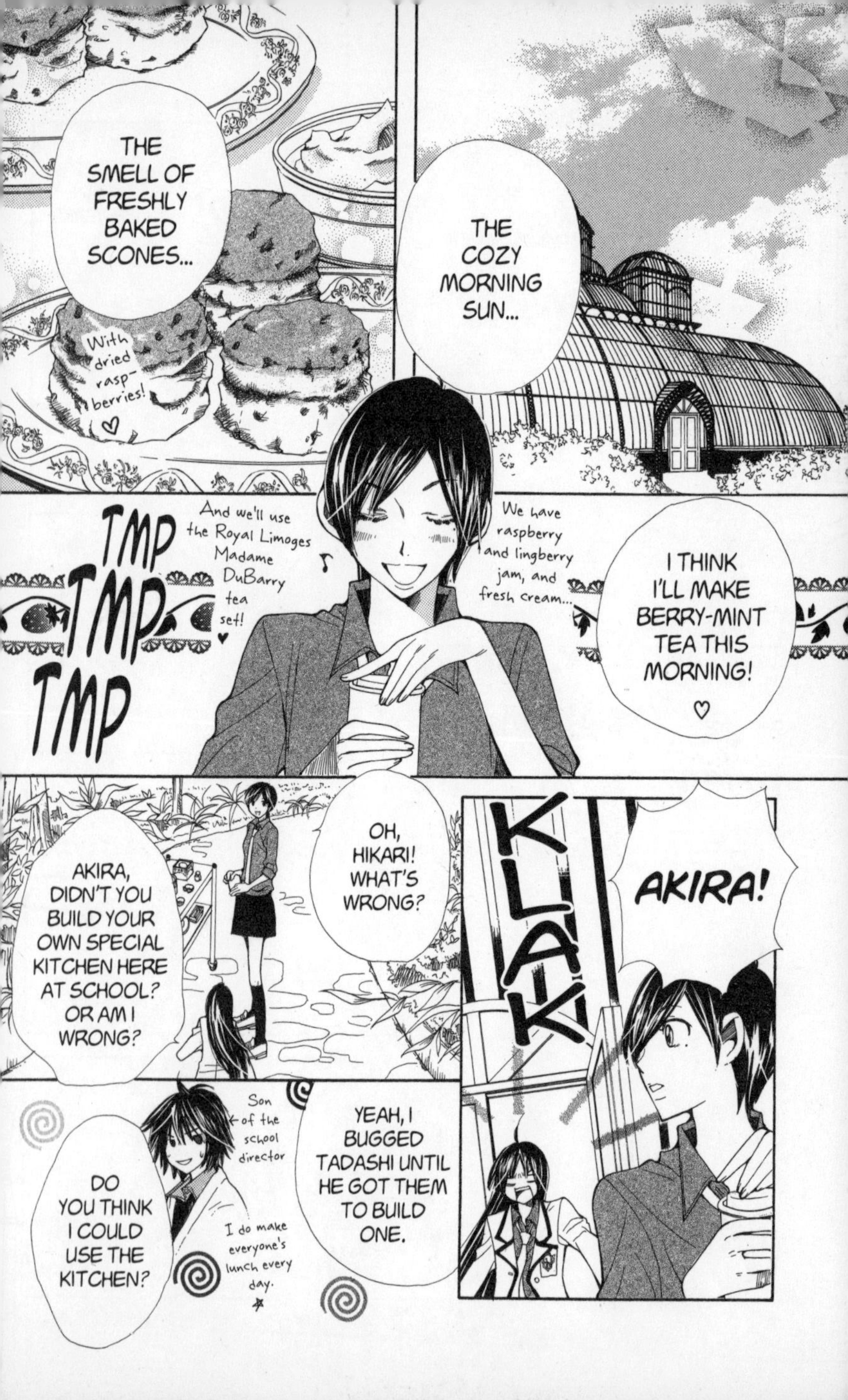
THE COZY MORNING SUN...
THE SMELL OF FRESHLY BAKED SCONES...
With dried rasp-berries! ♡
I THINK I'LL MAKE BERRY-MINT TEA THIS MORNING! ♡
We have raspberry and lingberry jam, and fresh cream...
And we'll use the Royal Limoges Madame DuBarry tea set! ♥
TMP TMP TMP
AKIRA!
KLAK
OH, HIKARI! WHAT'S WRONG?
AKIRA, DIDN'T YOU BUILD YOUR OWN SPECIAL KITCHEN HERE AT SCHOOL? OR AM I WRONG?
YEAH, I BUGGED TADASHI UNTIL HE GOT THEM TO BUILD ONE.
Son of the school director
I do make everyone's lunch every day.
DO YOU THINK I COULD USE THE KITCHEN?

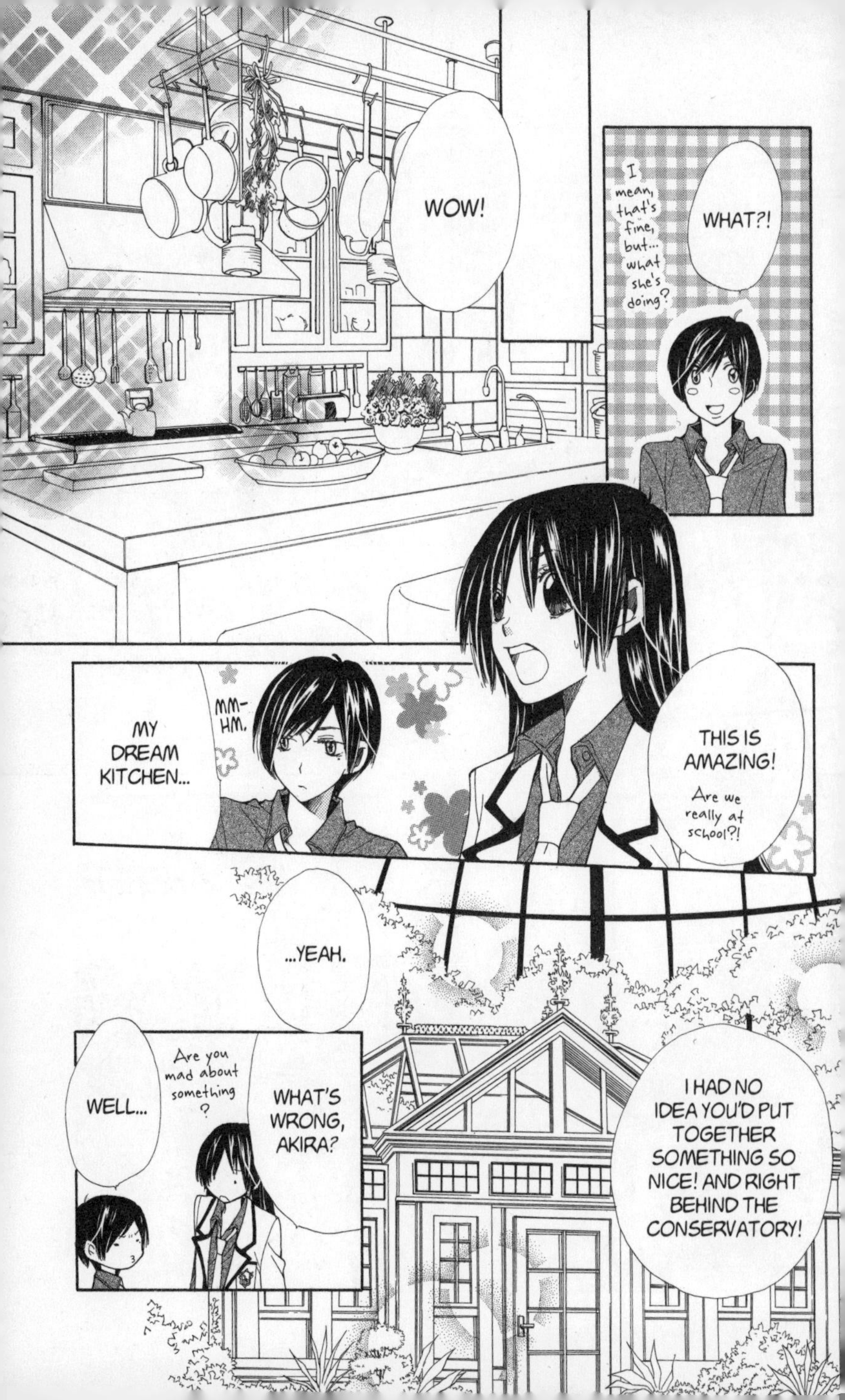
WHAT?!
I mean, that's fine, but... what she's doing?
WOW!
THIS IS AMAZING!
Are we really at school?!
MM-HM.
MY DREAM KITCHEN...
I HAD NO IDEA YOU'D PUT TOGETHER SOMETHING SO NICE! AND RIGHT BEHIND THE CONSERVATORY!
...YEAH.
WHAT'S WRONG, AKIRA?
Are you mad about something?
WELL...

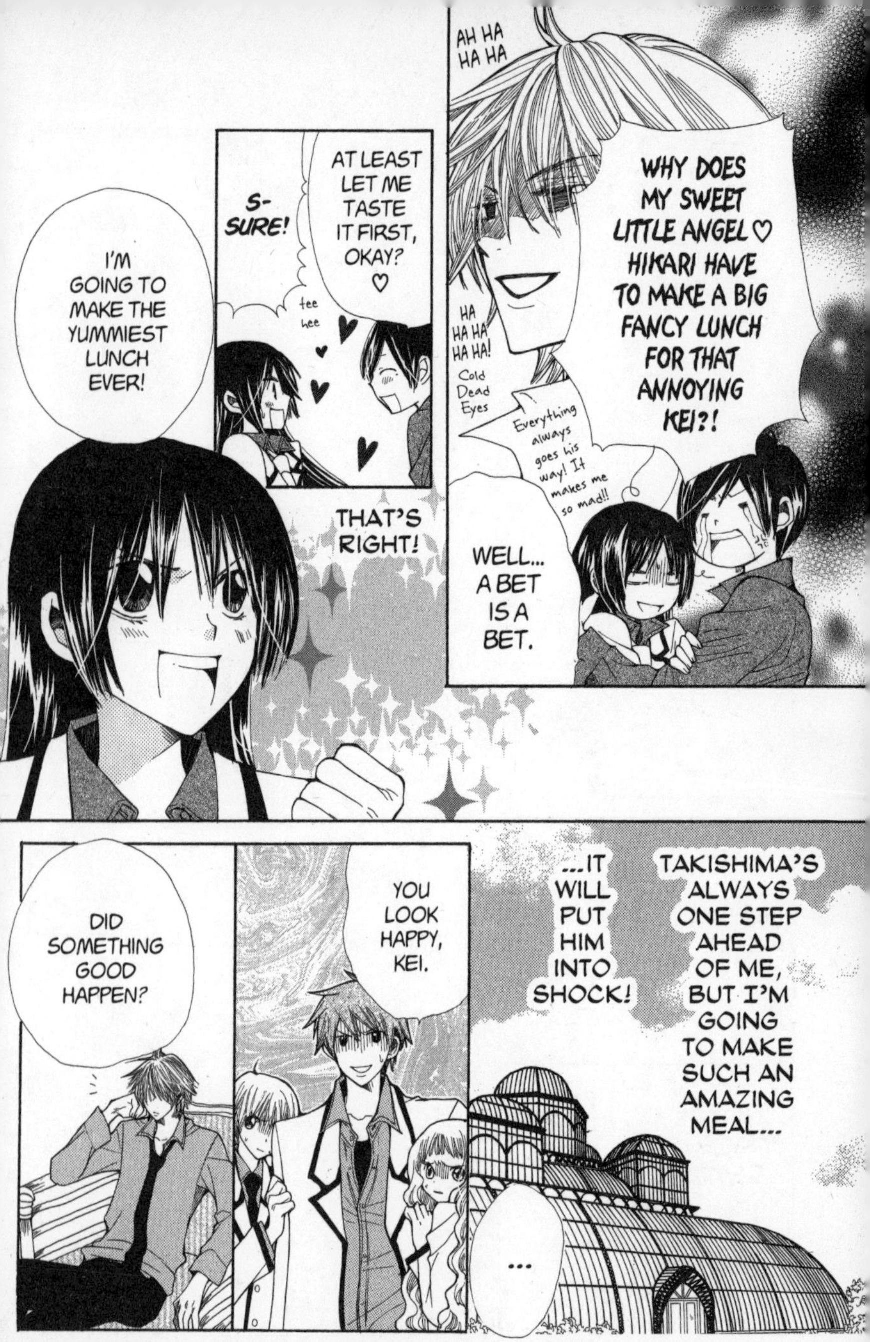
AH HA HA HA
WHY DOES MY SWEET LITTLE ANGEL ♡ HIKARI HAVE TO MAKE A BIG FANCY LUNCH FOR THAT ANNOYING KEI?!
HA HA HA HA HA!
Cold Dead Eyes
Everything always goes his way! It makes me so mad!!
WELL... A BET IS A BET.
AT LEAST LET ME TASTE IT FIRST, OKAY? ♡
S-SURE!
tee hee
THAT'S RIGHT!
I'M GOING TO MAKE THE YUMMIEST LUNCH EVER!
TAKISHIMA'S ALWAYS ONE STEP AHEAD OF ME, BUT I'M GOING TO MAKE SUCH AN AMAZING MEAL...
...IT WILL PUT HIM INTO SHOCK!
...
YOU LOOK HAPPY, KEI.
DID SOMETHING GOOD HAPPEN?

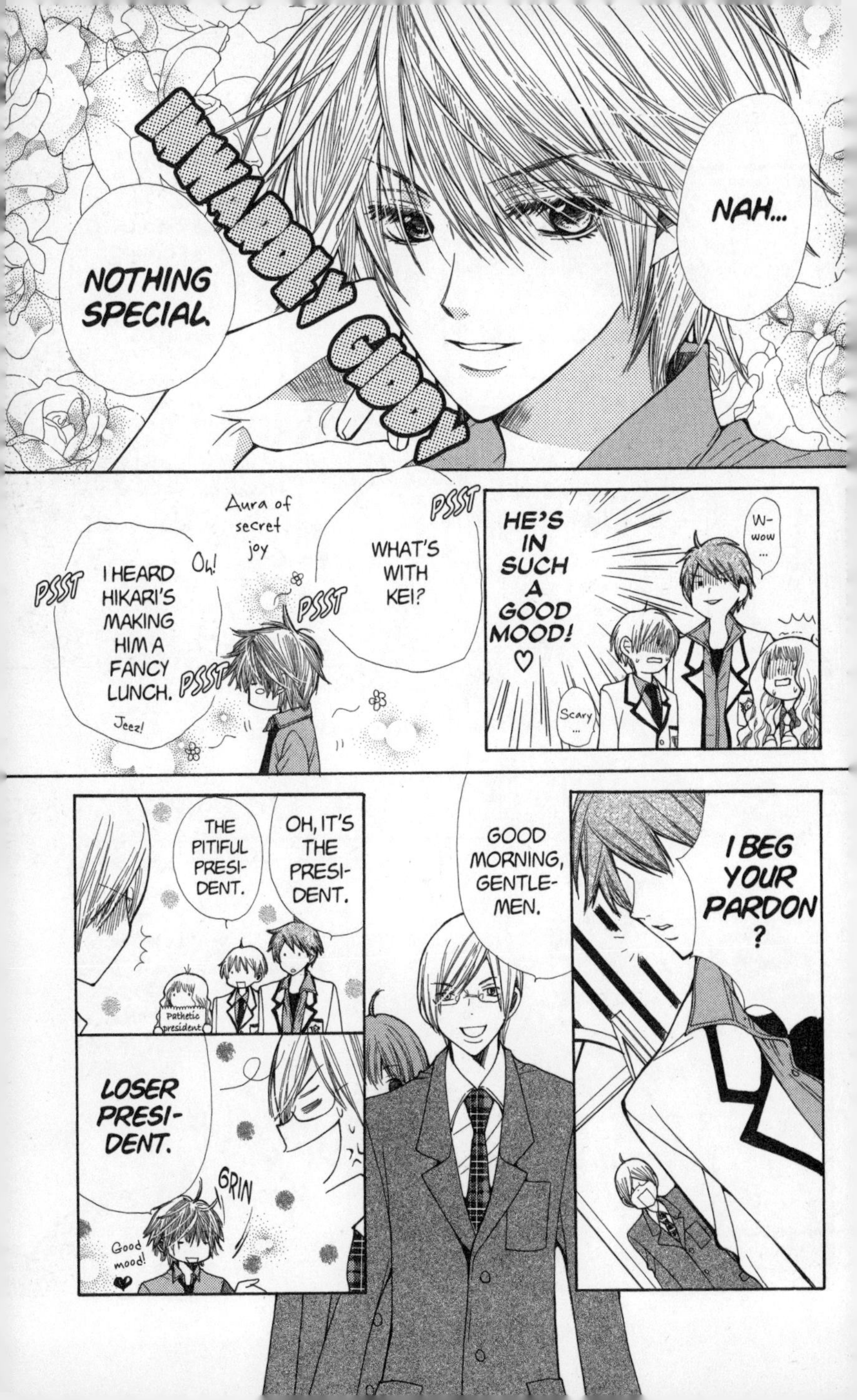
NAH...
NOTHING SPECIAL.
HE'S IN SUCH A GOOD MOOD! ♡
W-wow...
Scary...
PSSST
WHAT'S WITH KEI?
PSSST
Aura of secret joy
Oh!
PSSST
I HEARD HIKARI'S MAKING HIM A FANCY LUNCH.
PSSST
Jeez!
I BEG YOUR PARDON?
GOOD MORNING, GENTLEMEN.
OH, IT'S THE PRESIDENT.
THE PITIFUL PRESIDENT.
Pathetic president
LOSER PRESIDENT.
GRIN
Good mood!

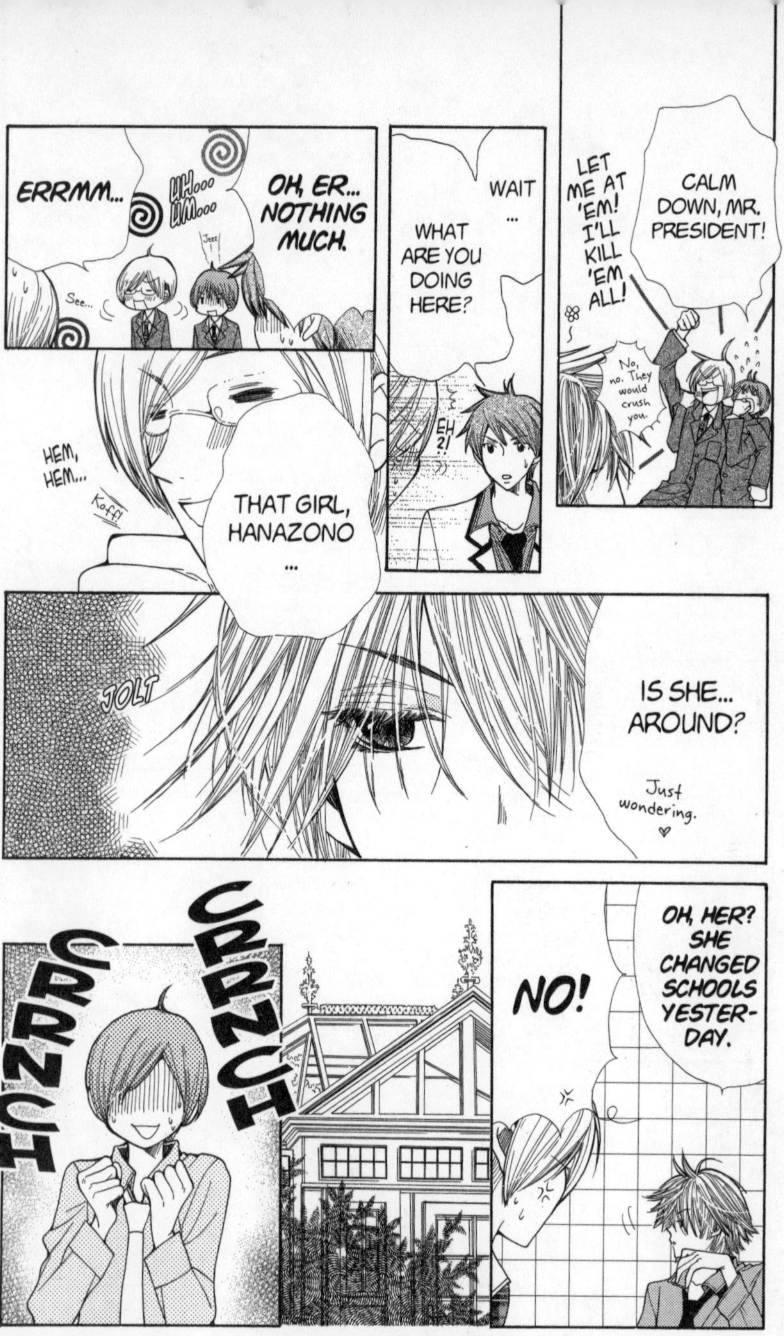
CALM DOWN, MR. PRESIDENT!
LET ME AT 'EM! I'LL KILL 'EM ALL!
No, no. They would crush you.
WAIT ...
WHAT ARE YOU DOING HERE?
EH?!
OH, ER... NOTHING MUCH.
Jeez
UHooo
UMooo
ERRMM...
See...
HEM, HEM...
Koff!
THAT GIRL, HANAZONO ...
IS SHE... AROUND?
Just wondering.
JOLT
OH, HER? SHE CHANGED SCHOOLS YESTER-DAY.
NO!
CRRNCH
CRRNCH

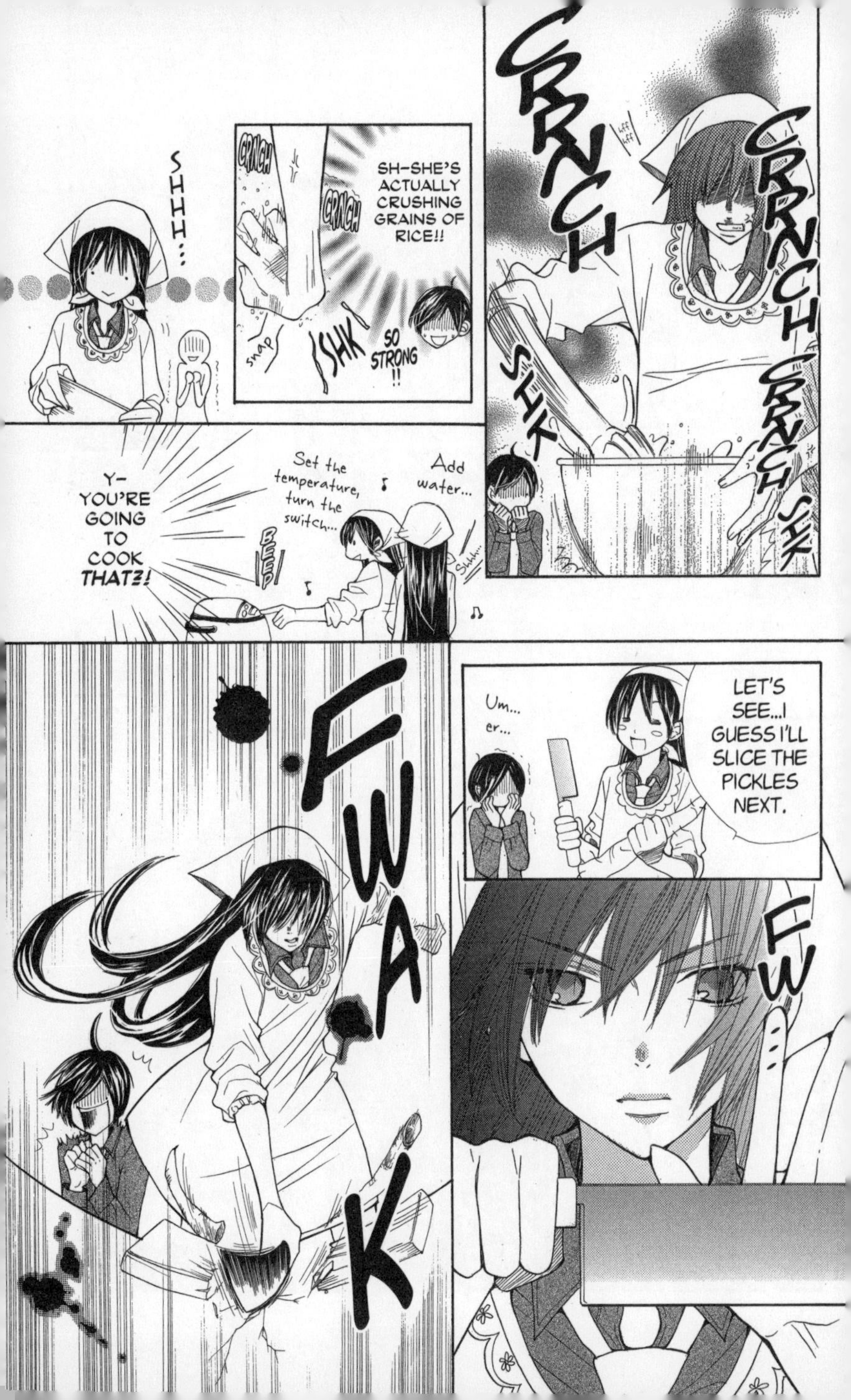
CRNCH
hff hff
CRNCH
SHK
CRNCH
SHK
CRNCH
CRNCH
SH-SHE'S ACTUALLY CRUSHING GRAINS OF RICE!!
snap
SHK
SO STRONG !!
SHHH...
Add water...
Set the temperature, turn the switch...
BEEP
Shhh...
Y-YOU'RE GOING TO COOK THAT?!
LET'S SEE...I GUESS I'LL SLICE THE PICKLES NEXT.
Um... er...
FW
FWAK

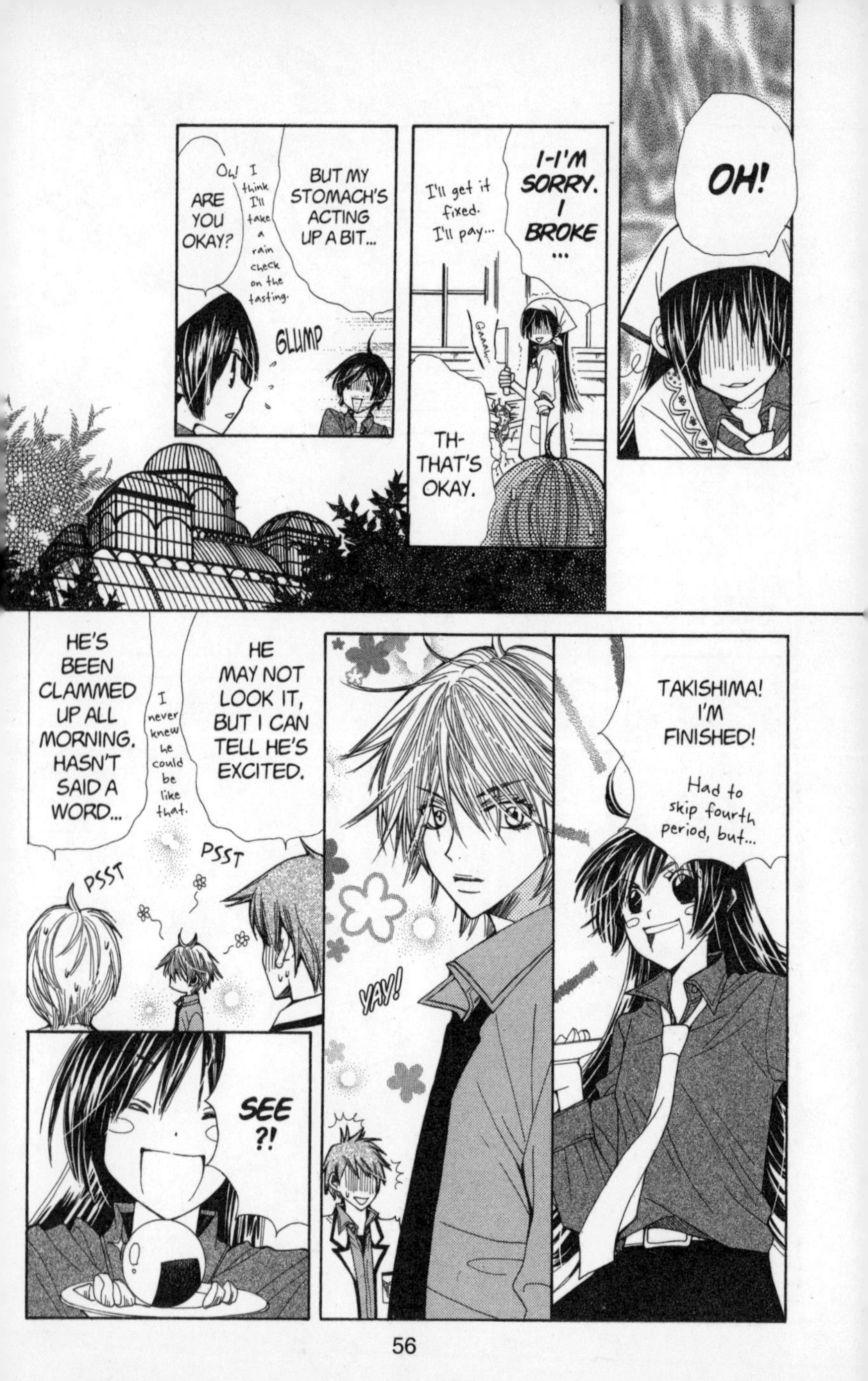

OH!
I-I'M SORRY. I BROKE...
I'll get it fixed. I'll pay...
TH-THAT'S OKAY.
BUT MY STOMACH'S ACTING UP A BIT...
Oh! I think I'll take a rain check on the tasting.
ARE YOU OKAY?
GLUMP
TAKISHIMA! I'M FINISHED!
Had to skip fourth period, but...
YAY!
HE MAY NOT LOOK IT, BUT I CAN TELL HE'S EXCITED.
I never knew he could be like that.
HE'S BEEN CLAMMED UP ALL MORNING. HASN'T SAID A WORD...
PSST
PSST
SEE?!

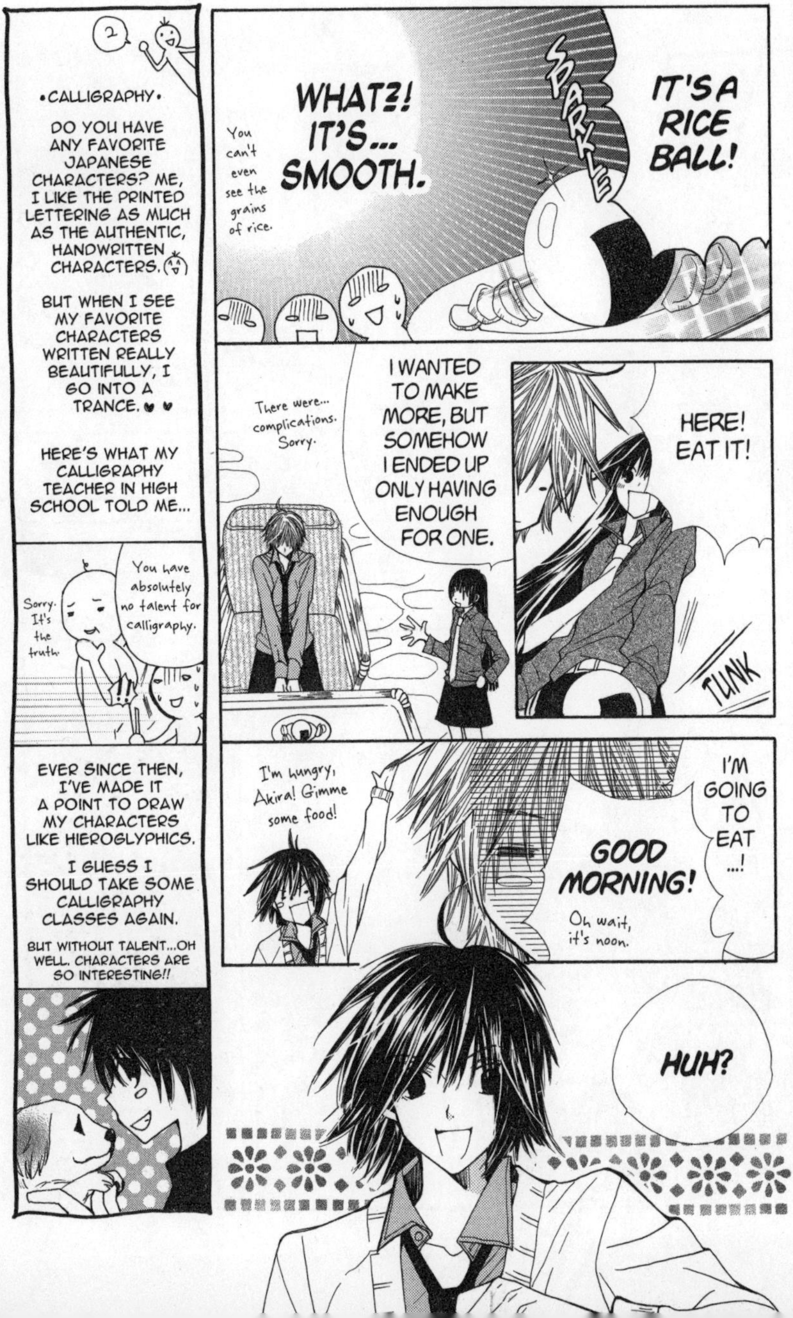
IT'S A RICE BALL!
SPARKLE
WHAT?! IT'S... SMOOTH.
You can't even see the grains of rice.
HERE! EAT IT!
TUNK
I WANTED TO MAKE MORE, BUT SOMEHOW I ENDED UP ONLY HAVING ENOUGH FOR ONE.
There were... complications. Sorry.
I'M GOING TO EAT ...!
GOOD MORNING!
Oh wait, it's noon.
I'm hungry, Akira! Gimme some food!
HUH?
2
•CALLIGRAPHY•
DO YOU HAVE ANY FAVORITE JAPANESE CHARACTERS? ME, I LIKE THE PRINTED LETTERING AS MUCH AS THE AUTHENTIC, HANDWRITTEN CHARACTERS.
BUT WHEN I SEE MY FAVORITE CHARACTERS WRITTEN REALLY BEAUTIFULLY, I GO INTO A TRANCE.
HERE'S WHAT MY CALLIGRAPHY TEACHER IN HIGH SCHOOL TOLD ME...
You have absolutely no talent for calligraphy.
Sorry. It's the truth.
EVER SINCE THEN, I'VE MADE IT A POINT TO DRAW MY CHARACTERS LIKE HIEROGLYPHICS.
I GUESS I SHOULD TAKE SOME CALLIGRAPHY CLASSES AGAIN.
BUT WITHOUT TALENT...OH WELL. CHARACTERS ARE SO INTERESTING!!

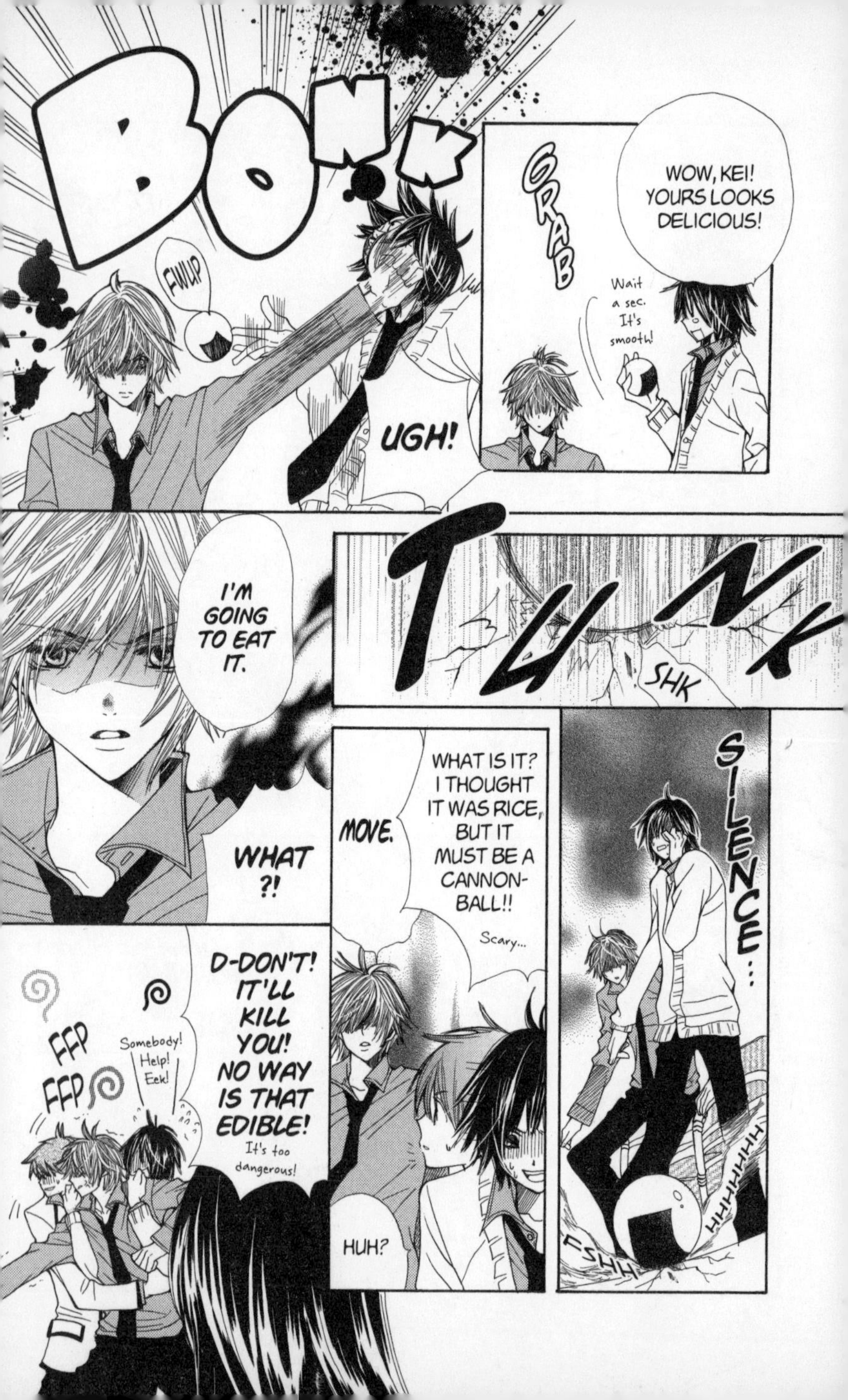
GRAB
WOW, KEI! YOURS LOOKS DELICIOUS!
Wait a sec. It's smooth!
BONK
FWUP
UGH!
TUNK
SHK
SILENCE...
FSHH
HHHHHHH
WHAT IS IT? I THOUGHT IT WAS RICE, BUT IT MUST BE A CANNON-BALL!!
Scary...
MOVE.
HUH?
I'M GOING TO EAT IT.
WHAT?!
D-DON'T! IT'LL KILL YOU! NO WAY IS THAT EDIBLE!
It's too dangerous!
Somebody! Help! Eek!
FFP FFP

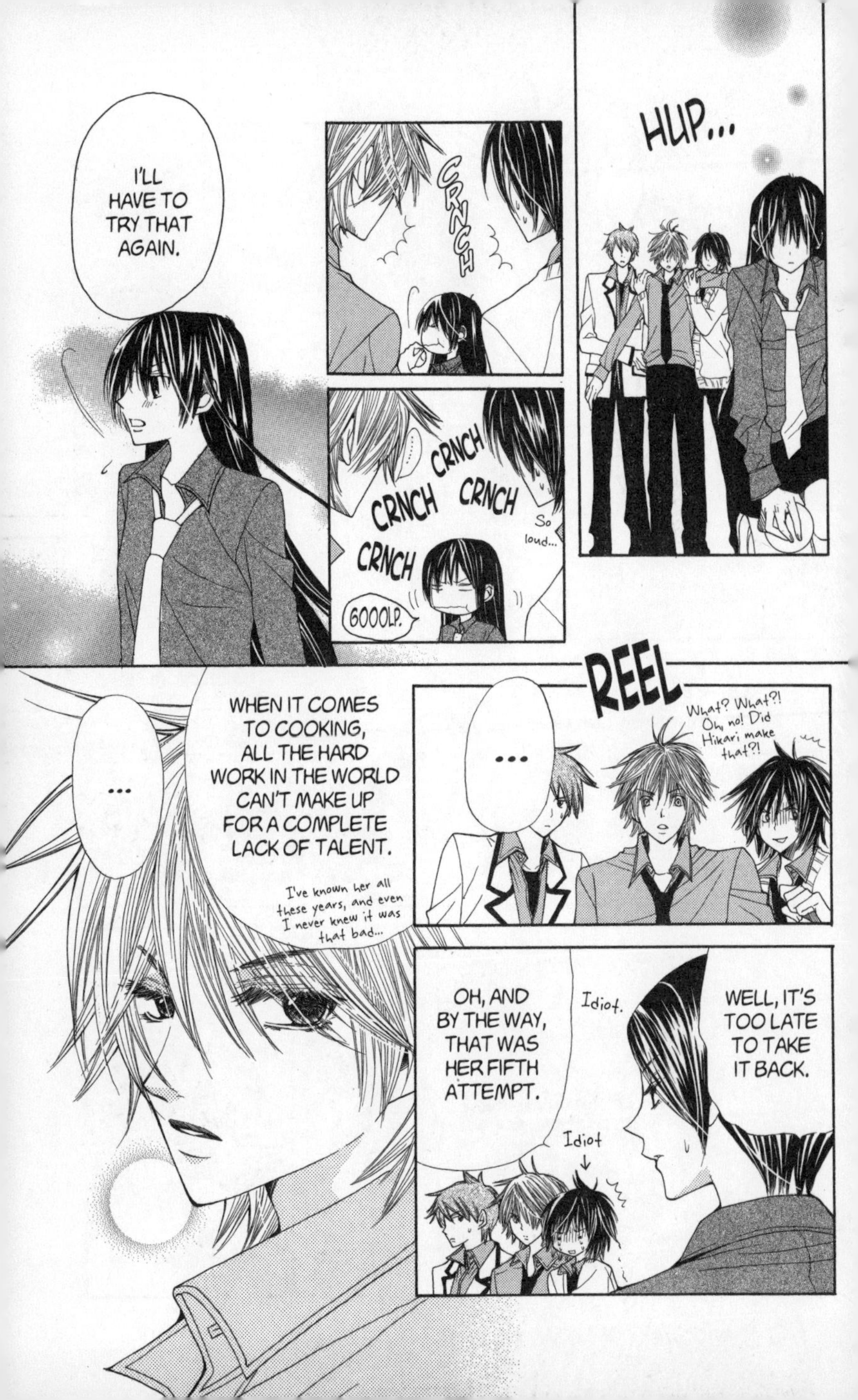
HUP...
CRNCH
So loud...
CRNCH
CRNCH
CRNCH
CRNCH
GOOOLP.
I'LL HAVE TO TRY THAT AGAIN.
REEL
What? What?! Oh, no! Did Hikari make that?!
...
WELL, IT'S TOO LATE TO TAKE IT BACK.
Idiot.
OH, AND BY THE WAY, THAT WAS HER FIFTH ATTEMPT.
Idiot
WHEN IT COMES TO COOKING, ALL THE HARD WORK IN THE WORLD CAN'T MAKE UP FOR A COMPLETE LACK OF TALENT.
I've known her all these years, and even I never knew it was that bad...
...

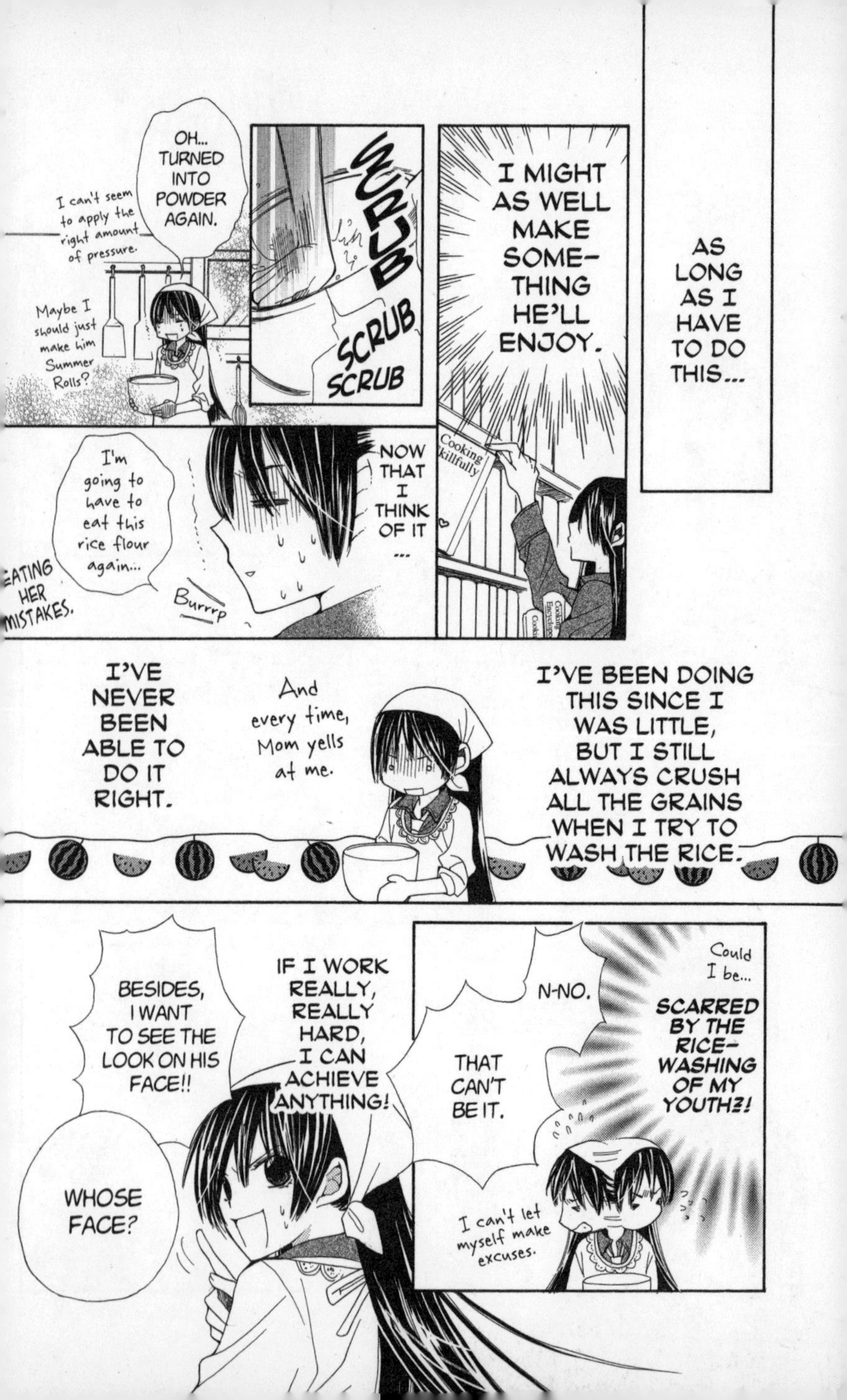

AS LONG AS I HAVE TO DO THIS...
I MIGHT AS WELL MAKE SOMETHING HE'LL ENJOY.
Cooking Skillfully
SCRUB
SCRUB
SCRUB
OH... TURNED INTO POWDER AGAIN.
I can't seem to apply the right amount of pressure.
Maybe I should just make him Summer Rolls?
NOW THAT I THINK OF IT...
I'm going to have to eat this rice flour again...
Burrrp
EATING HER MISTAKES.
I'VE BEEN DOING THIS SINCE I WAS LITTLE, BUT I STILL ALWAYS CRUSH ALL THE GRAINS WHEN I TRY TO WASH THE RICE.
And every time, Mom yells at me.
I'VE NEVER BEEN ABLE TO DO IT RIGHT.
Could I be...
SCARRED BY THE RICE-WASHING OF MY YOUTH?!
N-NO.
THAT CAN'T BE IT.
I can't let myself make excuses.
IF I WORK REALLY, REALLY HARD, I CAN ACHIEVE ANYTHING!
BESIDES, I WANT TO SEE THE LOOK ON HIS FACE!!
WHOSE FACE?

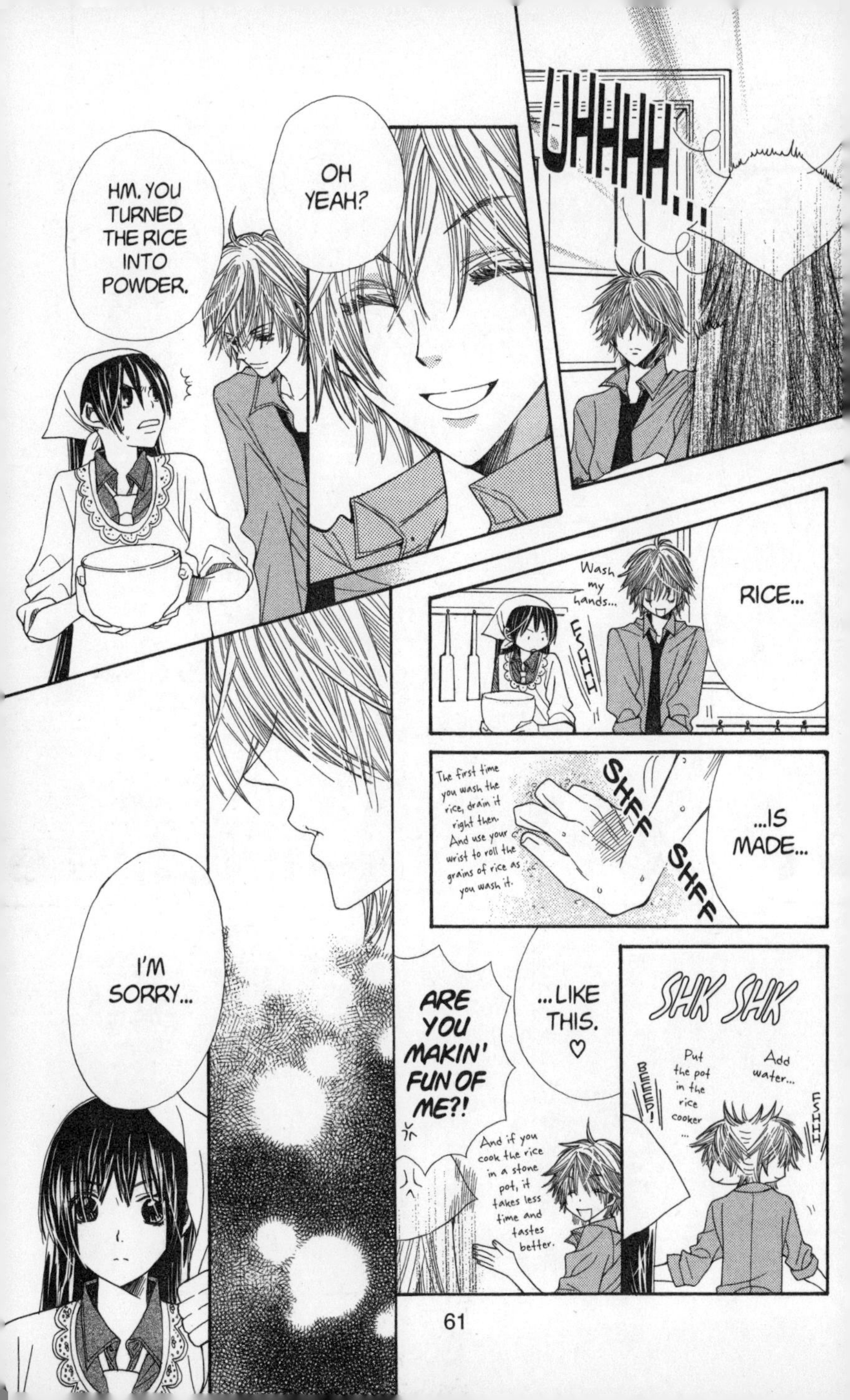
UHHHH...
OH YEAH?
HM. YOU TURNED THE RICE INTO POWDER.
RICE...
Wash my hands...
FSHHH
...IS MADE...
SHFF SHFF
The first time you wash the rice, drain it right then. And use your wrist to roll the grains of rice as you wash it.
...LIKE THIS. ♡
SHK SHK
Add water...
FSHHH
Put the pot in the rice cooker...
BEEP!
ARE YOU MAKIN' FUN OF ME?!
And if you cook the rice in a stone pot, it takes less time and tastes better.
I'M SORRY...

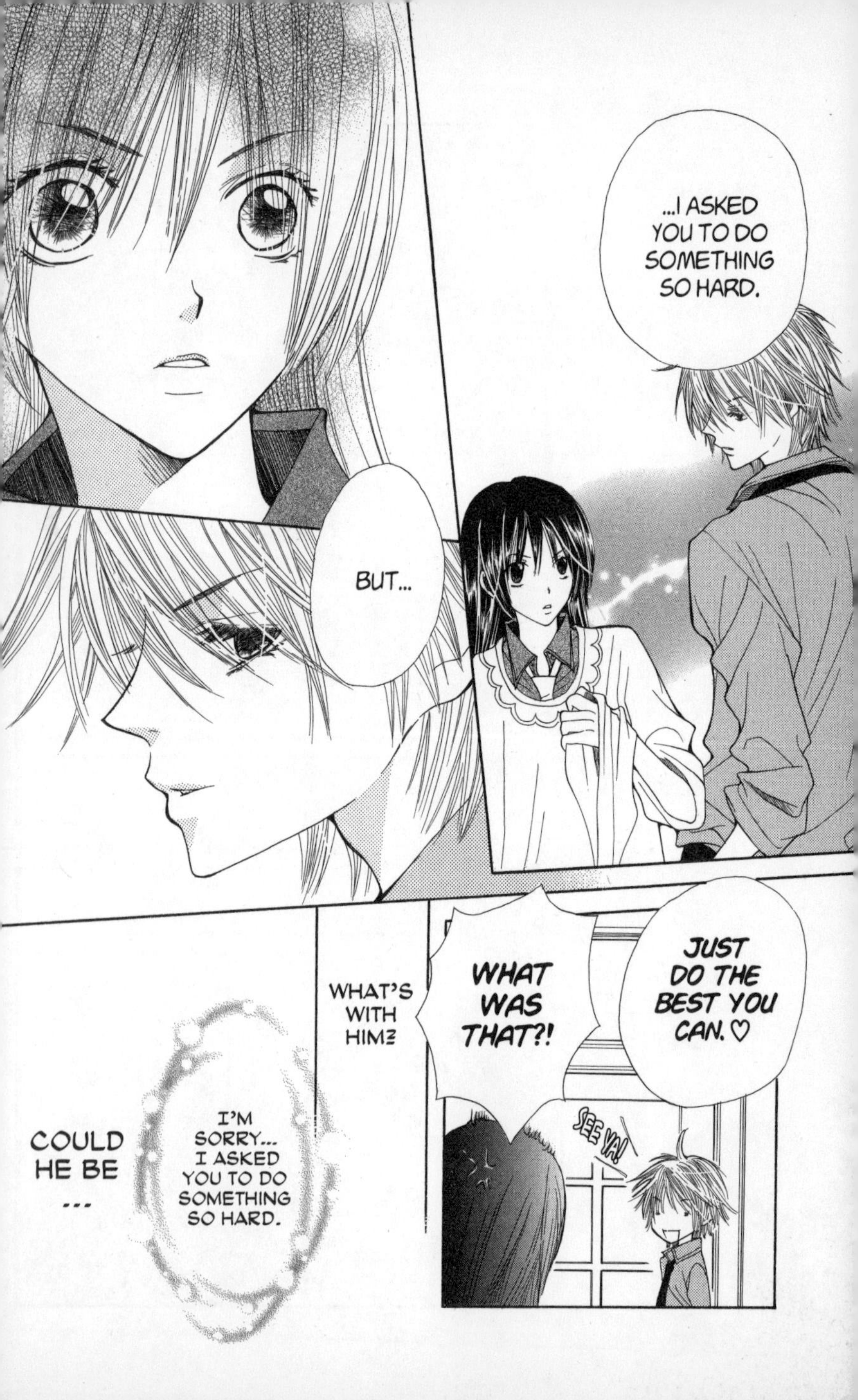
...I ASKED YOU TO DO SOMETHING SO HARD.
BUT...
JUST DO THE BEST YOU CAN. ♡
SEE YA!
WHAT WAS THAT?!
WHAT'S WITH HIM?
I'M SORRY... I ASKED YOU TO DO SOMETHING SO HARD.
COULD HE BE ...

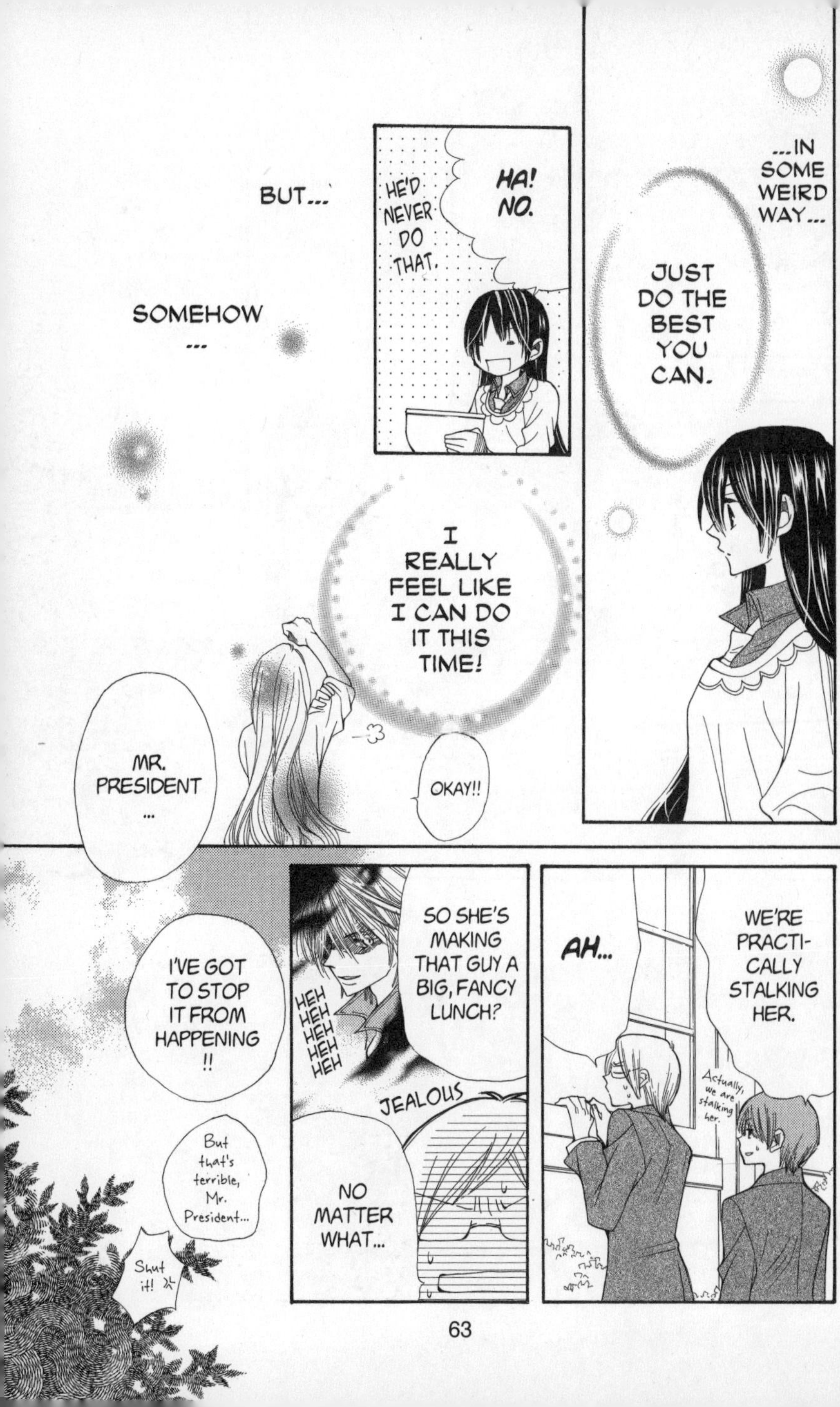
...IN SOME WEIRD WAY...
JUST DO THE BEST YOU CAN.
HA! NO.
HE'D NEVER DO THAT.
BUT...
SOMEHOW ...
I REALLY FEEL LIKE I CAN DO IT THIS TIME!
OKAY!!
MR. PRESIDENT ...
WE'RE PRACTI-CALLY STALKING HER.
AH...
Actually, we are stalking her.
SO SHE'S MAKING THAT GUY A BIG, FANCY LUNCH?
HEH HEH HEH HEH HEH
JEALOUS
NO MATTER WHAT...
I'VE GOT TO STOP IT FROM HAPPENING !!
But that's terrible, Mr. President...
Shut it!

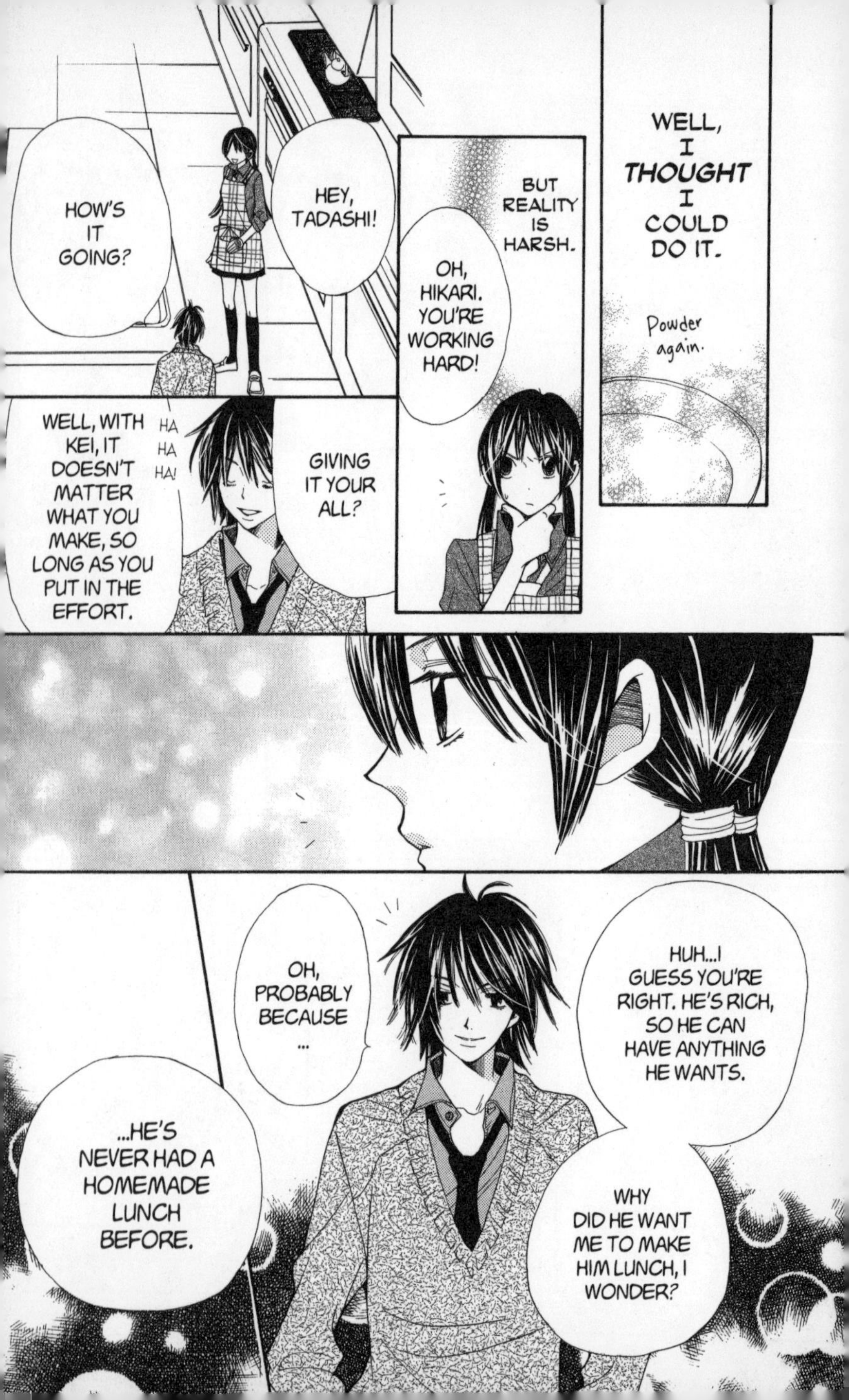
WELL, I *THOUGHT* I COULD DO IT.
Powder again.
BUT REALITY IS HARSH.
OH, HIKARI. YOU'RE WORKING HARD!
HEY, TADASHI!
HOW'S IT GOING?
GIVING IT YOUR ALL?
HA HA HA!
WELL, WITH KEI, IT DOESN'T MATTER WHAT YOU MAKE, SO LONG AS YOU PUT IN THE EFFORT.
HUH...I GUESS YOU'RE RIGHT. HE'S RICH, SO HE CAN HAVE ANYTHING HE WANTS.
WHY DID HE WANT ME TO MAKE HIM LUNCH, I WONDER?
OH, PROBABLY BECAUSE ...
...HE'S NEVER HAD A HOMEMADE LUNCH BEFORE.

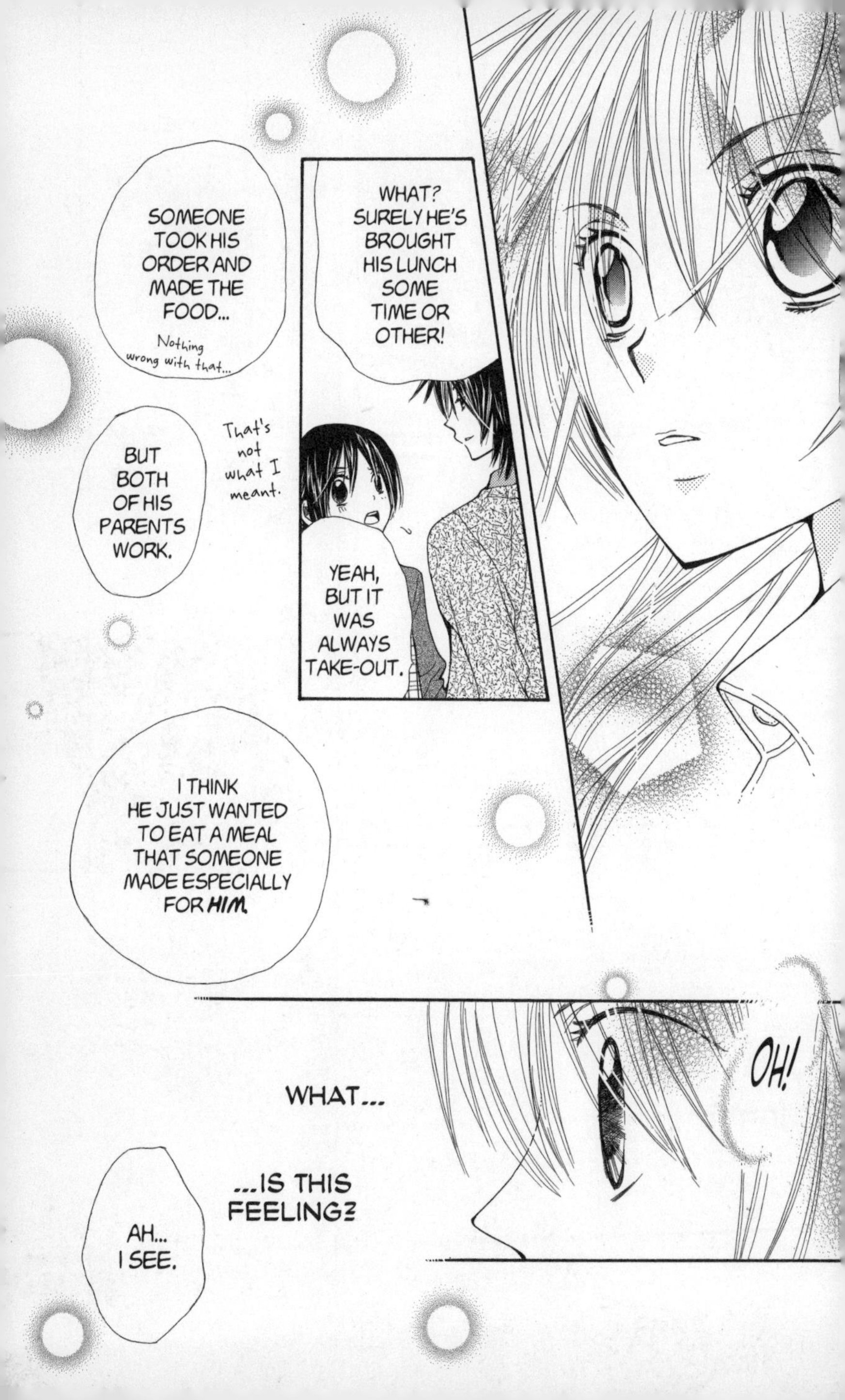
WHAT? SURELY HE'S BROUGHT HIS LUNCH SOME TIME OR OTHER!
YEAH, BUT IT WAS ALWAYS TAKE-OUT.
SOMEONE TOOK HIS ORDER AND MADE THE FOOD...
Nothing wrong with that...
BUT BOTH OF HIS PARENTS WORK.
That's not what I meant.
I THINK HE JUST WANTED TO EAT A MEAL THAT SOMEONE MADE ESPECIALLY FOR HIM.
OH!
WHAT...
...IS THIS FEELING?
AH... I SEE.

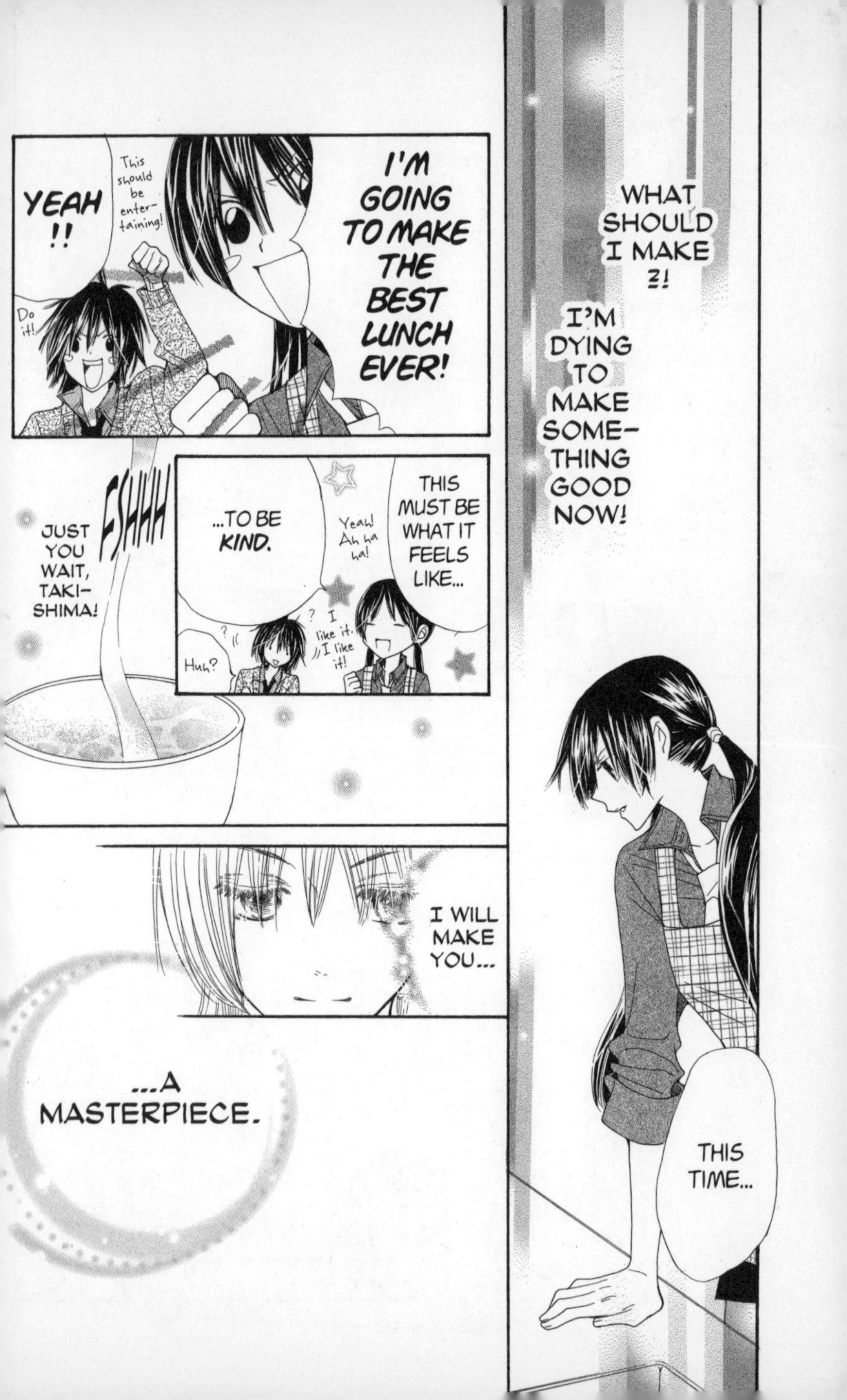
WHAT SHOULD I MAKE?!
I'M DYING TO MAKE SOMETHING GOOD NOW!
THIS TIME...
I'M GOING TO MAKE THE BEST LUNCH EVER!
This should be entertaining!
YEAH!!
Do it!
THIS MUST BE WHAT IT FEELS LIKE...
Yeah! Ah ha ha!
...TO BE KIND.
I like it. I like it!
Huh?
FSHHH
JUST YOU WAIT, TAKISHIMA!
I WILL MAKE YOU...
...A MASTERPIECE.

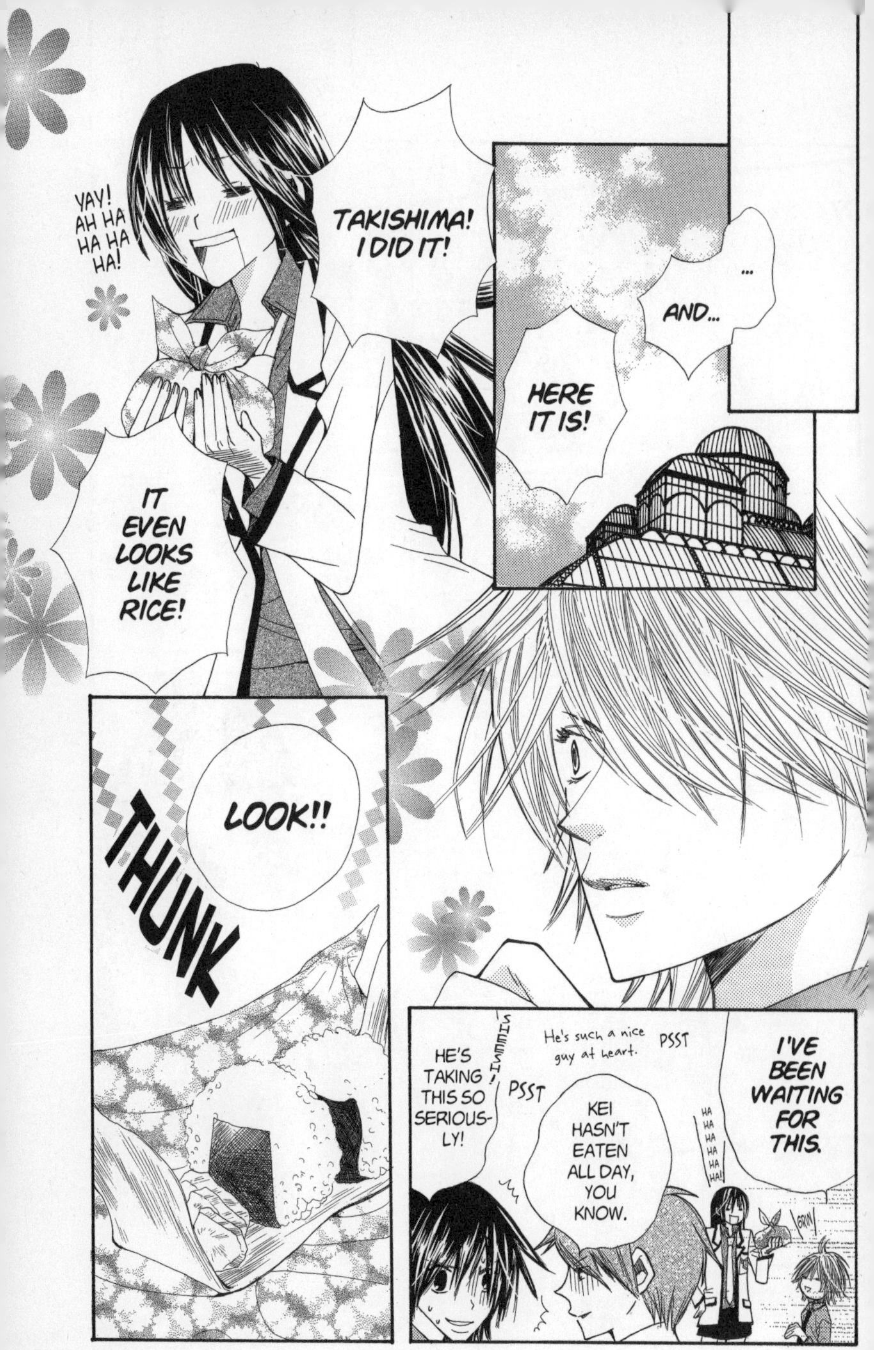
...
AND...
HERE IT IS!
TAKISHIMA! I DID IT!
YAY! AH HA HA HA HA!
IT EVEN LOOKS LIKE RICE!
I'VE BEEN WAITING FOR THIS.
HA HA HA HA HA HA!
GRIN
PSST
He's such a nice guy at heart.
KEI HASN'T EATEN ALL DAY, YOU KNOW.
PSST
SHEESH!
HE'S TAKING THIS SO SERIOUS-LY!
LOOK!!
THUNK

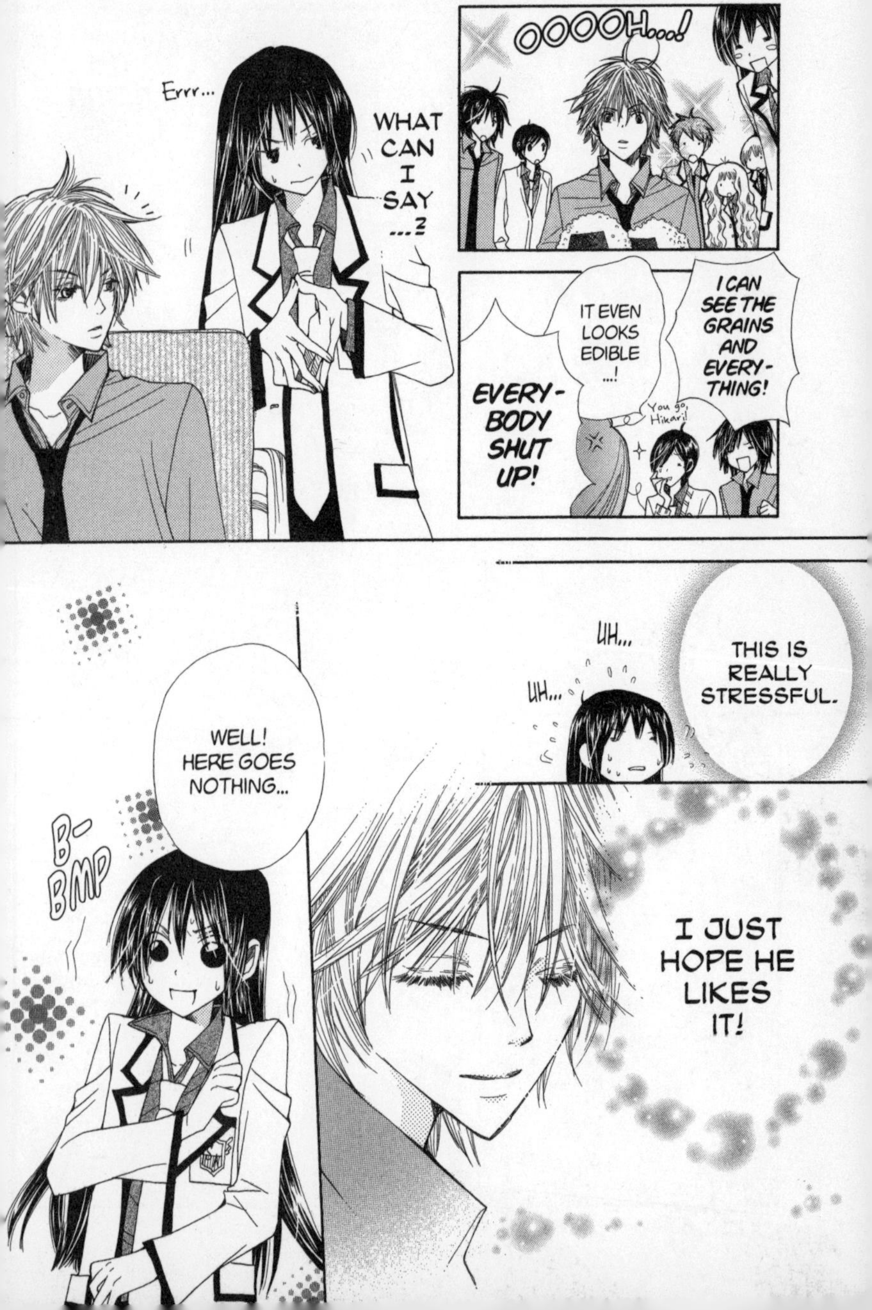
OOOOH...!
I CAN SEE THE GRAINS AND EVERY-THING!
IT EVEN LOOKS EDIBLE ...!
You go, Hikari!
EVERY-BODY SHUT UP!
WHAT CAN I SAY ...?
Errr...
UH...
UH...
THIS IS REALLY STRESSFUL.
I JUST HOPE HE LIKES IT!
B-BMP
WELL! HERE GOES NOTHING...

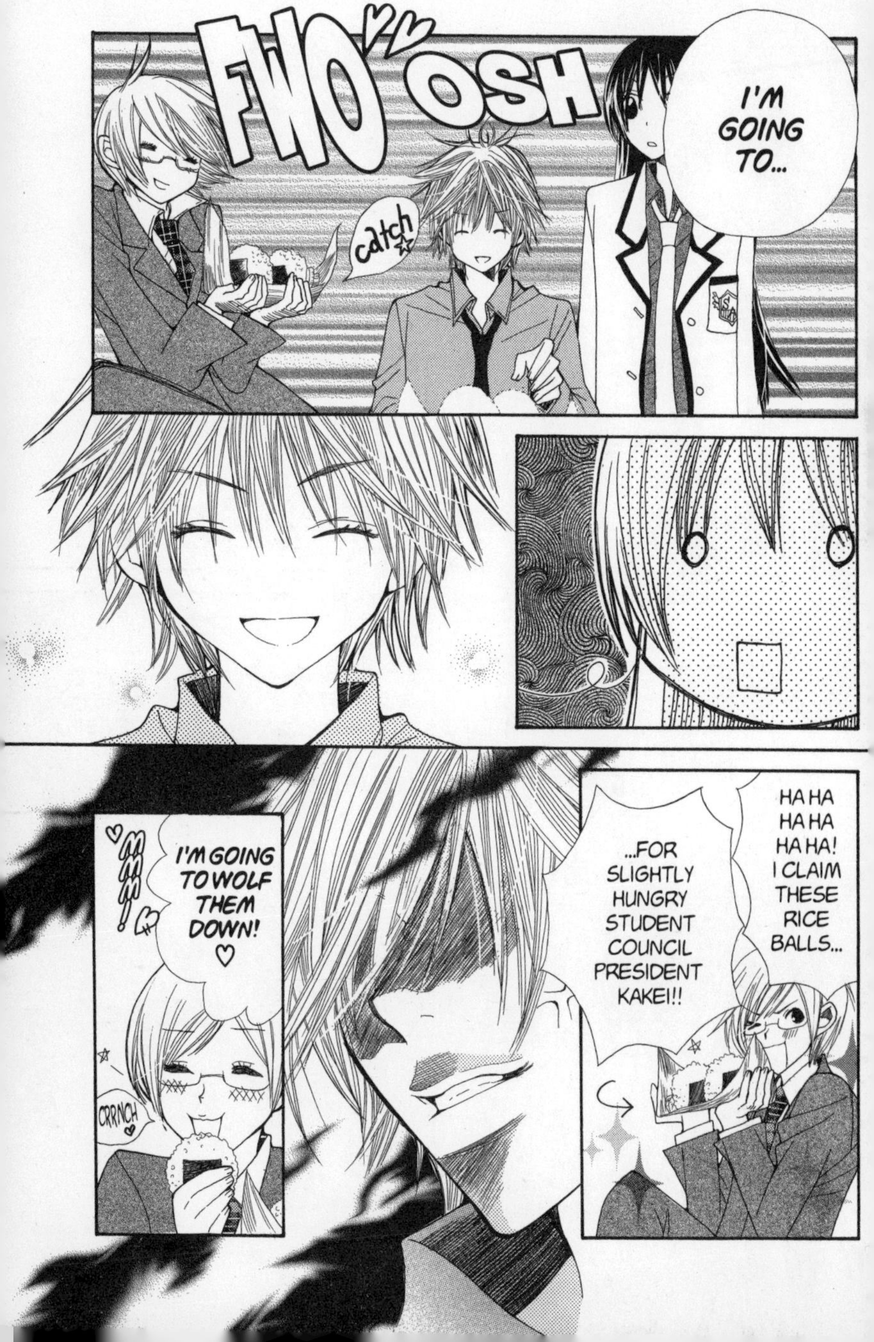
I'M GOING TO...
FWOOSH
catch☆
HA HA HA HA HA HA! I CLAIM THESE RICE BALLS...
...FOR SLIGHTLY HUNGRY STUDENT COUNCIL PRESIDENT KAKEI!!
I'M GOING TO WOLF THEM DOWN! ♡
MMM!
CRRNCH

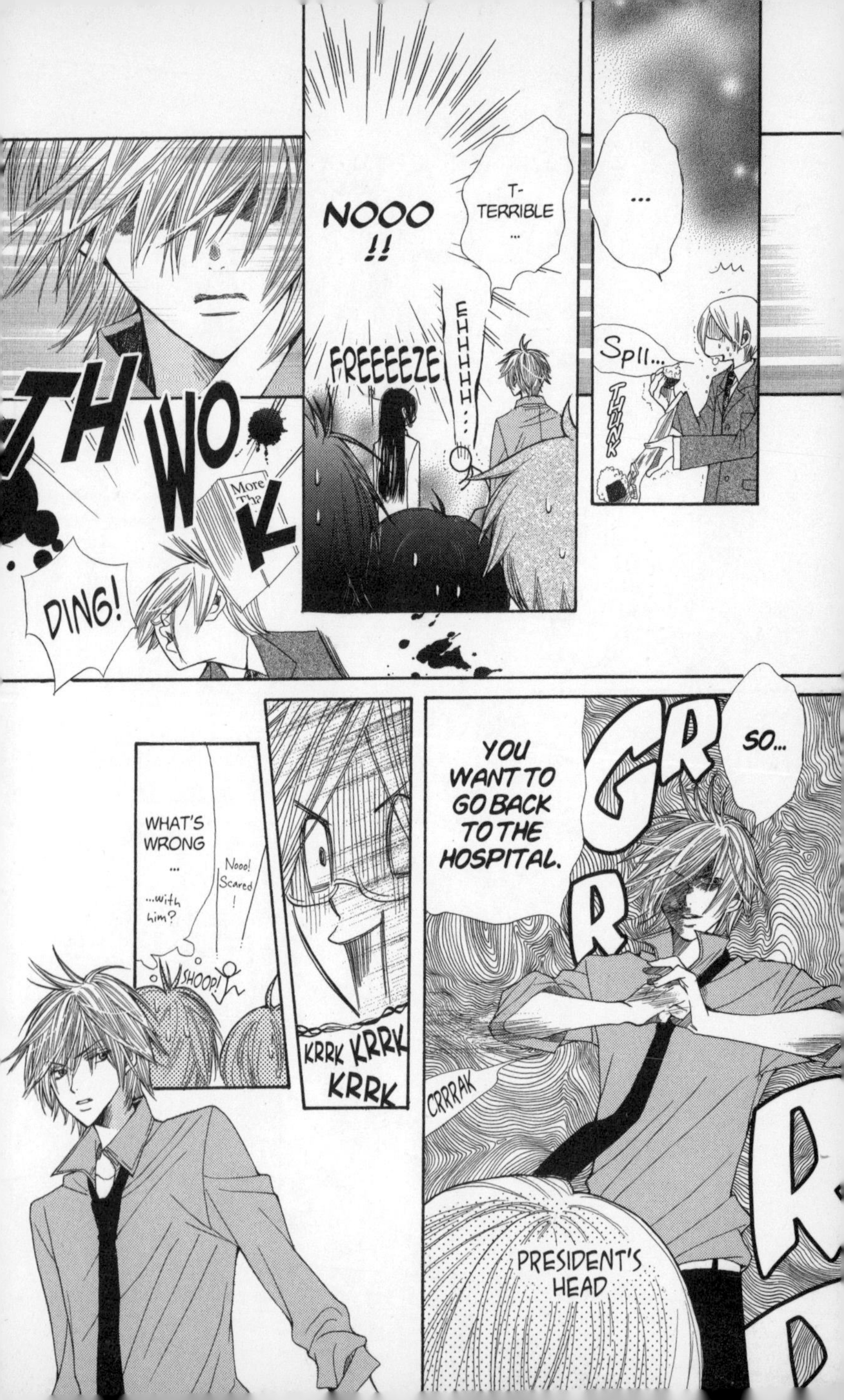
...
Spll...
THUNK
T-TERRIBLE ...
NOOO !!
EHHHHH...
FREEEEZE
THWOK
More Th
DING!
SO...
GRR
YOU WANT TO GO BACK TO THE HOSPITAL.
CRRRAK
PRESIDENT'S HEAD
KRRK KRRK KRRK
WHAT'S WRONG ...
...with him?
Nooo! Scared!
SHOOP!

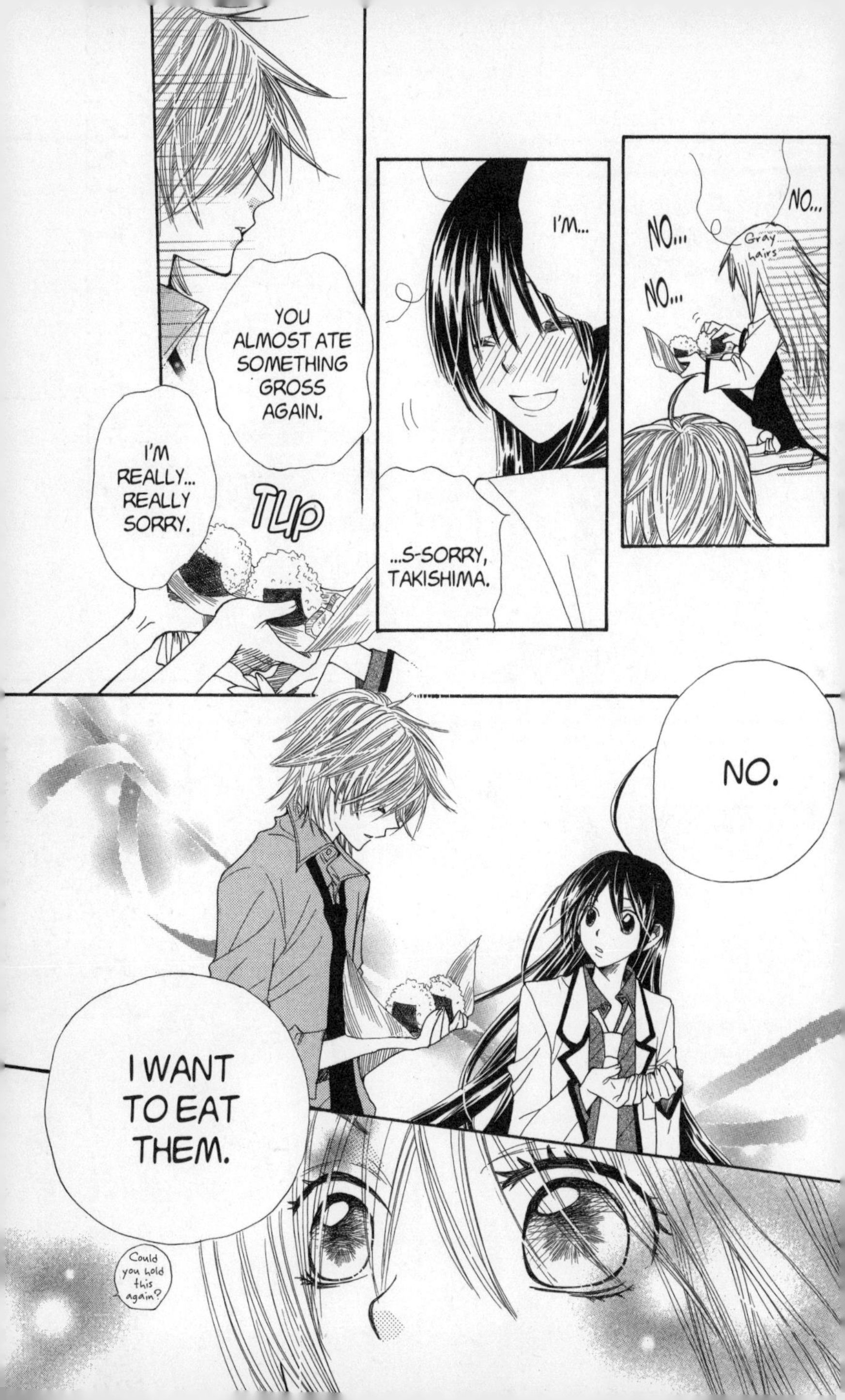
NO...
NO...
Gray hairs
NO...
I'M...
...S-SORRY, TAKISHIMA.
YOU ALMOST ATE SOMETHING GROSS AGAIN.
I'M REALLY... REALLY SORRY.
TLUP
NO.
I WANT TO EAT THEM.
Could you hold this again?

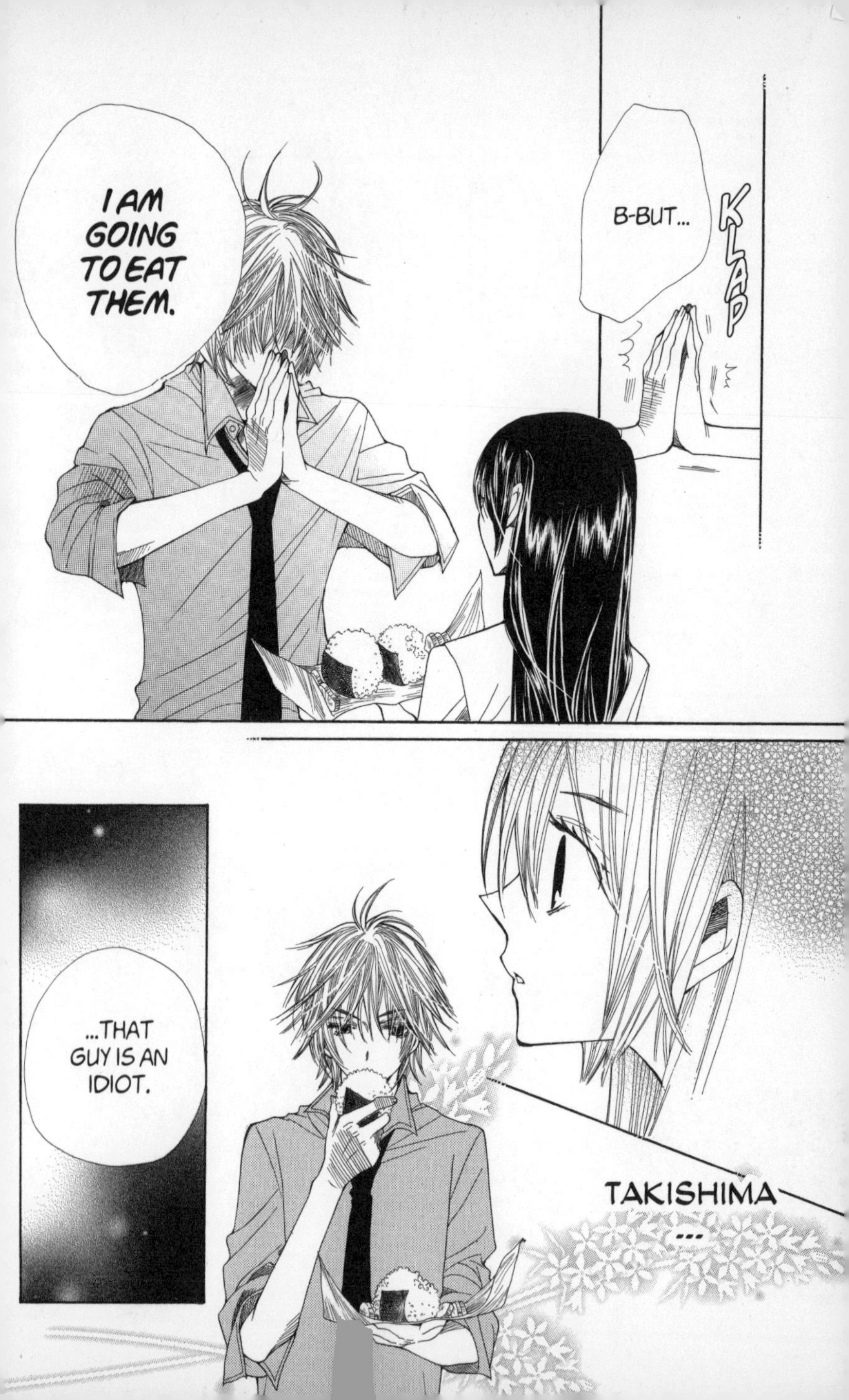
B-BUT...
KLAP
I AM GOING TO EAT THEM.
TAKISHIMA ...
...THAT GUY IS AN IDIOT.

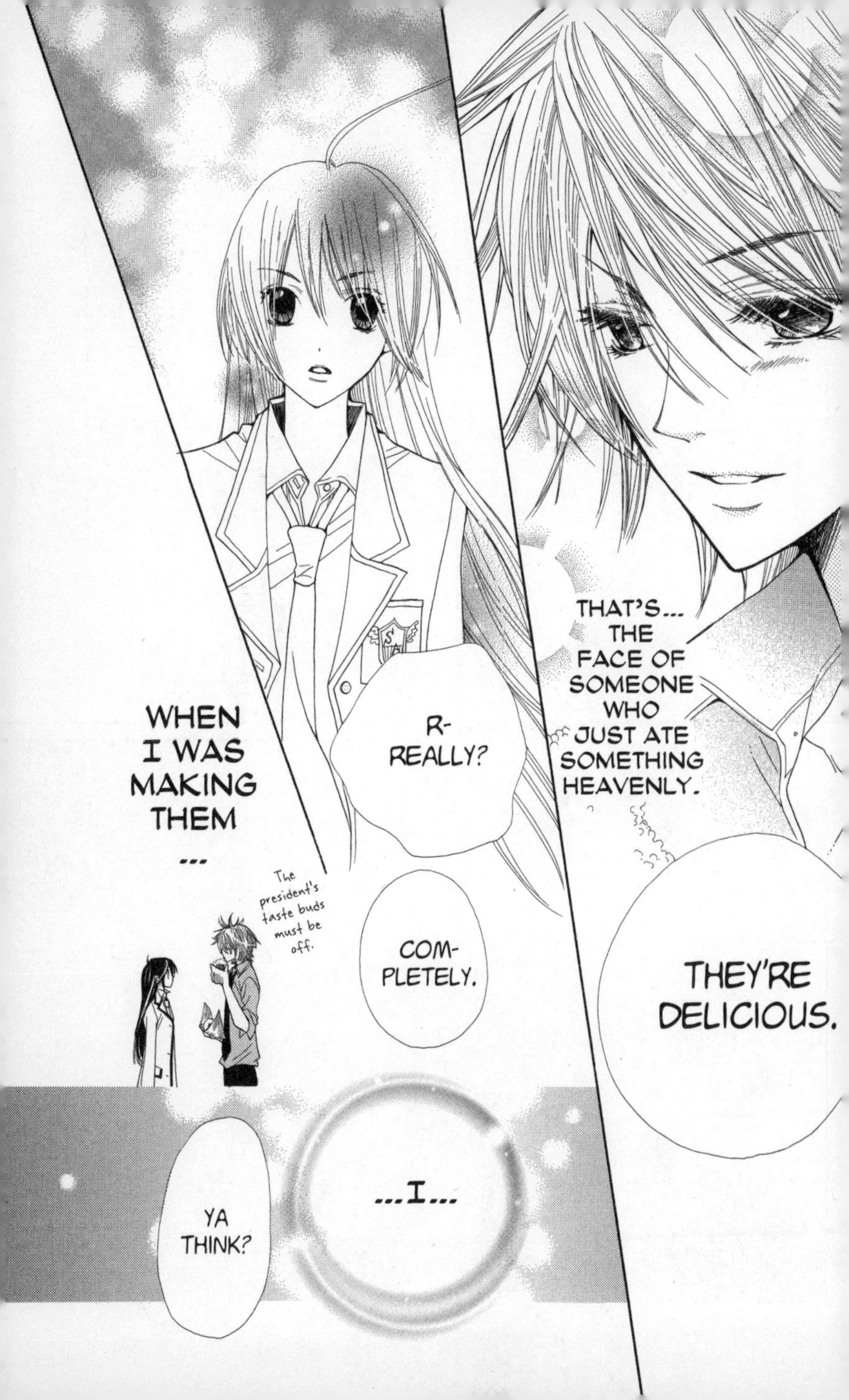
THAT'S... THE FACE OF SOMEONE WHO JUST ATE SOMETHING HEAVENLY.
THEY'RE DELICIOUS.
R-REALLY?
COM-PLETELY.
WHEN I WAS MAKING THEM ...
The president's taste buds must be off.
...I...
YA THINK?

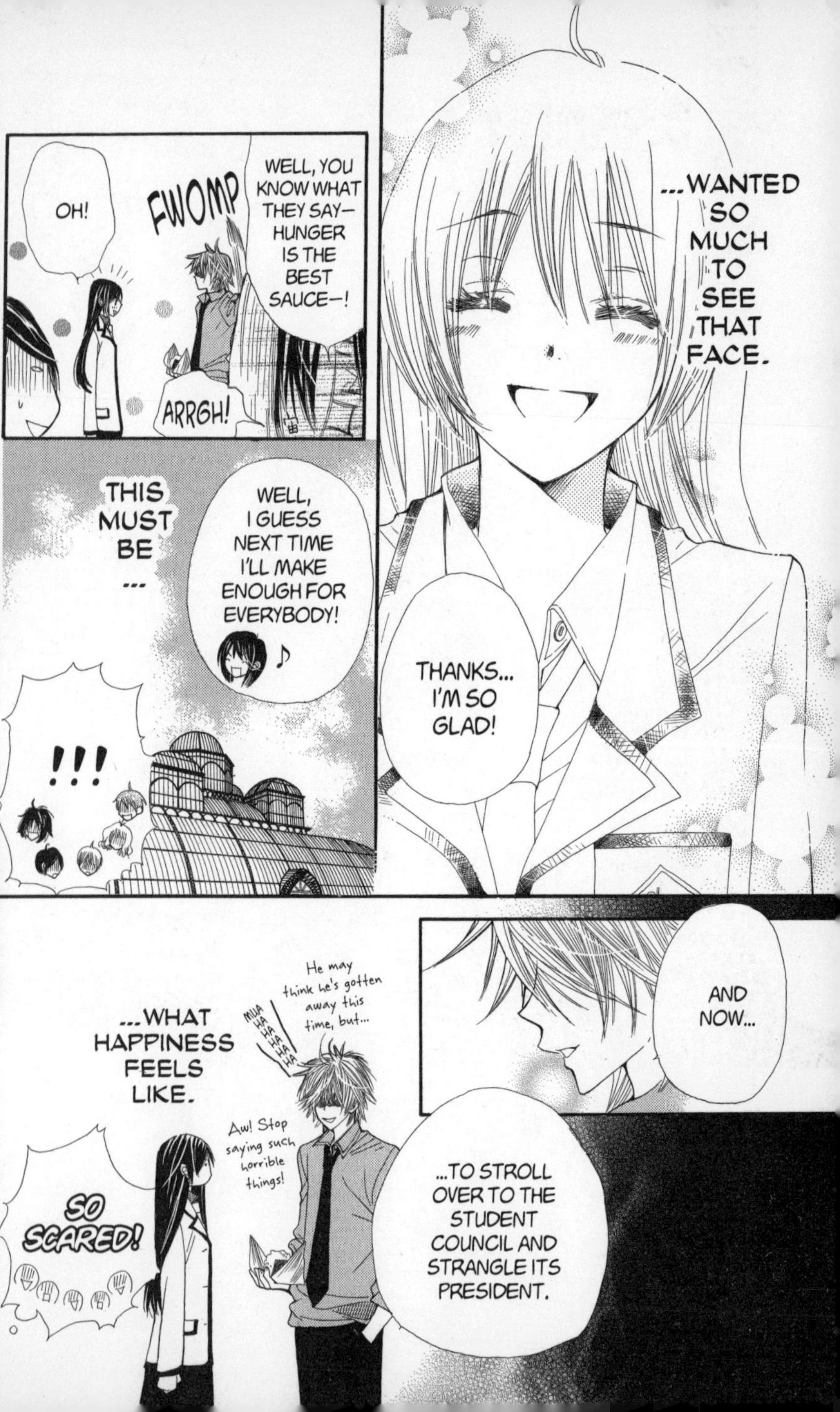
...WANTED SO MUCH TO SEE THAT FACE.
THANKS... I'M SO GLAD!
WELL, YOU KNOW WHAT THEY SAY— HUNGER IS THE BEST SAUCE—!
FWOMP
OH!
ARRGH!
WELL, I GUESS NEXT TIME I'LL MAKE ENOUGH FOR EVERYBODY! ♪
THIS MUST BE ...
!!!
AND NOW...
...TO STROLL OVER TO THE STUDENT COUNCIL AND STRANGLE ITS PRESIDENT.
...WHAT HAPPINESS FEELS LIKE.
He may think he's gotten away this time, but...
MUA HA HA HA HA HA HA
Aw! Stop saying such horrible things!
SO SCARED!

Chapter 7

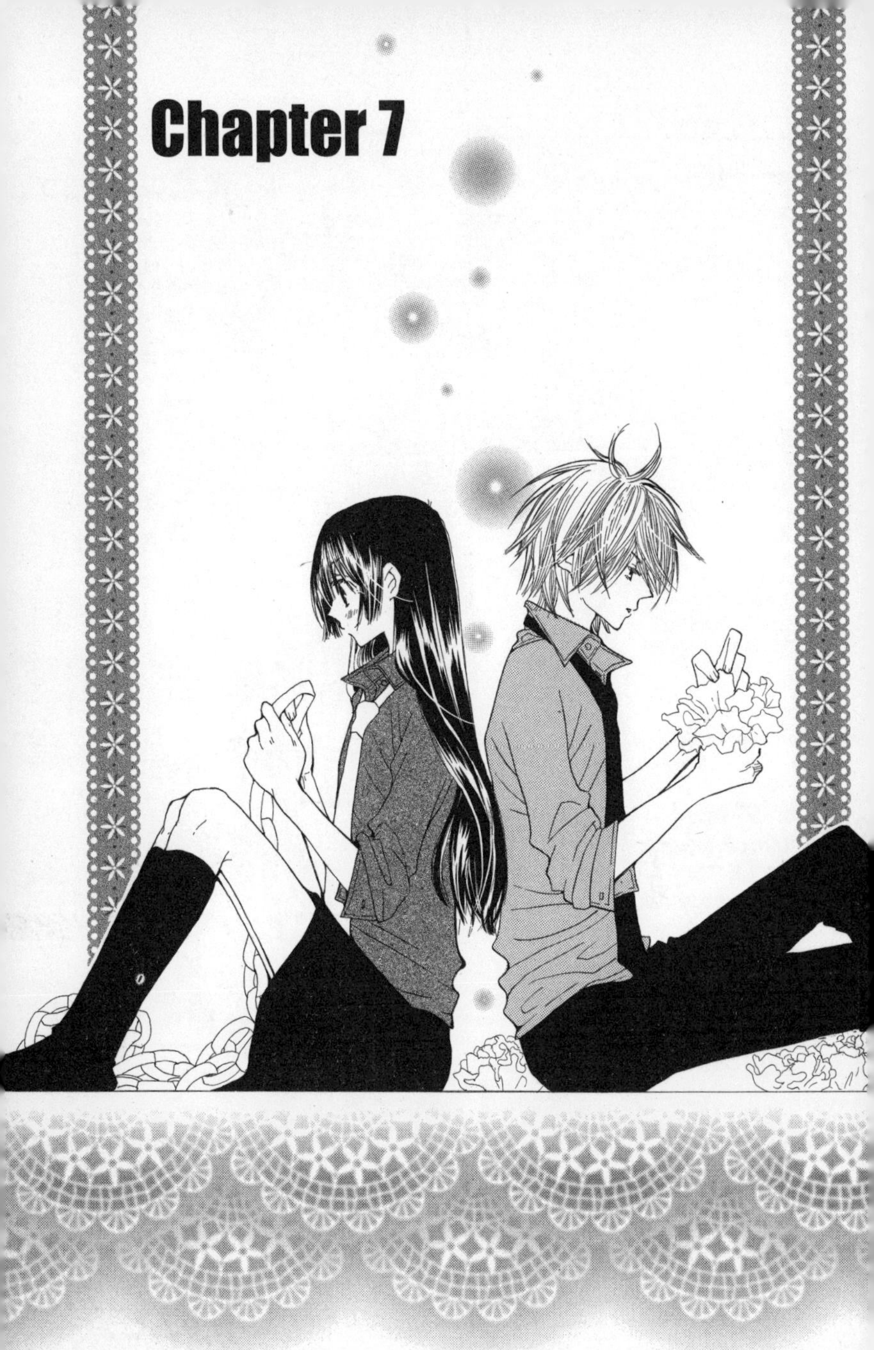

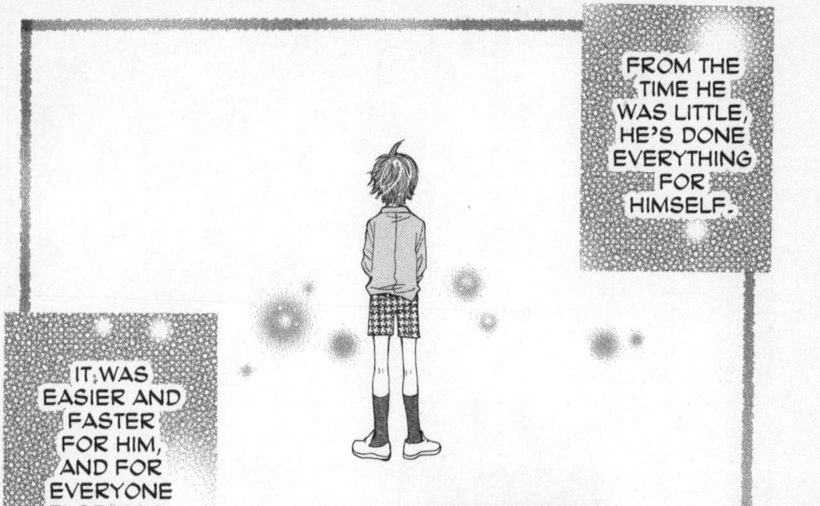
FROM THE TIME HE WAS LITTLE, HE'S DONE EVERYTHING FOR HIMSELF.
IT WAS EASIER AND FASTER FOR HIM, AND FOR EVERYONE ELSE, TOO.
OOH!
ANOTHER CHALLENGE FROM THE STUDENT COUNCIL.

• PROFILE •

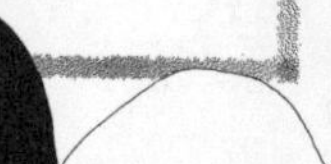
B

EVERY NOW AND THEN, I GET A LETTER ASKING ME TO DO CHARACTER PROFILES. THANK YOU SO MUCH FOR BEING THAT INTERESTED!

IT REALLY MAKES ME HAPPY. I'LL THINK ABOUT IT ONCE THE THIRD VOLUME IS PUBLISHED...

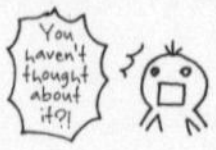
You haven't thought about it?!

BUT AT LEAST AS OF VOLUME TWO, WE FINALLY KNOW TADASHI'S BIRTHDAY. HE WAS BORN ON SEPTEMBER 9! HUFF, HUFF...

What am I going to do about everyone else?

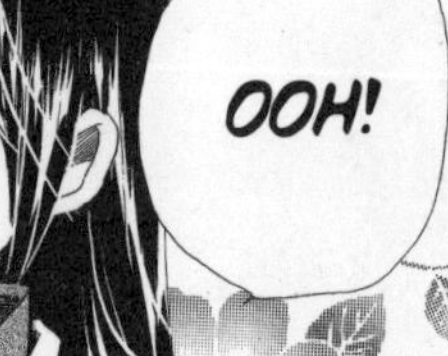
I'm a Virgo?
That means... virgin...

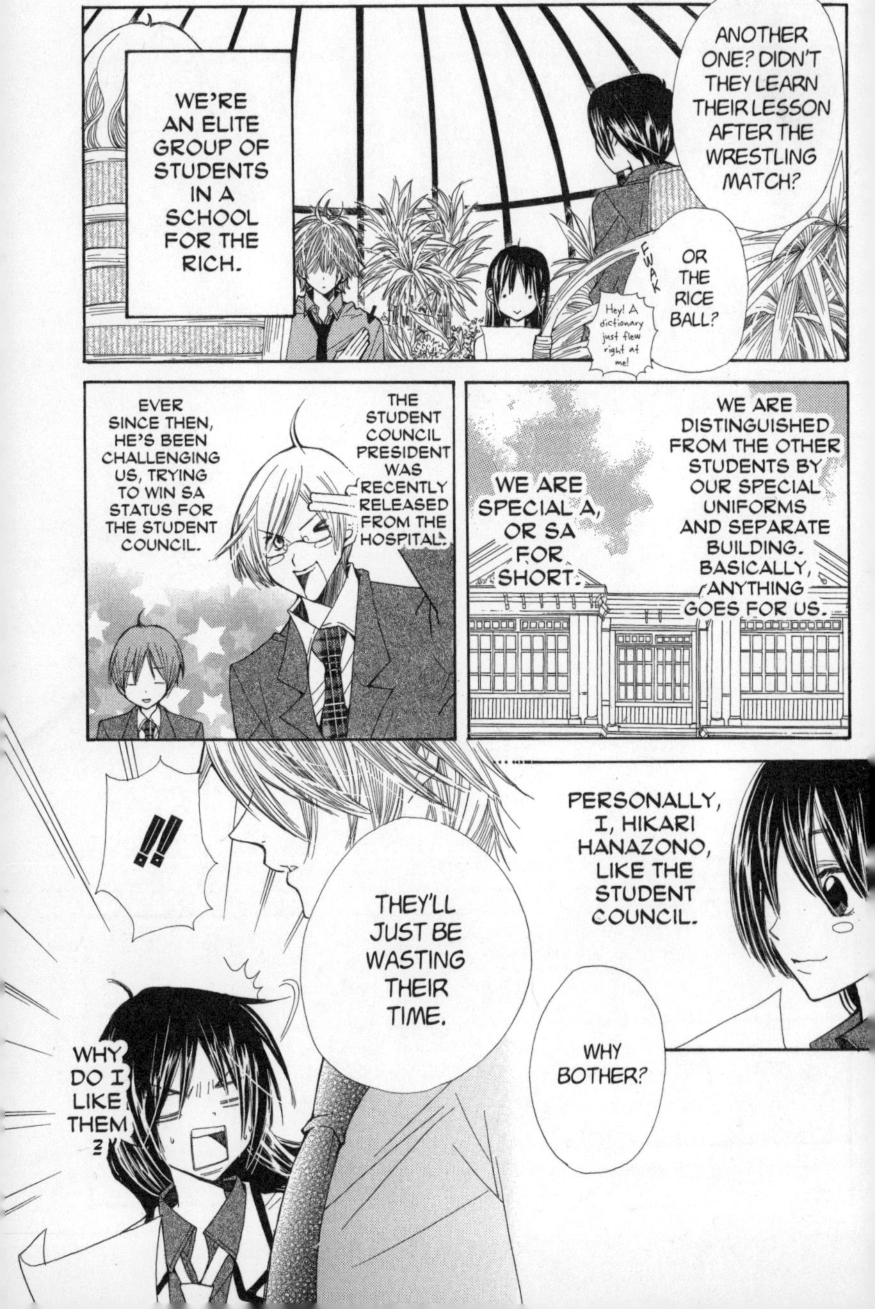
ANOTHER ONE? DIDN'T THEY LEARN THEIR LESSON AFTER THE WRESTLING MATCH?
OR THE RICE BALL?
FWAK
Hey! A dictionary just flew right at me!
WE'RE AN ELITE GROUP OF STUDENTS IN A SCHOOL FOR THE RICH.
WE ARE DISTINGUISHED FROM THE OTHER STUDENTS BY OUR SPECIAL UNIFORMS AND SEPARATE BUILDING. BASICALLY, ANYTHING GOES FOR US.
WE ARE SPECIAL A, OR SA FOR SHORT.
THE STUDENT COUNCIL PRESIDENT WAS RECENTLY RELEASED FROM THE HOSPITAL.
EVER SINCE THEN, HE'S BEEN CHALLENGING US, TRYING TO WIN SA STATUS FOR THE STUDENT COUNCIL.
PERSONALLY, I, HIKARI HANAZONO, LIKE THE STUDENT COUNCIL.
WHY BOTHER?
THEY'LL JUST BE WASTING THEIR TIME.
!!
WHY DO I LIKE THEM?

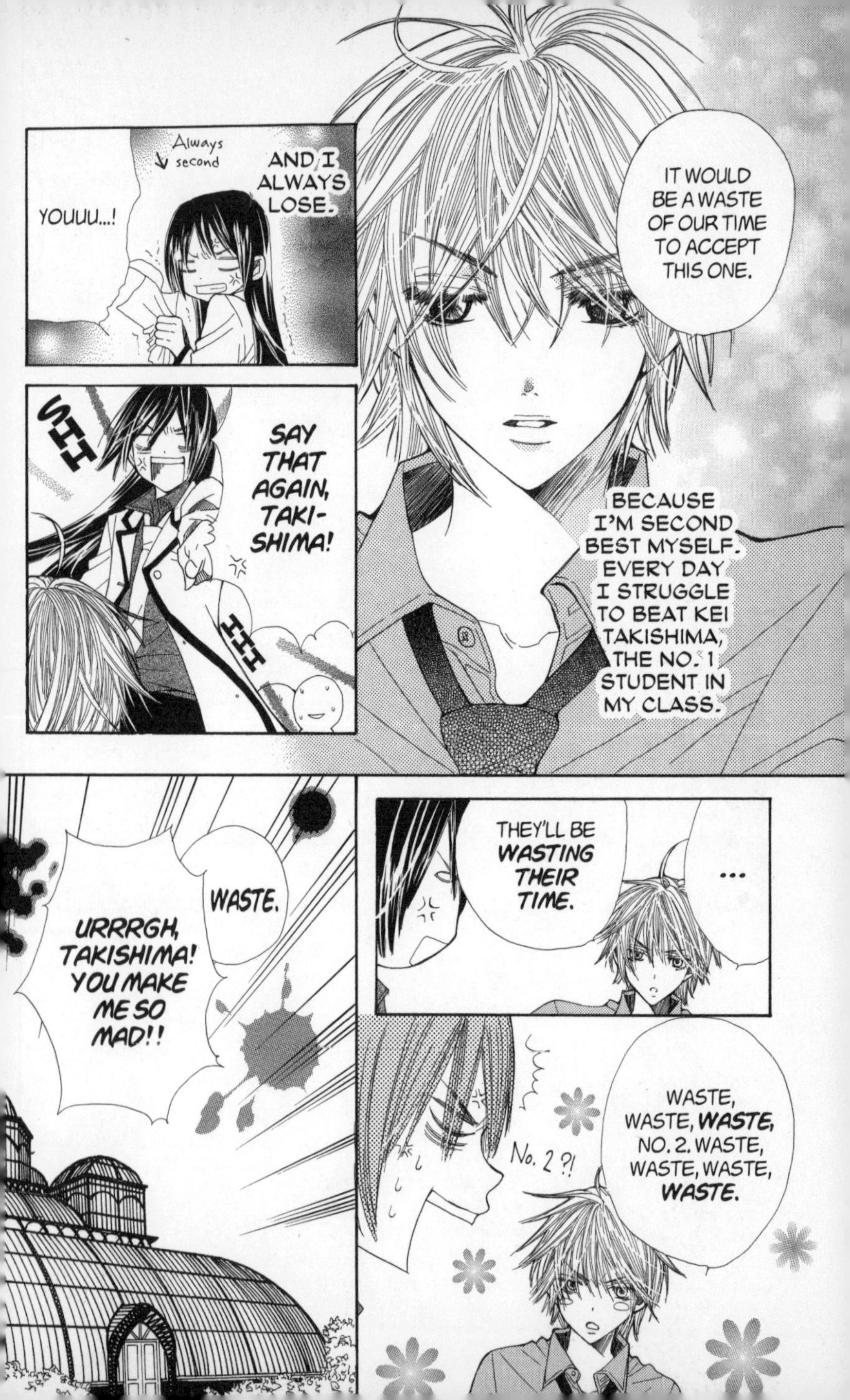
IT WOULD BE A WASTE OF OUR TIME TO ACCEPT THIS ONE.
BECAUSE I'M SECOND BEST MYSELF. EVERY DAY I STRUGGLE TO BEAT KEI TAKISHIMA, THE NO. 1 STUDENT IN MY CLASS.
AND I ALWAYS LOSE.
Always second
YOUUU...!
SHH
SAY THAT AGAIN, TAKI-SHIMA!
SHH
THEY'LL BE WASTING THEIR TIME.
...
WASTE, WASTE, WASTE, NO. 2. WASTE, WASTE, WASTE, WASTE.
No. 2 ?!
WASTE.
URRRGH, TAKISHIMA! YOU MAKE ME SO MAD!!

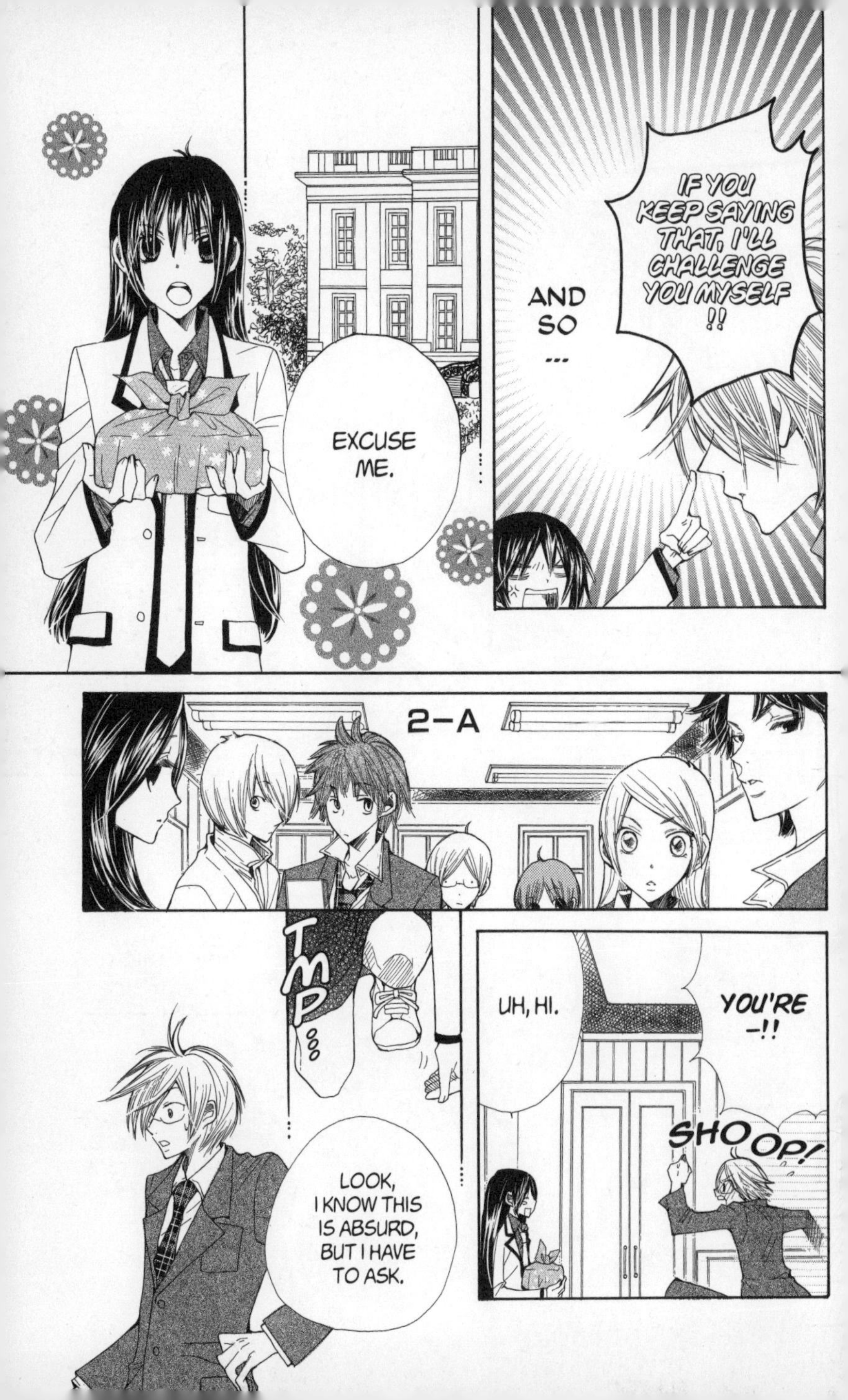
IF YOU KEEP SAYING THAT, I'LL CHALLENGE YOU MYSELF!!
AND SO...
EXCUSE ME.
2-A
YOU'RE—!!
UH, HI.
SHOOP!
TMP...
LOOK, I KNOW THIS IS ABSURD, BUT I HAVE TO ASK.

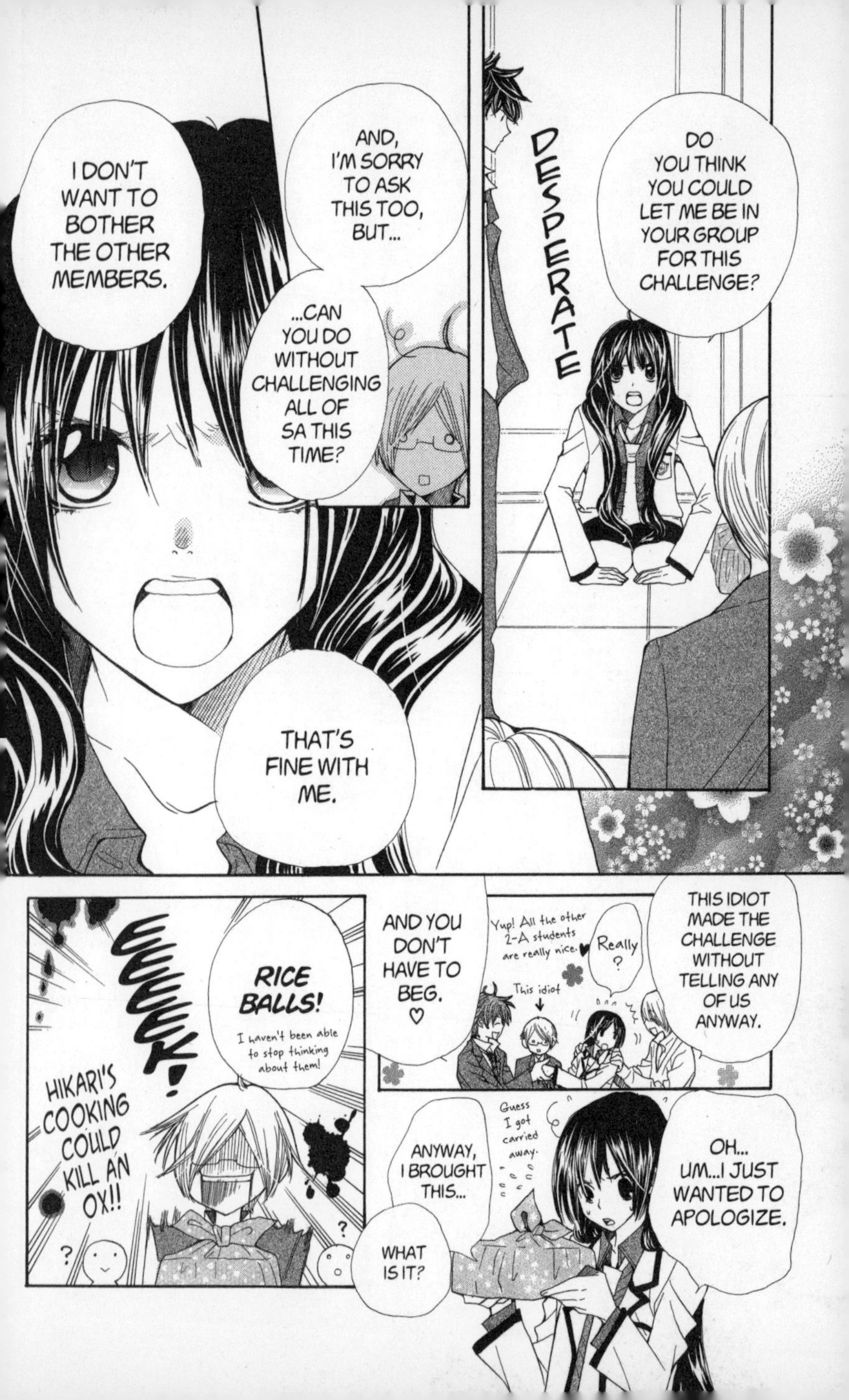
DESPERATE
DO YOU THINK YOU COULD LET ME BE IN YOUR GROUP FOR THIS CHALLENGE?
AND, I'M SORRY TO ASK THIS TOO, BUT...
...CAN YOU DO WITHOUT CHALLENGING ALL OF SA THIS TIME?
I DON'T WANT TO BOTHER THE OTHER MEMBERS.
THAT'S FINE WITH ME.
THIS IDIOT MADE THE CHALLENGE WITHOUT TELLING ANY OF US ANYWAY.
Really ?
Yup! All the other 2-A students are really nice.
This idiot
AND YOU DON'T HAVE TO BEG.
OH... UM...I JUST WANTED TO APOLOGIZE.
Guess I got carried away.
ANYWAY, I BROUGHT THIS...
WHAT IS IT?
RICE BALLS!
I haven't been able to stop thinking about them!
EEEEEK!
HIKARI'S COOKING COULD KILL AN OX!!

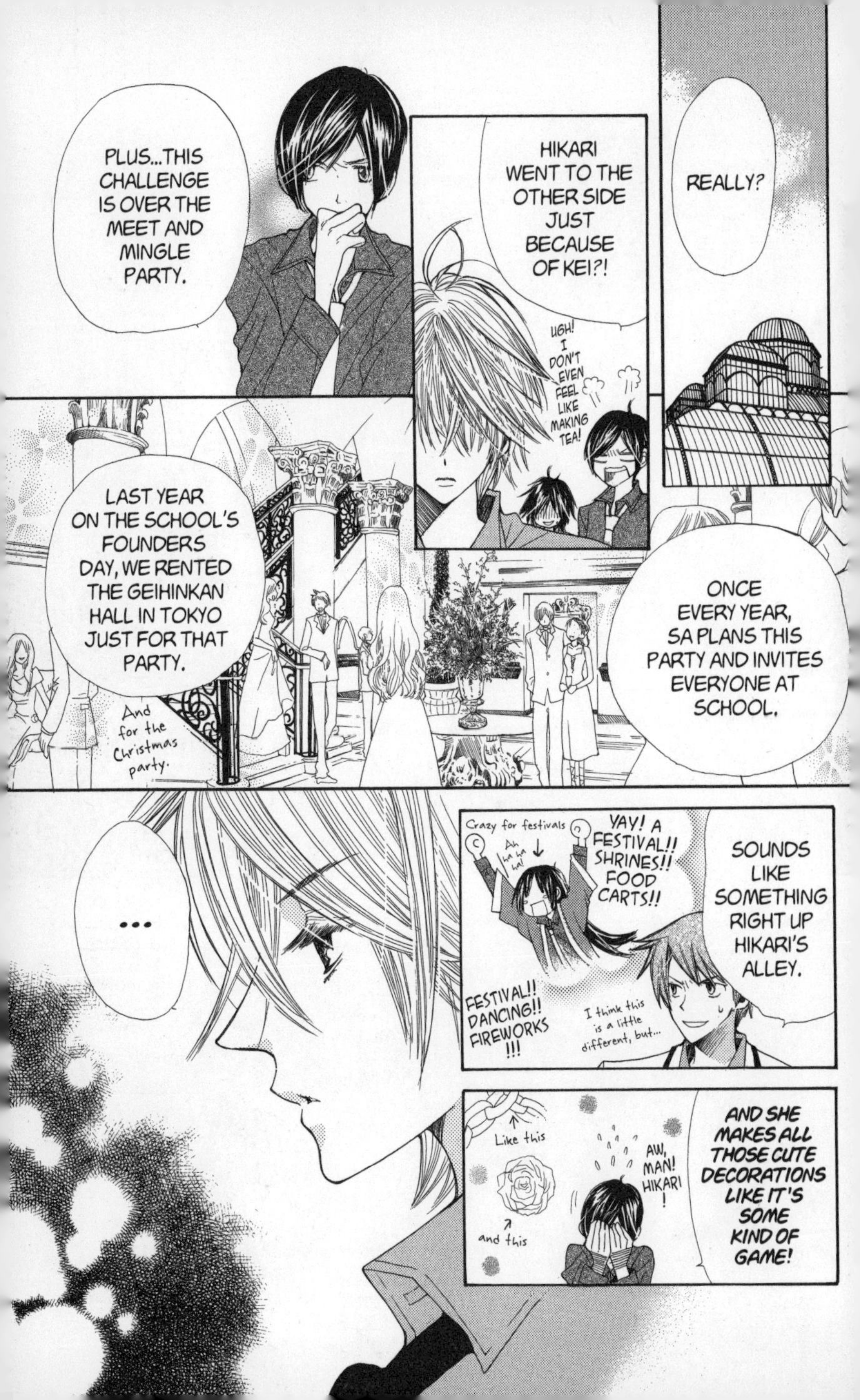
REALLY?
HIKARI WENT TO THE OTHER SIDE JUST BECAUSE OF KEI?!
UGH! I DON'T EVEN FEEL LIKE MAKING TEA!
PLUS...THIS CHALLENGE IS OVER THE MEET AND MINGLE PARTY.
ONCE EVERY YEAR, SA PLANS THIS PARTY AND INVITES EVERYONE AT SCHOOL.
LAST YEAR ON THE SCHOOL'S FOUNDERS DAY, WE RENTED THE GEIHINKAN HALL IN TOKYO JUST FOR THAT PARTY.
And for the Christmas party.
SOUNDS LIKE SOMETHING RIGHT UP HIKARI'S ALLEY.
YAY! A FESTIVAL!! SHRINES!! FOOD CARTS!!
Crazy for festivals
Ah ha ha ha!
FESTIVAL!! DANCING!! FIREWORKS!!!
I think this is a little different, but...
AND SHE MAKES ALL THOSE CUTE DECORATIONS LIKE IT'S SOME KIND OF GAME!
AW, MAN! HIKARI!
Like this
and this
...

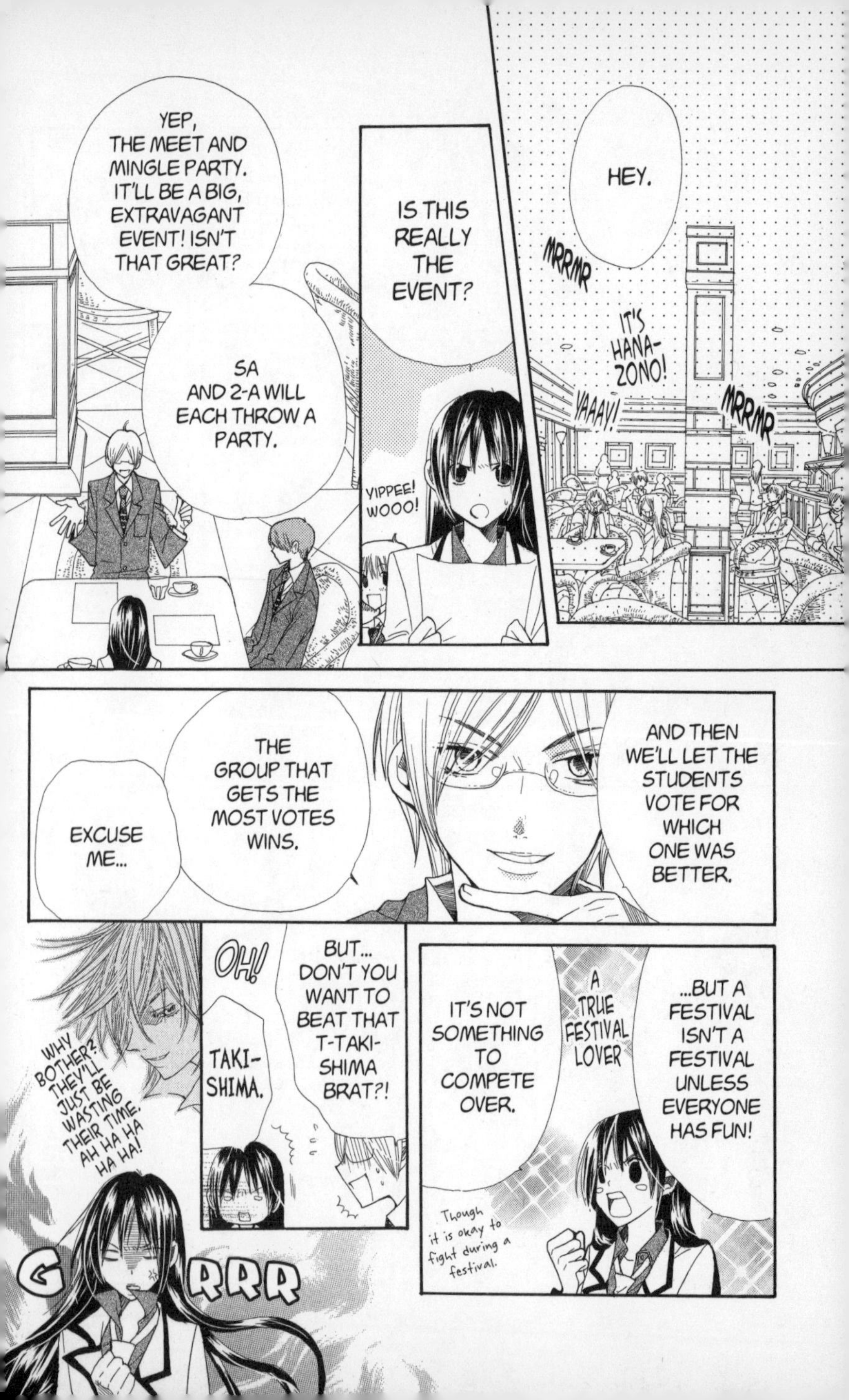
HEY.
MRRMR
IT'S HANA-ZONO!
YAAAY!
MRRMR
IS THIS REALLY THE EVENT?
YIPPEE! WOOO!
YEP, THE MEET AND MINGLE PARTY. IT'LL BE A BIG, EXTRAVAGANT EVENT! ISN'T THAT GREAT?
SA AND 2-A WILL EACH THROW A PARTY.
AND THEN WE'LL LET THE STUDENTS VOTE FOR WHICH ONE WAS BETTER.
THE GROUP THAT GETS THE MOST VOTES WINS.
EXCUSE ME...
...BUT A FESTIVAL ISN'T A FESTIVAL UNLESS EVERYONE HAS FUN!
A TRUE FESTIVAL LOVER
IT'S NOT SOMETHING TO COMPETE OVER.
Though it is okay to fight during a festival.
BUT... DON'T YOU WANT TO BEAT THAT T-TAKI-SHIMA BRAT?!
OH!
TAKI-SHIMA.
WHY BOTHER? THEY'LL JUST BE WASTING THEIR TIME. AH HA HA HA HA!
GRRR

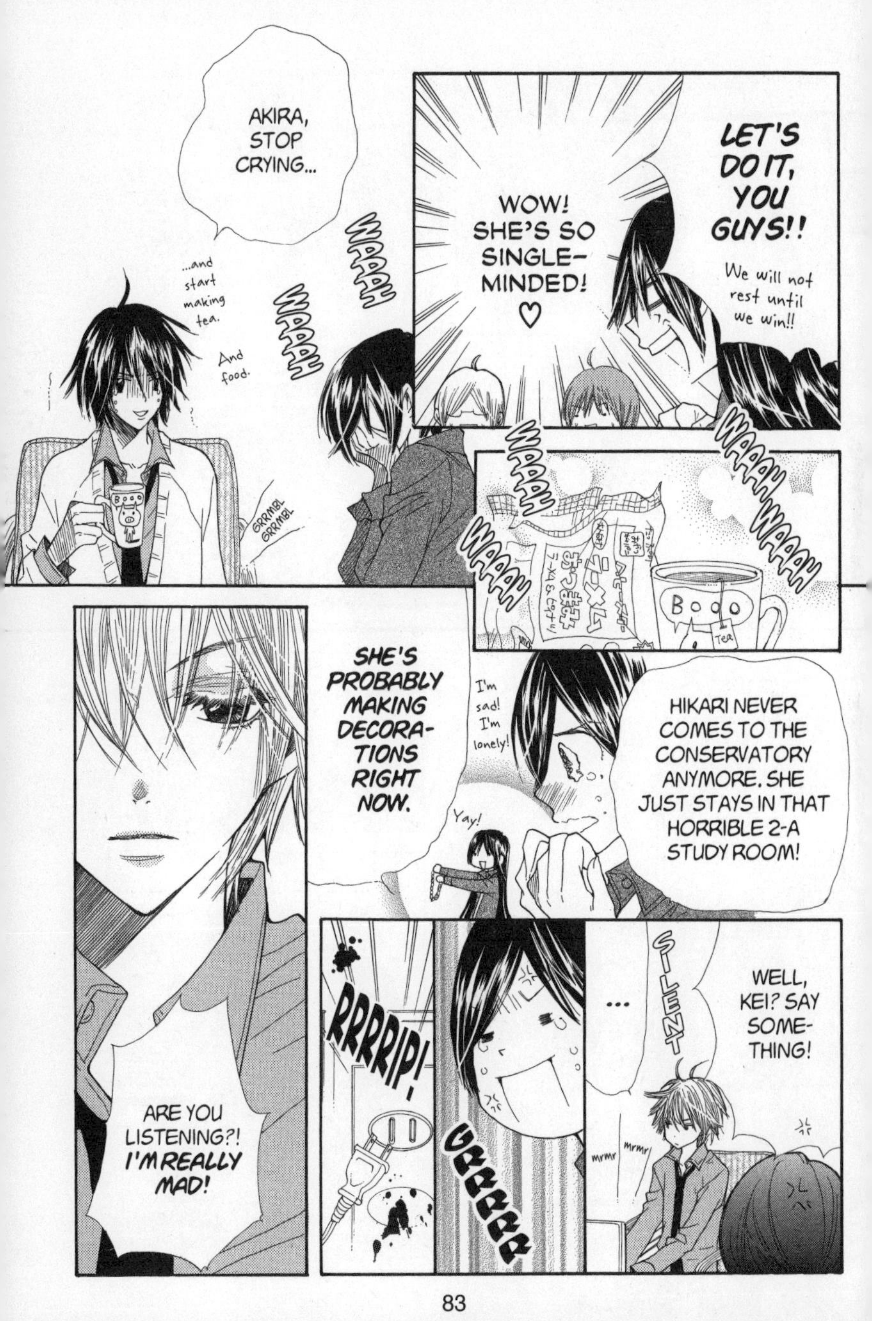
LET'S DO IT, YOU GUYS!!
We will not rest until we win!!
WOW! SHE'S SO SINGLE-MINDED! ♡
WAAAH WAAAH
WAAAH
WAAAH
AKIRA, STOP CRYING...
WAAAH
WAAAH
...and start making tea.
And food.
GRRMBL GRRMBL
Boo
HIKARI NEVER COMES TO THE CONSERVATORY ANYMORE. SHE JUST STAYS IN THAT HORRIBLE 2-A STUDY ROOM!
I'm sad! I'm lonely!
SHE'S PROBABLY MAKING DECORATIONS RIGHT NOW.
Yay!
WELL, KEI? SAY SOMETHING!
SILENT
...
mrmr mrmr
GRRRRR
RRRRIP!
ARE YOU LISTENING?! I'M REALLY MAD!

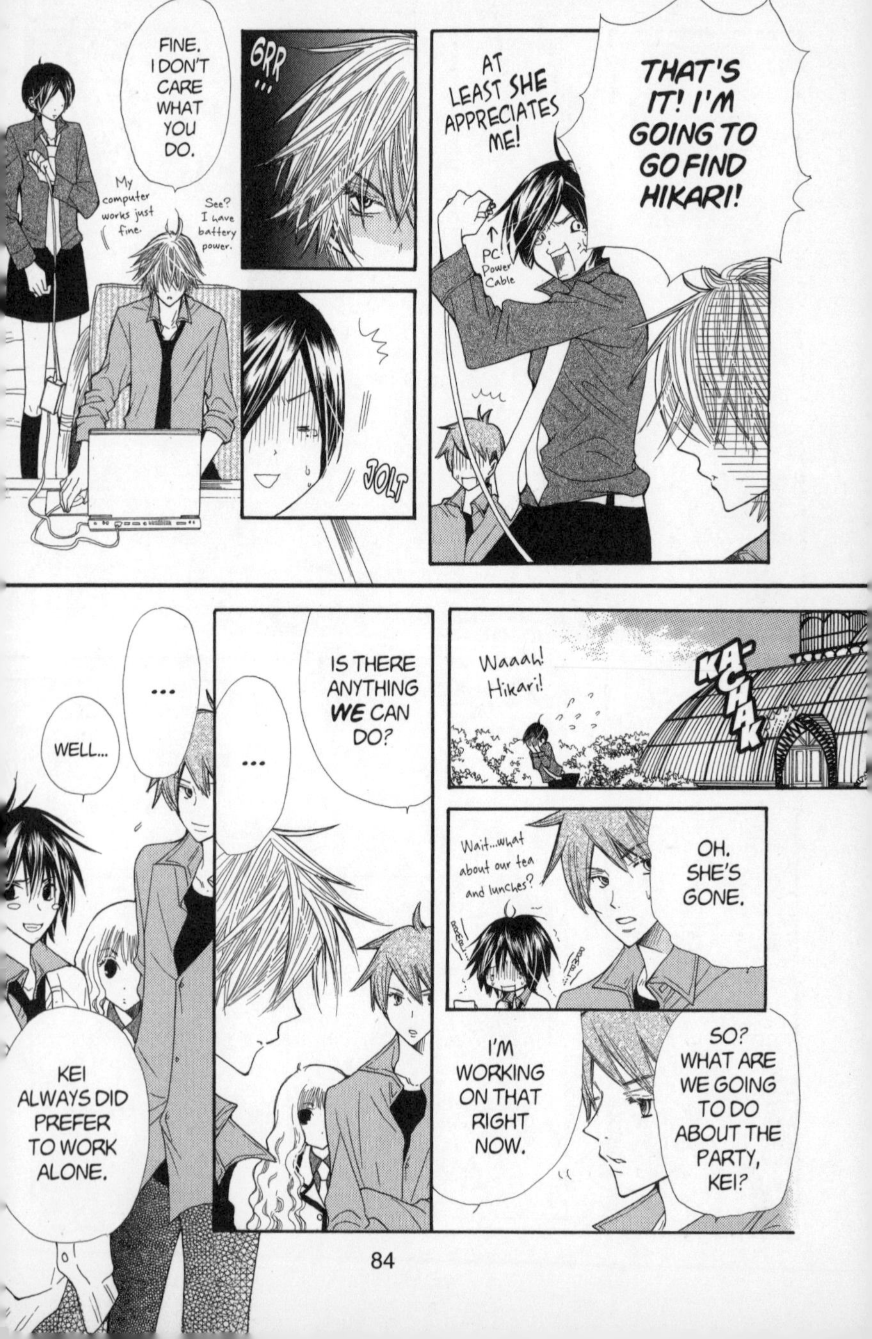
THAT'S IT! I'M GOING TO GO FIND HIKARI!
AT LEAST SHE APPRECIATES ME!
PC Power Cable
GRR...
JOLT
FINE. I DON'T CARE WHAT YOU DO.
See? I have battery power.
My computer works just fine.
KA-CHAK
Waaah! Hikari!
OH. SHE'S GONE.
Wait...what about our tea and lunches?
SO? WHAT ARE WE GOING TO DO ABOUT THE PARTY, KEI?
I'M WORKING ON THAT RIGHT NOW.
IS THERE ANYTHING WE CAN DO?
...
...
WELL...
KEI ALWAYS DID PREFER TO WORK ALONE.

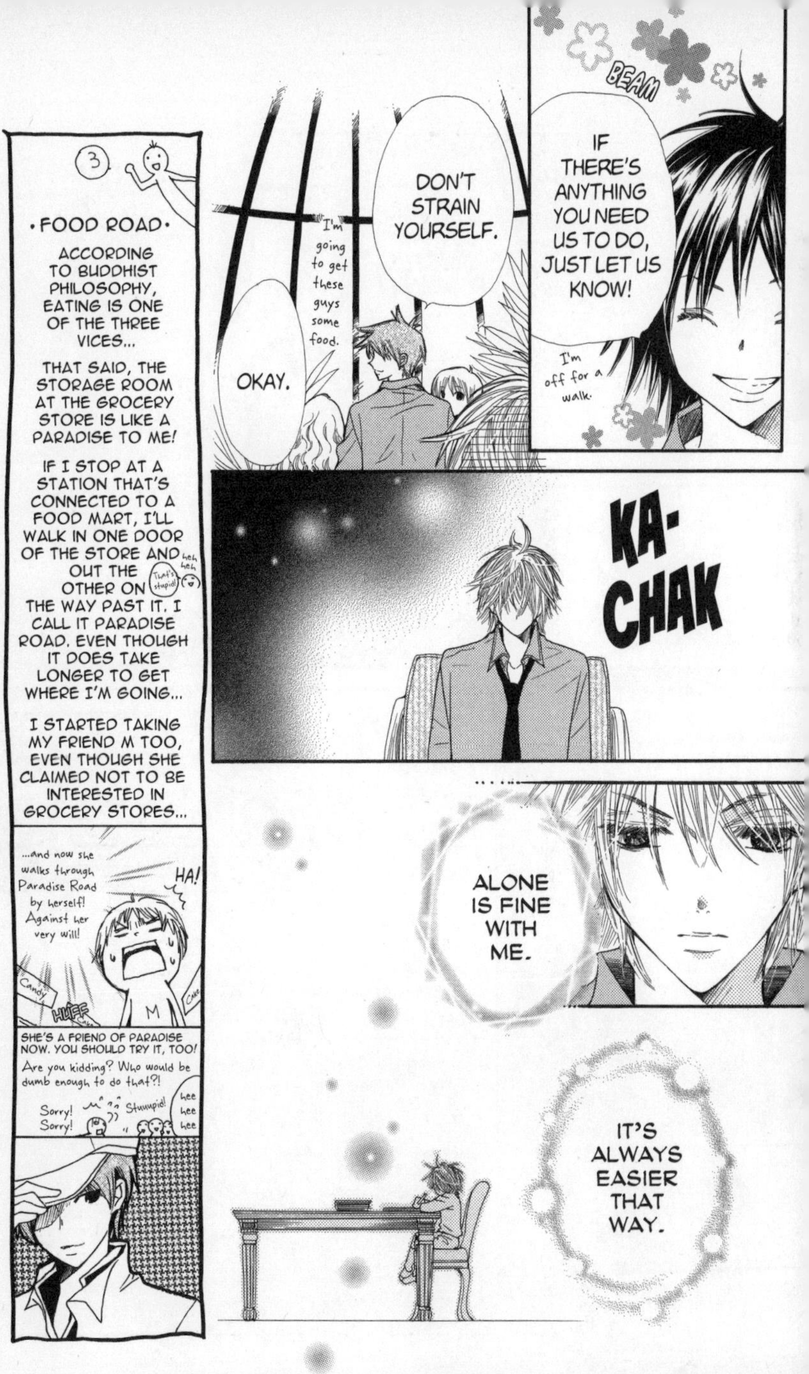
BEAM
IF THERE'S ANYTHING YOU NEED US TO DO, JUST LET US KNOW!
I'm off for a walk.
DON'T STRAIN YOURSELF.
I'm going to get these guys some food.
OKAY.
KA-CHAK
......
ALONE IS FINE WITH ME.
IT'S ALWAYS EASIER THAT WAY.
3
•FOOD ROAD•
ACCORDING TO BUDDHIST PHILOSOPHY, EATING IS ONE OF THE THREE VICES...
THAT SAID, THE STORAGE ROOM AT THE GROCERY STORE IS LIKE A PARADISE TO ME!
IF I STOP AT A STATION THAT'S CONNECTED TO A FOOD MART, I'LL WALK IN ONE DOOR OF THE STORE AND OUT THE OTHER ON THE WAY PAST IT. I CALL IT PARADISE ROAD, EVEN THOUGH IT DOES TAKE LONGER TO GET WHERE I'M GOING...
heh heh
That's stupid!
I STARTED TAKING MY FRIEND M TOO, EVEN THOUGH SHE CLAIMED NOT TO BE INTERESTED IN GROCERY STORES...
...and now she walks through Paradise Road by herself! Against her very will!
HA!
Candy
HUFF
Cake
M
SHE'S A FRIEND OF PARADISE NOW. YOU SHOULD TRY IT, TOO!
Are you kidding? Who would be dumb enough to do that?!
Sorry! Sorry!
Stuuupid!
hee hee hee

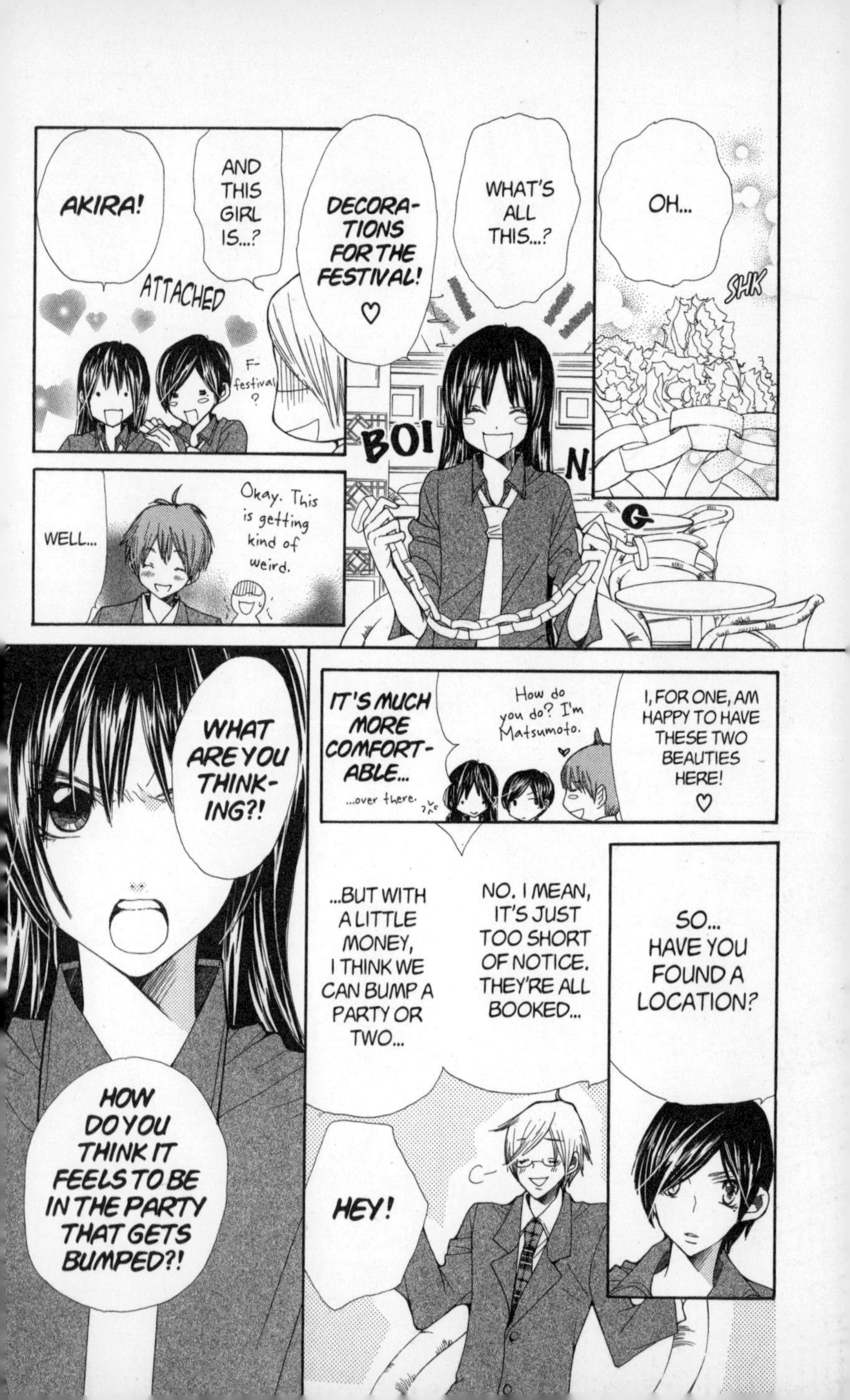
OH...
SHK
WHAT'S ALL THIS...?
DECORATIONS FOR THE FESTIVAL! ♡
BOING
AND THIS GIRL IS...?
AKIRA!
ATTACHED
F-festival?
Okay. This is getting kind of weird.
WELL...
I, FOR ONE, AM HAPPY TO HAVE THESE TWO BEAUTIES HERE! ♡
How do you do? I'm Matsumoto.
IT'S MUCH MORE COMFORTABLE...
...over there.
SO... HAVE YOU FOUND A LOCATION?
NO. I MEAN, IT'S JUST TOO SHORT OF NOTICE. THEY'RE ALL BOOKED...
...BUT WITH A LITTLE MONEY, I THINK WE CAN BUMP A PARTY OR TWO...
HEY!
WHAT ARE YOU THINKING?!
HOW DO YOU THINK IT FEELS TO BE IN THE PARTY THAT GETS BUMPED?!

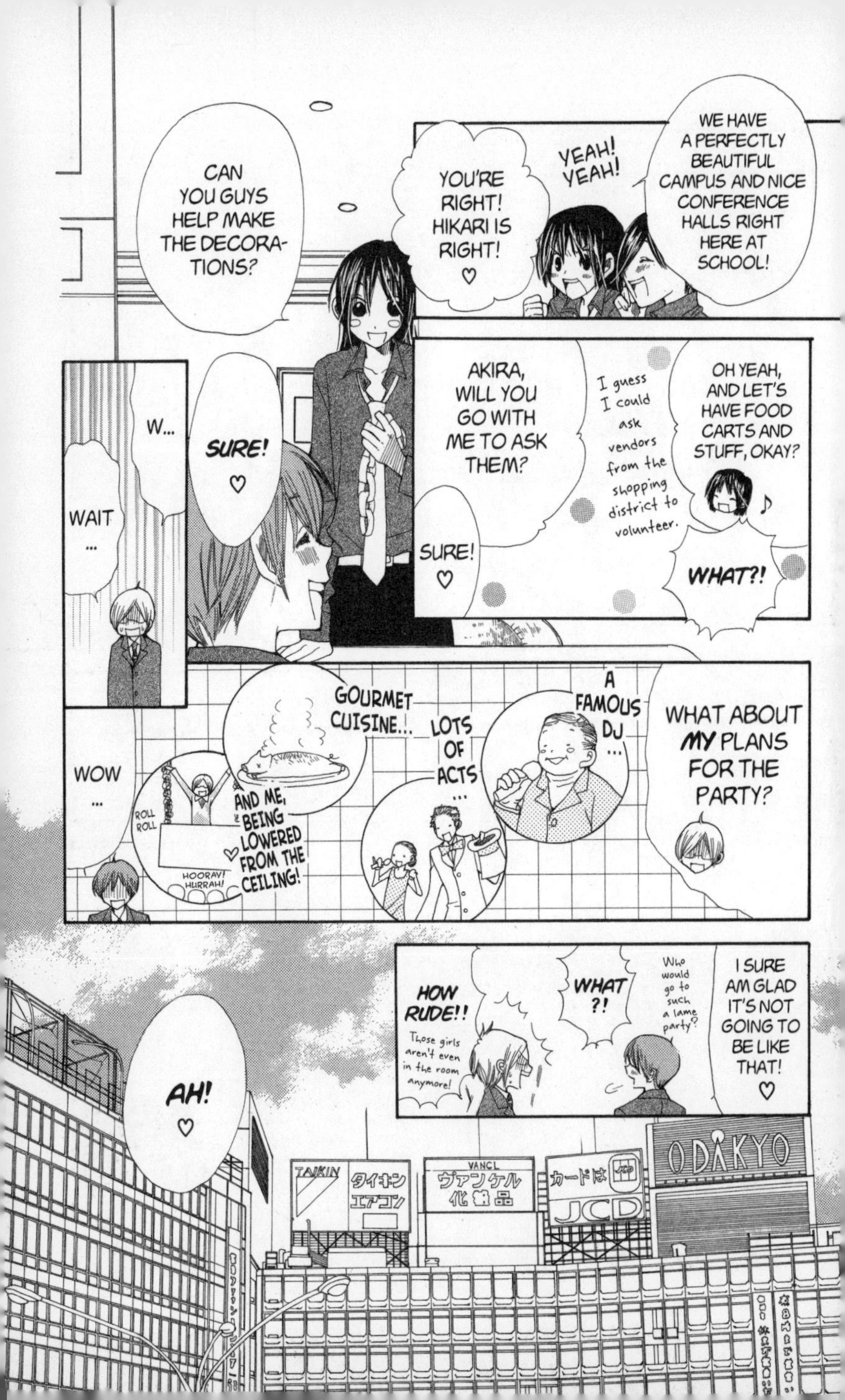

WE HAVE A PERFECTLY BEAUTIFUL CAMPUS AND NICE CONFERENCE HALLS RIGHT HERE AT SCHOOL!
YEAH! YEAH!
YOU'RE RIGHT! HIKARI IS RIGHT! ♡
CAN YOU GUYS HELP MAKE THE DECORATIONS?
OH YEAH, AND LET'S HAVE FOOD CARTS AND STUFF, OKAY? ♪
I guess I could ask vendors from the shopping district to volunteer.
WHAT?!
AKIRA, WILL YOU GO WITH ME TO ASK THEM?
SURE! ♡
SURE! ♡
W...
WAIT ...
WHAT ABOUT MY PLANS FOR THE PARTY?
A FAMOUS DJ ...
LOTS OF ACTS ...
GOURMET CUISINE...
AND ME, BEING LOWERED FROM THE CEILING! ♡
ROLL ROLL
HOORAY! HURRAH!
WOW ...
I SURE AM GLAD IT'S NOT GOING TO BE LIKE THAT! ♡
Who would go to such a lame party?
WHAT ?!
HOW RUDE!!
Those girls aren't even in the room anymore!
AH! ♡
ODAKYO
カードは JCD
VANCL ヴァンケル 化粧品
TAIKIN タイキン エアコン

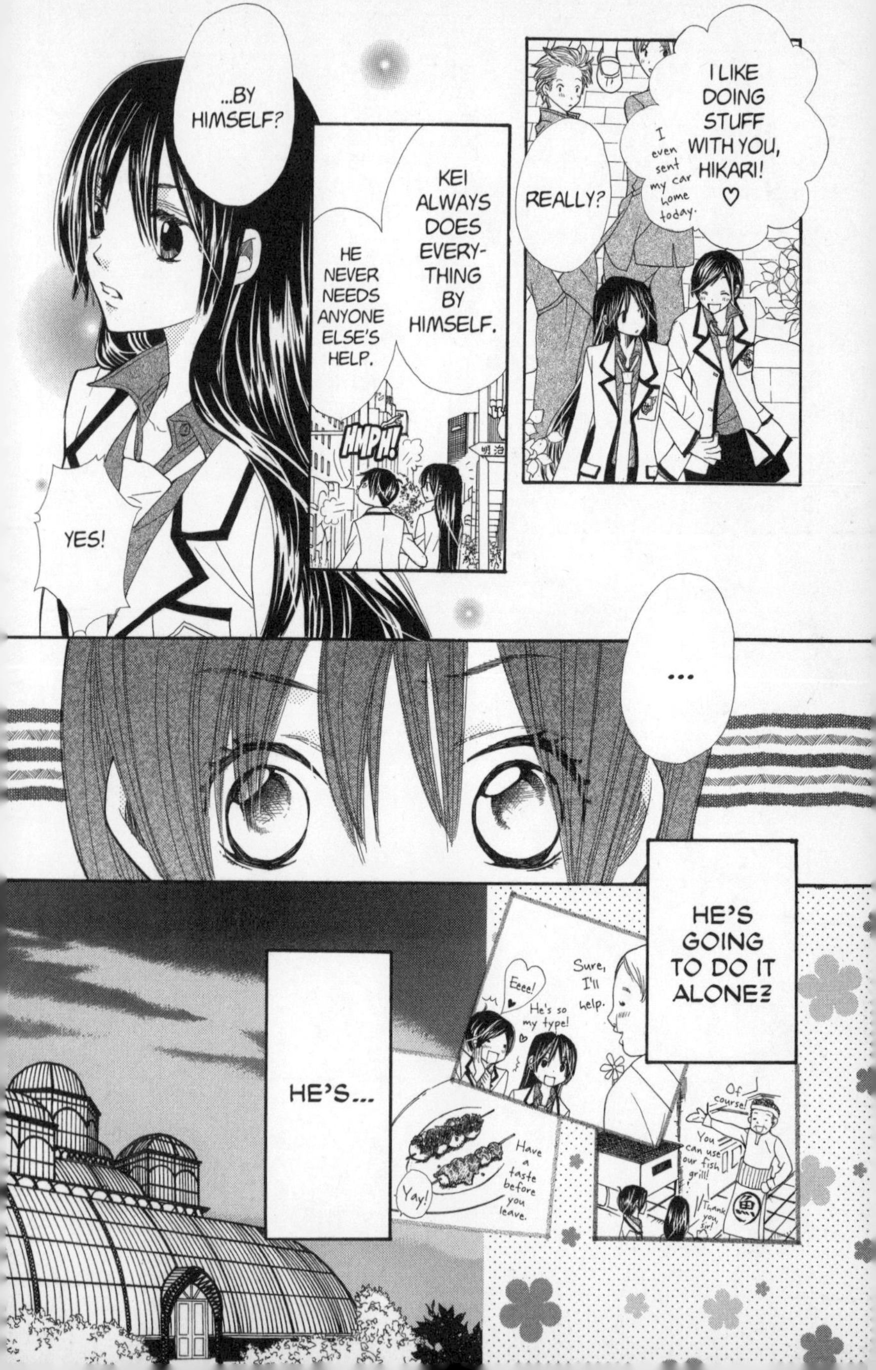
I LIKE DOING STUFF WITH YOU, HIKARI! ♡
I even sent my car home today.
REALLY?
KEI ALWAYS DOES EVERY-THING BY HIMSELF.
HE NEVER NEEDS ANYONE ELSE'S HELP.
HMPH!
...BY HIMSELF?
YES!
...
HE'S GOING TO DO IT ALONE?
Sure, I'll help.
Eeee! ♡
He's so my type! ♡
Of course!
You can use our fish grill!
Thank you, sir!
Have a taste before you leave.
Yay!
HE'S...

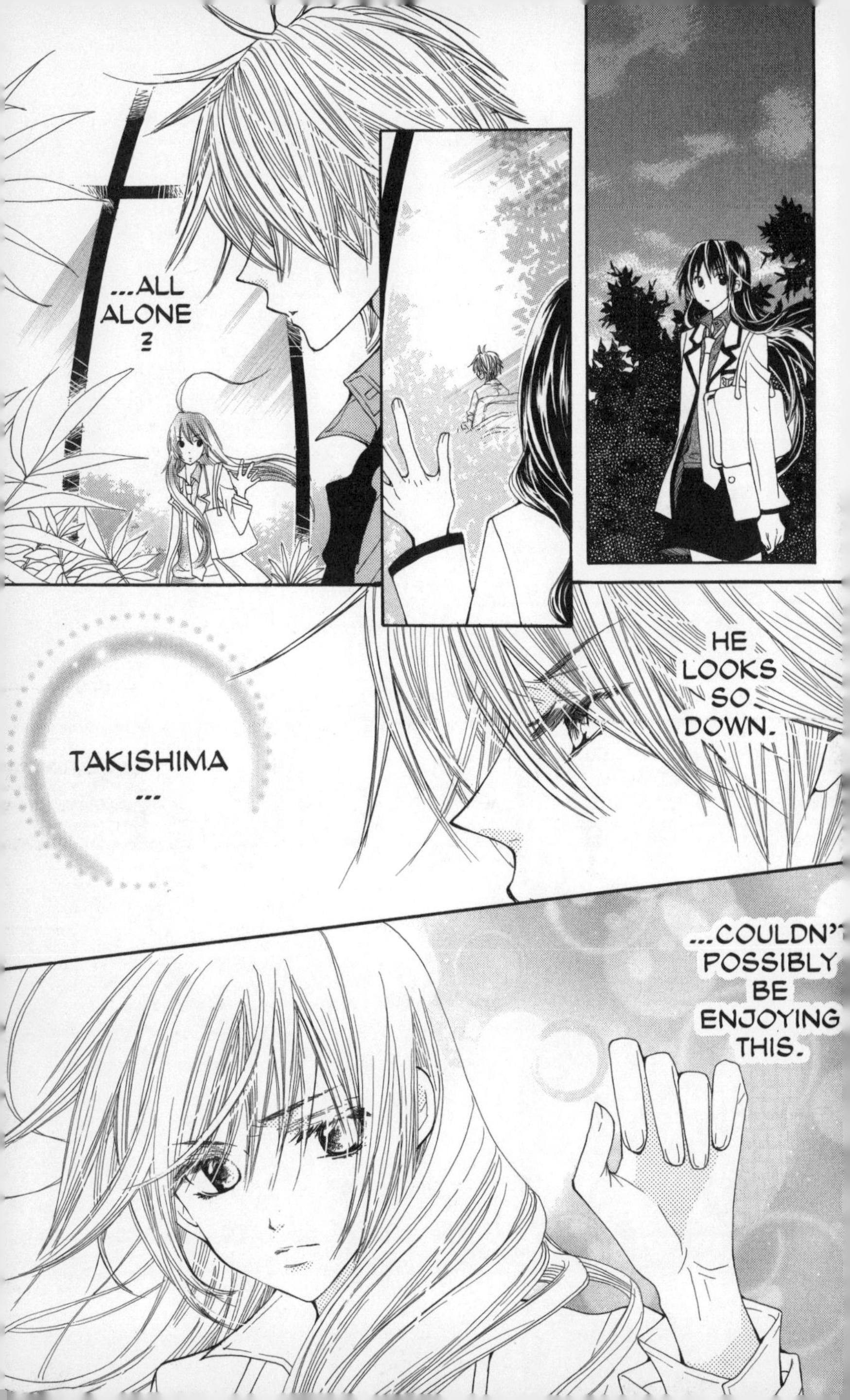
...ALL ALONE?
HE LOOKS SO DOWN.
TAKISHIMA...
...COULDN'T POSSIBLY BE ENJOYING THIS.

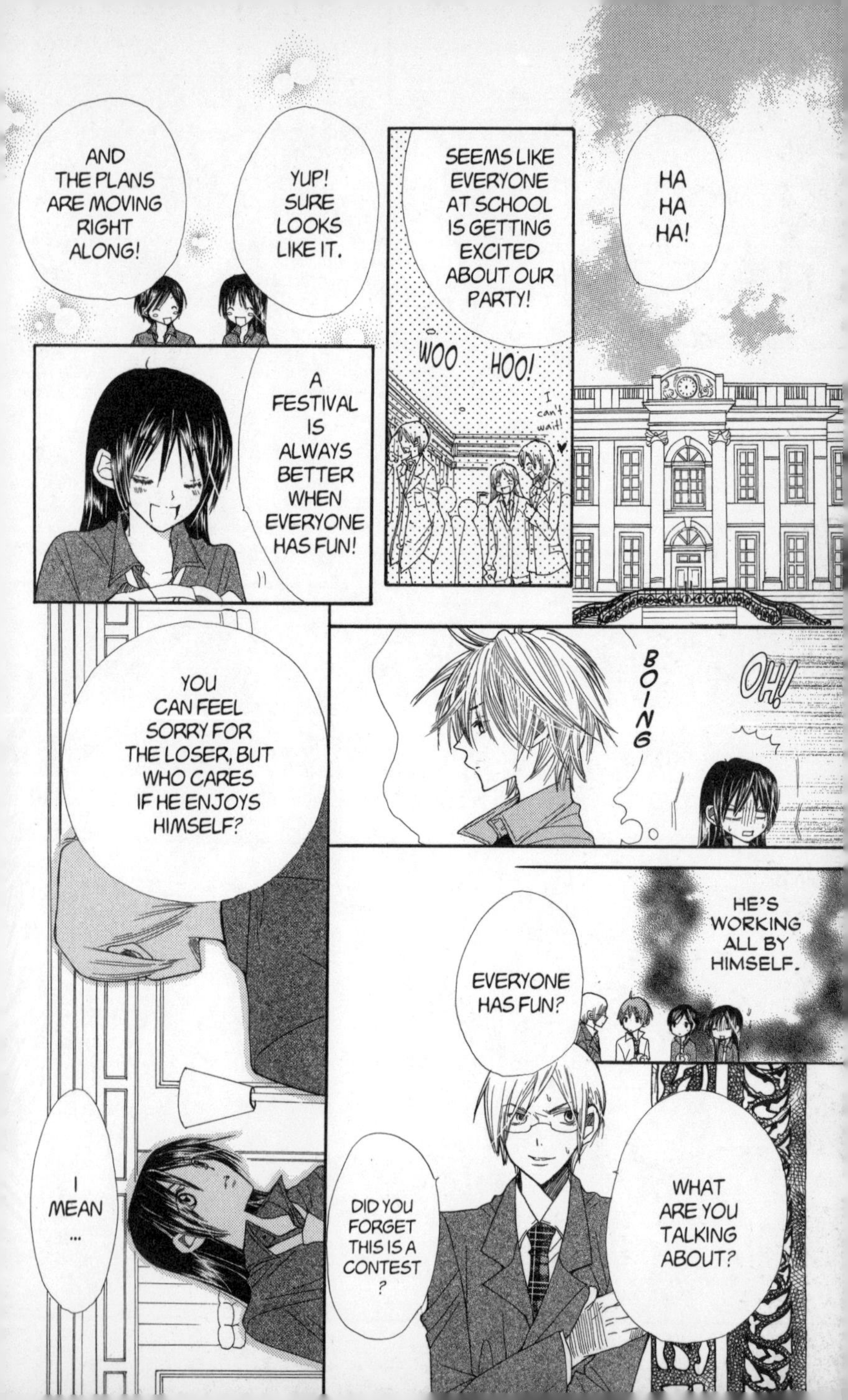
HA HA HA!
SEEMS LIKE EVERYONE AT SCHOOL IS GETTING EXCITED ABOUT OUR PARTY!
WOO HOO!
I can't wait!
YUP! SURE LOOKS LIKE IT.
AND THE PLANS ARE MOVING RIGHT ALONG!
A FESTIVAL IS ALWAYS BETTER WHEN EVERYONE HAS FUN!
BOING
OH!
HE'S WORKING ALL BY HIMSELF.
EVERYONE HAS FUN?
WHAT ARE YOU TALKING ABOUT?
DID YOU FORGET THIS IS A CONTEST?
YOU CAN FEEL SORRY FOR THE LOSER, BUT WHO CARES IF HE ENJOYS HIMSELF?
I MEAN...

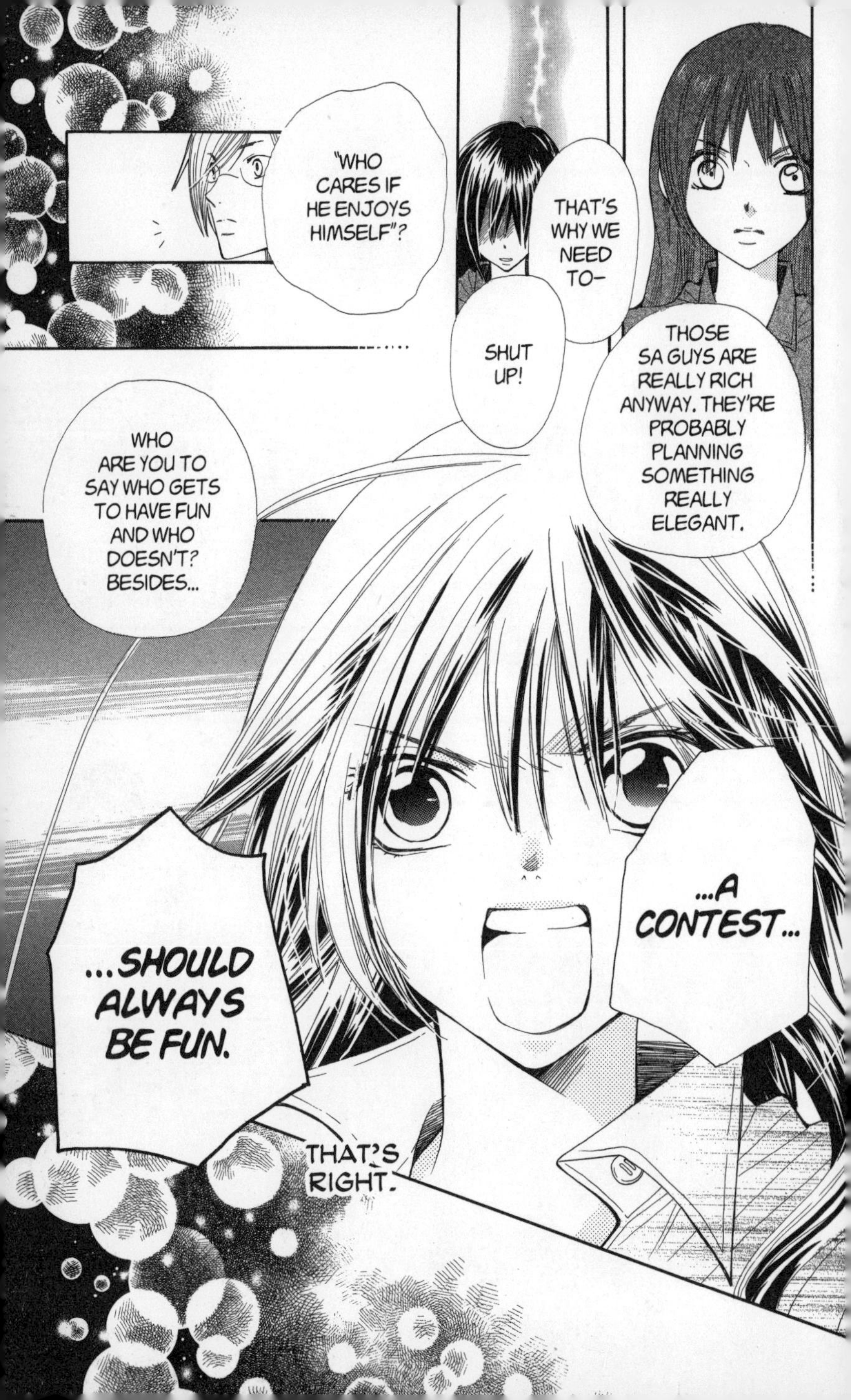
THOSE SA GUYS ARE REALLY RICH ANYWAY. THEY'RE PROBABLY PLANNING SOMETHING REALLY ELEGANT.
THAT'S WHY WE NEED TO—
SHUT UP!
"WHO CARES IF HE ENJOYS HIMSELF"?
WHO ARE YOU TO SAY WHO GETS TO HAVE FUN AND WHO DOESN'T? BESIDES...
...A CONTEST...
...SHOULD ALWAYS BE FUN.
THAT'S RIGHT.

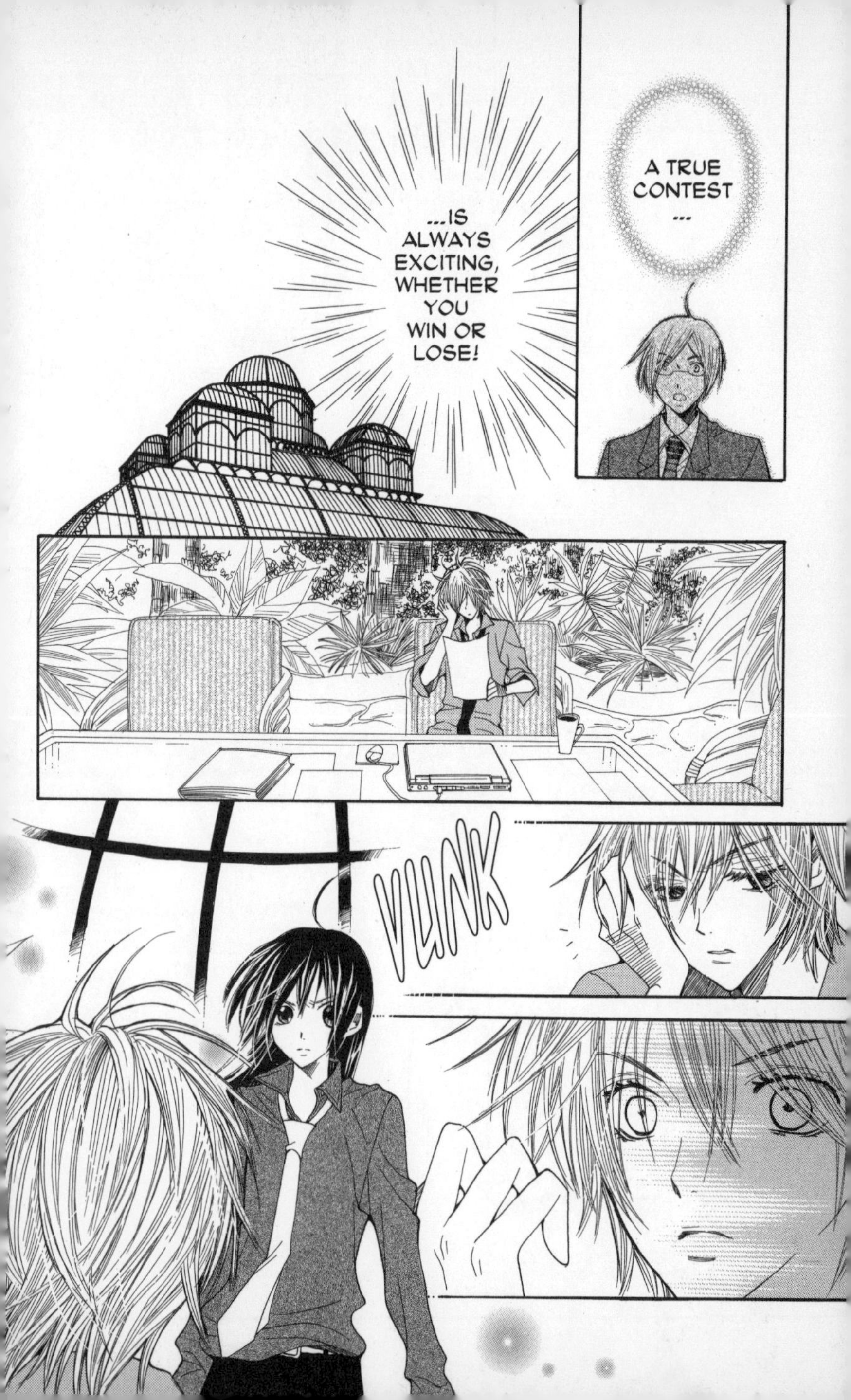
A TRUE CONTEST ...
...IS ALWAYS EXCITING, WHETHER YOU WIN OR LOSE!
VLINK

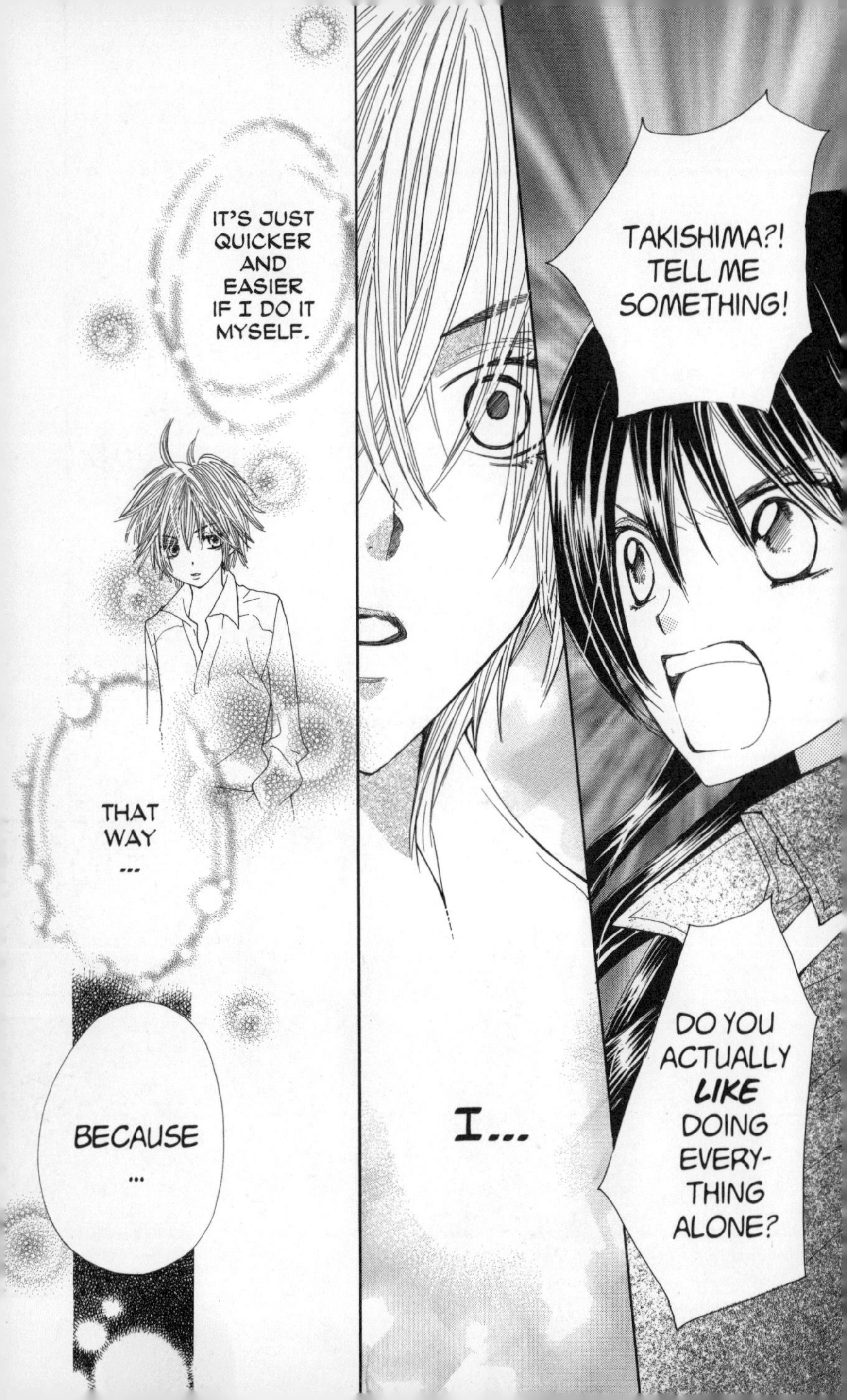
TAKISHIMA?! TELL ME SOMETHING!
DO YOU ACTUALLY **LIKE** DOING EVERY-THING ALONE?
I...
IT'S JUST QUICKER AND EASIER IF I DO IT MYSELF.
THAT WAY...
BECAUSE...

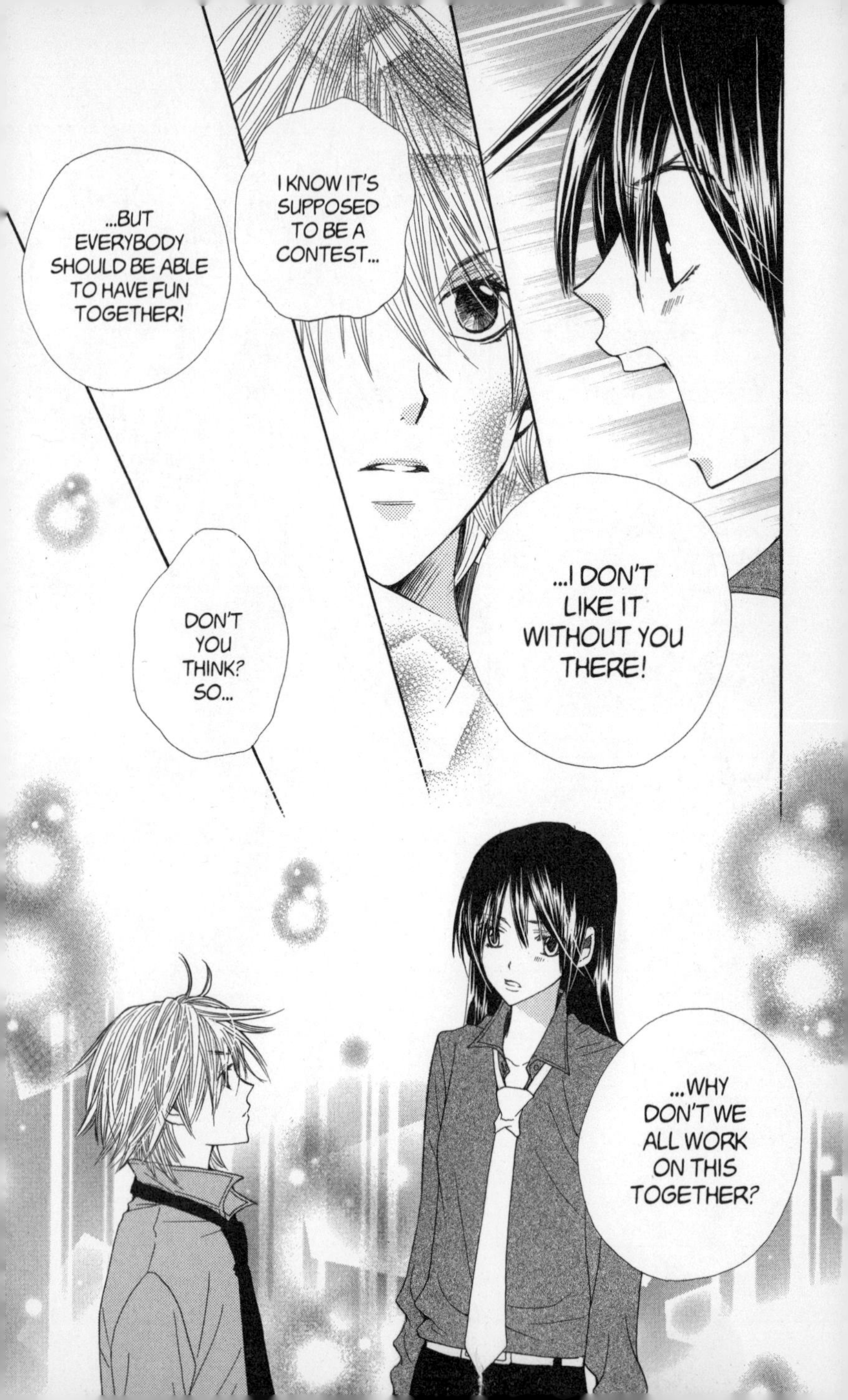
I KNOW IT'S SUPPOSED TO BE A CONTEST...
...BUT EVERYBODY SHOULD BE ABLE TO HAVE FUN TOGETHER!
DON'T YOU THINK? SO...
...I DON'T LIKE IT WITHOUT YOU THERE!
...WHY DON'T WE ALL WORK ON THIS TOGETHER?

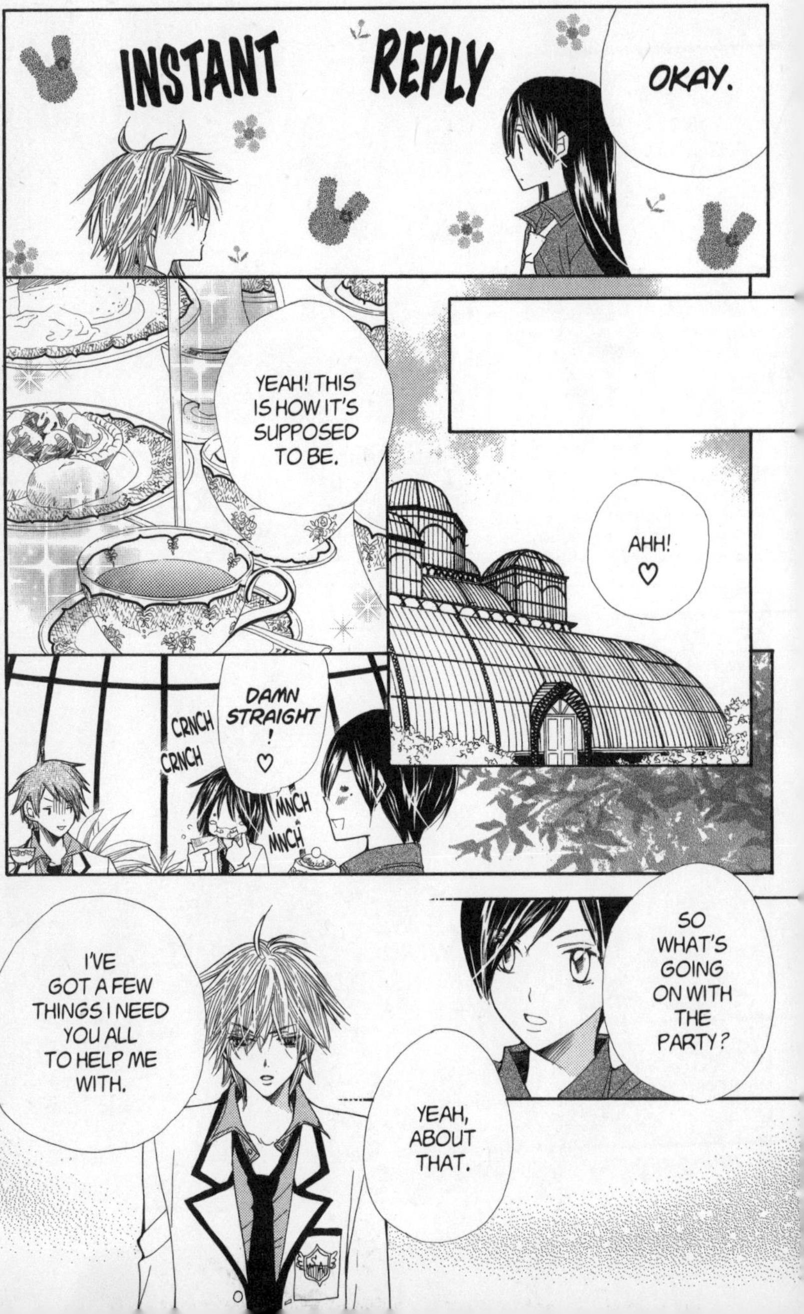
OKAY.
INSTANT REPLY
AHH! ♡
YEAH! THIS IS HOW IT'S SUPPOSED TO BE.
DAMN STRAIGHT! ♡
CRNCH CRNCH
MNCH MNCH
SO WHAT'S GOING ON WITH THE PARTY?
YEAH, ABOUT THAT.
I'VE GOT A FEW THINGS I NEED YOU ALL TO HELP ME WITH.

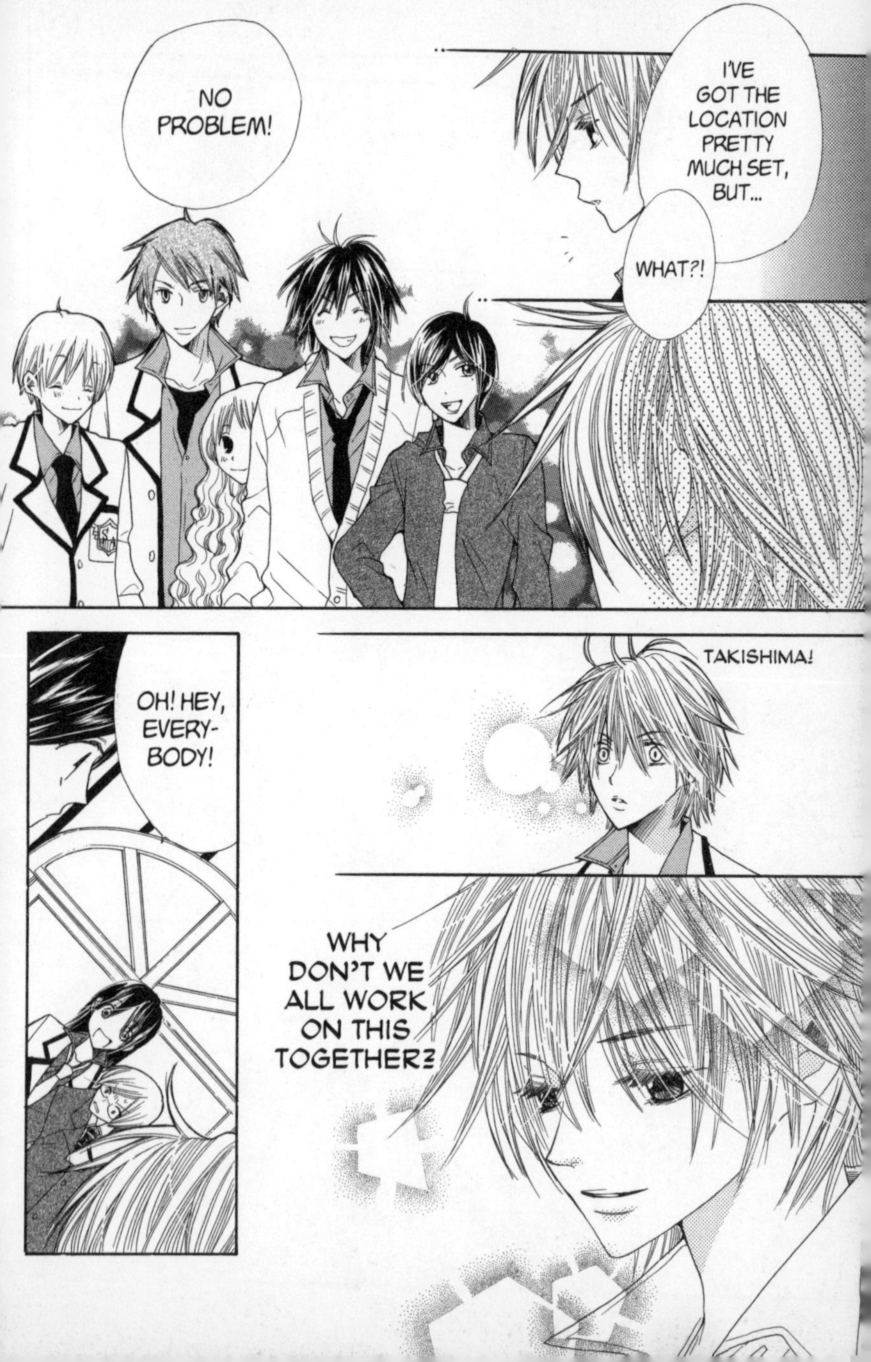
I'VE GOT THE LOCATION PRETTY MUCH SET, BUT...
WHAT?!
NO PROBLEM!
TAKISHIMA!
WHY DON'T WE ALL WORK ON THIS TOGETHER?
OH! HEY, EVERYBODY!

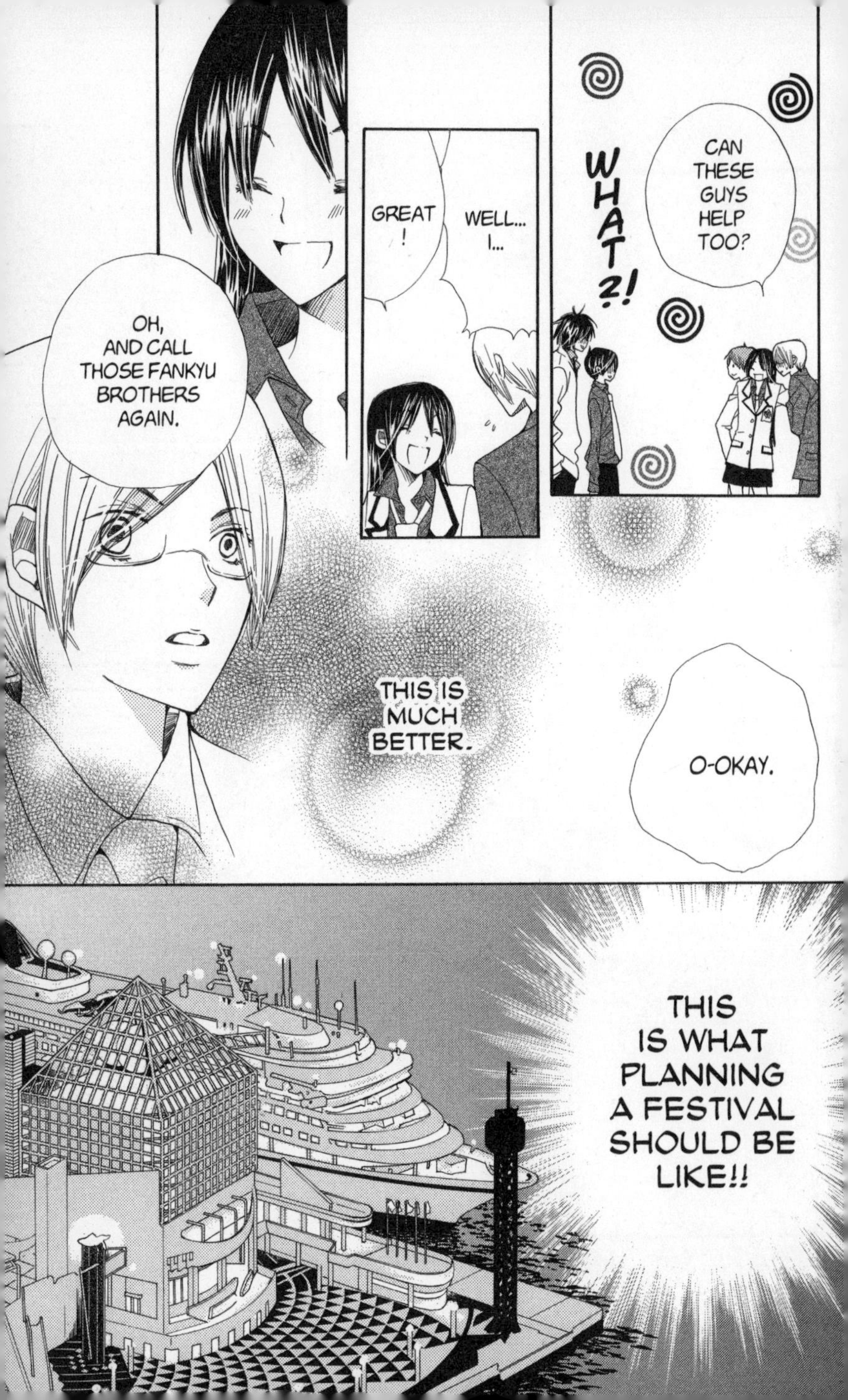
CAN THESE GUYS HELP TOO?
WHAT?!
WELL... I...
GREAT!
OH, AND CALL THOSE FANKYU BROTHERS AGAIN.
O-OKAY.
THIS IS MUCH BETTER.
THIS IS WHAT PLANNING A FESTIVAL SHOULD BE LIKE!!

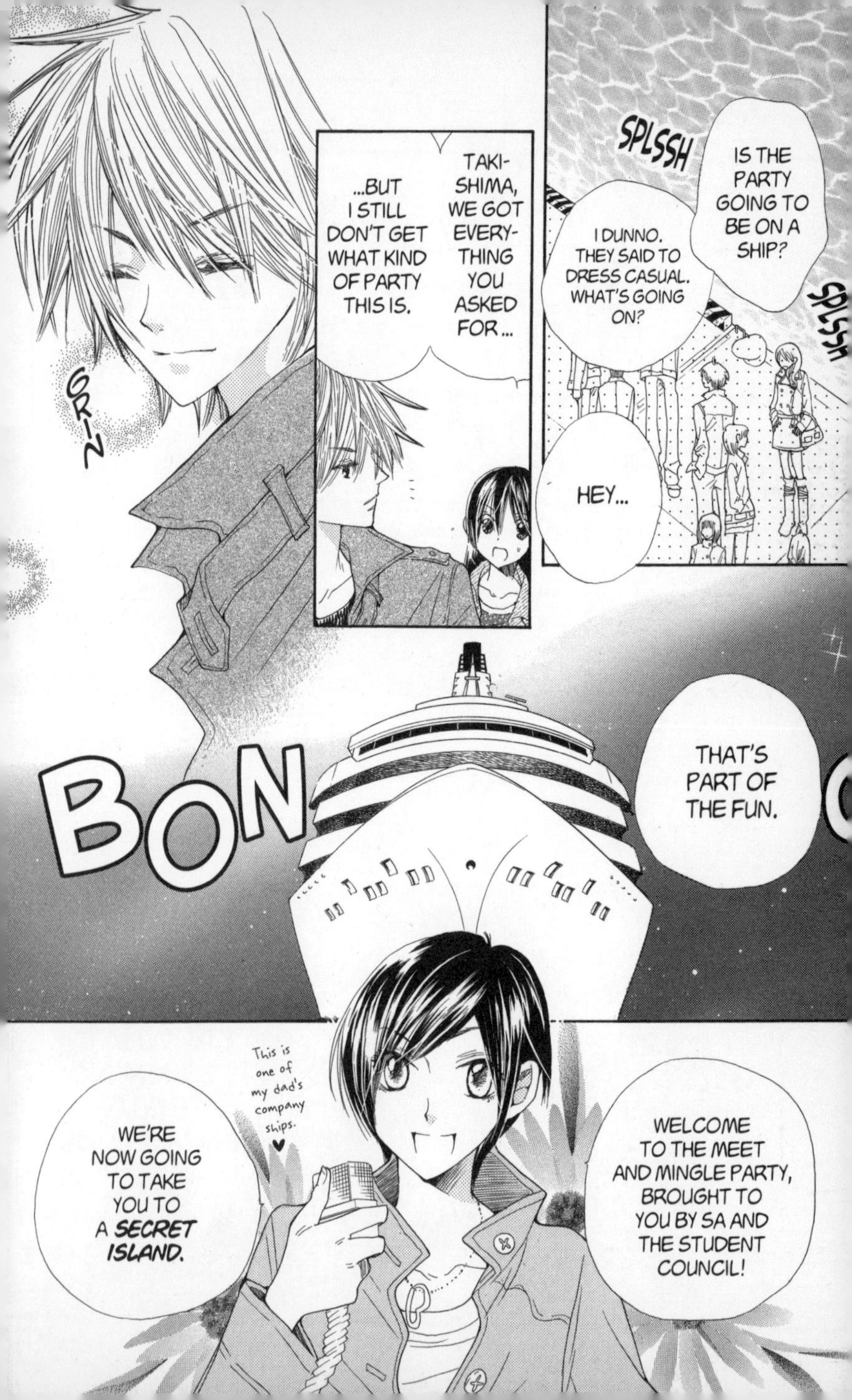
SPLSSH
IS THE PARTY GOING TO BE ON A SHIP?
SPLSSH
I DUNNO. THEY SAID TO DRESS CASUAL. WHAT'S GOING ON?
HEY...
TAKI-SHIMA, WE GOT EVERY-THING YOU ASKED FOR...
...BUT I STILL DON'T GET WHAT KIND OF PARTY THIS IS.
GRIN
THAT'S PART OF THE FUN.
BON
WELCOME TO THE MEET AND MINGLE PARTY, BROUGHT TO YOU BY SA AND THE STUDENT COUNCIL!
This is one of my dad's company ships.
WE'RE NOW GOING TO TAKE YOU TO A **SECRET ISLAND.**

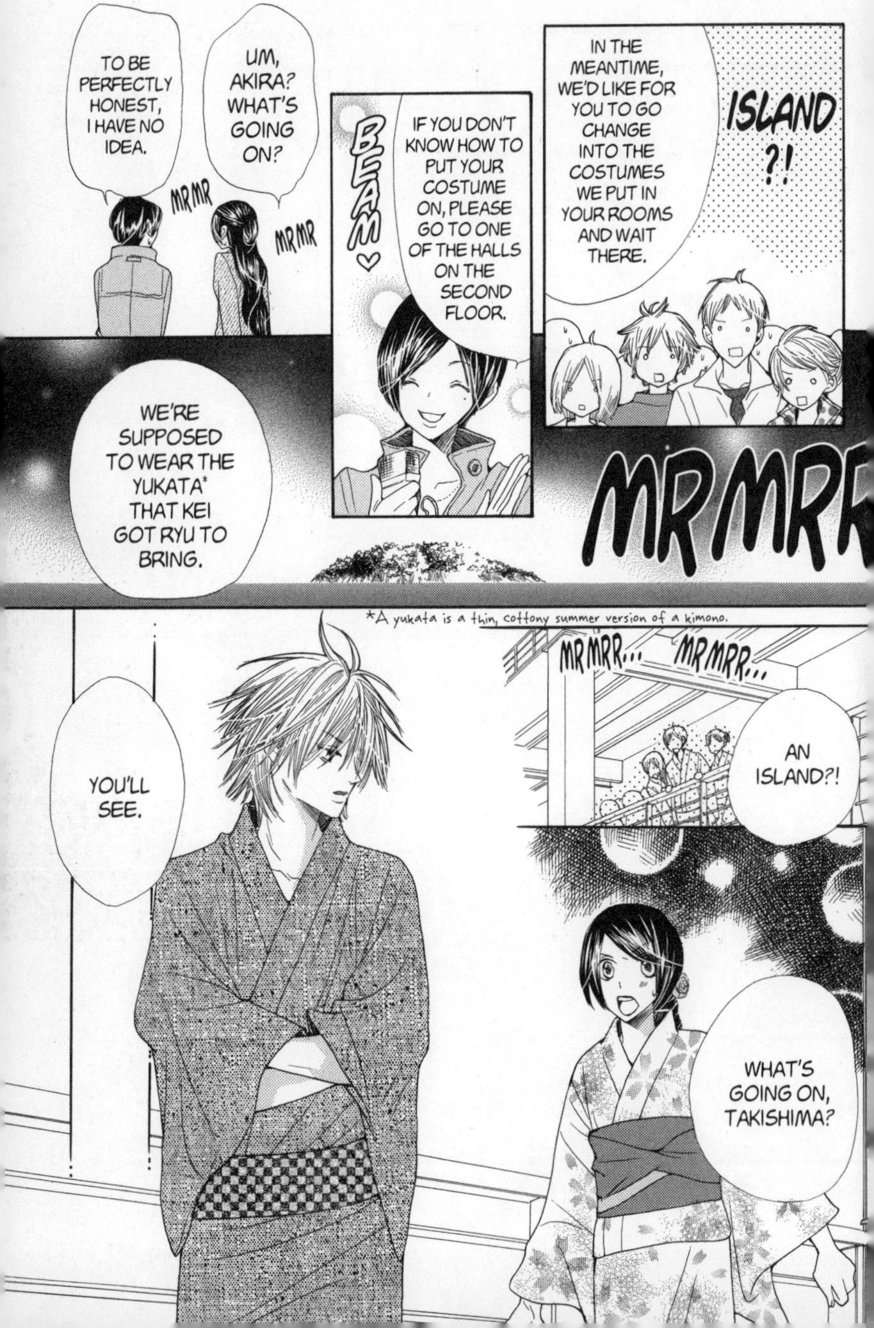
IN THE MEANTIME, WE'D LIKE FOR YOU TO GO CHANGE INTO THE COSTUMES WE PUT IN YOUR ROOMS AND WAIT THERE.
ISLAND?!
BEAM ♡
IF YOU DON'T KNOW HOW TO PUT YOUR COSTUME ON, PLEASE GO TO ONE OF THE HALLS ON THE SECOND FLOOR.
UM, AKIRA? WHAT'S GOING ON?
MRMR
MRMR
TO BE PERFECTLY HONEST, I HAVE NO IDEA.
MR MRR
WE'RE SUPPOSED TO WEAR THE YUKATA* THAT KEI GOT RYU TO BRING.
MRMRR... MRMRR...
AN ISLAND?!
WHAT'S GOING ON, TAKISHIMA?
YOU'LL SEE.
*A yukata is a thin, cottony summer version of a kimono.

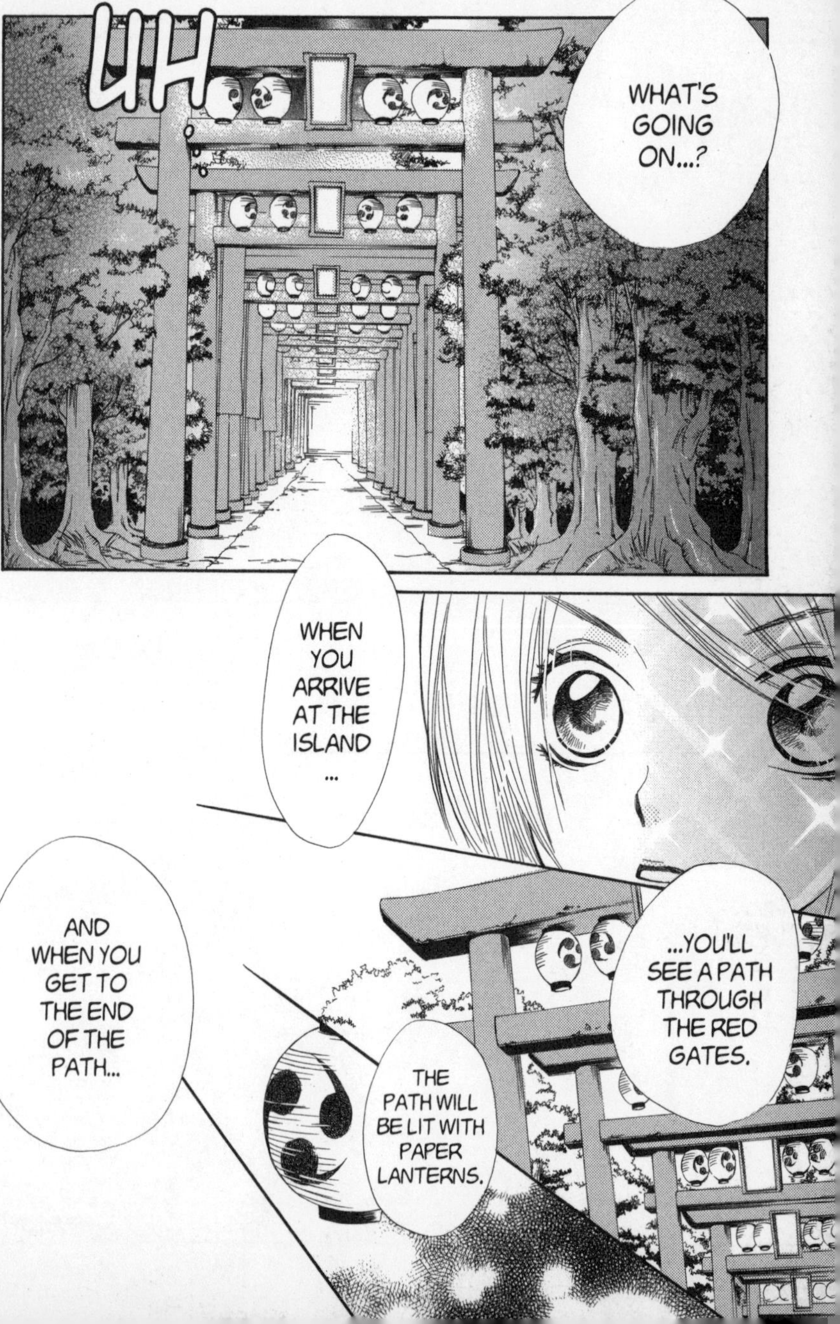
WHAT'S GOING ON...?
UH
WHEN YOU ARRIVE AT THE ISLAND ...
...YOU'LL SEE A PATH THROUGH THE RED GATES.
THE PATH WILL BE LIT WITH PAPER LANTERNS.
AND WHEN YOU GET TO THE END OF THE PATH...

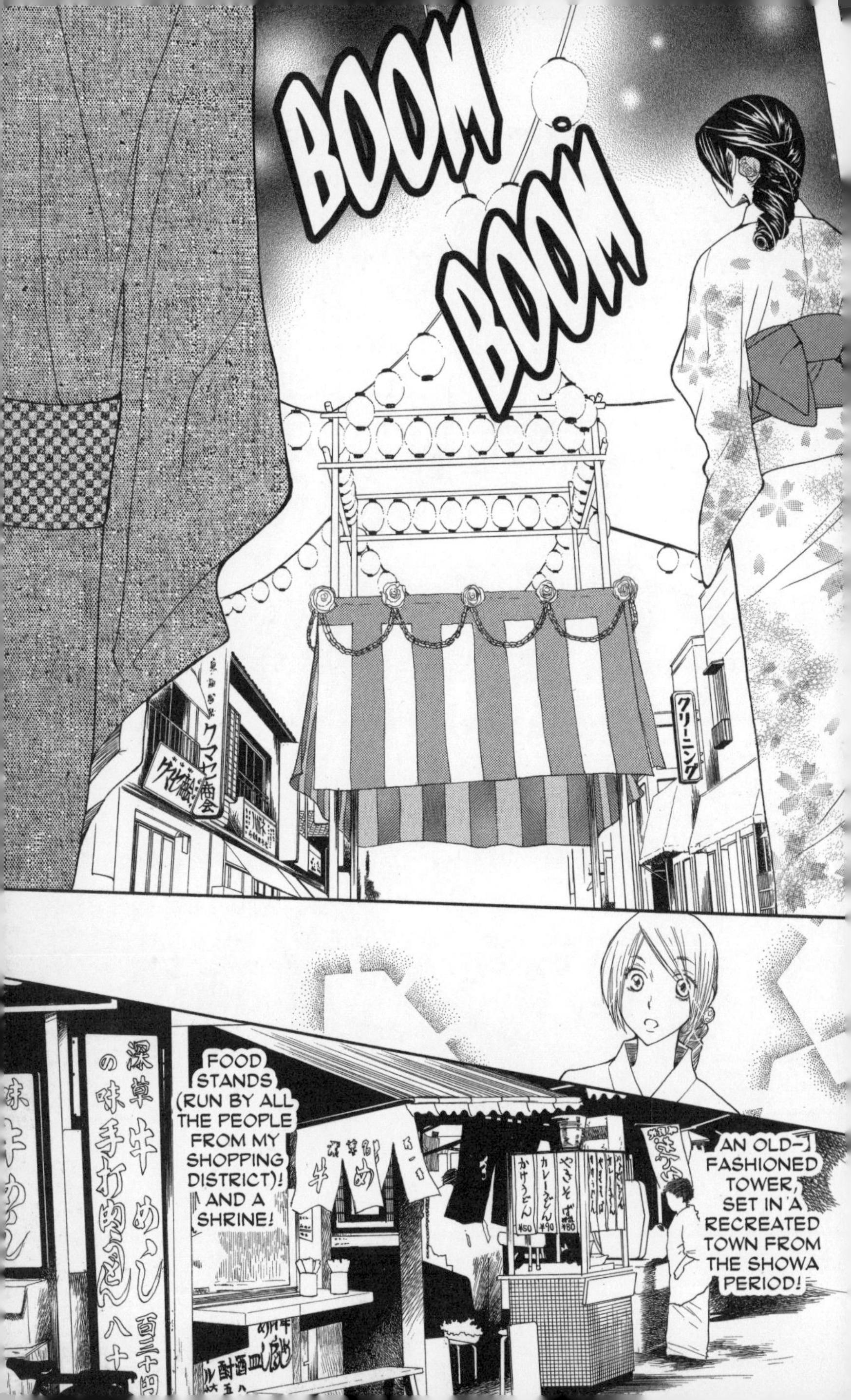
BOOM
BOOM
クマセ商会
クリーニング
AN OLD-FASHIONED TOWER, SET IN A RECREATED TOWN FROM THE SHOWA PERIOD!
やきそば
カレーうどん
かけうどん
¥80
¥90
¥50
FOOD STANDS (RUN BY ALL THE PEOPLE FROM MY SHOPPING DISTRICT)! AND A SHRINE!
深草牛めし 百三十円
の味手打うどん 八十

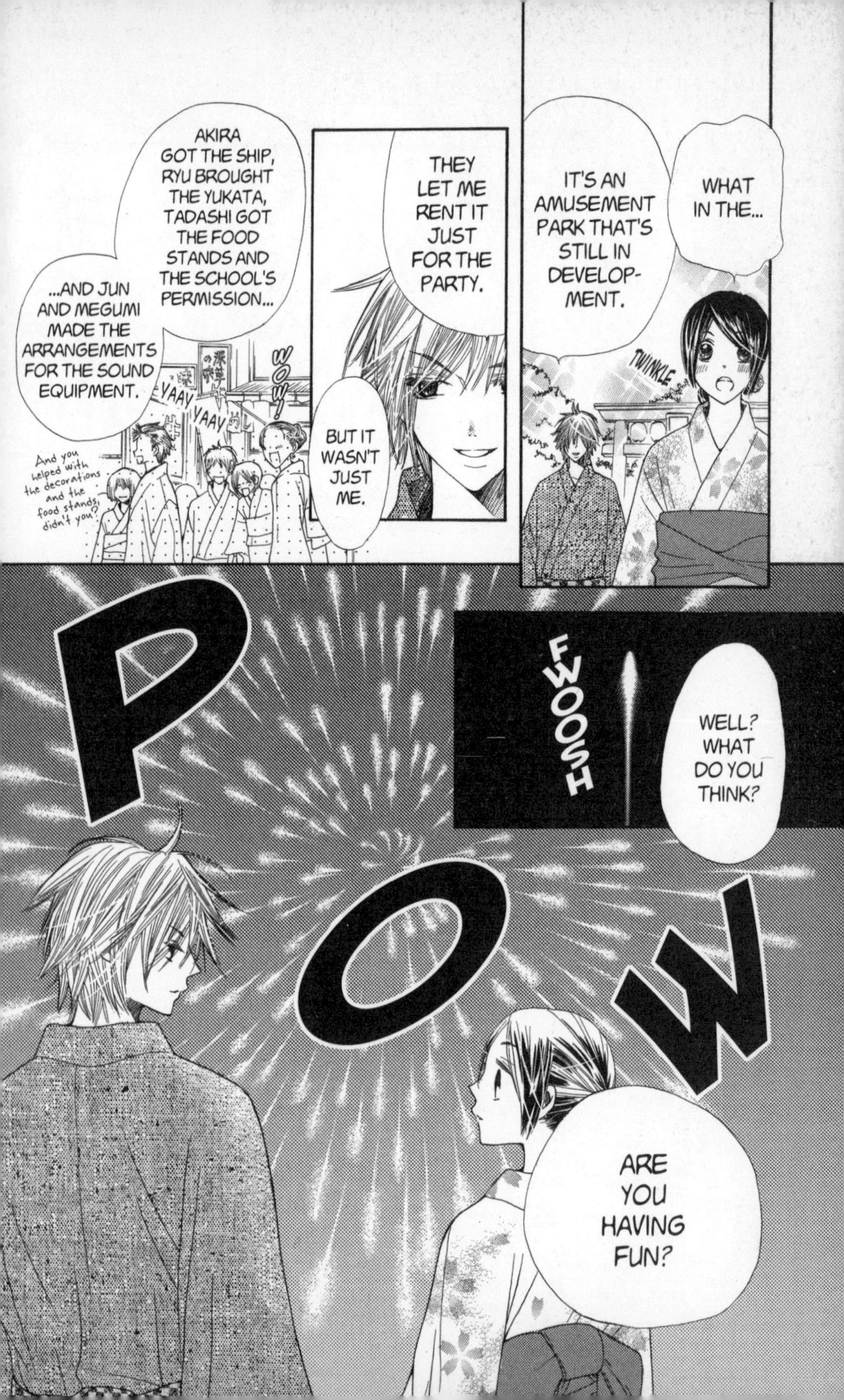
WHAT IN THE...
IT'S AN AMUSEMENT PARK THAT'S STILL IN DEVELOPMENT.
TWINKLE
THEY LET ME RENT IT JUST FOR THE PARTY.
BUT IT WASN'T JUST ME.
AKIRA GOT THE SHIP, RYU BROUGHT THE YUKATA, TADASHI GOT THE FOOD STANDS AND THE SCHOOL'S PERMISSION...
...AND JUN AND MEGUMI MADE THE ARRANGEMENTS FOR THE SOUND EQUIPMENT.
WOW!
YAAY
YAAY
And you helped with the decorations and the food stands, didn't you?
FWOOSH
WELL? WHAT DO YOU THINK?
POW
ARE YOU HAVING FUN?

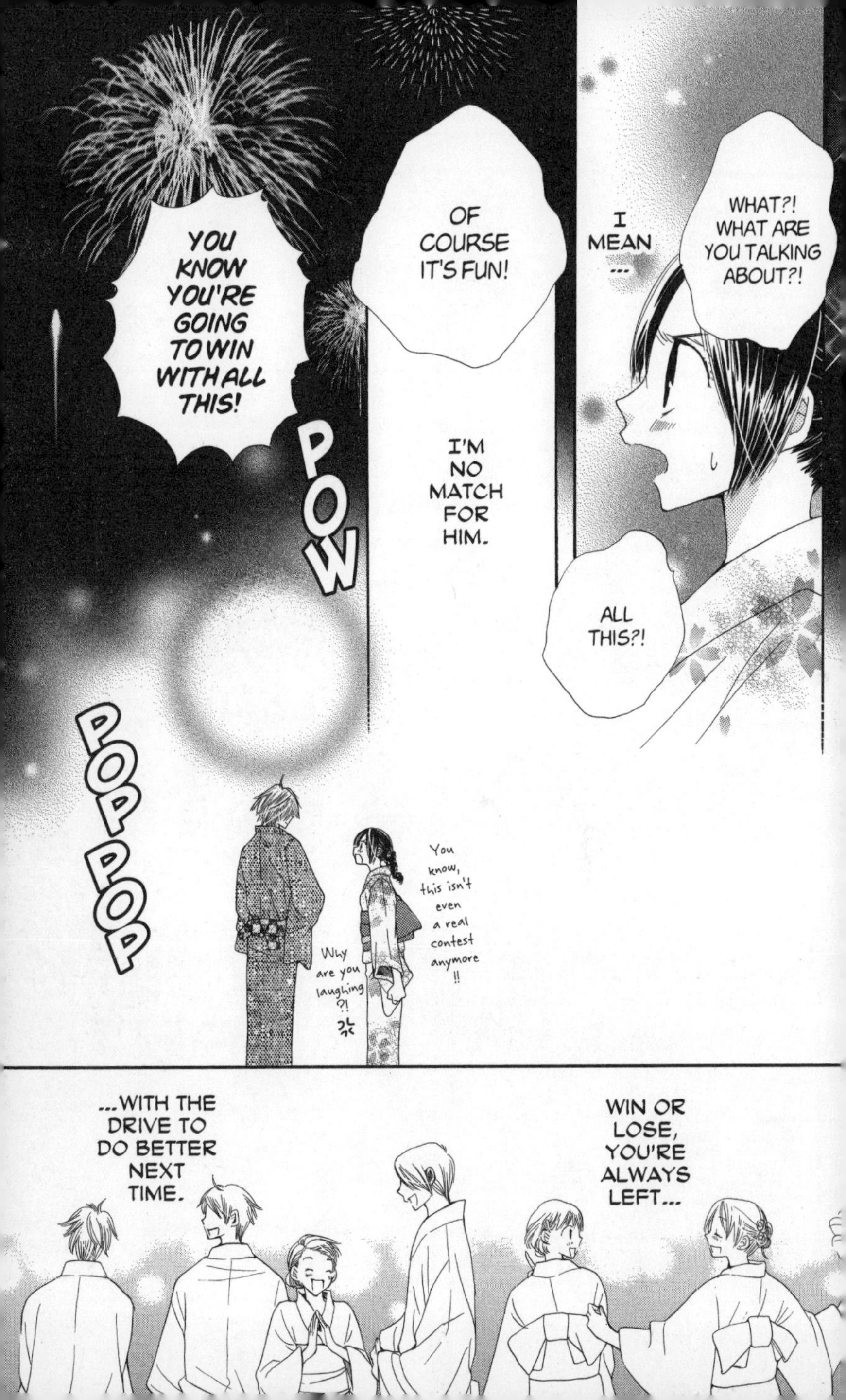
WHAT?! WHAT ARE YOU TALKING ABOUT?!
I MEAN...
ALL THIS?!
OF COURSE IT'S FUN!
I'M NO MATCH FOR HIM.
YOU KNOW YOU'RE GOING TO WIN WITH ALL THIS!
POW
POP POP
You know, this isn't even a real contest anymore!!
Why are you laughing?!
WIN OR LOSE, YOU'RE ALWAYS LEFT...
...WITH THE DRIVE TO DO BETTER NEXT TIME.

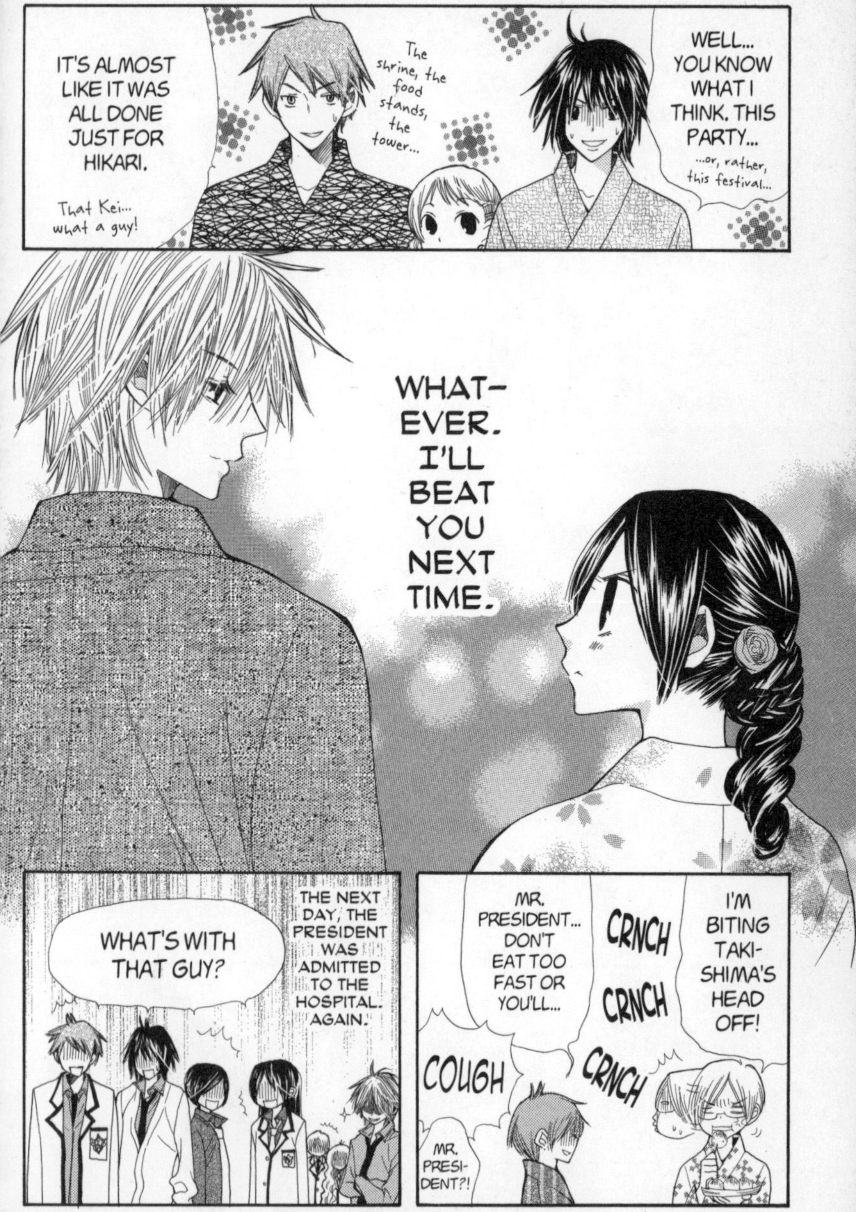
WELL... YOU KNOW WHAT I THINK. THIS PARTY...
...or, rather, this festival...
The shrine, the food stands, the tower...
IT'S ALMOST LIKE IT WAS ALL DONE JUST FOR HIKARI.
That Kei... what a guy!
WHAT-EVER. I'LL BEAT YOU NEXT TIME.
I'M BITING TAKI-SHIMA'S HEAD OFF!
CRNCH
CRNCH
CRNCH
MR. PRESIDENT... DON'T EAT TOO FAST OR YOU'LL...
COUGH
MR. PRESI-DENT?!
THE NEXT DAY, THE PRESIDENT WAS ADMITTED TO THE HOSPITAL. AGAIN.
WHAT'S WITH THAT GUY?

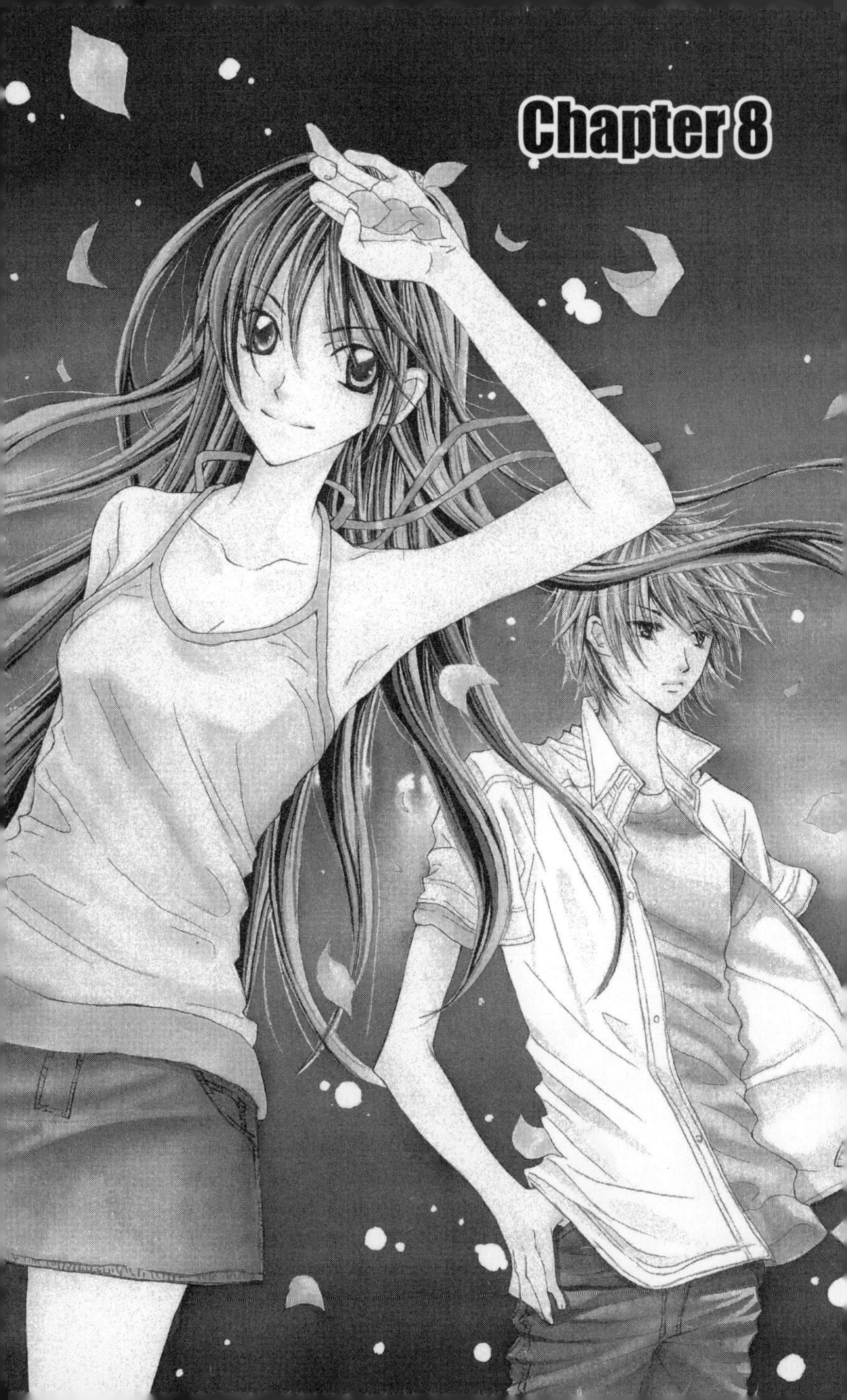
Chapter 8

Special · A

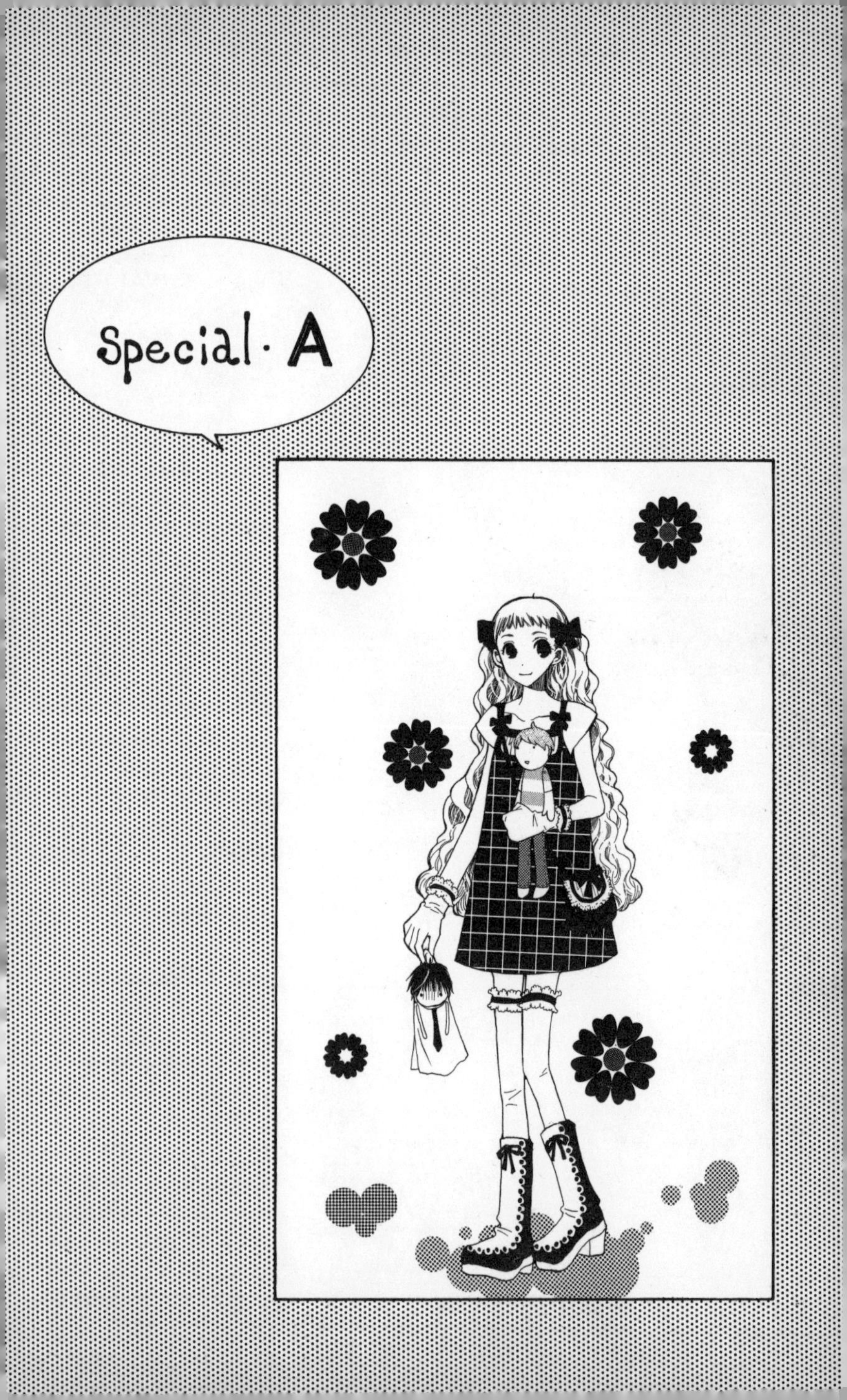

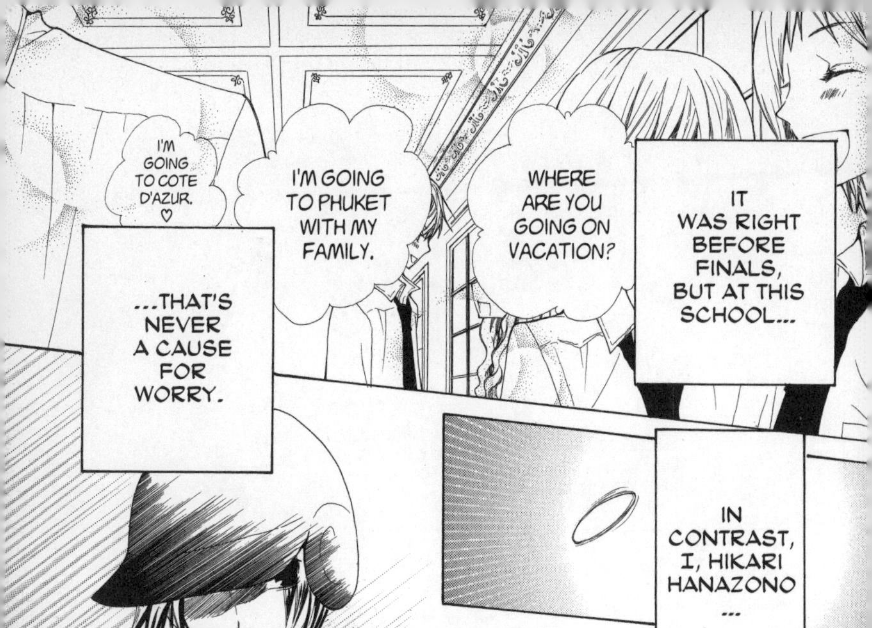
IT WAS RIGHT BEFORE FINALS, BUT AT THIS SCHOOL...
WHERE ARE YOU GOING ON VACATION?
I'M GOING TO PHUKET WITH MY FAMILY.
I'M GOING TO COTE D'AZUR. ♡
...THAT'S NEVER A CAUSE FOR WORRY.
IN CONTRAST, I, HIKARI HANAZONO...
...HAD NO TIME TO RELAX.
WHAP

• MY ASSISTANTS •

EVER SINCE THIS BECAME A SERIES, I HAVE HAD TO BRING IN ASSISTANTS FOR EACH VOLUME. I'M SO GRATEFUL THAT THEY ARE ALWAYS THERE FOR ME, AND I'D LIKE TO USE THIS SPACE TO THANK THEM. AKIKOU AND NISSHI, THANK YOU FOR MAKING THE OFFICE SO MUCH FUN. HAVING PEOPLE TO WORK WITH MAKES IT SO MUCH BETTER. REALLY, THANK YOU! AND THANKS TO ALL OF YOU WHO CAME IN TO HELP TEMPORARILY, AND TO ALL OF MY FRIENDS WHO HAVE COME TO HELP, TOO!

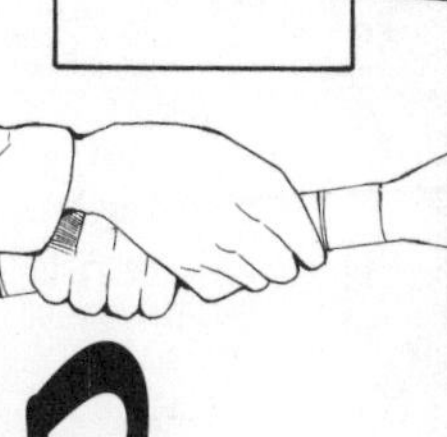
C
And finally, thank to Akikou, who keeps us laughing with her silly songs...
La la...
Black vinegar.
...and to Nisshi the health nut.
&
GRIN

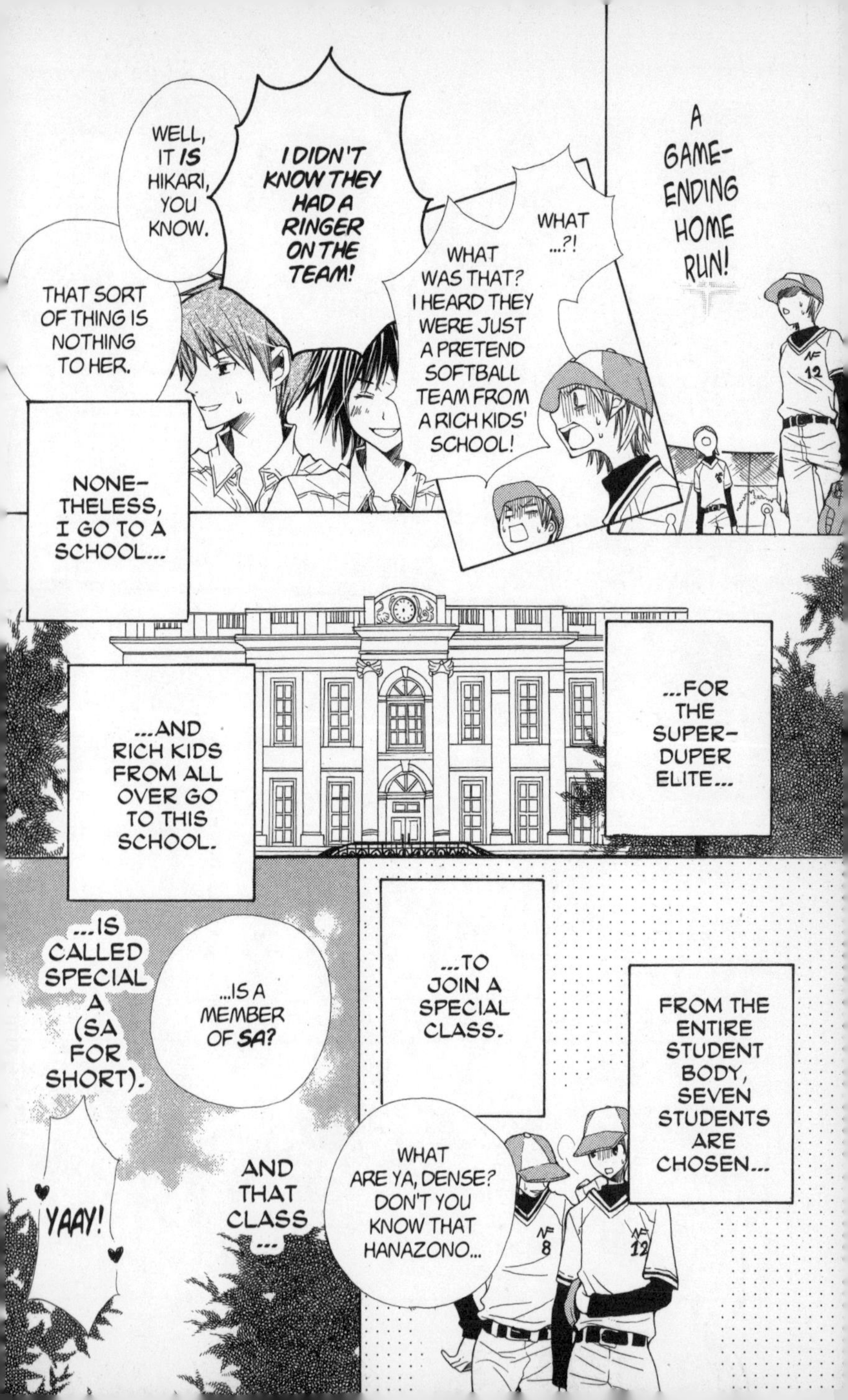
A GAME-ENDING HOME RUN!
WHAT ...?!
WHAT WAS THAT? I HEARD THEY WERE JUST A PRETEND SOFTBALL TEAM FROM A RICH KIDS' SCHOOL!
I DIDN'T KNOW THEY HAD A RINGER ON THE TEAM!
WELL, IT IS HIKARI, YOU KNOW.
THAT SORT OF THING IS NOTHING TO HER.
NONE-THELESS, I GO TO A SCHOOL...
...FOR THE SUPER-DUPER ELITE...
...AND RICH KIDS FROM ALL OVER GO TO THIS SCHOOL.
FROM THE ENTIRE STUDENT BODY, SEVEN STUDENTS ARE CHOSEN...
...TO JOIN A SPECIAL CLASS.
WHAT ARE YA, DENSE? DON'T YOU KNOW THAT HANAZONO...
...IS A MEMBER OF SA?
AND THAT CLASS ...
...IS CALLED SPECIAL A (SA FOR SHORT).
YAAY!

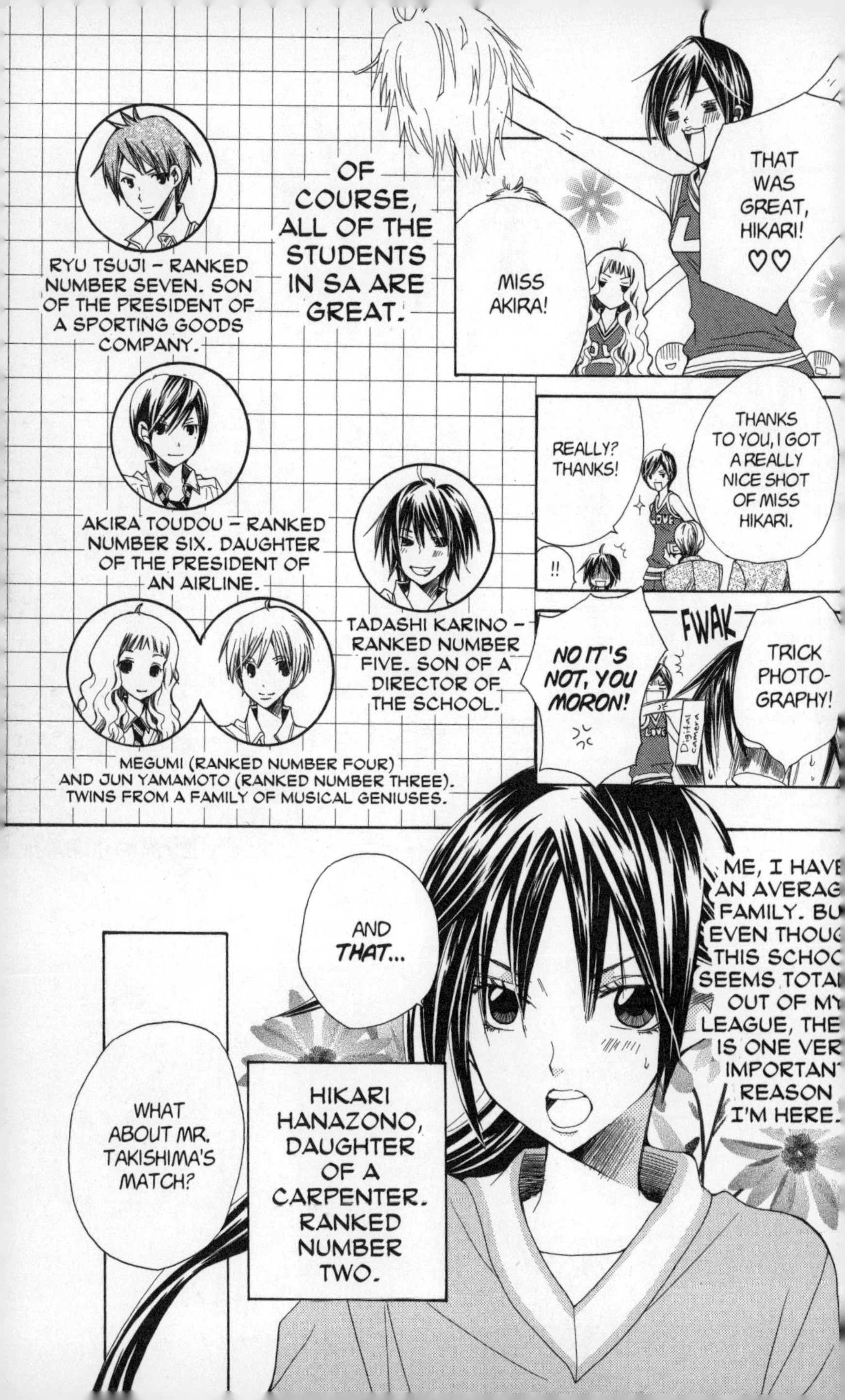
THAT WAS GREAT, HIKARI! ♡♡
MISS AKIRA!
THANKS TO YOU, I GOT A REALLY NICE SHOT OF MISS HIKARI.
REALLY? THANKS!
!!
TRICK PHOTOGRAPHY!
FWAK
NO IT'S NOT, YOU MORON!
Digital camera
OF COURSE, ALL OF THE STUDENTS IN SA ARE GREAT.
RYU TSUJI – RANKED NUMBER SEVEN. SON OF THE PRESIDENT OF A SPORTING GOODS COMPANY.
AKIRA TOUDOU – RANKED NUMBER SIX. DAUGHTER OF THE PRESIDENT OF AN AIRLINE.
TADASHI KARINO – RANKED NUMBER FIVE. SON OF A DIRECTOR OF THE SCHOOL.
MEGUMI (RANKED NUMBER FOUR) AND JUN YAMAMOTO (RANKED NUMBER THREE). TWINS FROM A FAMILY OF MUSICAL GENIUSES.
ME, I HAVE AN AVERAG FAMILY. BU EVEN THOUG THIS SCHOO SEEMS TOTA OUT OF MY LEAGUE, THE IS ONE VER IMPORTAN REASON I'M HERE.
AND THAT...
HIKARI HANAZONO, DAUGHTER OF A CARPENTER. RANKED NUMBER TWO.
WHAT ABOUT MR. TAKISHIMA'S MATCH?

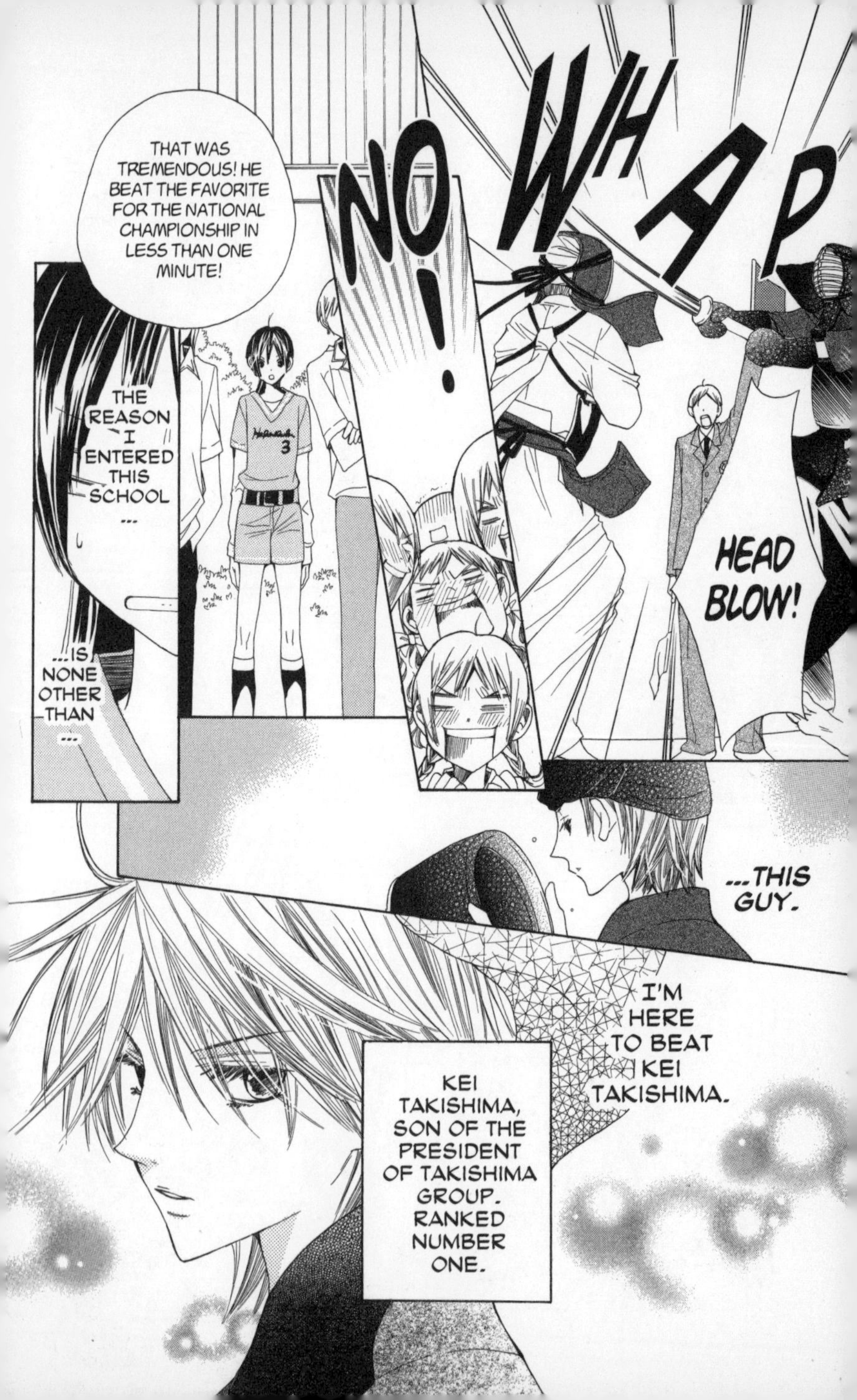
WHAP
HEAD BLOW!
NO!
THAT WAS TREMENDOUS! HE BEAT THE FAVORITE FOR THE NATIONAL CHAMPIONSHIP IN LESS THAN ONE MINUTE!
THE REASON I ENTERED THIS SCHOOL...
...IS NONE OTHER THAN...
...THIS GUY.
I'M HERE TO BEAT KEI TAKISHIMA.
KEI TAKISHIMA, SON OF THE PRESIDENT OF TAKISHIMA GROUP. RANKED NUMBER ONE.

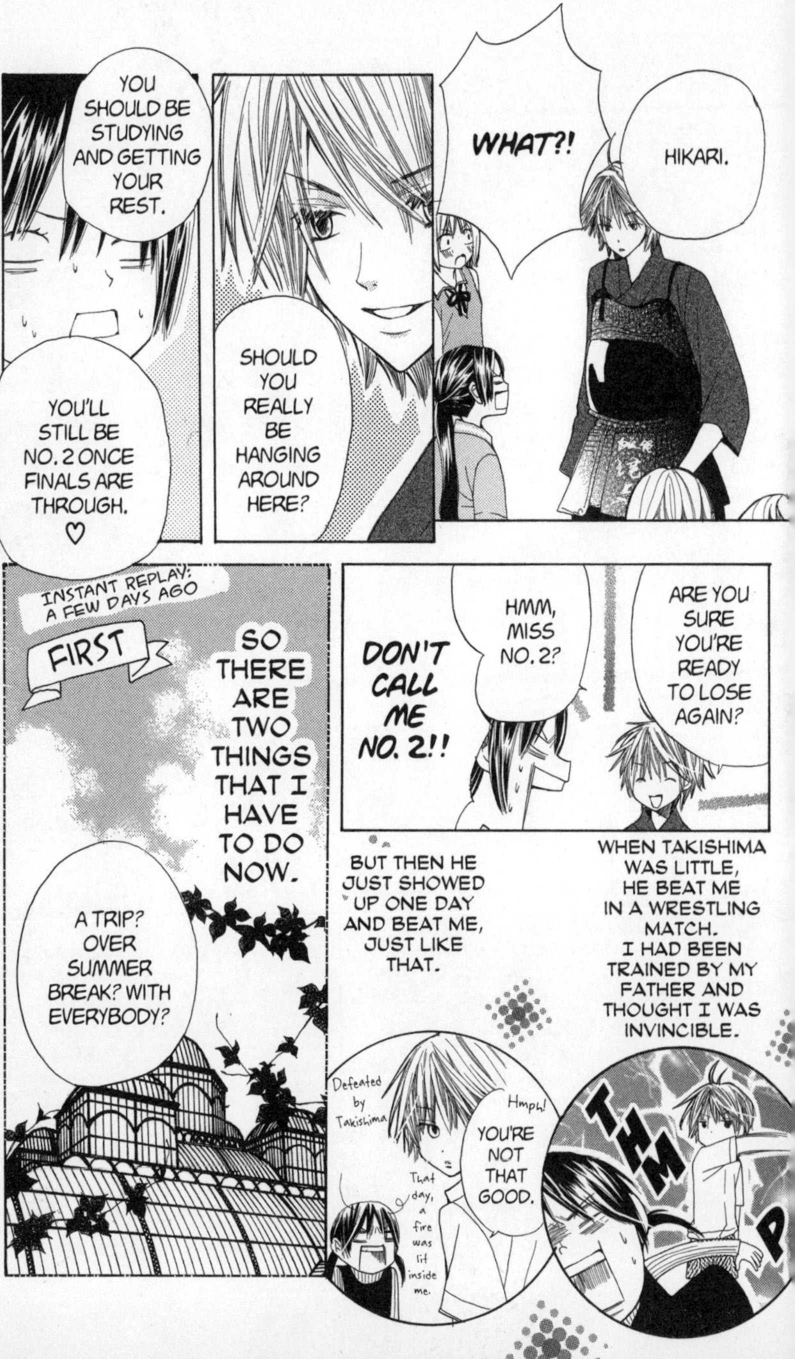
HIKARI.
WHAT?!
SHOULD YOU REALLY BE HANGING AROUND HERE?
YOU SHOULD BE STUDYING AND GETTING YOUR REST.
YOU'LL STILL BE NO. 2 ONCE FINALS ARE THROUGH. ♡
ARE YOU SURE YOU'RE READY TO LOSE AGAIN?
HMM, MISS NO. 2?
DON'T CALL ME NO. 2!!
WHEN TAKISHIMA WAS LITTLE, HE BEAT ME IN A WRESTLING MATCH. I HAD BEEN TRAINED BY MY FATHER AND THOUGHT I WAS INVINCIBLE.
BUT THEN HE JUST SHOWED UP ONE DAY AND BEAT ME, JUST LIKE THAT.
THMP
Hmph!
YOU'RE NOT THAT GOOD.
Defeated by Takishima
That day, a fire was lit inside me.
INSTANT REPLAY: A FEW DAYS AGO
FIRST
SO THERE ARE TWO THINGS THAT I HAVE TO DO NOW.
A TRIP? OVER SUMMER BREAK? WITH EVERYBODY?

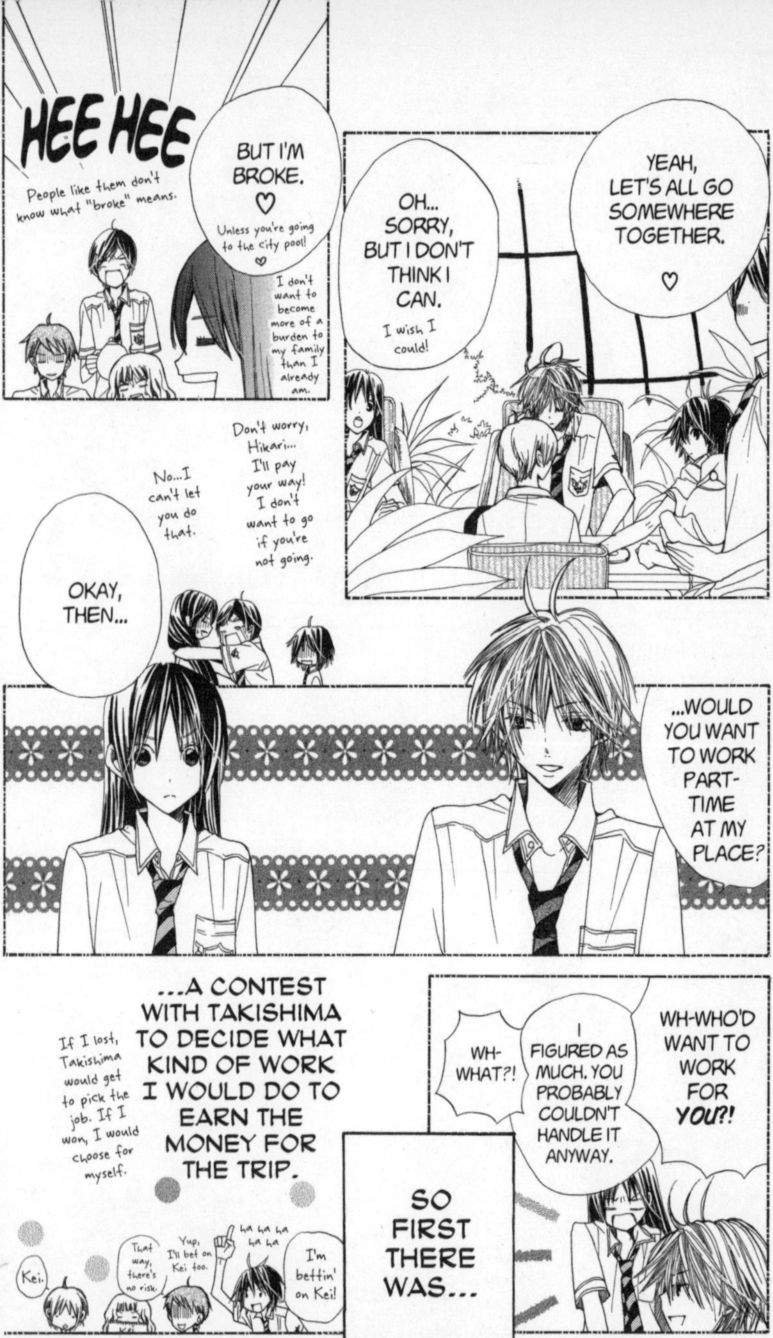
YEAH, LET'S ALL GO SOMEWHERE TOGETHER. ♡
OH... SORRY, BUT I DON'T THINK I CAN.
I wish I could!
BUT I'M BROKE. ♡
Unless you're going to the city pool! ♡
I don't want to become more of a burden to my family than I already am.
HEE HEE
People like them don't know what "broke" means.
Don't worry, Hikari... I'll pay your way! I don't want to go if you're not going.
No...I can't let you do that.
OKAY, THEN...
...WOULD YOU WANT TO WORK PART-TIME AT MY PLACE?
WH-WHO'D WANT TO WORK FOR *YOU?!*
I FIGURED AS MUCH. YOU PROBABLY COULDN'T HANDLE IT ANYWAY.
WH-WHAT?!
SO FIRST THERE WAS...
...A CONTEST WITH TAKISHIMA TO DECIDE WHAT KIND OF WORK I WOULD DO TO EARN THE MONEY FOR THE TRIP.
If I lost, Takishima would get to pick the job. If I won, I would choose for myself.
I'm bettin' on Kei!
ha ha ha ha ha
Yup, I'll bet on Kei too.
That way, there's no risk.
Kei.

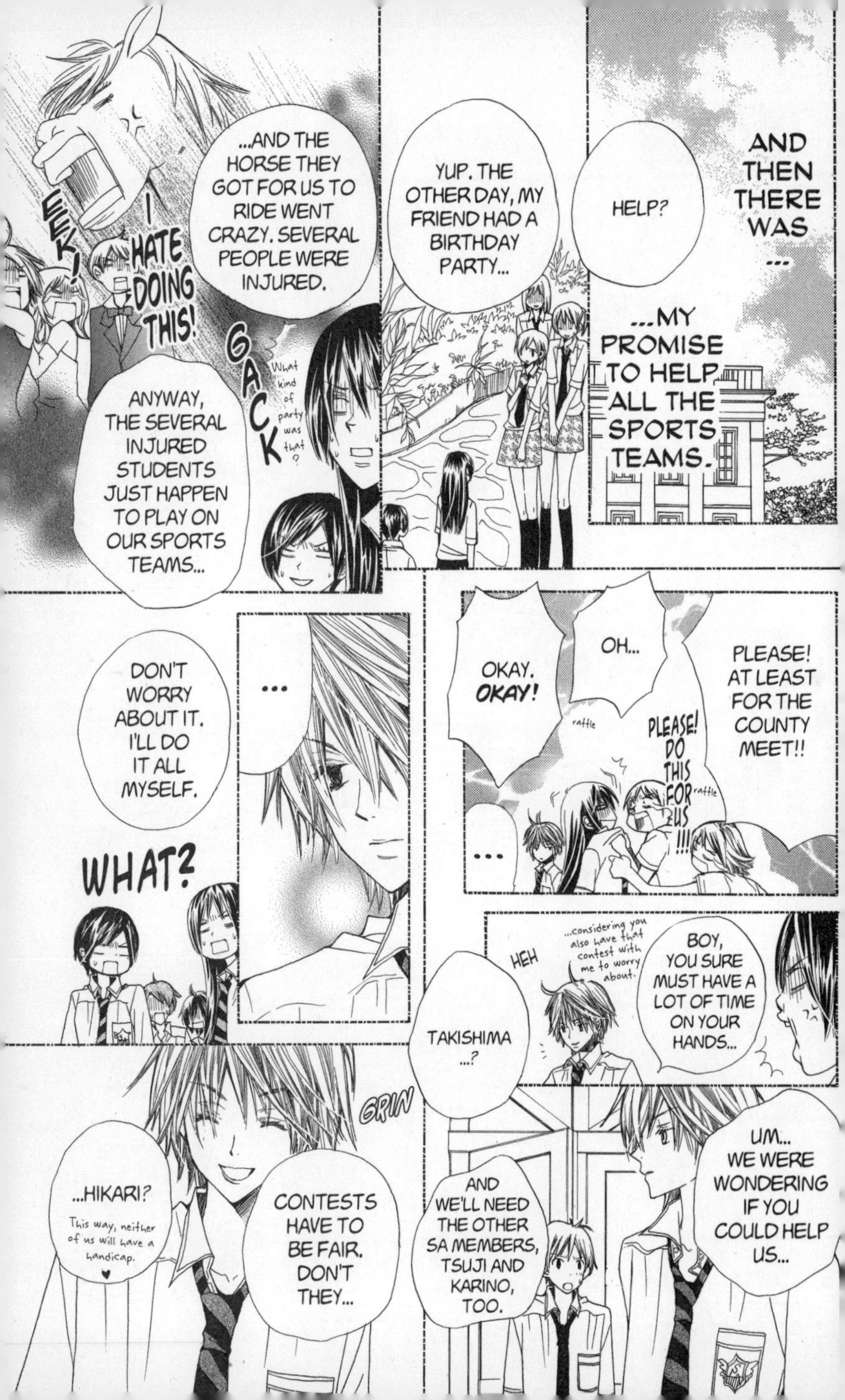
AND THEN THERE WAS...
...MY PROMISE TO HELP ALL THE SPORTS TEAMS.
HELP?
YUP. THE OTHER DAY, MY FRIEND HAD A BIRTHDAY PARTY...
...AND THE HORSE THEY GOT FOR US TO RIDE WENT CRAZY. SEVERAL PEOPLE WERE INJURED.
EEK!
I HATE DOING THIS!
GACK
What kind of party was that?
ANYWAY, THE SEVERAL INJURED STUDENTS JUST HAPPEN TO PLAY ON OUR SPORTS TEAMS...
PLEASE! AT LEAST FOR THE COUNTY MEET!!
OH...
OKAY. OKAY!
PLEASE! DO THIS FOR US!!!
rattle
rattle
...
BOY, YOU SURE MUST HAVE A LOT OF TIME ON YOUR HANDS...
...considering you also have that contest with me to worry about.
HEH
TAKISHIMA ...?
...
DON'T WORRY ABOUT IT. I'LL DO IT ALL MYSELF.
WHAT?
UM... WE WERE WONDERING IF YOU COULD HELP US...
AND WE'LL NEED THE OTHER SA MEMBERS, TSUJI AND KARINO, TOO.
GRIN
CONTESTS HAVE TO BE FAIR. DON'T THEY...
...HIKARI?
This way, neither of us will have a handicap.

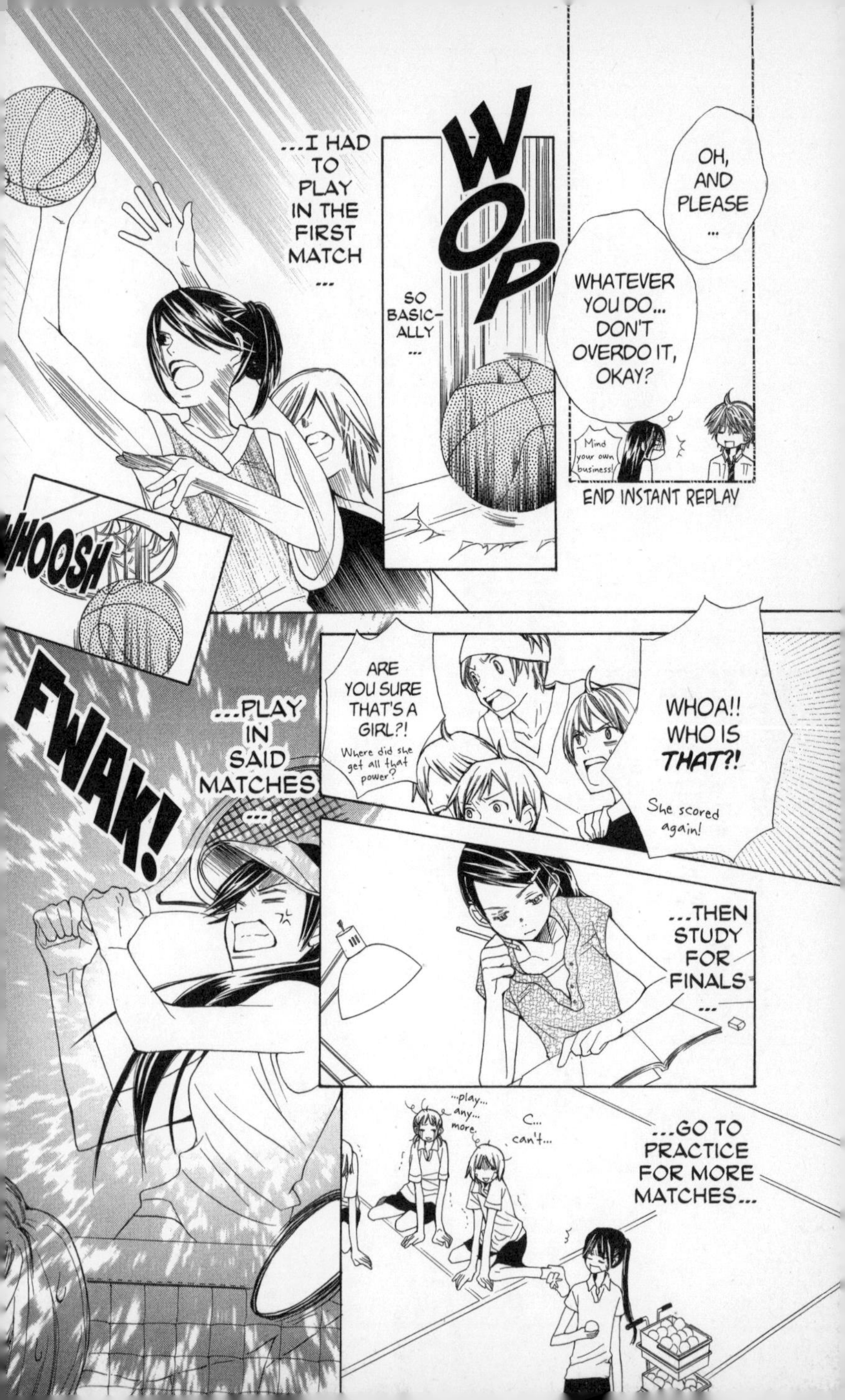
OH, AND PLEASE ...
WHATEVER YOU DO... DON'T OVERDO IT, OKAY?
Mind your own business!
END INSTANT REPLAY
WOP
SO BASIC-ALLY ...
...I HAD TO PLAY IN THE FIRST MATCH ...
WHOOSH
WHOA!! WHO IS THAT?!
She scored again!
ARE YOU SURE THAT'S A GIRL?!
Where did she get all that power?
...THEN STUDY FOR FINALS ...
...GO TO PRACTICE FOR MORE MATCHES...
C... can't...
...play... any... more.
FWAK!
...PLAY IN SAID MATCHES ...

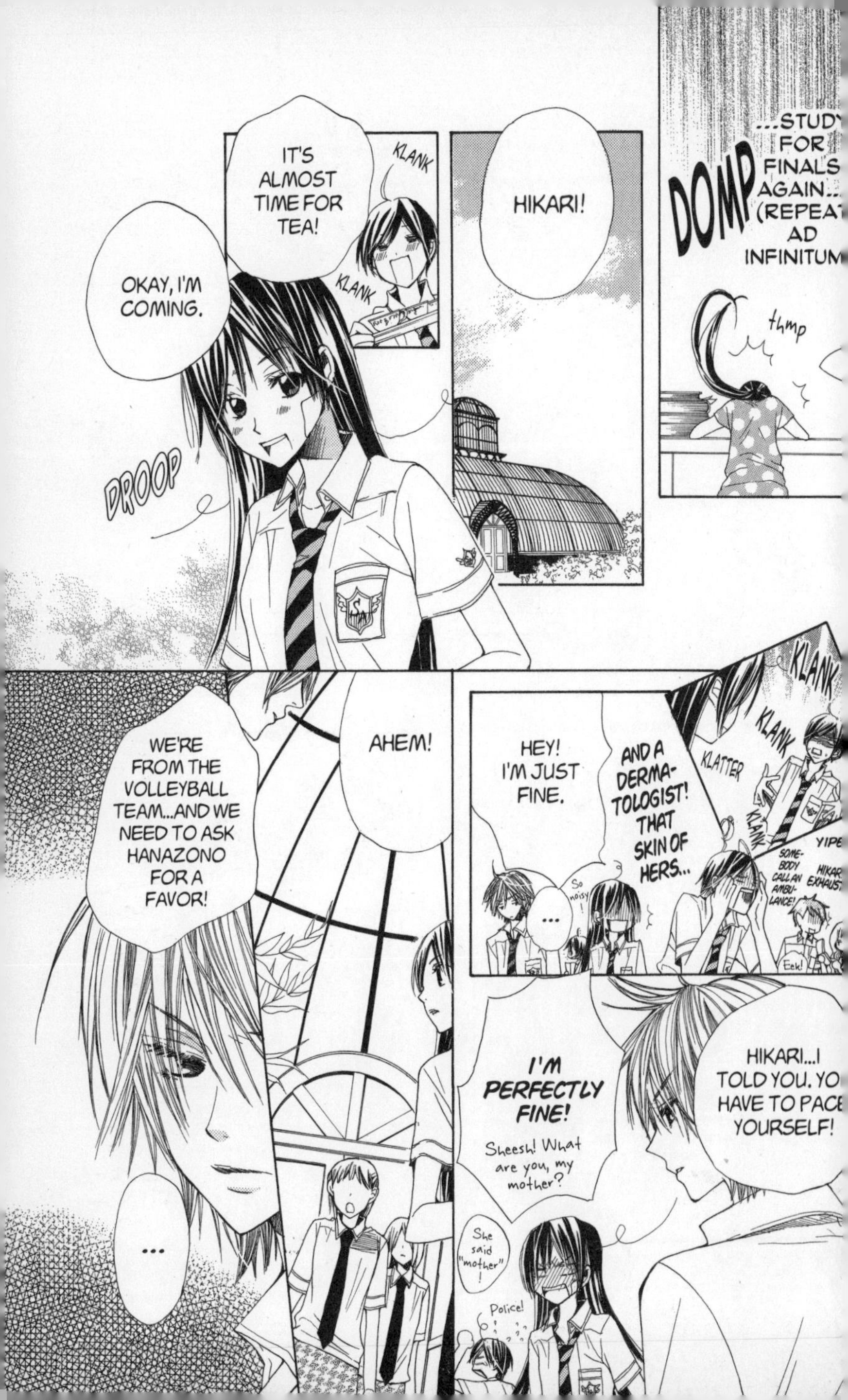
...STUDY FOR FINALS AGAIN... (REPEAT AD INFINITUM
DOMP
thmp
HIKARI!
IT'S ALMOST TIME FOR TEA!
KLANK
KLANK
OKAY, I'M COMING.
DROOP
KLANK
KLANK
KLATTER
KLANK
YIPE
SOME-BODY CALL AN AMBU-LANCE!
HIKAR EXHAUST
Eek!
AND A DERMA-TOLOGIST! THAT SKIN OF HERS...
HEY! I'M JUST FINE.
So noisy!
...
HIKARI...I TOLD YOU. YO HAVE TO PACE YOURSELF!
I'M PERFECTLY FINE!
Sheesh! What are you, my mother?
She said "mother"!
Police!
AHEM!
WE'RE FROM THE VOLLEYBALL TEAM...AND WE NEED TO ASK HANAZONO FOR A FAVOR!
...

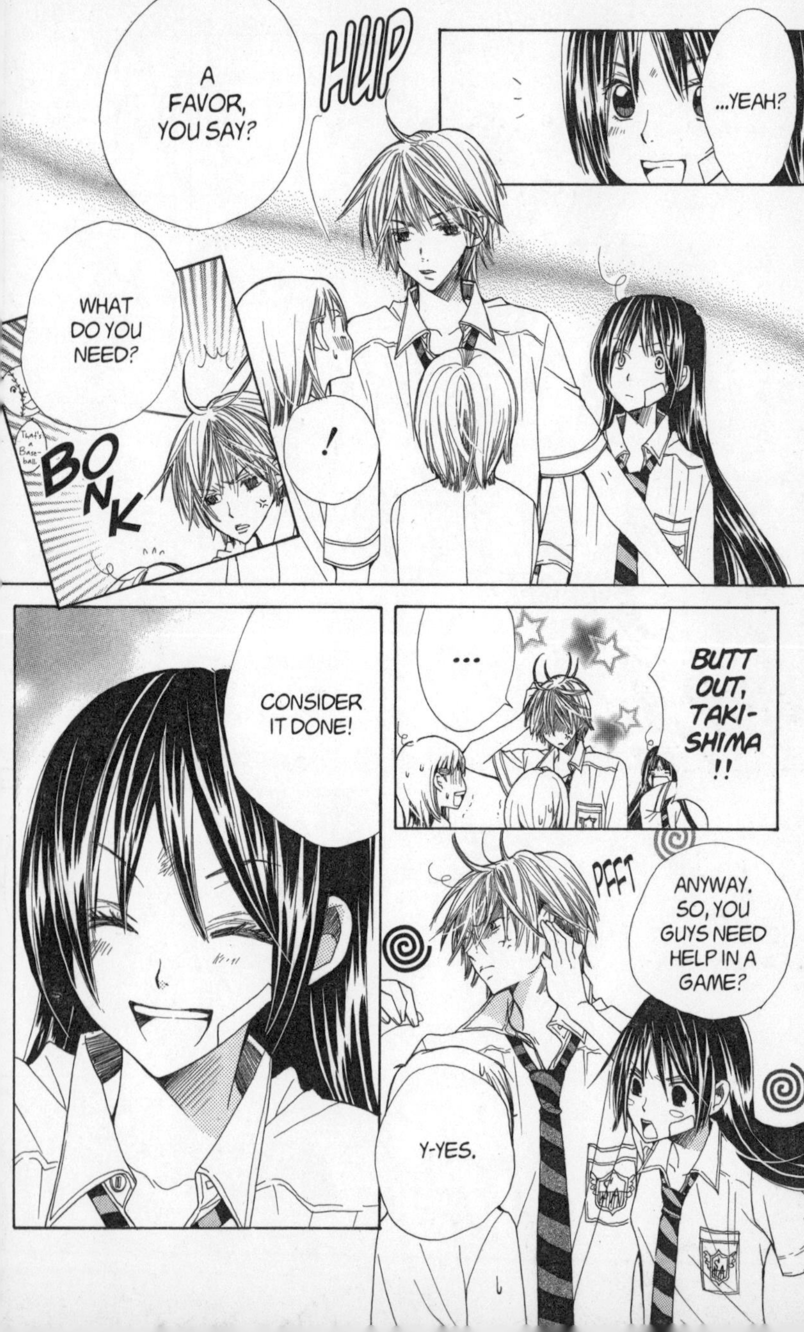
...YEAH?
HUP
A FAVOR, YOU SAY?
!
WHAT DO YOU NEED?
BONK
That's a Baseball
...
BUTT OUT, TAKISHIMA!!
PFFT
ANYWAY. SO, YOU GUYS NEED HELP IN A GAME?
Y-YES.
CONSIDER IT DONE!

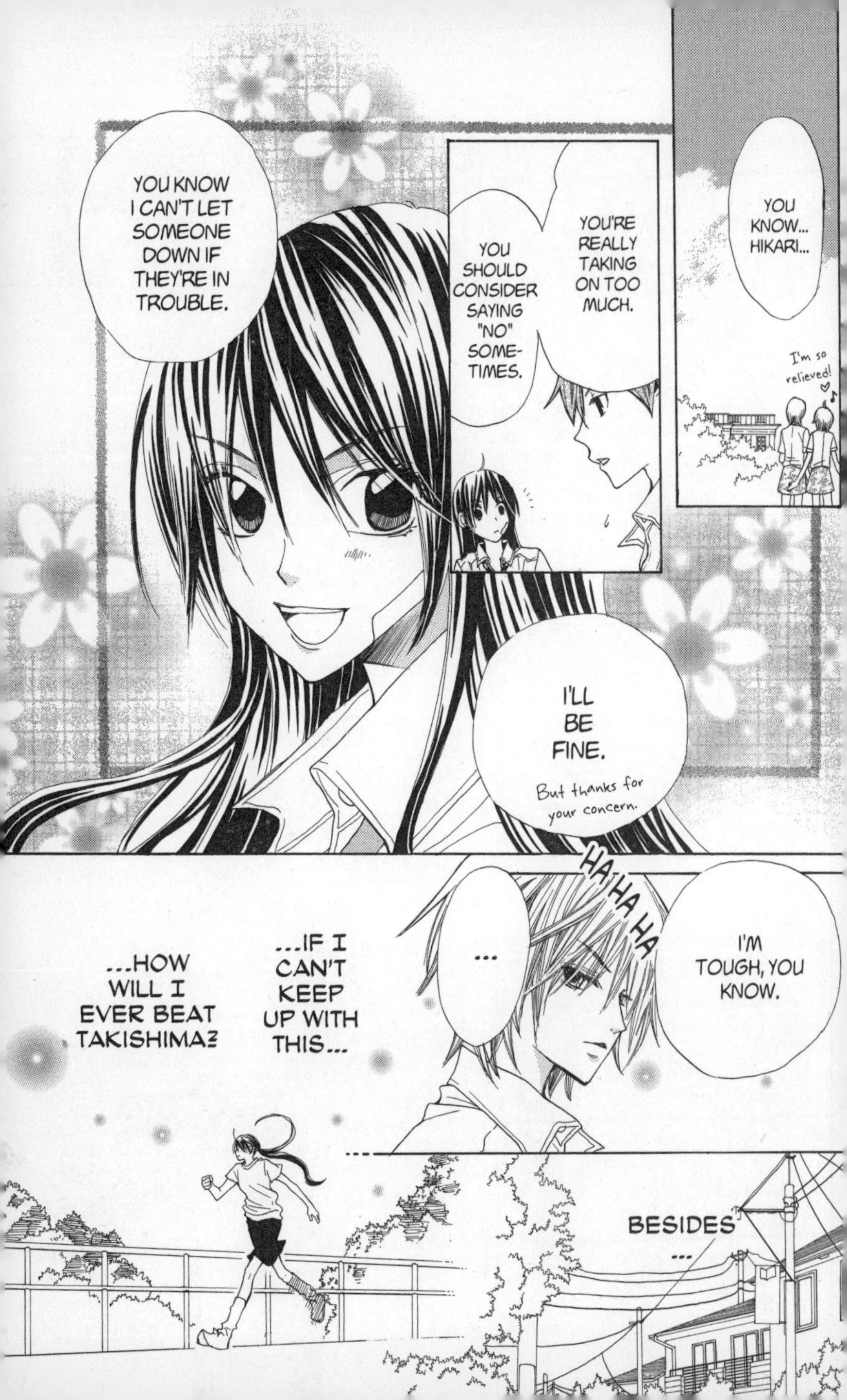
YOU KNOW... HIKARI...
I'm so relieved!
YOU'RE REALLY TAKING ON TOO MUCH.
YOU SHOULD CONSIDER SAYING "NO" SOME-TIMES.
YOU KNOW I CAN'T LET SOMEONE DOWN IF THEY'RE IN TROUBLE.
I'LL BE FINE.
But thanks for your concern.
HA HA HA
I'M TOUGH, YOU KNOW.
...
...IF I CAN'T KEEP UP WITH THIS...
...HOW WILL I EVER BEAT TAKISHIMA?
BESIDES ...
...

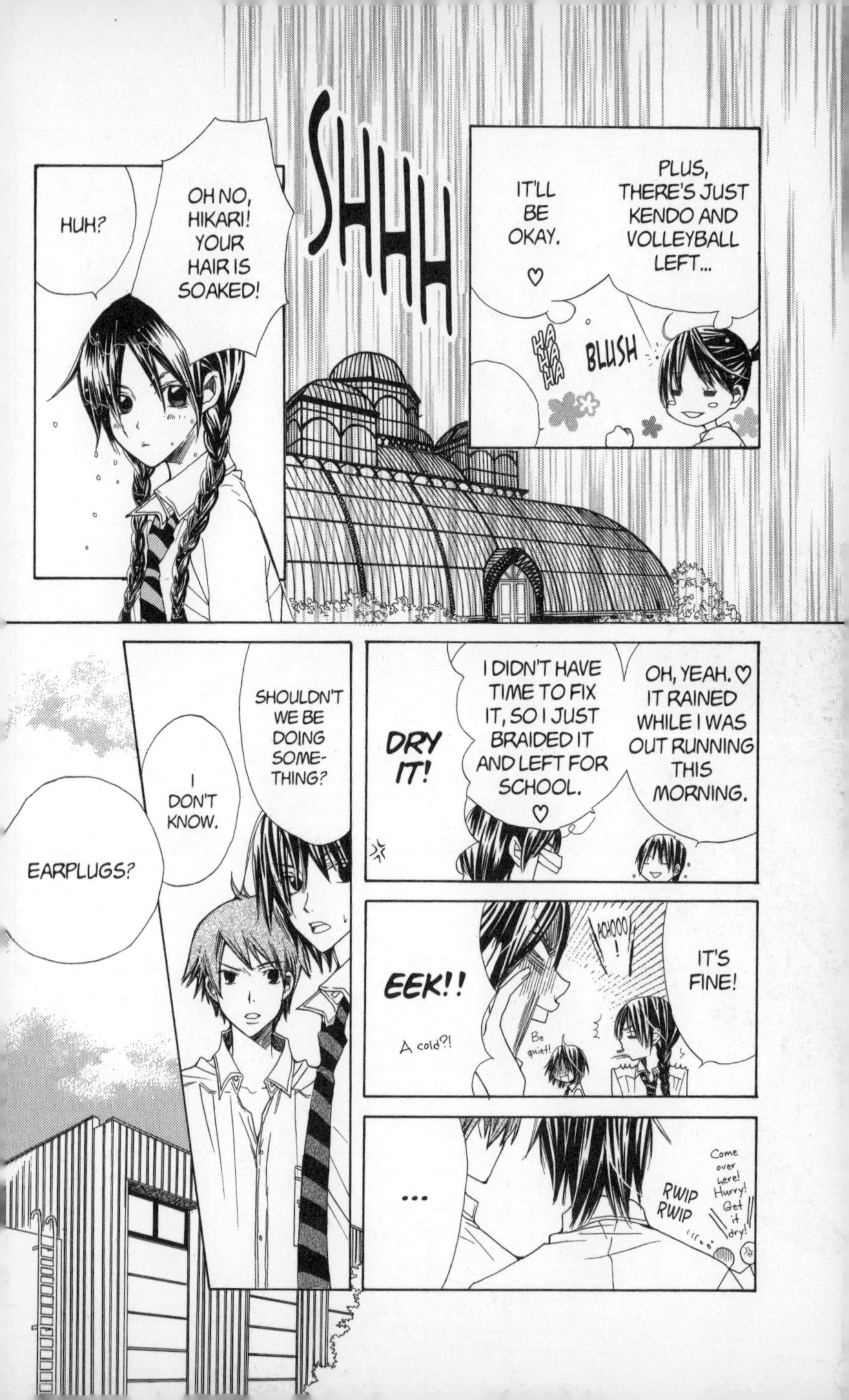
PLUS, THERE'S JUST KENDO AND VOLLEYBALL LEFT...
IT'LL BE OKAY. ♡
HA HA HA
BLUSH
SHHHH
OH NO, HIKARI! YOUR HAIR IS SOAKED!
HUH?
OH, YEAH. ♡ IT RAINED WHILE I WAS OUT RUNNING THIS MORNING.
I DIDN'T HAVE TIME TO FIX IT, SO I JUST BRAIDED IT AND LEFT FOR SCHOOL. ♡
DRY IT!
ACHOOO!
IT'S FINE!
Be quiet!
EEK!!
A cold?!
Come over here! Hurry! Get it dry!
RWIP RWIP
...
SHOULDN'T WE BE DOING SOME-THING?
I DON'T KNOW.
EARPLUGS?

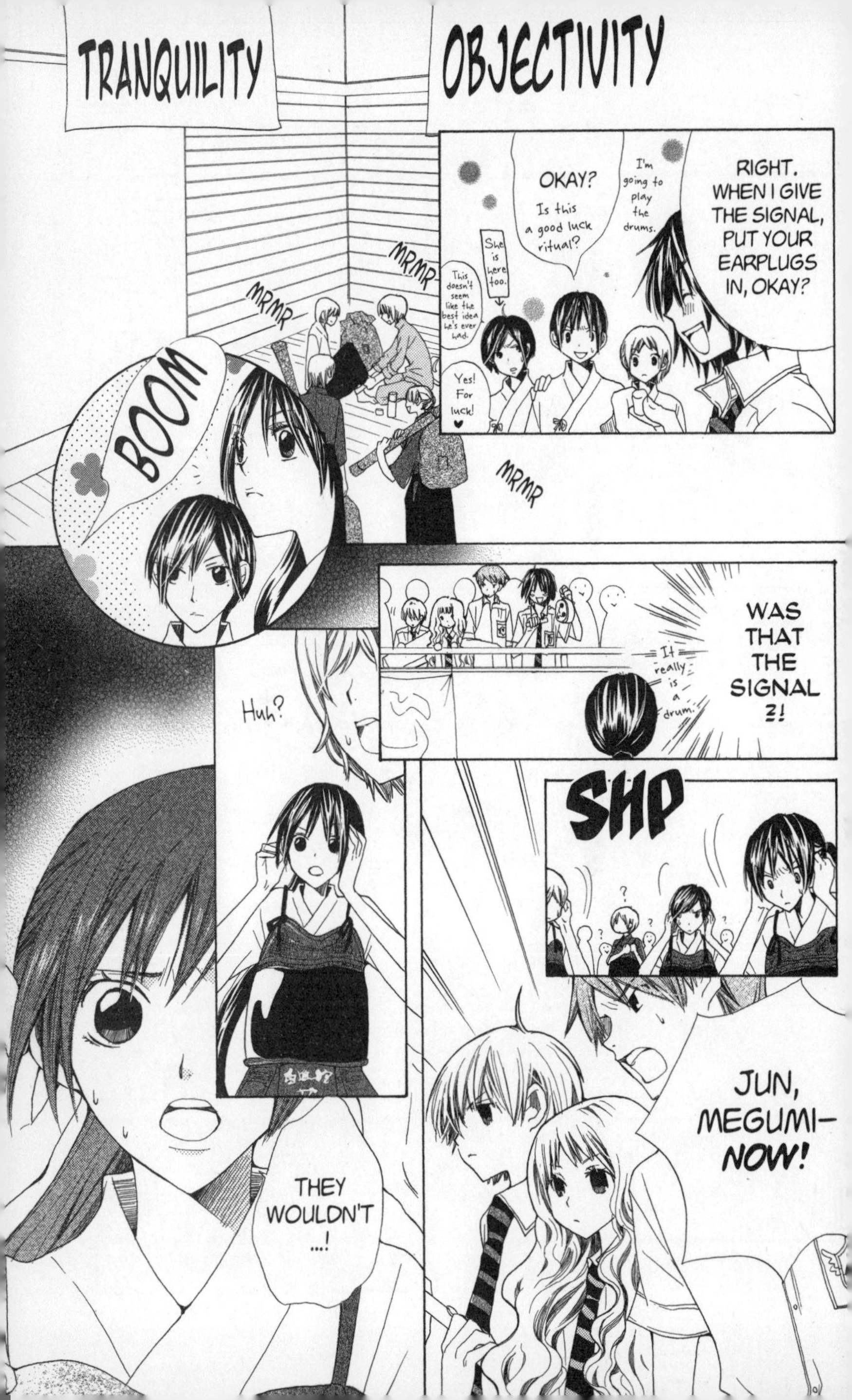
OBJECTIVITY
TRANQUILITY
RIGHT. WHEN I GIVE THE SIGNAL, PUT YOUR EARPLUGS IN, OKAY?
I'm going to play the drums.
OKAY? Is this a good luck ritual?
She is here too.
This doesn't seem like the best idea he's ever had.
Yes! For luck!
MRMR
MRMR
MRMR
BOOM
WAS THAT THE SIGNAL ?!
It really is a drum.
Huh?
SHP
JUN, MEGUMI—NOW!
THEY WOULDN'T ...!

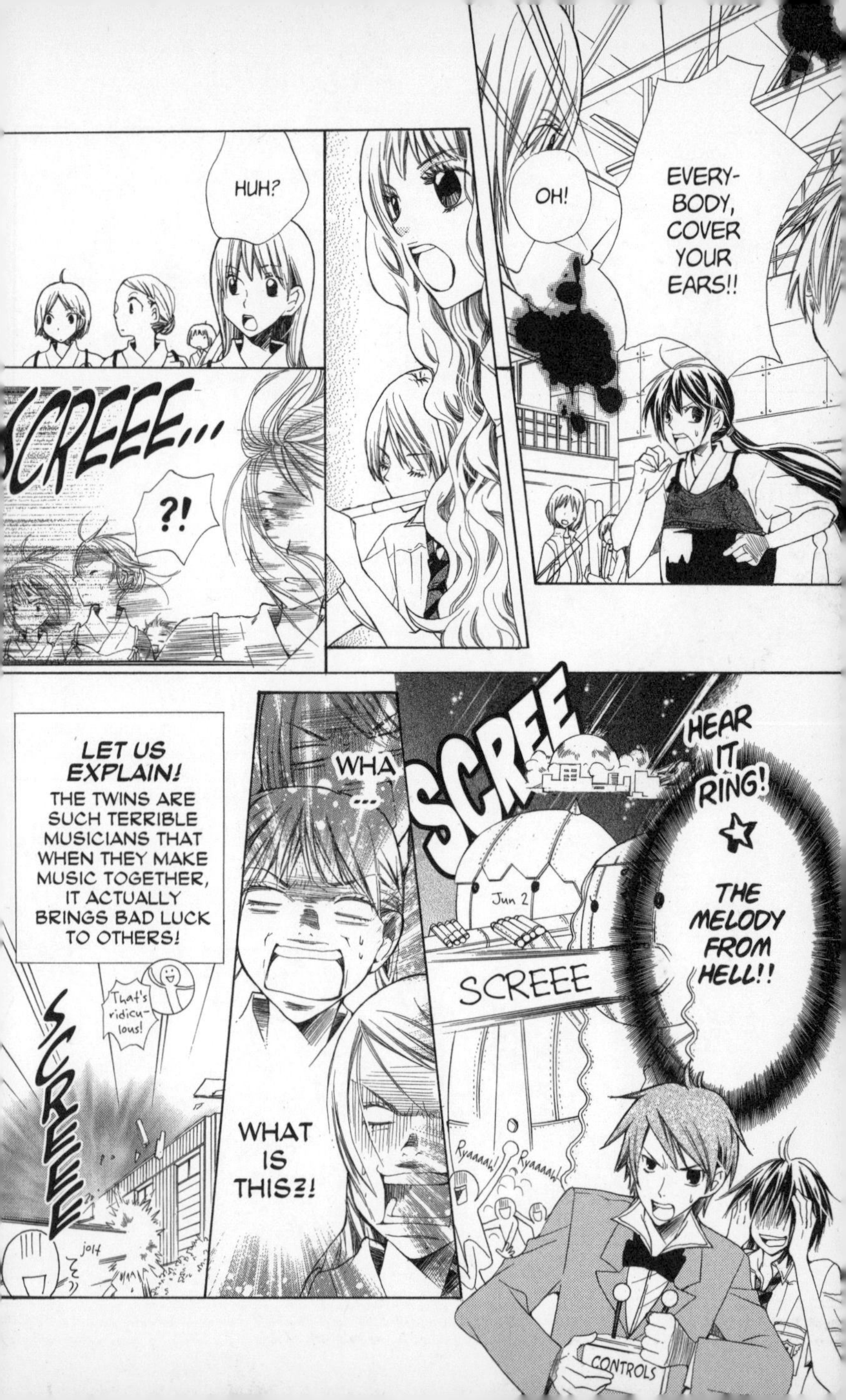
EVERY-BODY, COVER YOUR EARS!!
OH!
HUH?
SCREEE...
?!
HEAR IT RING! ☆
THE MELODY FROM HELL!!
SCREE
Jun 2
SCREEE
Ryaaaah! Ryaaaah!
CONTROLS
WHA...
WHAT IS THIS?!
LET US EXPLAIN! THE TWINS ARE SUCH TERRIBLE MUSICIANS THAT WHEN THEY MAKE MUSIC TOGETHER, IT ACTUALLY BRINGS BAD LUCK TO OTHERS!
That's ridiculous!
SCREEE
jolt

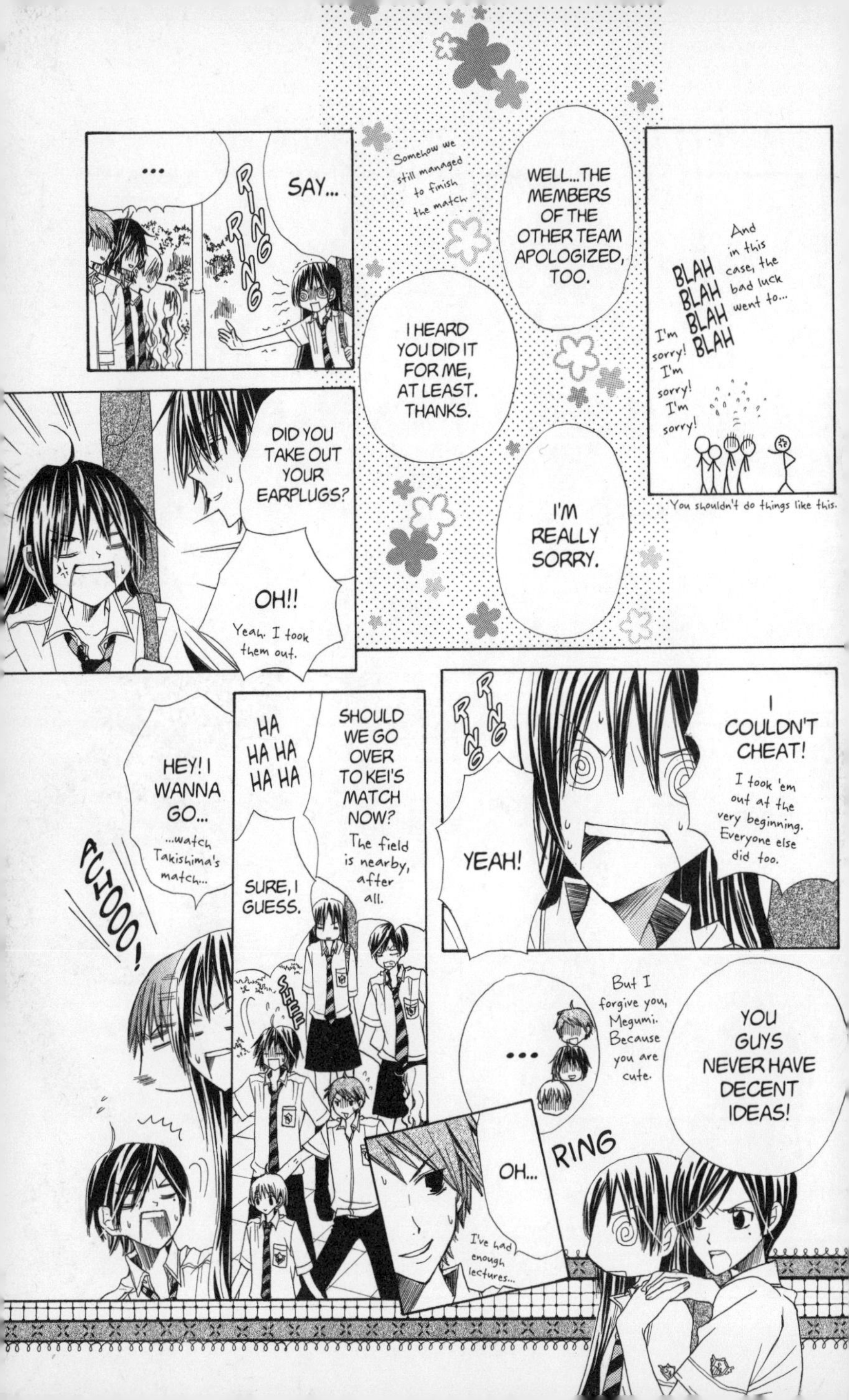

And in this case, the bad luck went to...
BLAH BLAH BLAH BLAH
I'm sorry! I'm sorry! I'm sorry!
You shouldn't do things like this.
WELL...THE MEMBERS OF THE OTHER TEAM APOLOGIZED, TOO.
Somehow we still managed to finish the match
I HEARD YOU DID IT FOR ME, AT LEAST. THANKS.
I'M REALLY SORRY.
SAY...
RING RING
...
DID YOU TAKE OUT YOUR EARPLUGS?
OH!!
Yeah. I took them out.
I COULDN'T CHEAT!
I took 'em out at the very beginning. Everyone else did too.
RING RING
YEAH!
SHOULD WE GO OVER TO KEI'S MATCH NOW?
The field is nearby, after all.
HA HA HA HA HA
SURE, I GUESS.
HEY! I WANNA GO...
...watch Takishima's match...
FUIOOO!
YOU GUYS NEVER HAVE DECENT IDEAS!
But I forgive you, Megumi. Because you are cute.
...
RING
OH...
I've had enough lectures...

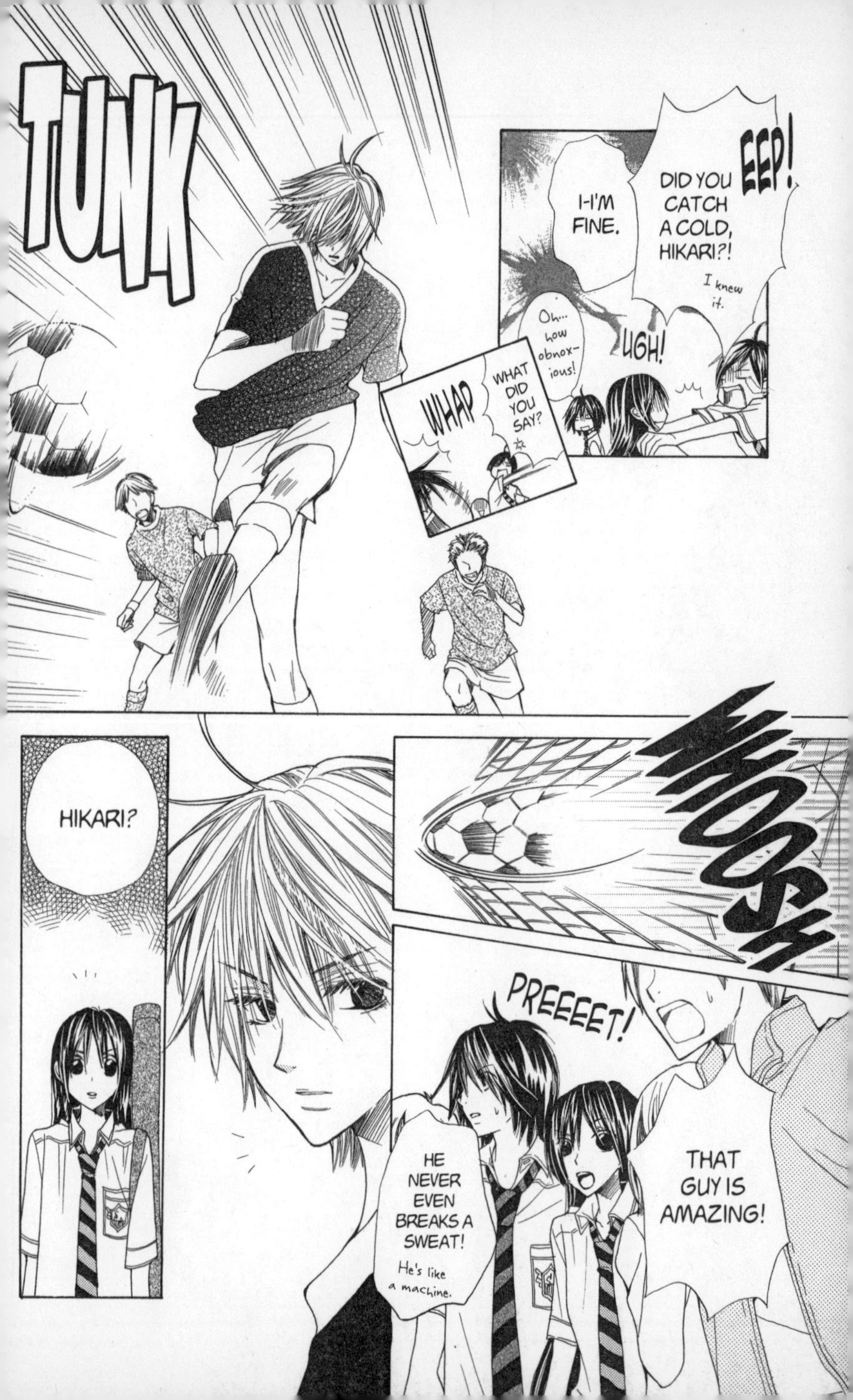
EEP!
DID YOU CATCH A COLD, HIKARI?!
I knew it.
I-I'M FINE.
UGH!
Oh... how obnoxious!
WHAT DID YOU SAY?
WHAP
TUNK
WHOOSH
PREEEEET!
THAT GUY IS AMAZING!
HE NEVER EVEN BREAKS A SWEAT!
He's like a machine.
HIKARI?

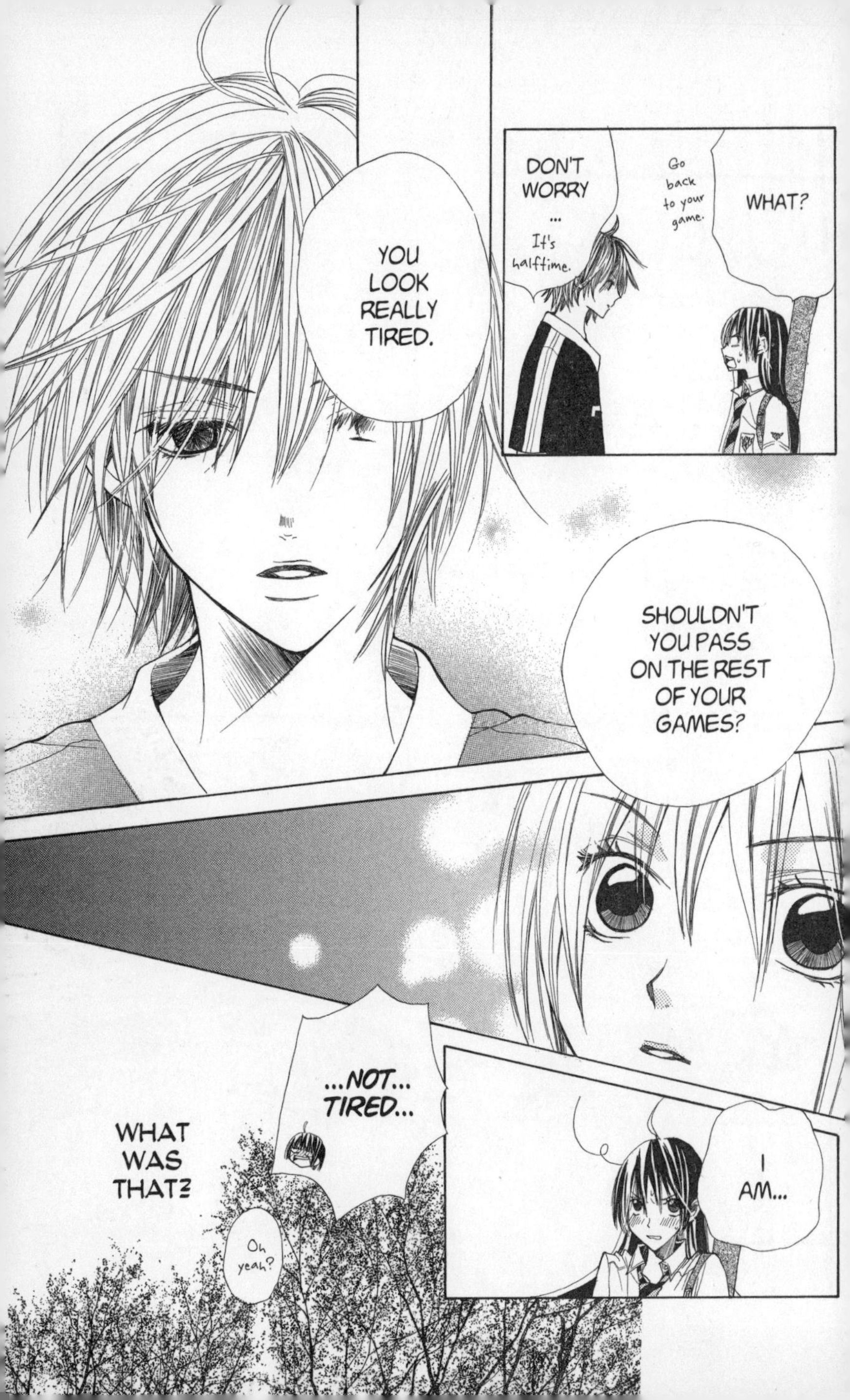
WHAT?
Go back to your game.
DON'T WORRY ... It's halftime.
YOU LOOK REALLY TIRED.
SHOULDN'T YOU PASS ON THE REST OF YOUR GAMES?
I AM...
...NOT... TIRED...
WHAT WAS THAT?!
Oh yeah?

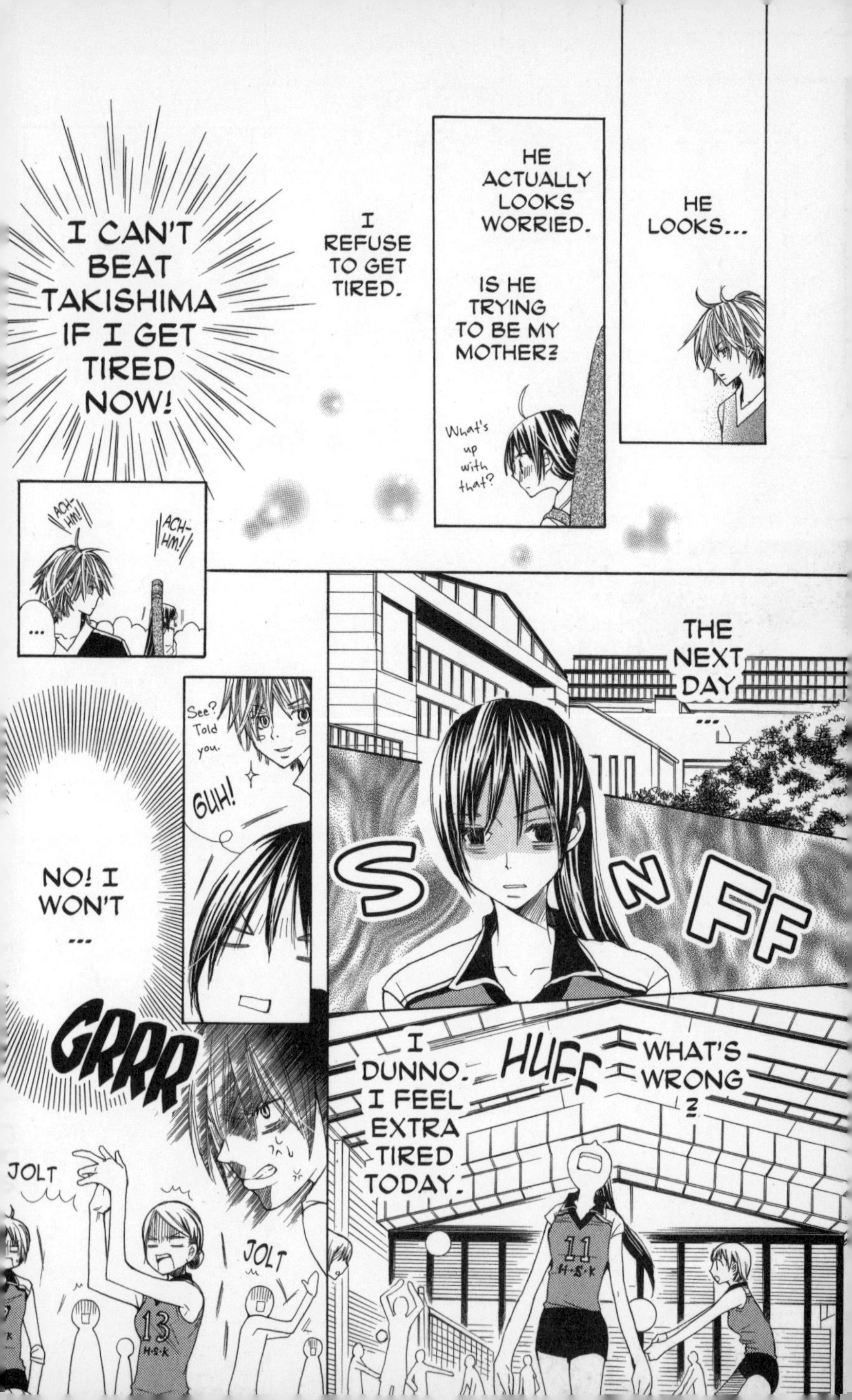
HE LOOKS...
HE ACTUALLY LOOKS WORRIED.
IS HE TRYING TO BE MY MOTHER?
What's up with that?
I REFUSE TO GET TIRED.
I CAN'T BEAT TAKISHIMA IF I GET TIRED NOW!
ACH-HM!
ACH-HM!
...
THE NEXT DAY...
SNFF
WHAT'S WRONG?
HUFF
I DUNNO. I FEEL EXTRA TIRED TODAY.
See? Told you.
GUH!
NO! I WON'T...
GRRR
JOLT
JOLT

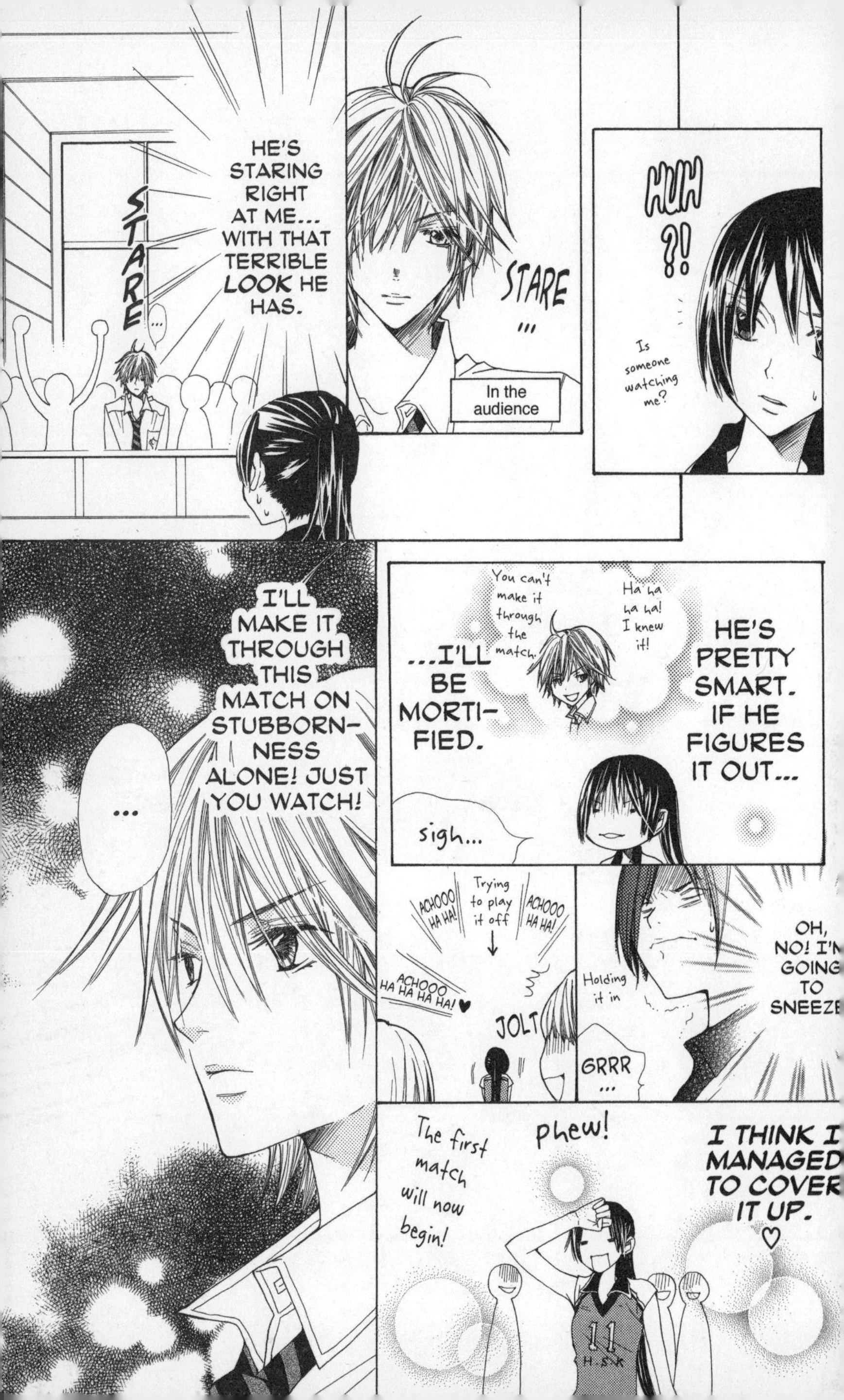
HUH ?!
Is someone watching me?
STARE ...
In the audience
HE'S STARING RIGHT AT ME... WITH THAT TERRIBLE LOOK HE HAS.
STARE
...
HE'S PRETTY SMART. IF HE FIGURES IT OUT...
...I'LL BE MORTIFIED.
Ha ha ha ha! I knew it!
You can't make it through the match.
sigh...
OH, NO! I'M GOING TO SNEEZE
Holding it in
GRRR ...
ACHOOO HA HA!
Trying to play it off
ACHOOO HA HA!
ACHOOO HA HA HA HA!
JOLT
I THINK I MANAGED TO COVER IT UP.
Phew!
The first match will now begin!
I'LL MAKE IT THROUGH THIS MATCH ON STUBBORNNESS ALONE! JUST YOU WATCH!
...

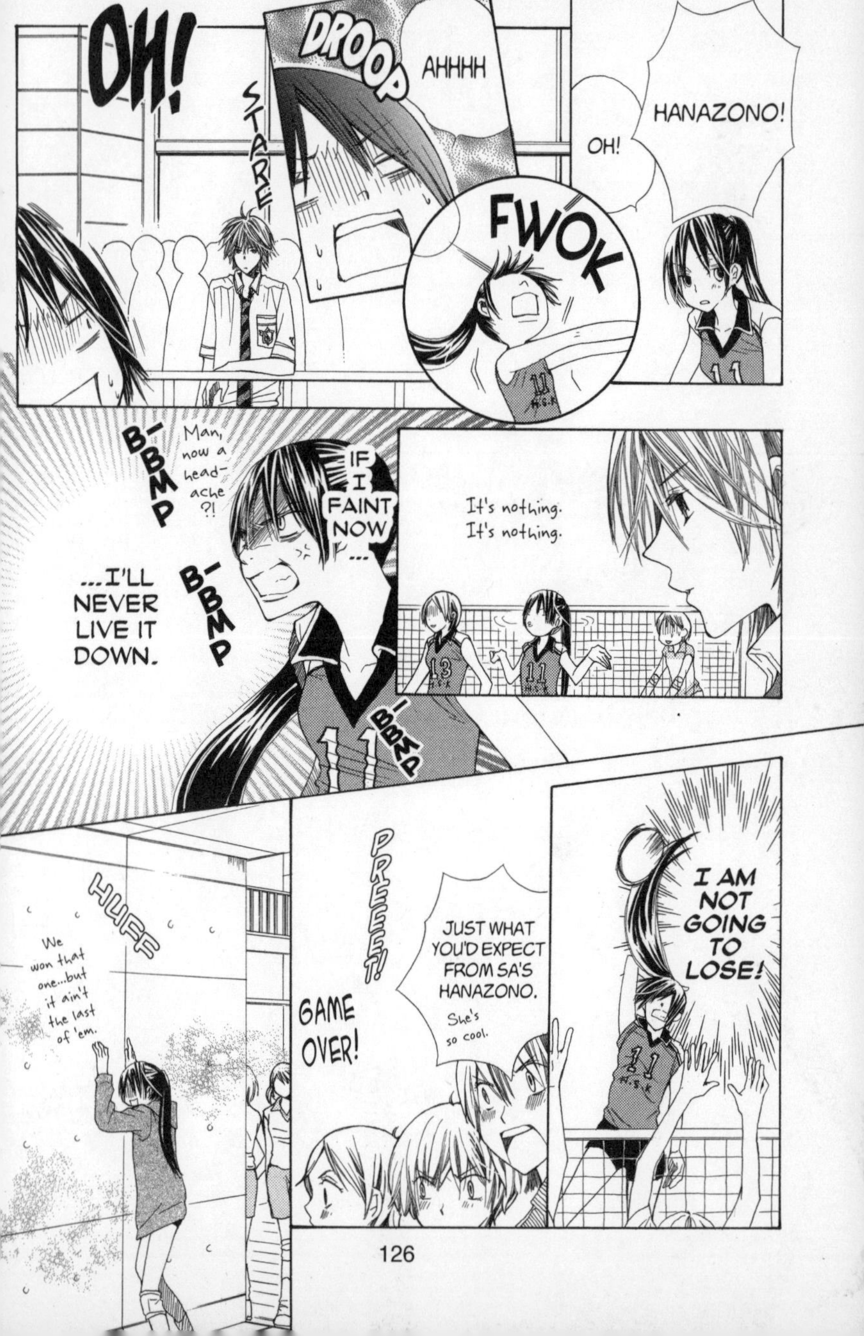
HANAZONO!
OH!
FWOK
DROOP
AHHHH
OH!
STARE
It's nothing. It's nothing.
IF I FAINT NOW...
Man, now a head-ache?!
B-BMP
B-BMP
...I'LL NEVER LIVE IT DOWN.
B-BMP
I AM NOT GOING TO LOSE!
PREEET!
JUST WHAT YOU'D EXPECT FROM SA'S HANAZONO.
She's so cool.
GAME OVER!
HUFF
We won that one...but it ain't the last of 'em.

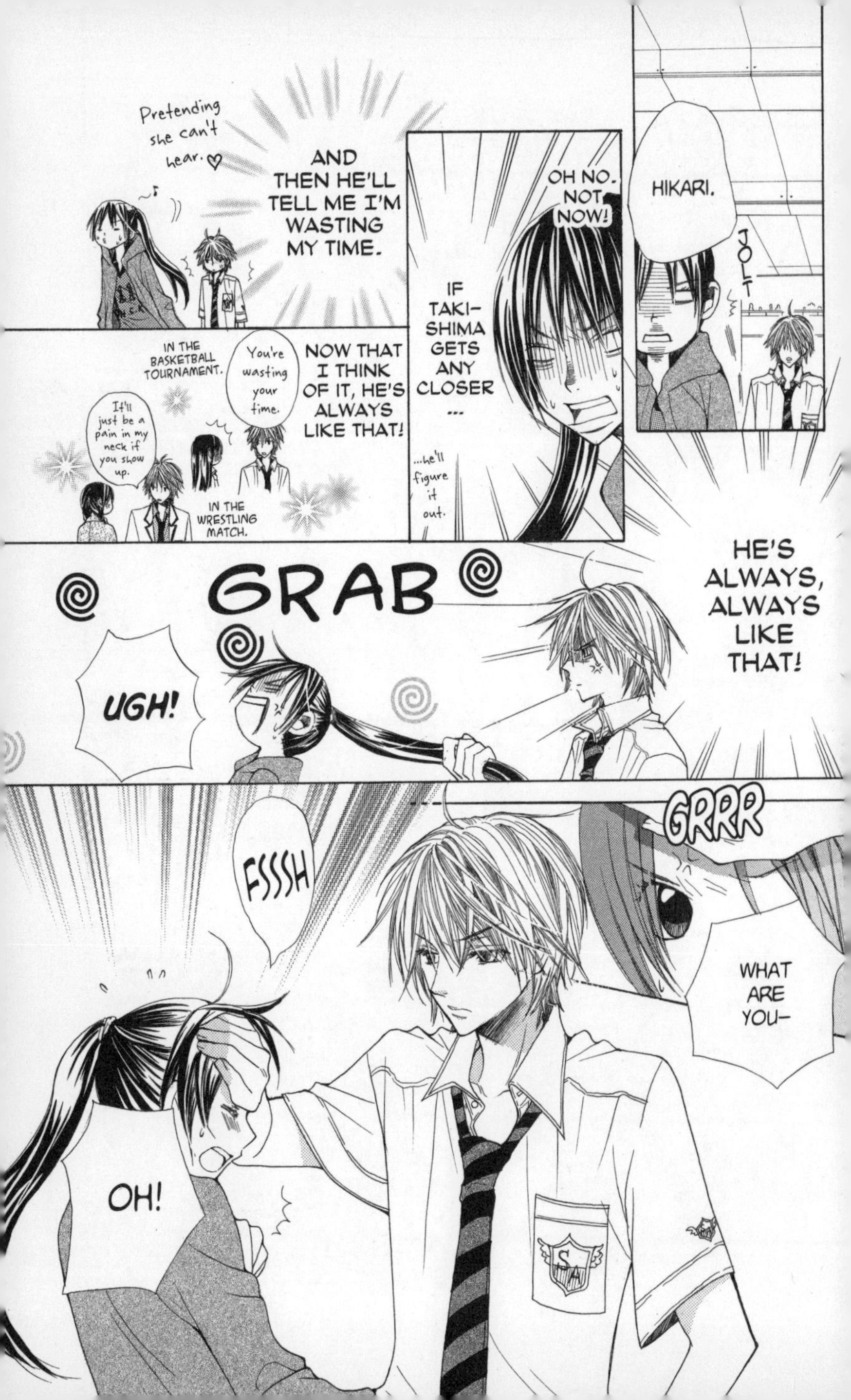
HIKARI.
JOLT
OH NO. NOT NOW!
IF TAKI-SHIMA GETS ANY CLOSER...
...he'll figure it out.
AND THEN HE'LL TELL ME I'M WASTING MY TIME.
Pretending she can't hear. ♡
NOW THAT I THINK OF IT, HE'S ALWAYS LIKE THAT!
You're wasting your time.
IN THE BASKETBALL TOURNAMENT.
It'll just be a pain in my neck if you show up.
IN THE WRESTLING MATCH.
HE'S ALWAYS, ALWAYS LIKE THAT!
GRAB
UGH!
GRRR
WHAT ARE YOU-
FSSSH
OH!

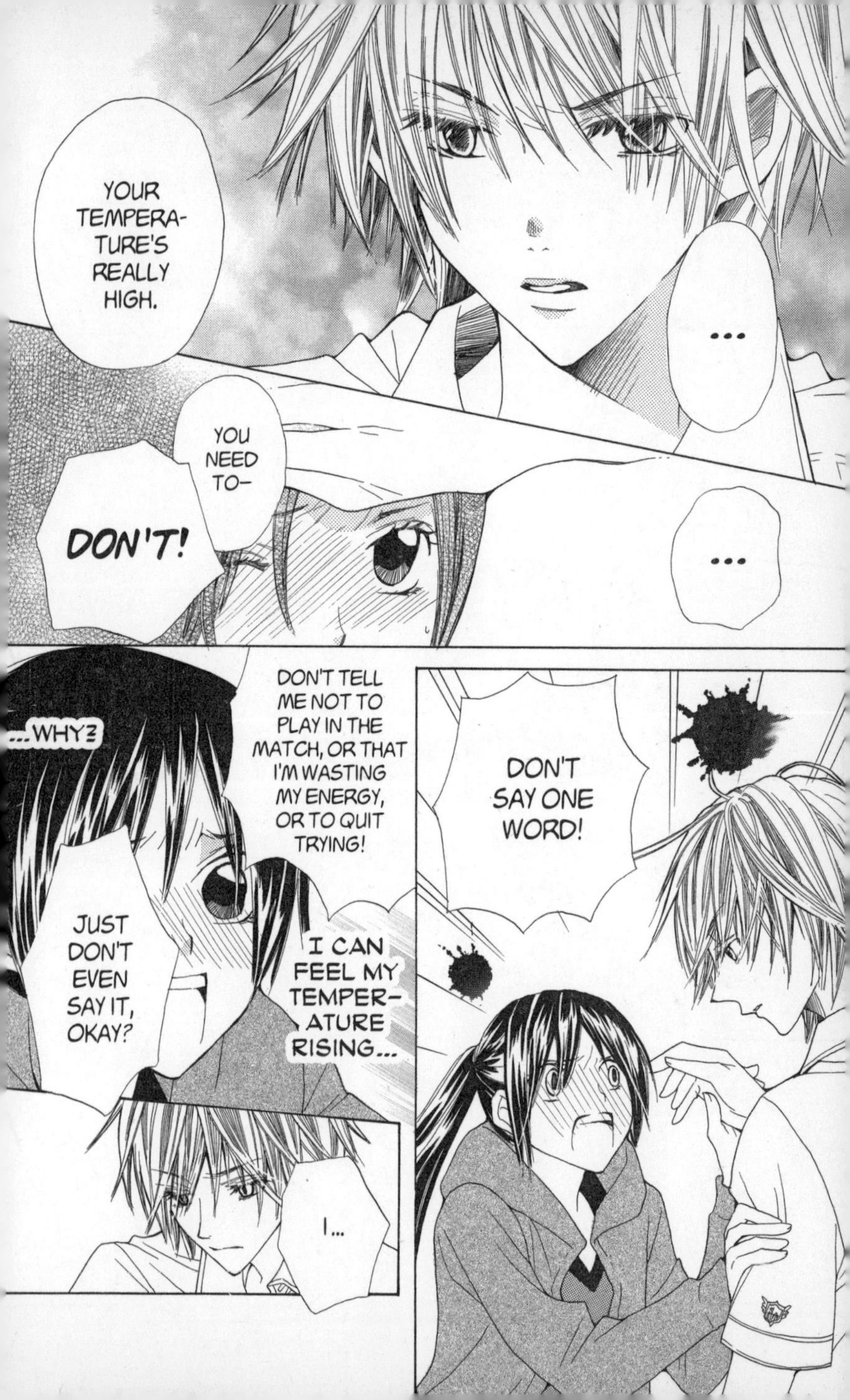
...
YOUR TEMPERATURE'S REALLY HIGH.
...
YOU NEED TO–
DON'T!
DON'T SAY ONE WORD!
DON'T TELL ME NOT TO PLAY IN THE MATCH, OR THAT I'M WASTING MY ENERGY, OR TO QUIT TRYING!
...WHY?
I CAN FEEL MY TEMPERATURE RISING...
JUST DON'T EVEN SAY IT, OKAY?
I...

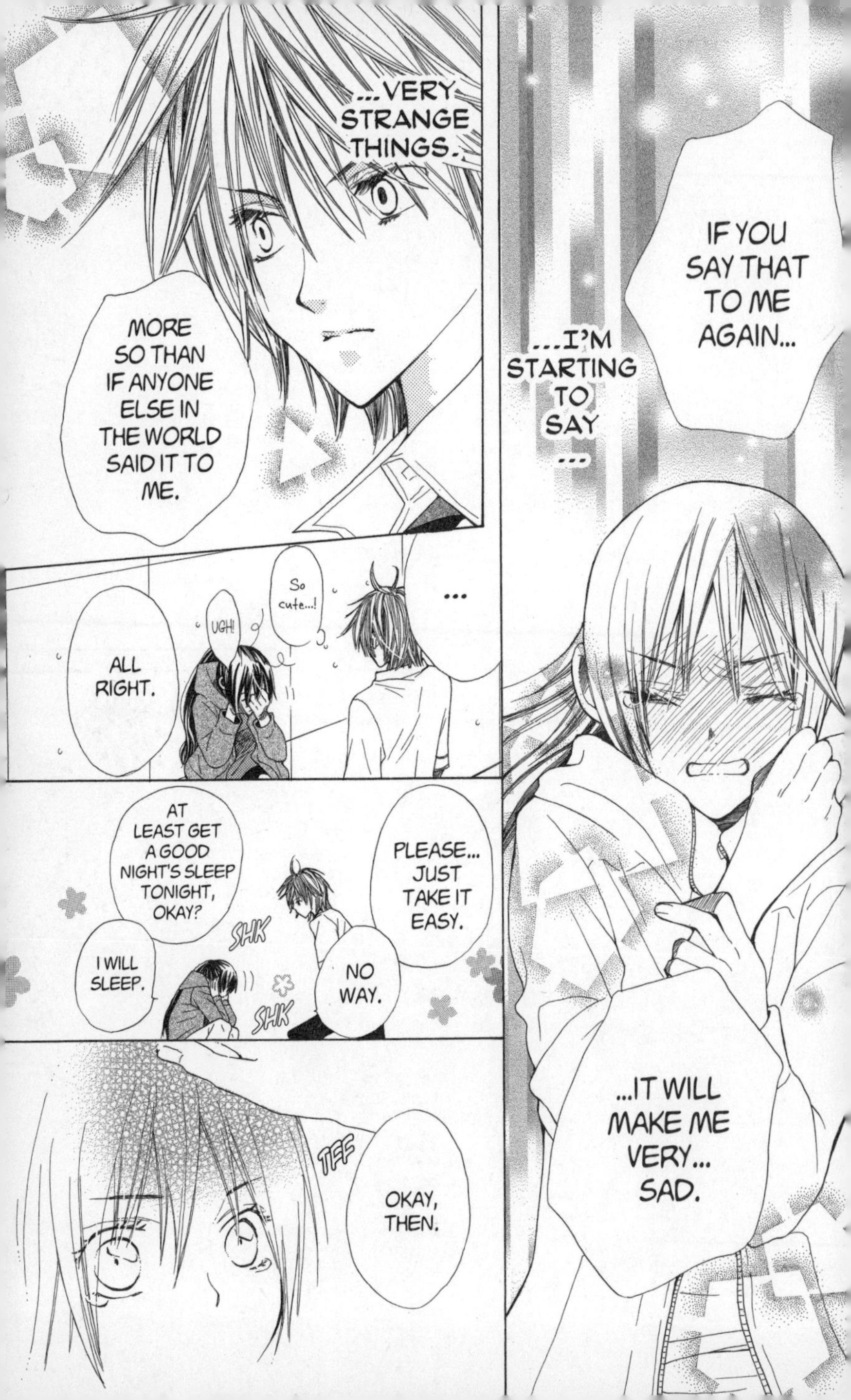
IF YOU SAY THAT TO ME AGAIN...
...I'M STARTING TO SAY ...
...IT WILL MAKE ME VERY... SAD.
...VERY STRANGE THINGS.
MORE SO THAN IF ANYONE ELSE IN THE WORLD SAID IT TO ME.
...
So cute...!
UGH!
ALL RIGHT.
PLEASE... JUST TAKE IT EASY.
AT LEAST GET A GOOD NIGHT'S SLEEP TONIGHT, OKAY?
NO WAY.
SHK
SHK
I WILL SLEEP.
TFF
OKAY, THEN.

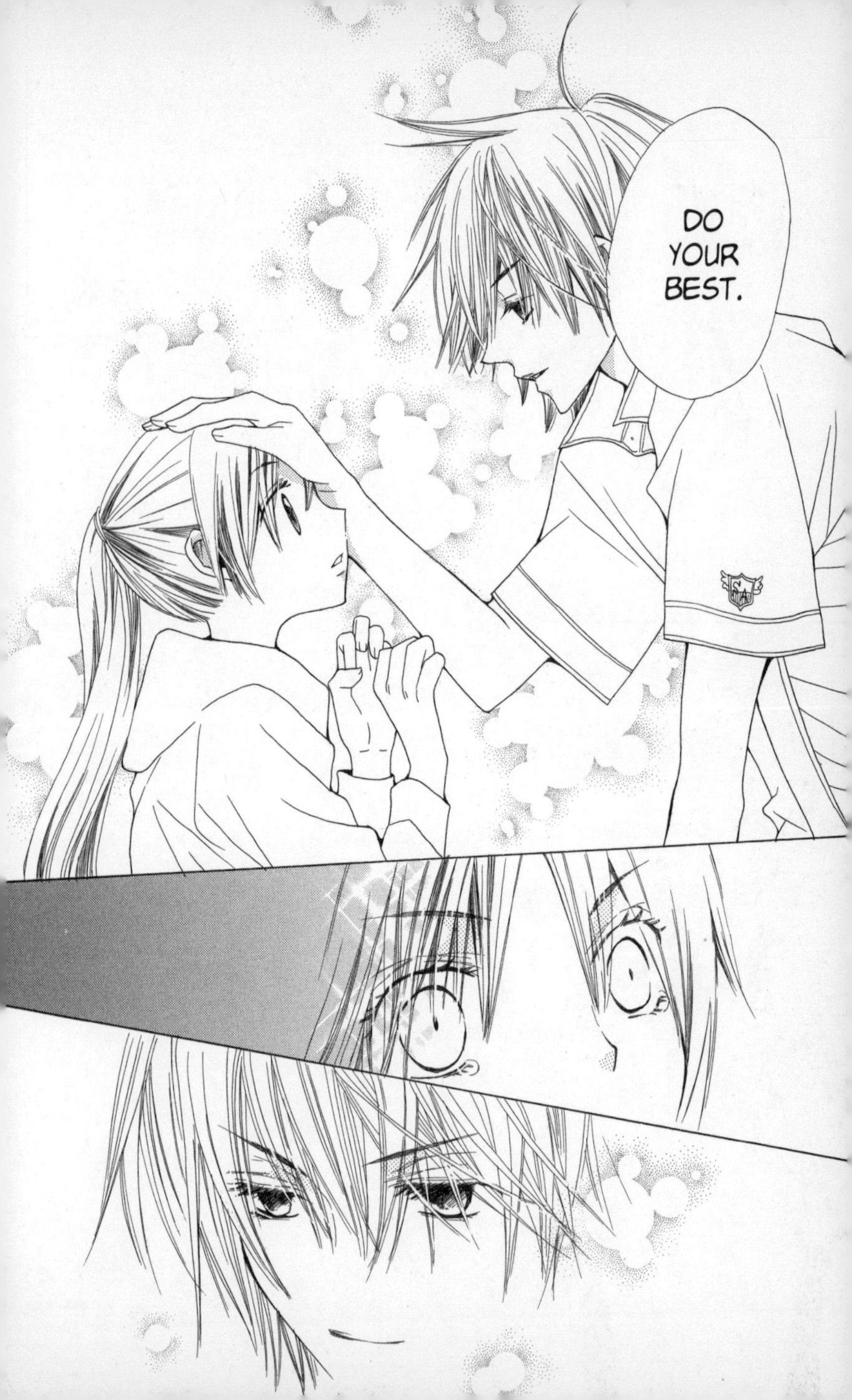
DO YOUR BEST.

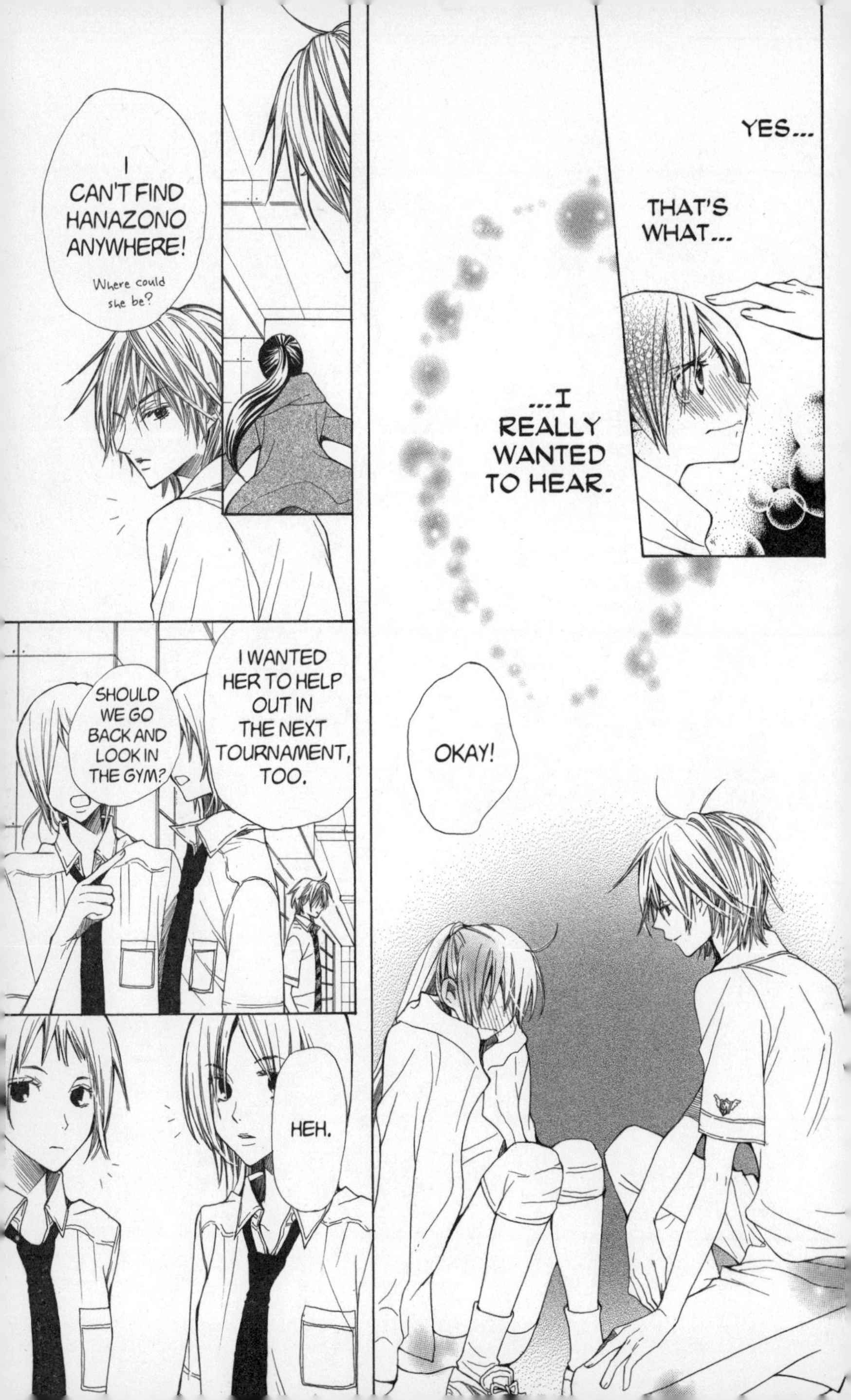
YES...
THAT'S WHAT...
...I REALLY WANTED TO HEAR.
OKAY!
I CAN'T FIND HANAZONO ANYWHERE!
Where could she be?
I WANTED HER TO HELP OUT IN THE NEXT TOURNAMENT, TOO.
SHOULD WE GO BACK AND LOOK IN THE GYM?
HEH.

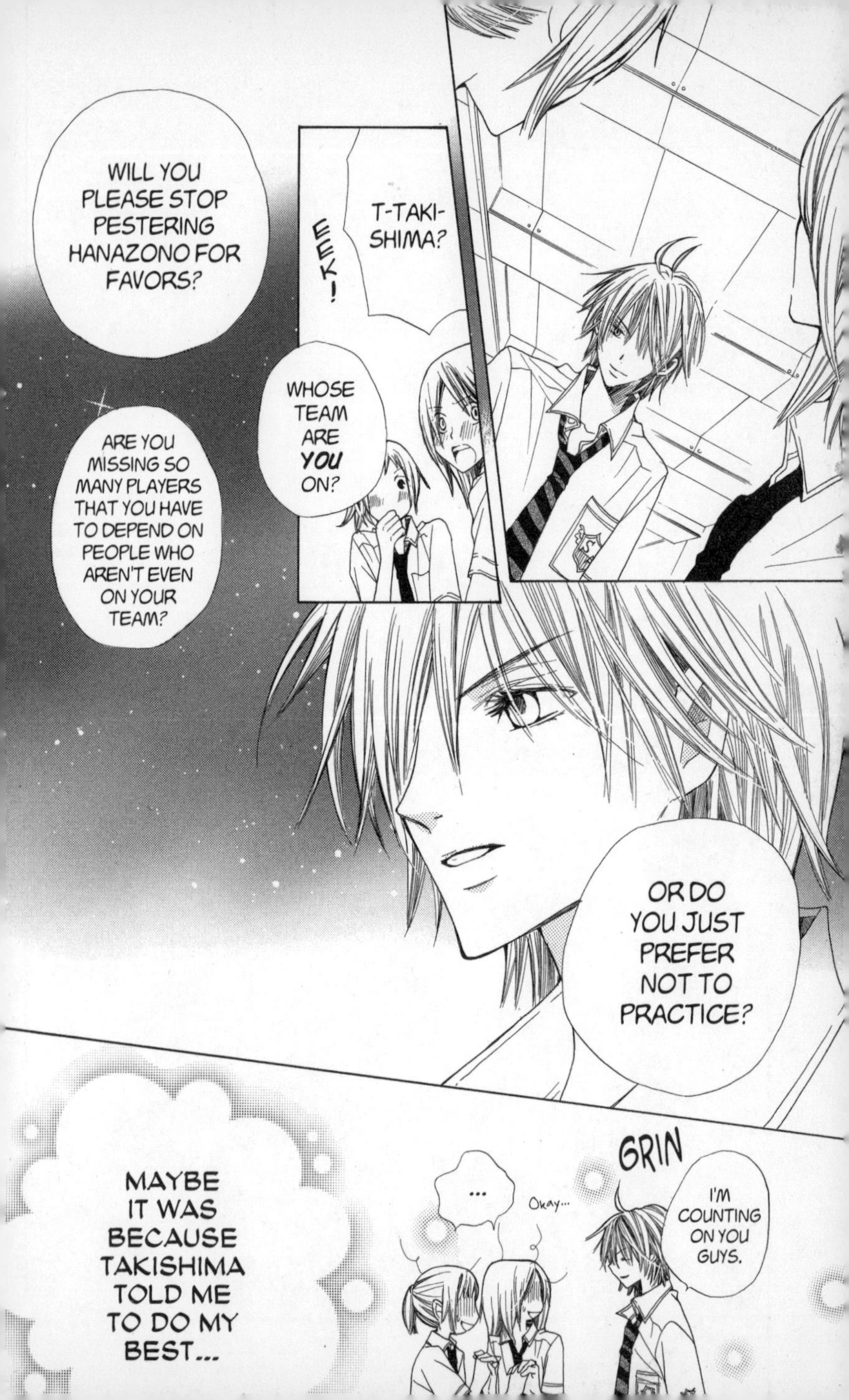
T-TAKI-SHIMA?
EEK!
WHOSE TEAM ARE YOU ON?
WILL YOU PLEASE STOP PESTERING HANAZONO FOR FAVORS?
ARE YOU MISSING SO MANY PLAYERS THAT YOU HAVE TO DEPEND ON PEOPLE WHO AREN'T EVEN ON YOUR TEAM?
OR DO YOU JUST PREFER NOT TO PRACTICE?
GRIN
I'M COUNTING ON YOU GUYS.
Okay...
...
MAYBE IT WAS BECAUSE TAKISHIMA TOLD ME TO DO MY BEST...

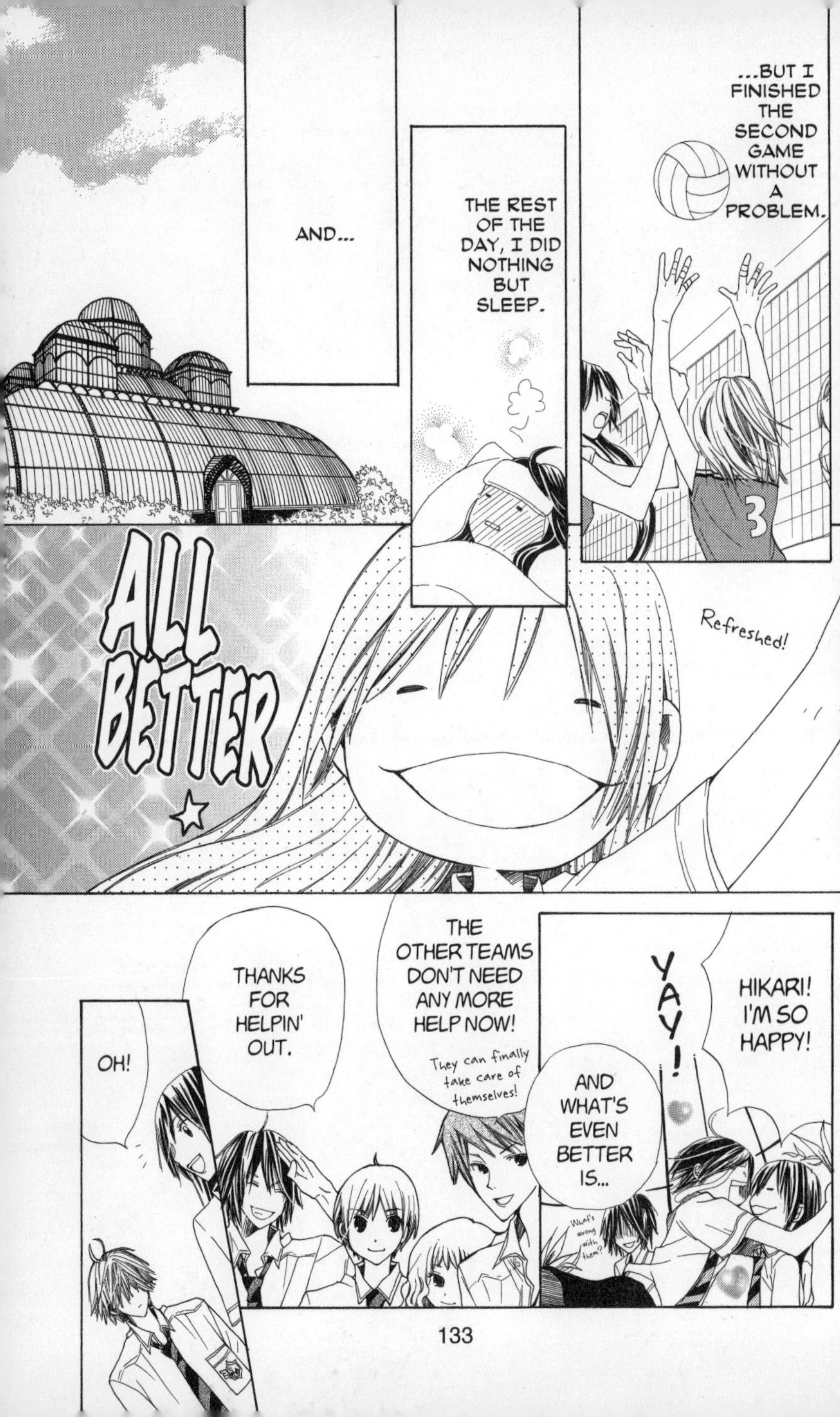
...BUT I FINISHED THE SECOND GAME WITHOUT A PROBLEM.
THE REST OF THE DAY, I DID NOTHING BUT SLEEP.
AND...
ALL BETTER
Refreshed!
HIKARI! I'M SO HAPPY!
YAY!
AND WHAT'S EVEN BETTER IS...
What's wrong with them?
THE OTHER TEAMS DON'T NEED ANY MORE HELP NOW!
They can finally take care of themselves!
THANKS FOR HELPIN' OUT.
OH!

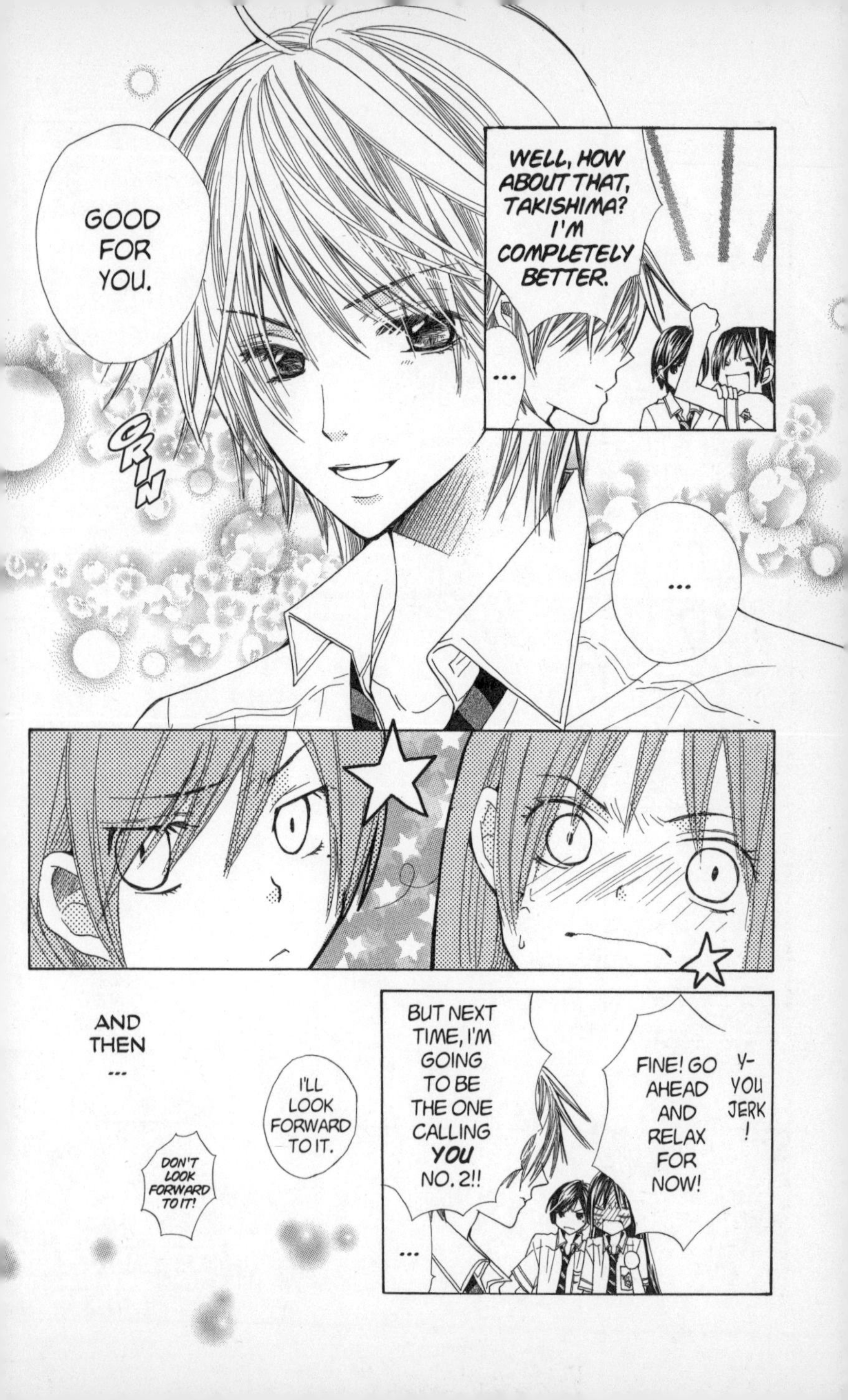
WELL, HOW ABOUT THAT, TAKISHIMA? I'M COMPLETELY BETTER.
...
GOOD FOR YOU.
GRIN
...
Y-YOU JERK!
FINE! GO AHEAD AND RELAX FOR NOW!
BUT NEXT TIME, I'M GOING TO BE THE ONE CALLING YOU NO. 2!!
...
I'LL LOOK FORWARD TO IT.
DON'T LOOK FORWARD TO IT!
AND THEN ...

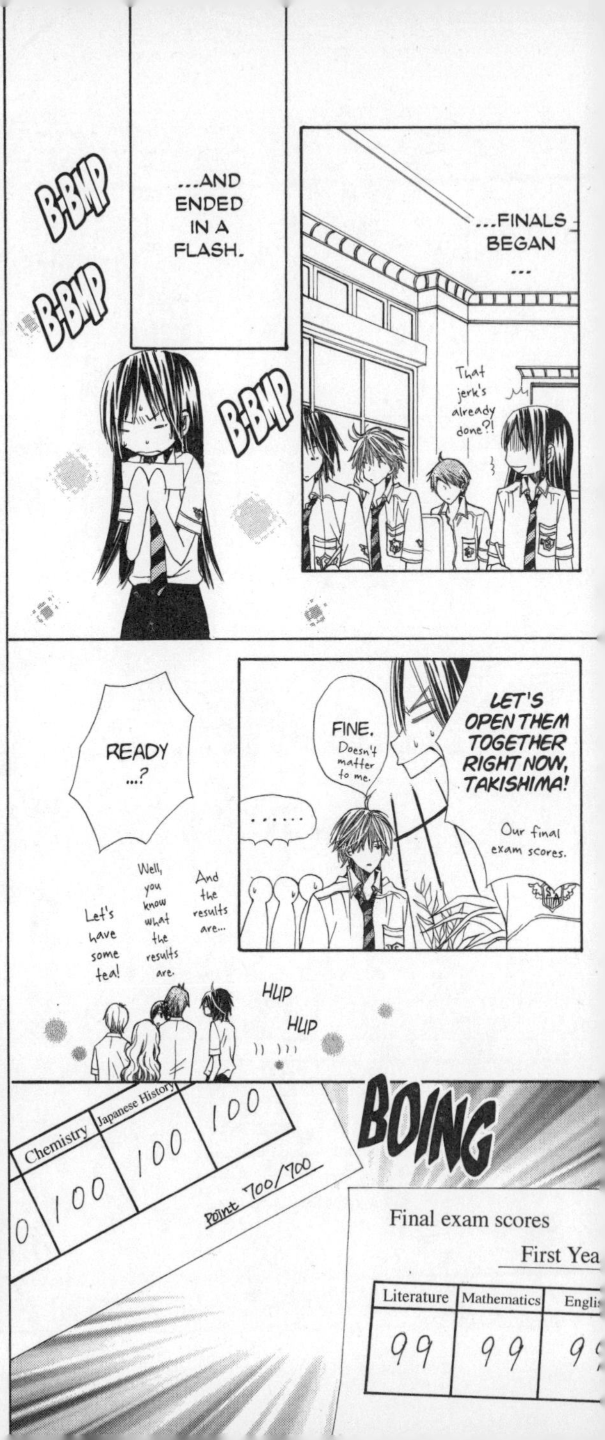
...FINALS BEGAN ...
That jerk's already done?!
...AND ENDED IN A FLASH.
B-BMP
B-BMP
B-BMP
LET'S OPEN THEM TOGETHER RIGHT NOW, TAKISHIMA!
Our final exam scores.
FINE. Doesn't matter to me.
......
READY ...?
And the results are...
Well, you know what the results are.
Let's have some tea!
HUP
HUP
BOING
Final exam scores
First Yea
Literature
Mathematics
Englis
99
99
Chemistry
Japanese History
100
100
100
Point 700/700

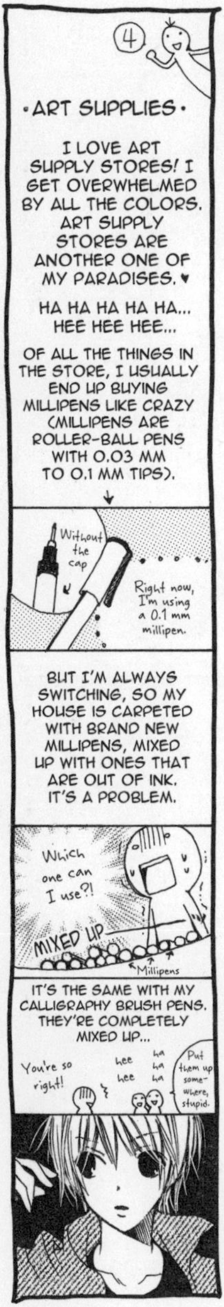
4
•ART SUPPLIES•
I LOVE ART SUPPLY STORES! I GET OVERWHELMED BY ALL THE COLORS. ART SUPPLY STORES ARE ANOTHER ONE OF MY PARADISES. ♥
HA HA HA HA HA... HEE HEE HEE...
OF ALL THE THINGS IN THE STORE, I USUALLY END UP BUYING MILLIPENS LIKE CRAZY (MILLIPENS ARE ROLLER-BALL PENS WITH 0.03 MM TO 0.1 MM TIPS).
Without the cap
Right now, I'm using a 0.1 mm millipen.
BUT I'M ALWAYS SWITCHING, SO MY HOUSE IS CARPETED WITH BRAND NEW MILLIPENS, MIXED UP WITH ONES THAT ARE OUT OF INK. IT'S A PROBLEM.
Which one can I use?!
MIXED UP
Millipens
IT'S THE SAME WITH MY CALLIGRAPHY BRUSH PENS. THEY'RE COMPLETELY MIXED UP...
You're so right!
hee hee
ha ha ha
Put them up somewhere, stupid.

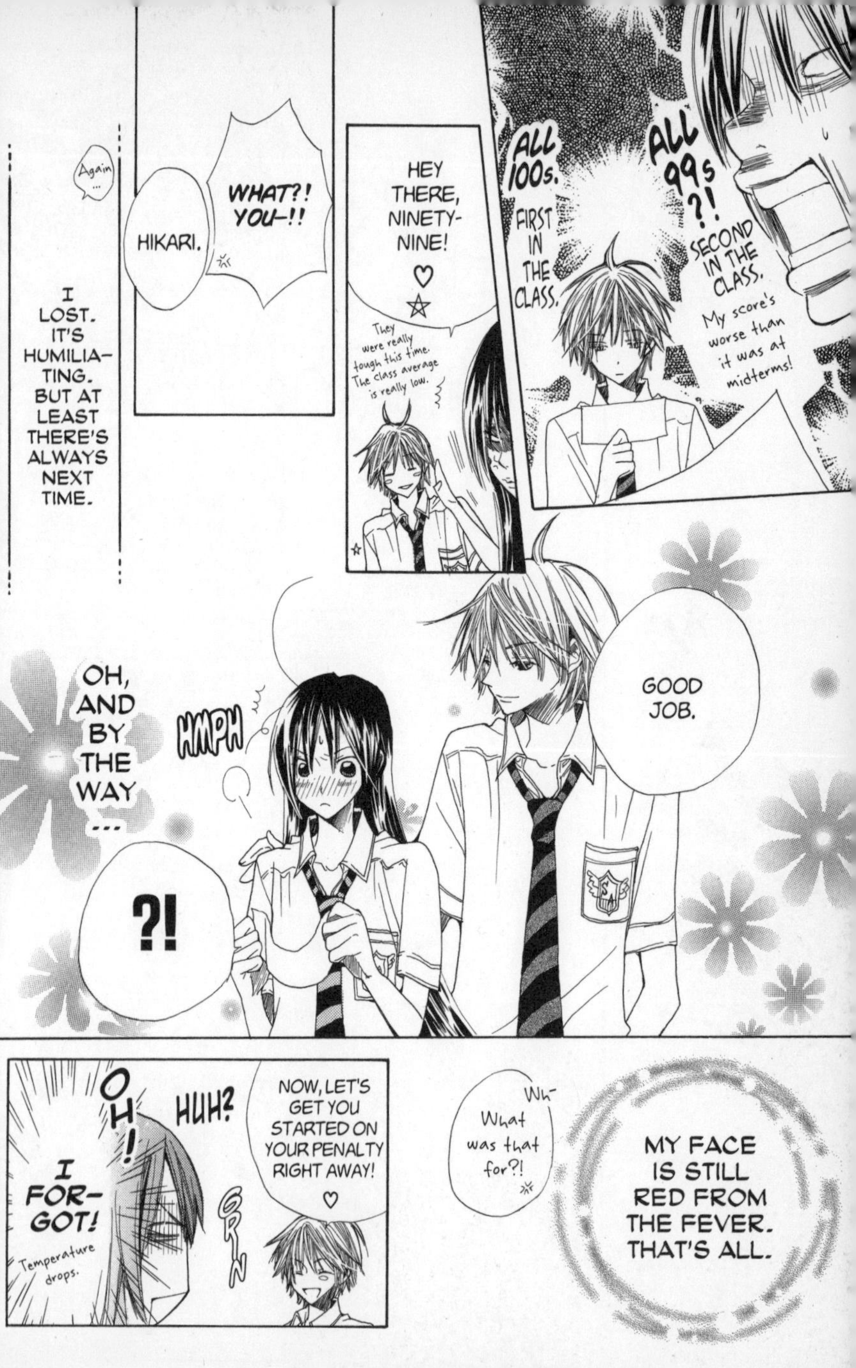
ALL 99s?!
SECOND IN THE CLASS.
My score's worse than it was at midterms!
ALL 100s.
FIRST IN THE CLASS.
HEY THERE, NINETY-NINE! ♡ ☆
They were really tough this time. The class average is really low.
WHAT?! YOU-!!
HIKARI.
Again...
I LOST. IT'S HUMILIATING. BUT AT LEAST THERE'S ALWAYS NEXT TIME.
GOOD JOB.
HMPH
OH, AND BY THE WAY...
?!
MY FACE IS STILL RED FROM THE FEVER. THAT'S ALL.
Wh- What was that for?!
NOW, LET'S GET YOU STARTED ON YOUR PENALTY RIGHT AWAY! ♡
HUH?
OH! I FORGOT!
GRIN
Temperature drops.

Chapter 9

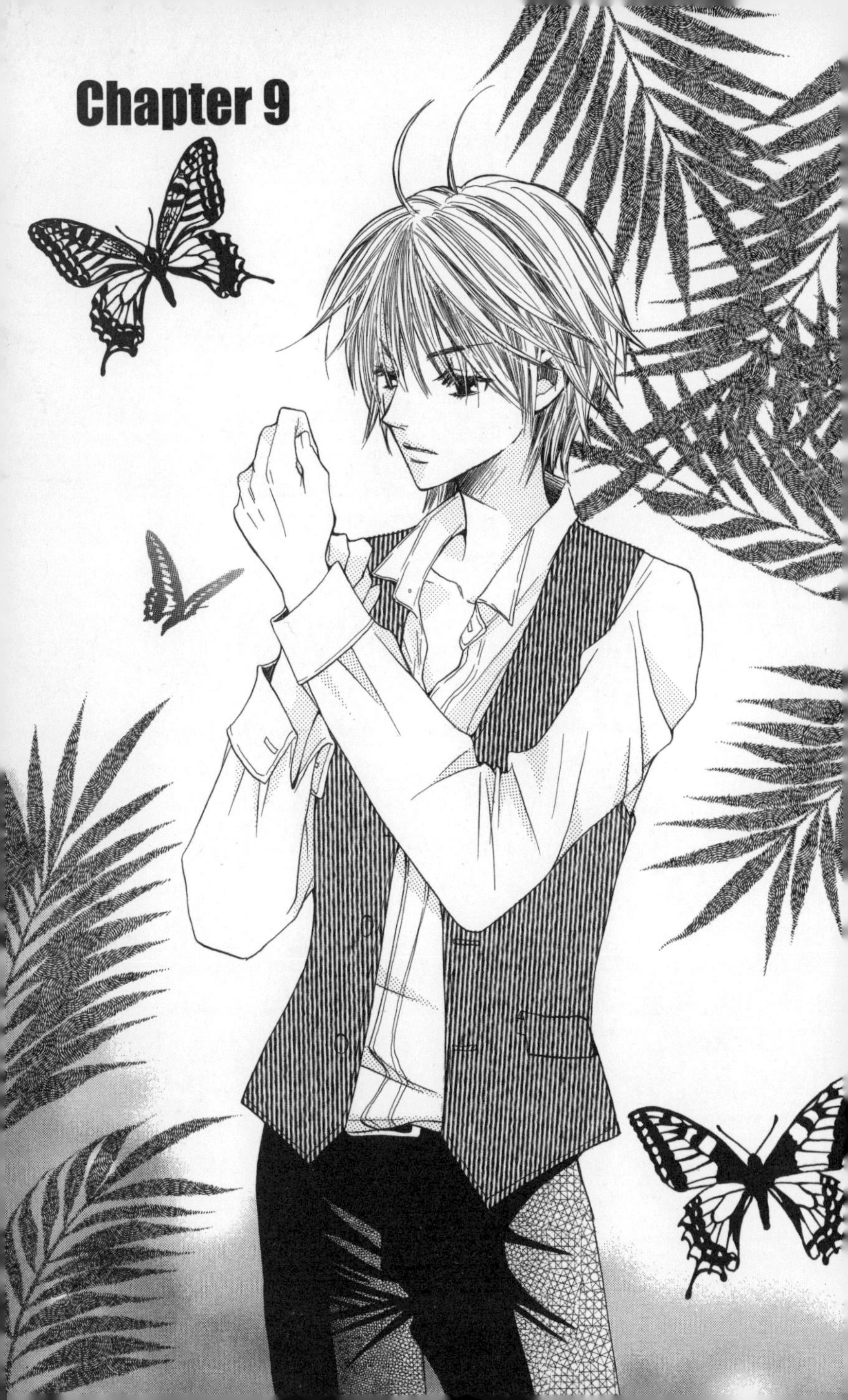

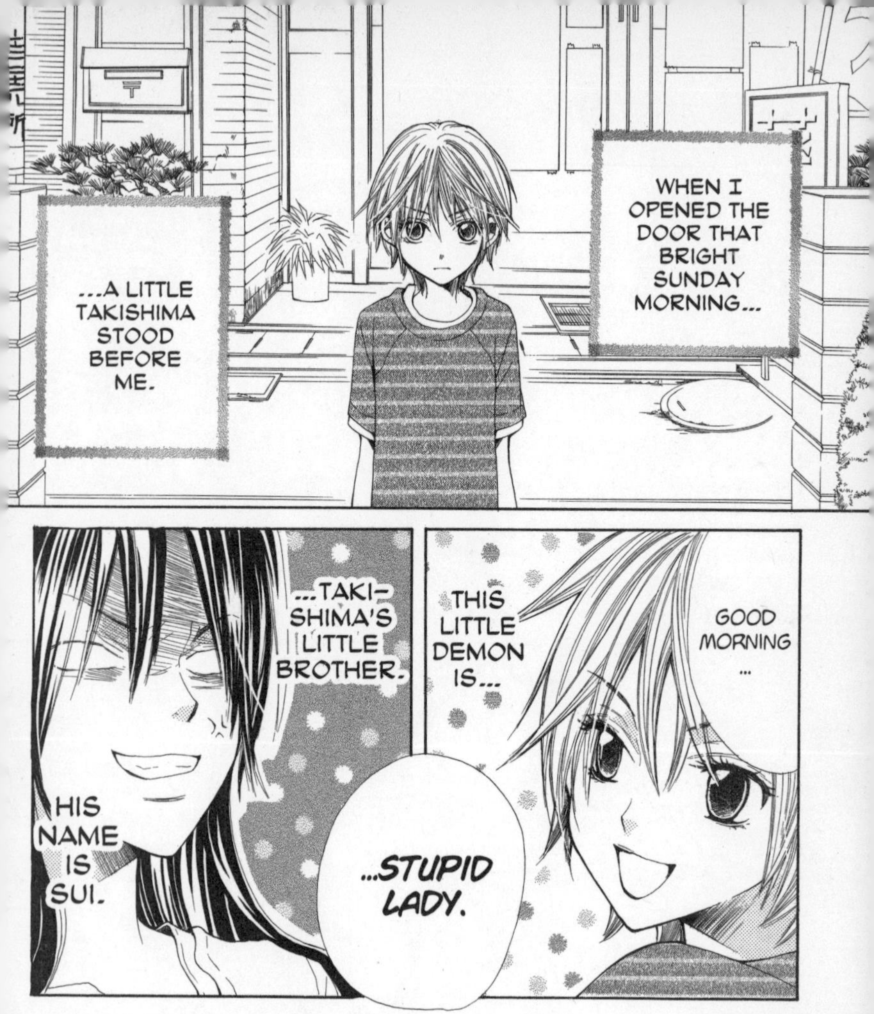
WHEN I OPENED THE DOOR THAT BRIGHT SUNDAY MORNING...
...A LITTLE TAKISHIMA STOOD BEFORE ME.
GOOD MORNING...
THIS LITTLE DEMON IS...
...STUPID LADY.
...TAKI-SHIMA'S LITTLE BROTHER.
HIS NAME IS SUI.

• LETTERS •

THANK YOU FOR ALL OF THEM! I AM GOING TO READ EVERY SINGLE ONE!

I'M SORRY IT ALWAYS TAKES ME SO LONG TO ANSWER THEM. BUT I WILL ALWAYS WRITE YOU BACK, EVENTUALLY. THEY GIVE ME SO MUCH OF MY INSPIRATION! SO THANK YOU VERY, VERY MUCH!

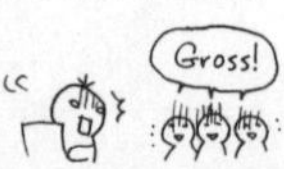
Gross!

I'm using this space just to thank you.

And thanks for all the presents, too! ♥

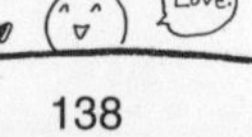
Love.

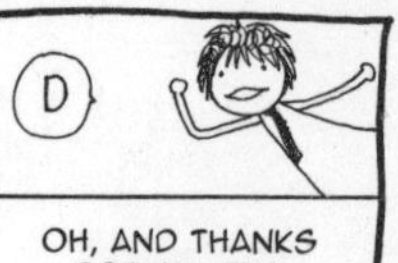
D

OH, AND THANKS FOR ALL THE FASCINATING DRAWINGS AND PURIKURA!

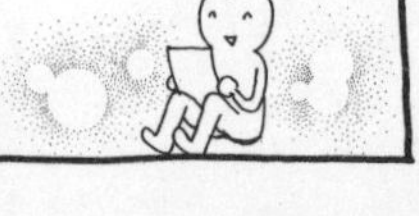

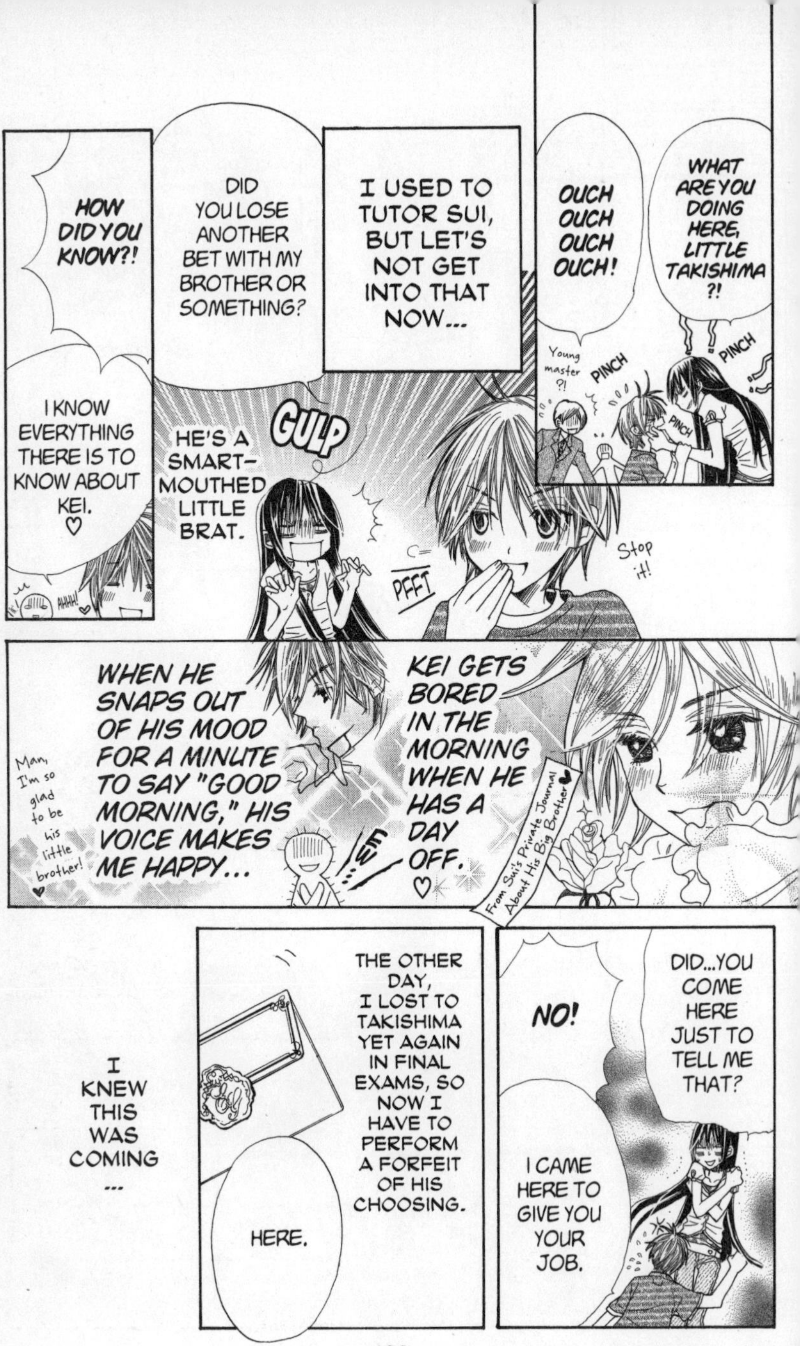
WHAT ARE YOU DOING HERE, LITTLE TAKISHIMA?!
OUCH OUCH OUCH OUCH!
PINCH
PINCH
PINCH
Young master ?!
I USED TO TUTOR SUI, BUT LET'S NOT GET INTO THAT NOW...
DID YOU LOSE ANOTHER BET WITH MY BROTHER OR SOMETHING?
GULP
Stop it!
PFFT
HE'S A SMART-MOUTHED LITTLE BRAT.
HOW DID YOU KNOW?!
I KNOW EVERYTHING THERE IS TO KNOW ABOUT KEI. ♡
AHHH!
KEI GETS BORED IN THE MORNING WHEN HE HAS A DAY OFF. ♡
From Sui's Private Journal About His Big Brother
WHEN HE SNAPS OUT OF HIS MOOD FOR A MINUTE TO SAY "GOOD MORNING," HIS VOICE MAKES ME HAPPY...
Man, I'm so glad to be his little brother! ♥
DID...YOU COME HERE JUST TO TELL ME THAT?
NO!
I CAME HERE TO GIVE YOU YOUR JOB.
THE OTHER DAY, I LOST TO TAKISHIMA YET AGAIN IN FINAL EXAMS, SO NOW I HAVE TO PERFORM A FORFEIT OF HIS CHOOSING.
HERE.
I KNEW THIS WAS COMING ...

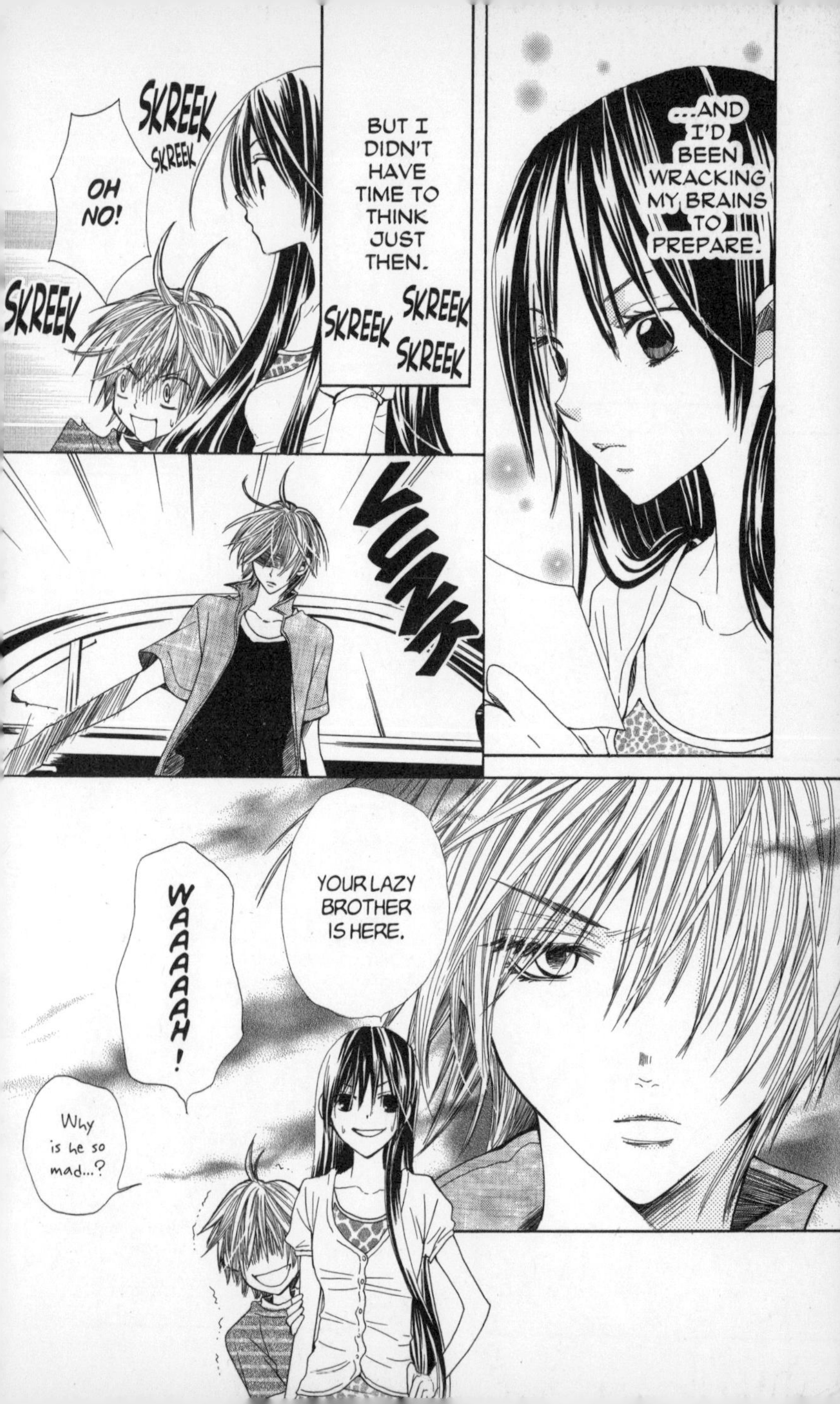
...AND I'D BEEN WRACKING MY BRAINS TO PREPARE.
BUT I DIDN'T HAVE TIME TO THINK JUST THEN.
SKREEK
SKREEK
SKREEK
SKREEK
SKREEK
SKREEK
OH NO!
SKREEK
VUNK
YOUR LAZY BROTHER IS HERE.
WAAAAAAH!
Why is he so mad...?

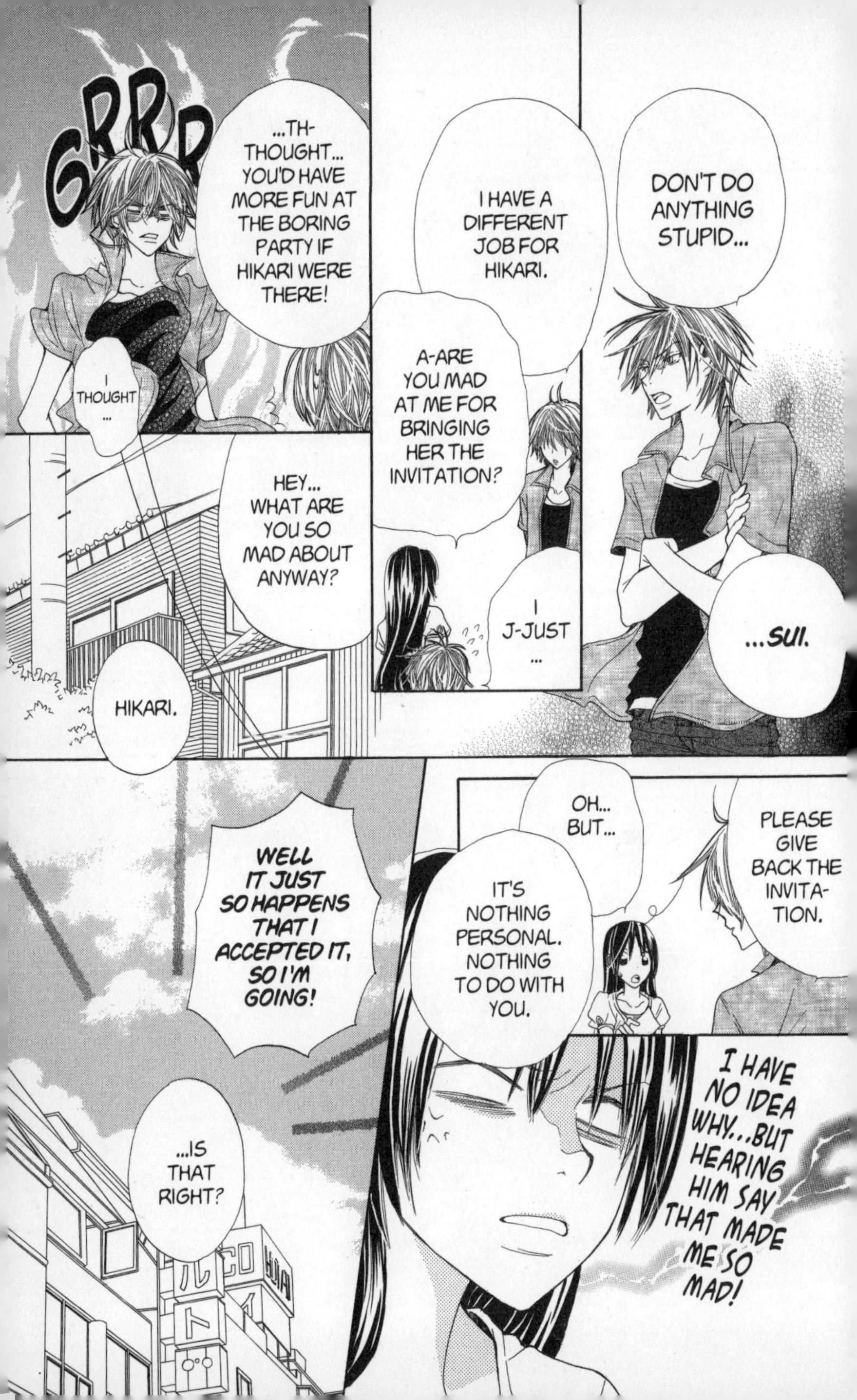
DON'T DO ANYTHING STUPID...
...SUI.
I HAVE A DIFFERENT JOB FOR HIKARI.
A-ARE YOU MAD AT ME FOR BRINGING HER THE INVITATION?
I J-JUST ...
...TH-THOUGHT... YOU'D HAVE MORE FUN AT THE BORING PARTY IF HIKARI WERE THERE!
GRRR
I THOUGHT ...
HEY... WHAT ARE YOU SO MAD ABOUT ANYWAY?
HIKARI.
PLEASE GIVE BACK THE INVITA-TION.
OH... BUT...
IT'S NOTHING PERSONAL. NOTHING TO DO WITH YOU.
I HAVE NO IDEA WHY...BUT HEARING HIM SAY THAT MADE ME SO MAD!
WELL IT JUST SO HAPPENS THAT I ACCEPTED IT, SO I'M GOING!
...IS THAT RIGHT?

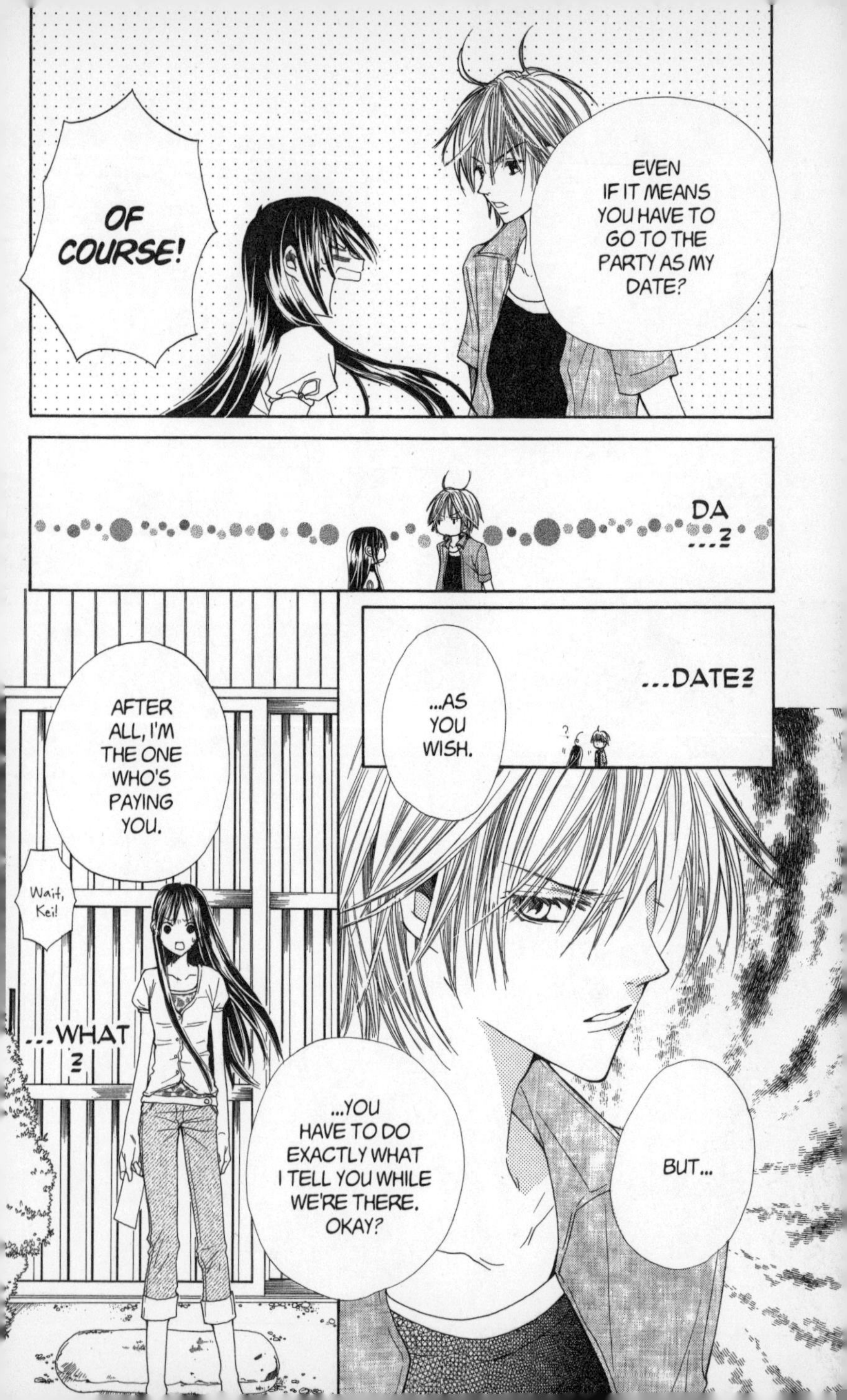

EVEN IF IT MEANS YOU HAVE TO GO TO THE PARTY AS MY DATE?
OF COURSE!
DA...?
...DATE?
...AS YOU WISH.
BUT...
...YOU HAVE TO DO EXACTLY WHAT I TELL YOU WHILE WE'RE THERE. OKAY?
AFTER ALL, I'M THE ONE WHO'S PAYING YOU.
Wait, Kei!
...WHAT?

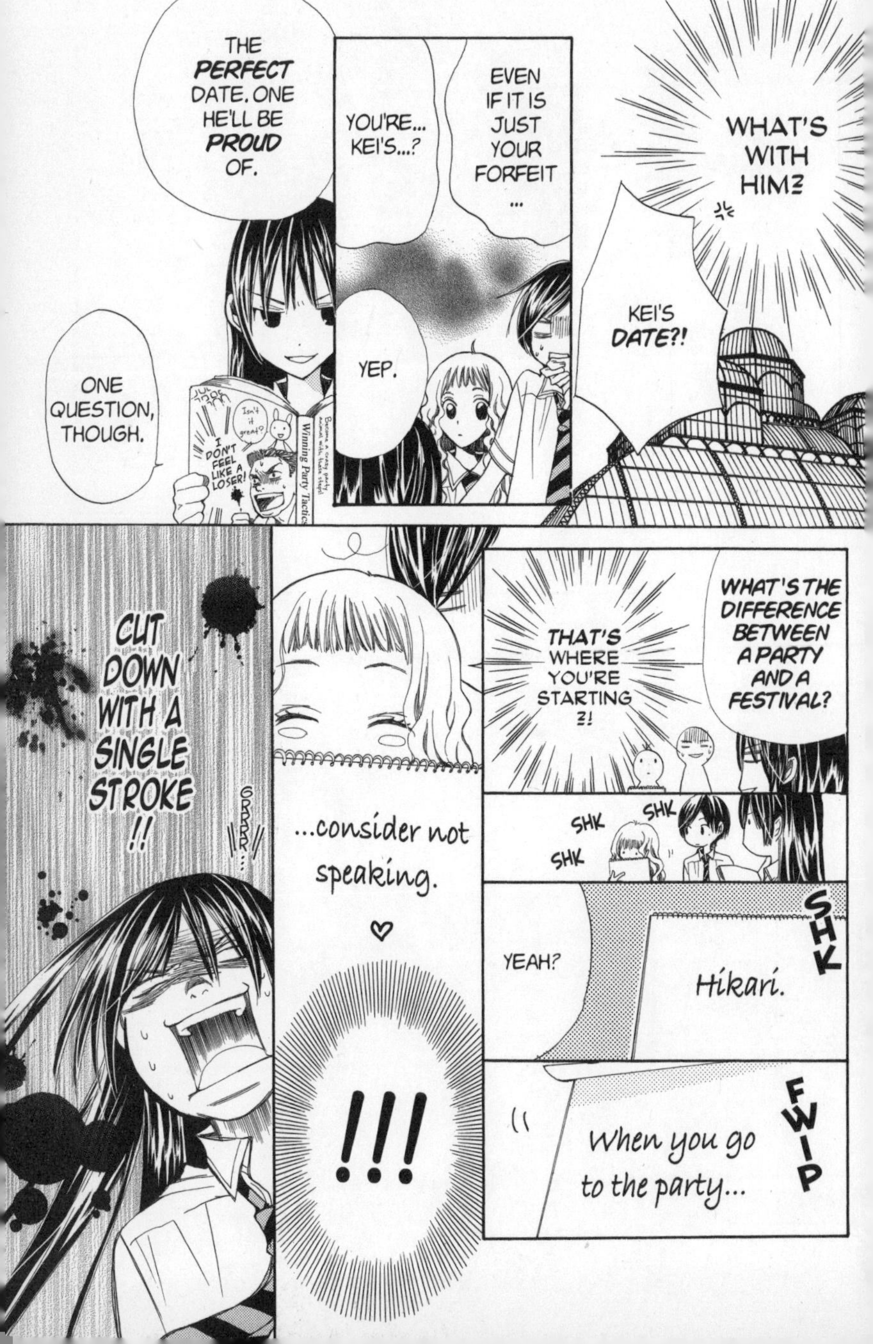

WHAT'S WITH HIM?
KEI'S DATE?!
EVEN IF IT IS JUST YOUR FORFEIT ...
YOU'RE... KEI'S...?
YEP.
THE PERFECT DATE. ONE HE'LL BE PROUD OF.
Winning Party Tactics
Isn't it great?!
I DON'T FEEL LIKE A LOSER!
ONE QUESTION, THOUGH.
WHAT'S THE DIFFERENCE BETWEEN A PARTY AND A FESTIVAL?
THAT'S WHERE YOU'RE STARTING?!
SHK
SHK
SHK
SHK
YEAH?
Hikari.
FWIP
When you go to the party...
...consider not speaking. ♡
!!!
CUT DOWN WITH A SINGLE STROKE!!
GRRRR...

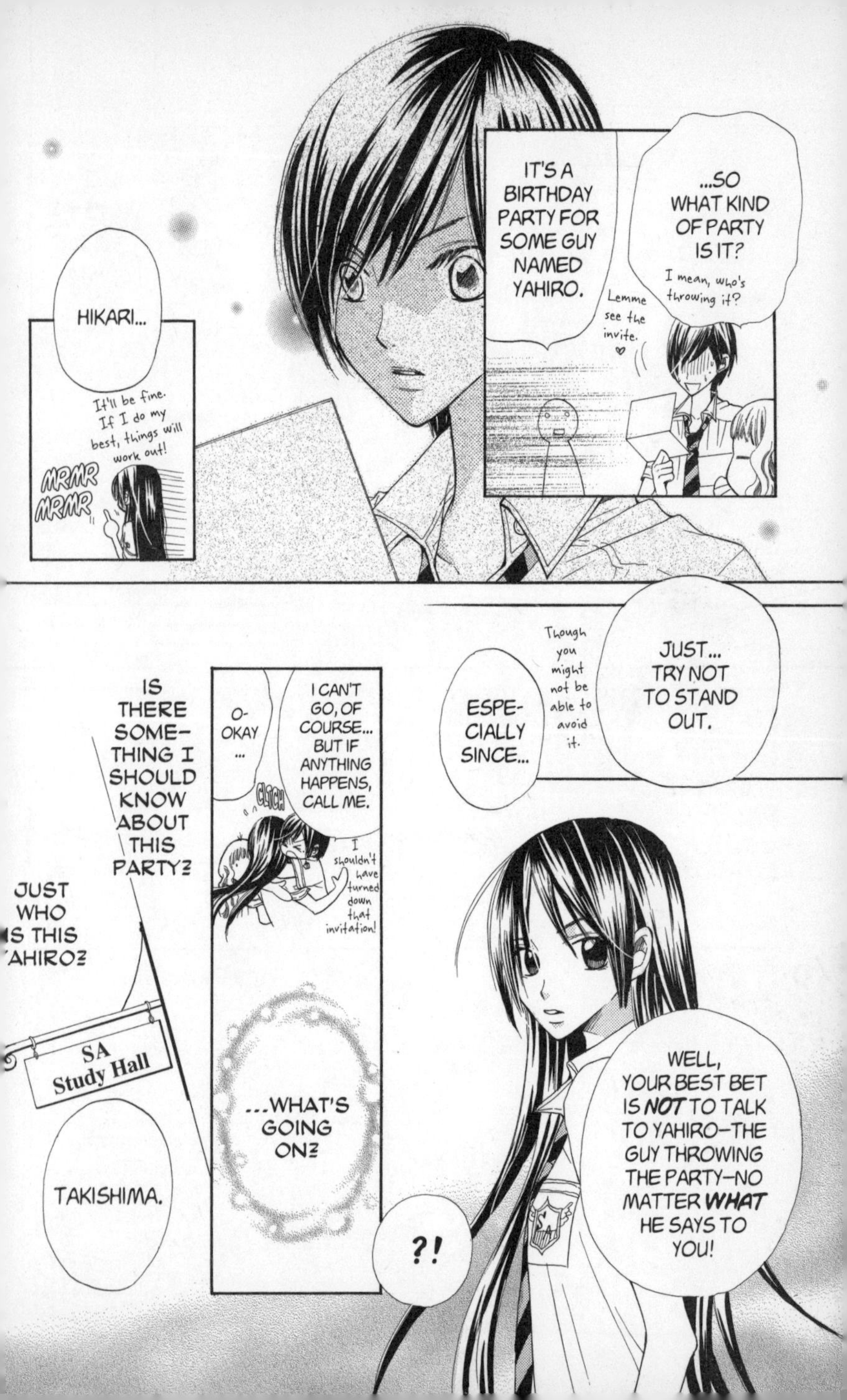
...SO WHAT KIND OF PARTY IS IT?
I mean, who's throwing it?
Lemme see the invite.
IT'S A BIRTHDAY PARTY FOR SOME GUY NAMED YAHIRO.
HIKARI...
It'll be fine. If I do my best, things will work out!
MRMR MRMR
JUST... TRY NOT TO STAND OUT.
Though you might not be able to avoid it.
ESPE-CIALLY SINCE...
WELL, YOUR BEST BET IS NOT TO TALK TO YAHIRO—THE GUY THROWING THE PARTY—NO MATTER WHAT HE SAYS TO YOU!
?!
I CAN'T GO, OF COURSE... BUT IF ANYTHING HAPPENS, CALL ME.
O-OKAY...
CLICH
I shouldn't have turned down that invitation!
...WHAT'S GOING ON?
IS THERE SOMETHING I SHOULD KNOW ABOUT THIS PARTY?
JUST WHO IS THIS YAHIRO?
SA Study Hall
TAKISHIMA.

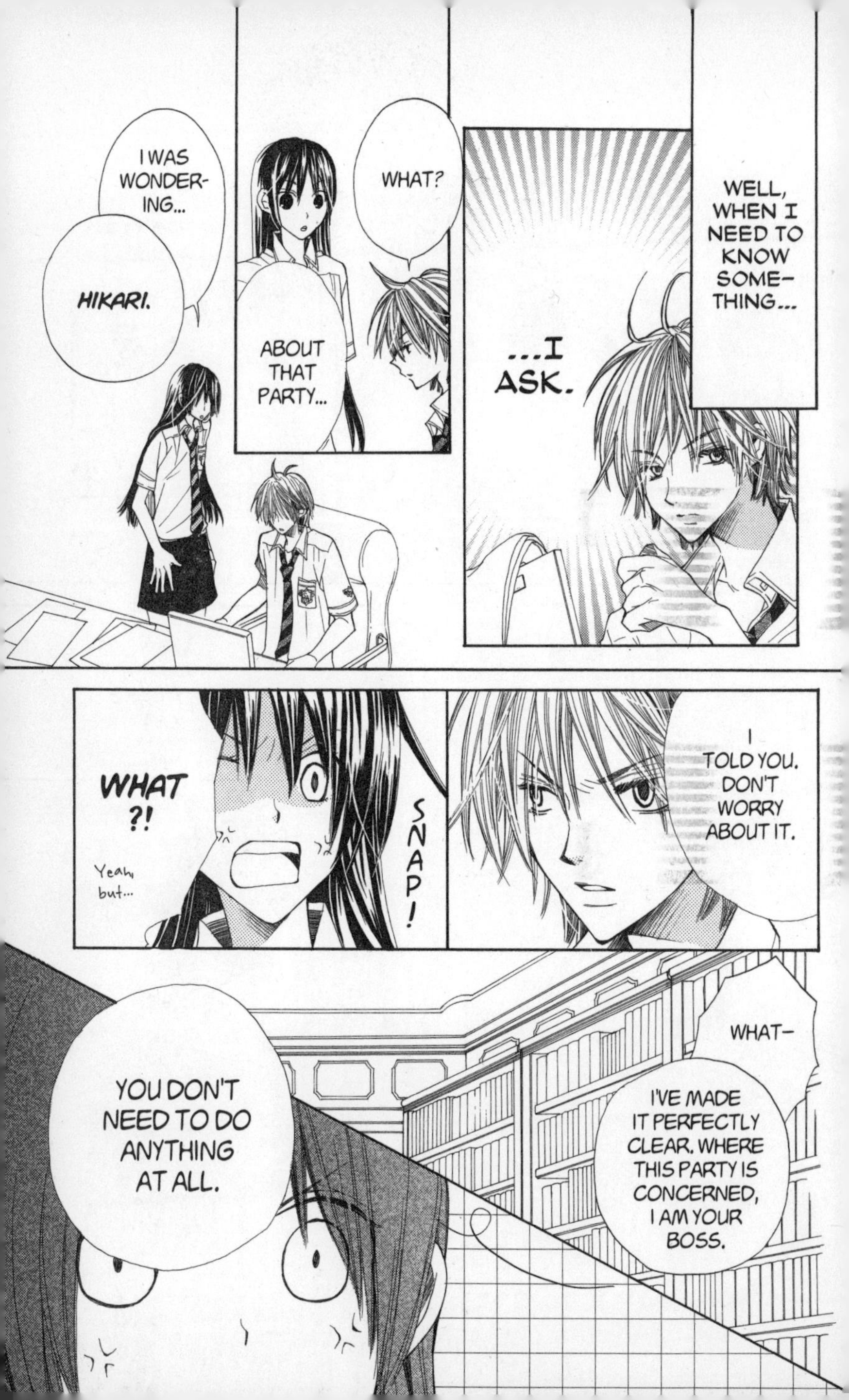
WELL, WHEN I NEED TO KNOW SOME-THING...
...I ASK.
WHAT?
ABOUT THAT PARTY...
I WAS WONDER-ING...
HIKARI.
I TOLD YOU. DON'T WORRY ABOUT IT.
SNAP!
WHAT ?!
Yeah, but...
WHAT-
I'VE MADE IT PERFECTLY CLEAR. WHERE THIS PARTY IS CONCERNED, I AM YOUR BOSS.
YOU DON'T NEED TO DO ANYTHING AT ALL.

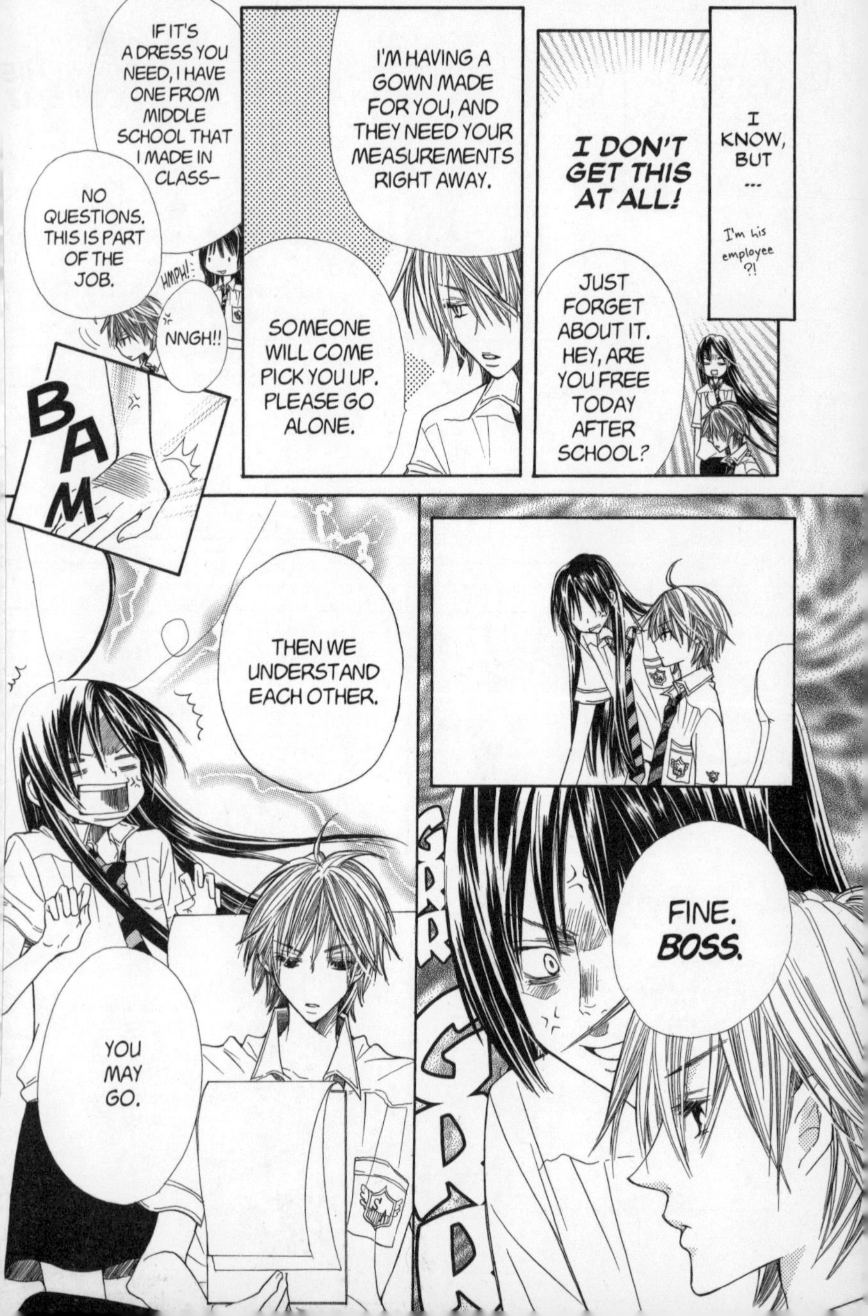

I KNOW, BUT ...
I'm his employee ?!
I DON'T GET THIS AT ALL!
JUST FORGET ABOUT IT. HEY, ARE YOU FREE TODAY AFTER SCHOOL?
I'M HAVING A GOWN MADE FOR YOU, AND THEY NEED YOUR MEASUREMENTS RIGHT AWAY.
SOMEONE WILL COME PICK YOU UP. PLEASE GO ALONE.
IF IT'S A DRESS YOU NEED, I HAVE ONE FROM MIDDLE SCHOOL THAT I MADE IN CLASS—
NO QUESTIONS. THIS IS PART OF THE JOB.
HMPH!
NNGH!!
BAM
GRRR
FINE. BOSS.
THEN WE UNDERSTAND EACH OTHER.
YOU MAY GO.

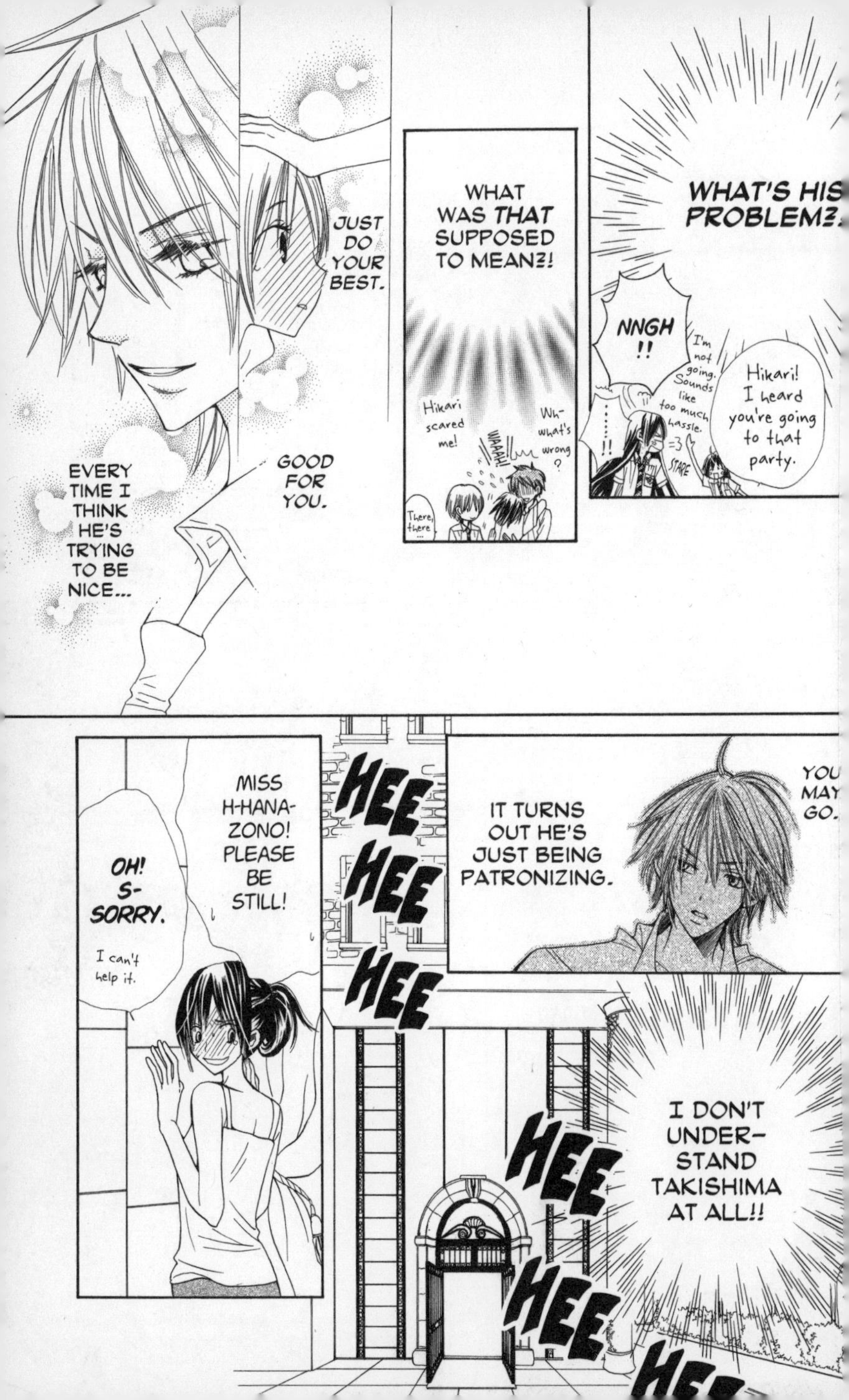
WHAT'S HIS PROBLEM?!
Hikari! I heard you're going to that party.
I'm not going. Sounds like too much hassle.
NNGH !!
STARE
!!
WHAT WAS THAT SUPPOSED TO MEAN?!
Wh-what's wrong?
WAAAH!
Hikari scared me!
There, there...
JUST DO YOUR BEST.
GOOD FOR YOU.
EVERY TIME I THINK HE'S TRYING TO BE NICE...
YOU MAY GO.
IT TURNS OUT HE'S JUST BEING PATRONIZING.
I DON'T UNDER-STAND TAKISHIMA AT ALL!!
HEE HEE HEE
HEE HEE HEE
MISS H-HANA-ZONO! PLEASE BE STILL!
OH! S-SORRY.
I can't help it.

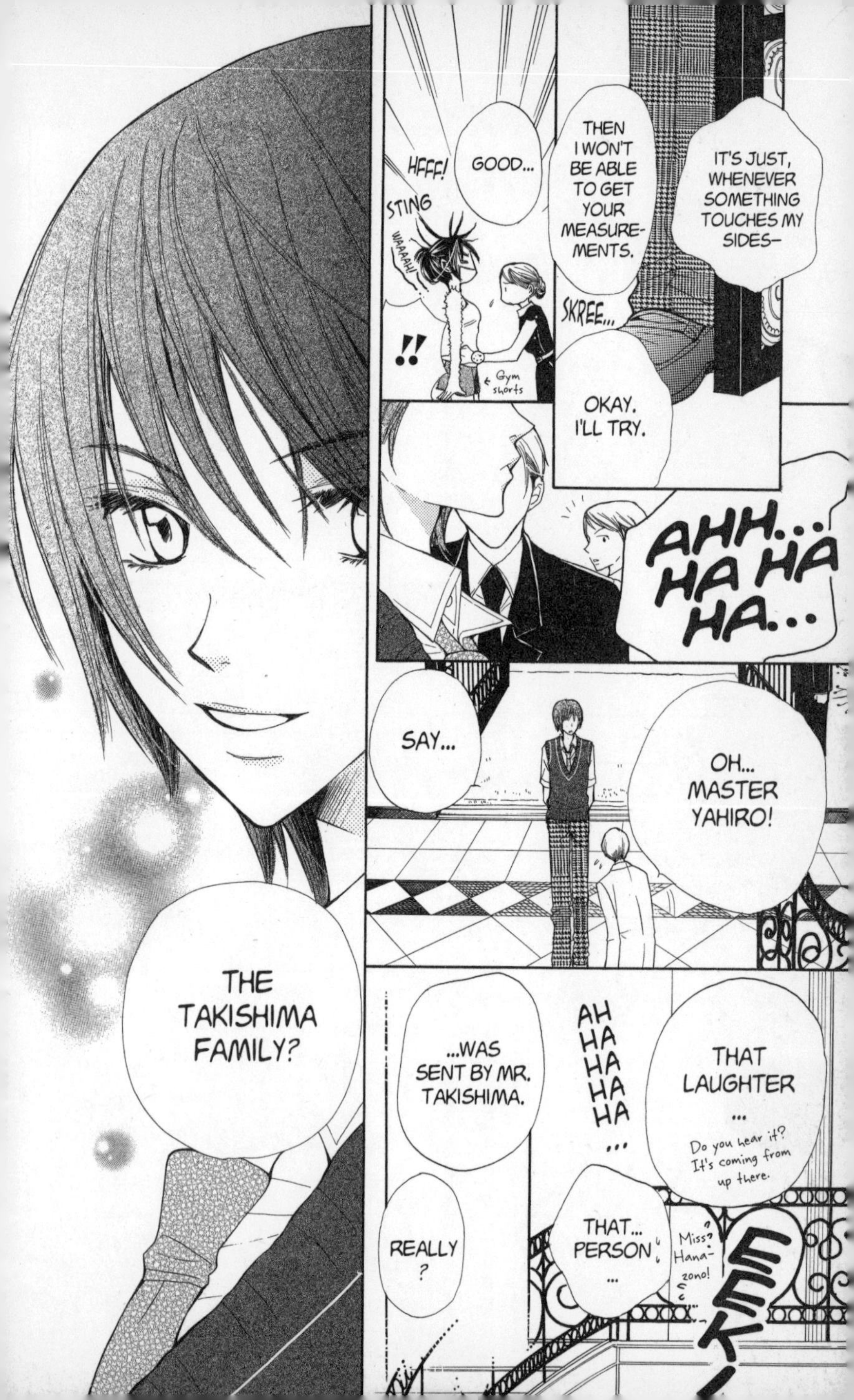
IT'S JUST, WHENEVER SOMETHING TOUCHES MY SIDES–
THEN I WON'T BE ABLE TO GET YOUR MEASUREMENTS.
SKREE...
OKAY. I'LL TRY.
GOOD...
HFFF!
STING
WAAAAH!
!!
← Gym shorts
AHH... HA HA HA...
OH... MASTER YAHIRO!
SAY...
THAT LAUGHTER ...
Do you hear it? It's coming from up there.
AH HA HA HA HA ...
...WAS SENT BY MR. TAKISHIMA.
EEEK!
Miss? Hana-zono!
THAT... PERSON ...
REALLY ?
THE TAKISHIMA FAMILY?

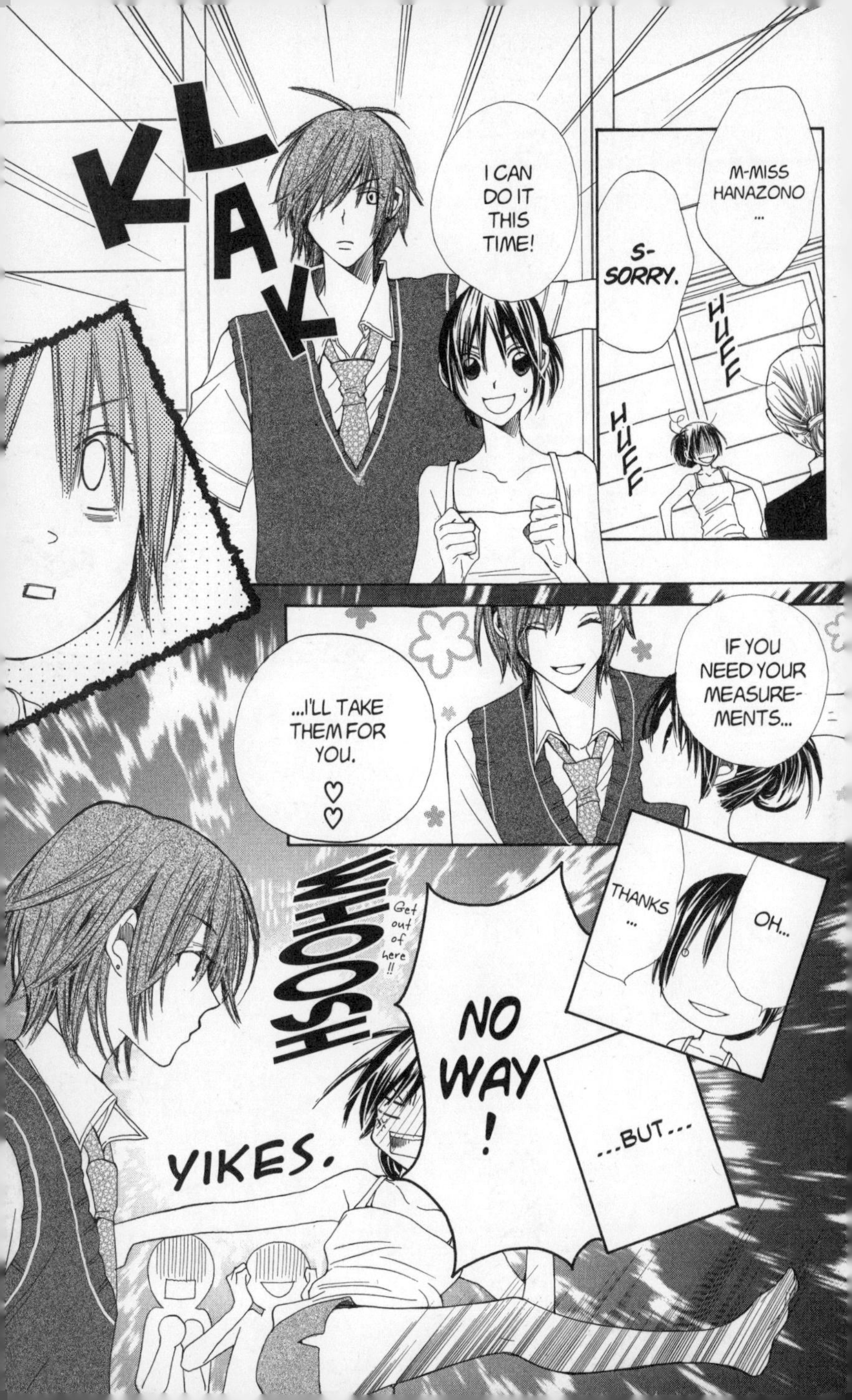
M-MISS HANAZONO ...
S-SORRY.
HUFF
HUFF
I CAN DO IT THIS TIME!
KLAK
IF YOU NEED YOUR MEASUREMENTS...
...I'LL TAKE THEM FOR YOU. ♡ ♡
OH...
THANKS ...
...BUT...
NO WAY!
Get out of here!!
WHOOSH
YIKES.

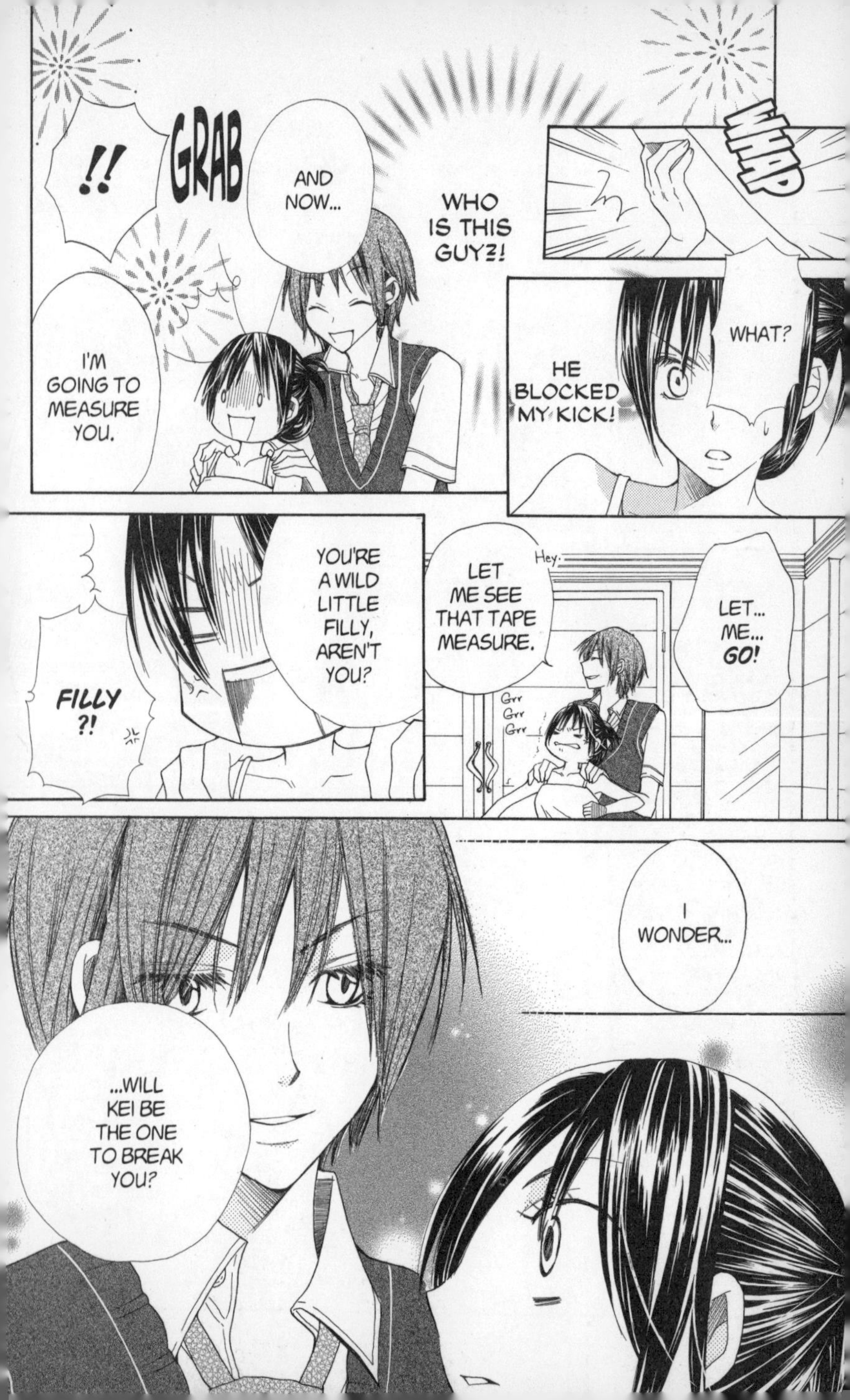
WHAP
WHAT?
HE BLOCKED MY KICK!
WHO IS THIS GUY?!
AND NOW...
GRAB
!!
I'M GOING TO MEASURE YOU.
LET... ME... GO!
Hey.
LET ME SEE THAT TAPE MEASURE.
Grr Grr Grr
YOU'RE A WILD LITTLE FILLY, AREN'T YOU?
FILLY?!
I WONDER...
...WILL KEI BE THE ONE TO BREAK YOU?

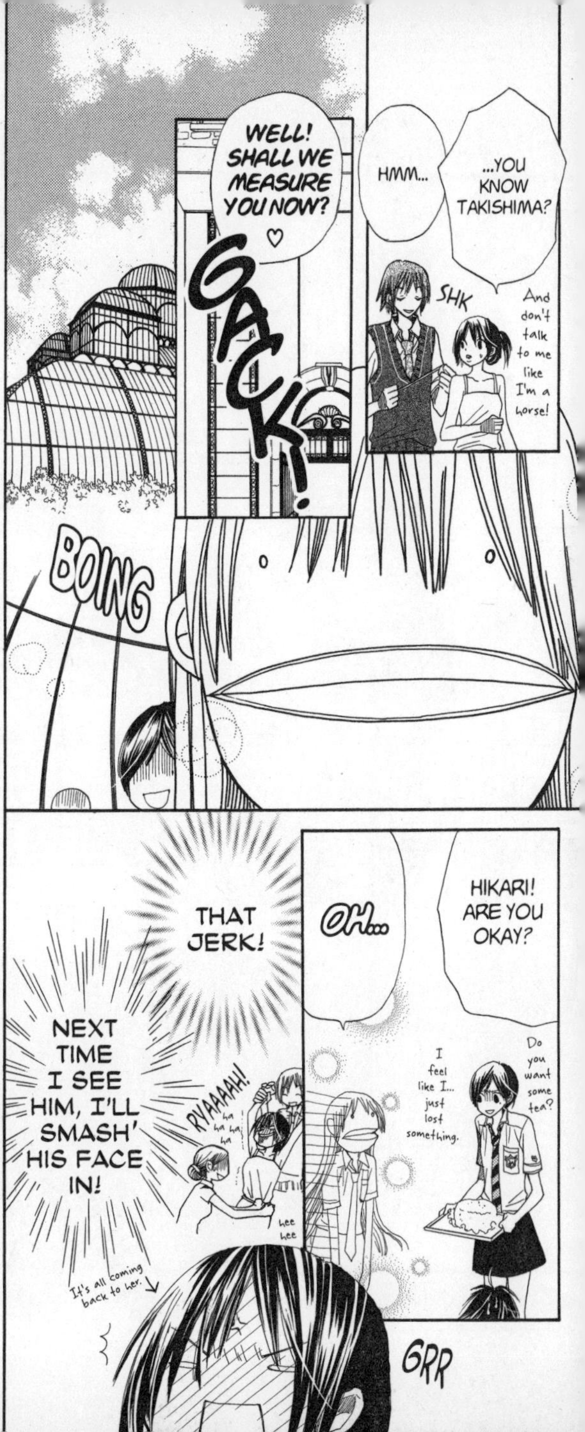
HMM...
...YOU KNOW TAKISHIMA?
SHK
And don't talk to me like I'm a horse!
WELL! SHALL WE MEASURE YOU NOW? ♡
GACK!
BOING
HIKARI! ARE YOU OKAY?
OH...
Do you want some tea?
I feel like I... just lost something.
THAT JERK!
NEXT TIME I SEE HIM, I'LL SMASH HIS FACE IN!
RYAAAAH!
ha ha ha
hee hee
It's all coming back to her.
GRR

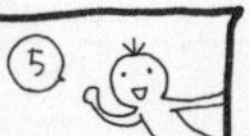
5

•CD SHOPS•

I LIKE CD STORES, TOO! WHEN I'M SHOPPING BY MYSELF, I USUALLY STOP BY ONE. I LOSE TRACK OF TIME LOOKING AT THE COVERS. AND I GO INTO A TRANCE WHEN I LISTEN TO THE SAMPLE SONGS...

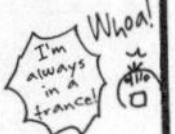
Whoa!
I'm always in a trance!

WHY ARE THE SONGS THEY HAVE ON SAMPLE PLAYLISTS ALWAYS SO GOOD?

THOUGH OCCASIONALLY SOMEONE LEAVES THE VOLUME SO HIGH THAT IT STARTLES YOU WHEN YOU PUT THE HEADPHONES ON.

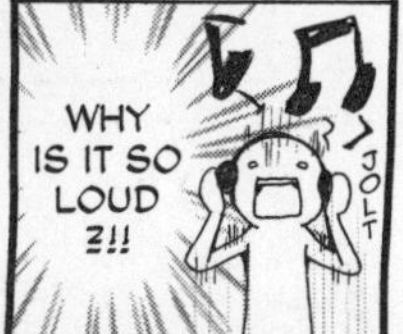
WHY IS IT SO LOUD ?!!
JOLT

I GUESS VOLUME LEVELS ARE A PERSONAL PREFERENCE.

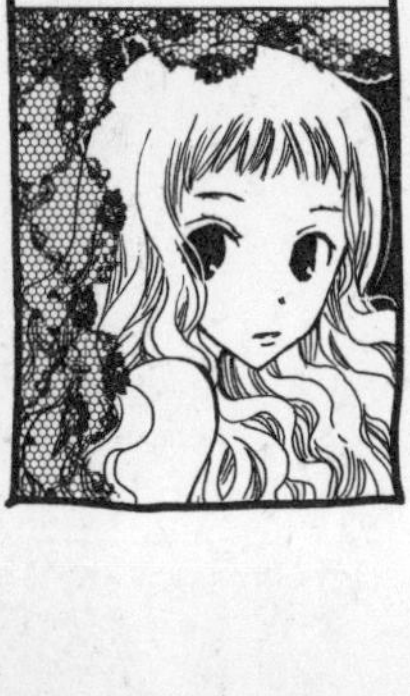

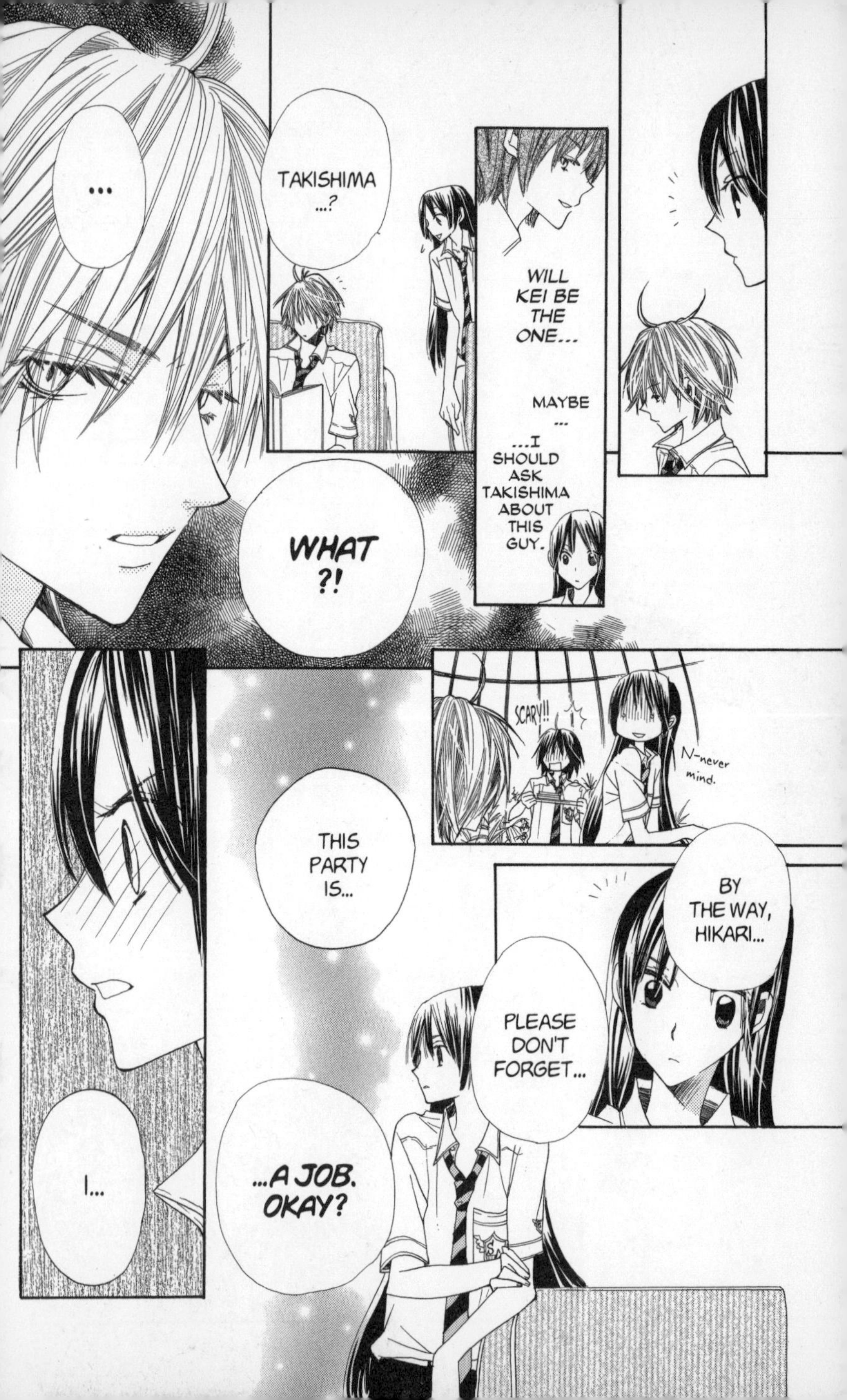
WILL KEI BE THE ONE...
MAYBE...
...I SHOULD ASK TAKISHIMA ABOUT THIS GUY.
TAKISHIMA ...?
...
WHAT ?!
SCARY!!
N-never mind.
BY THE WAY, HIKARI...
PLEASE DON'T FORGET...
THIS PARTY IS...
...A JOB. OKAY?
I...

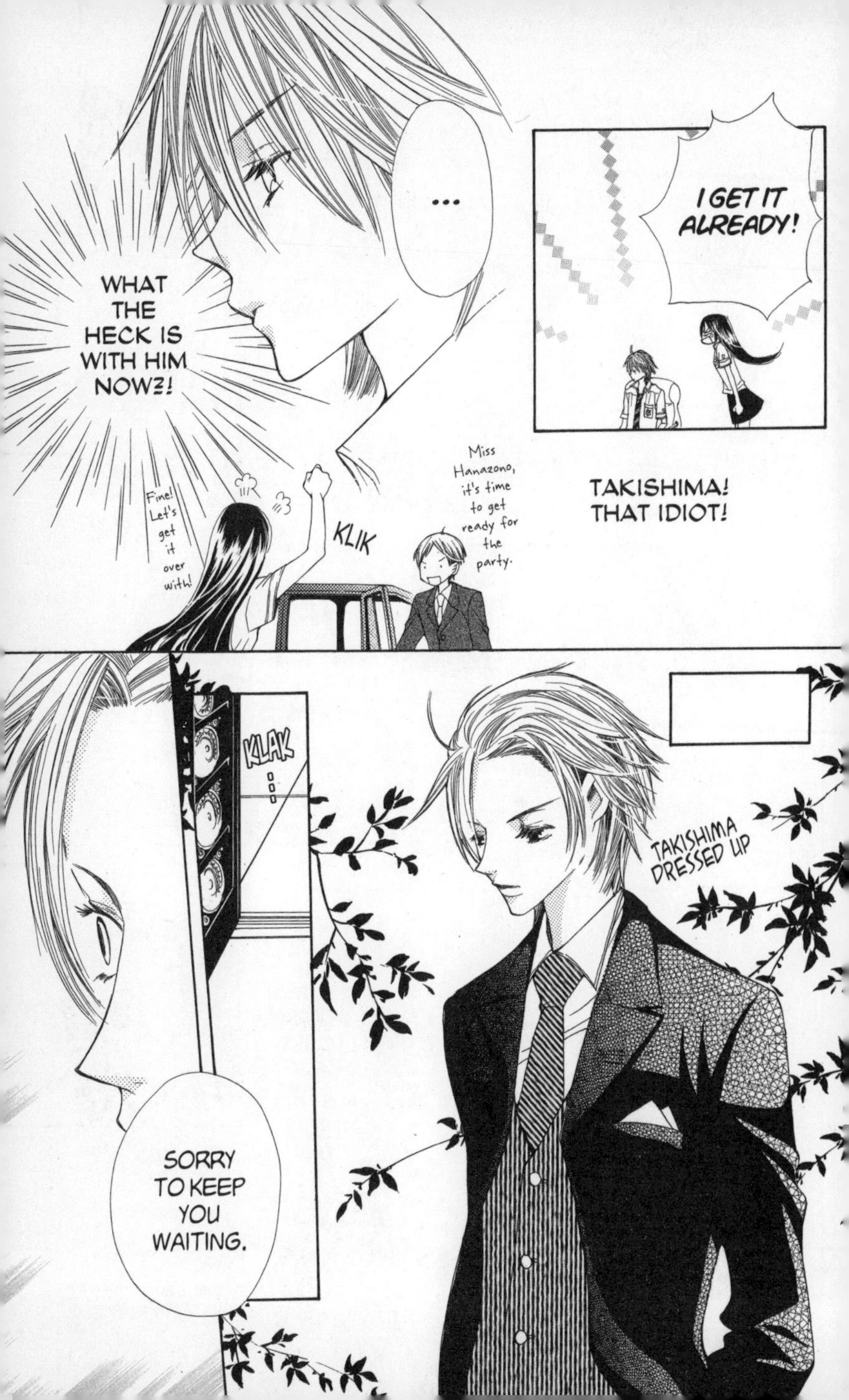
I GET IT ALREADY!
TAKISHIMA! THAT IDIOT!
...
WHAT THE HECK IS WITH HIM NOW?!
Miss Hanazono, it's time to get ready for the party.
KLIK
Fine! Let's get it over with!
TAKISHIMA DRESSED UP
KLAK
...
SORRY TO KEEP YOU WAITING.

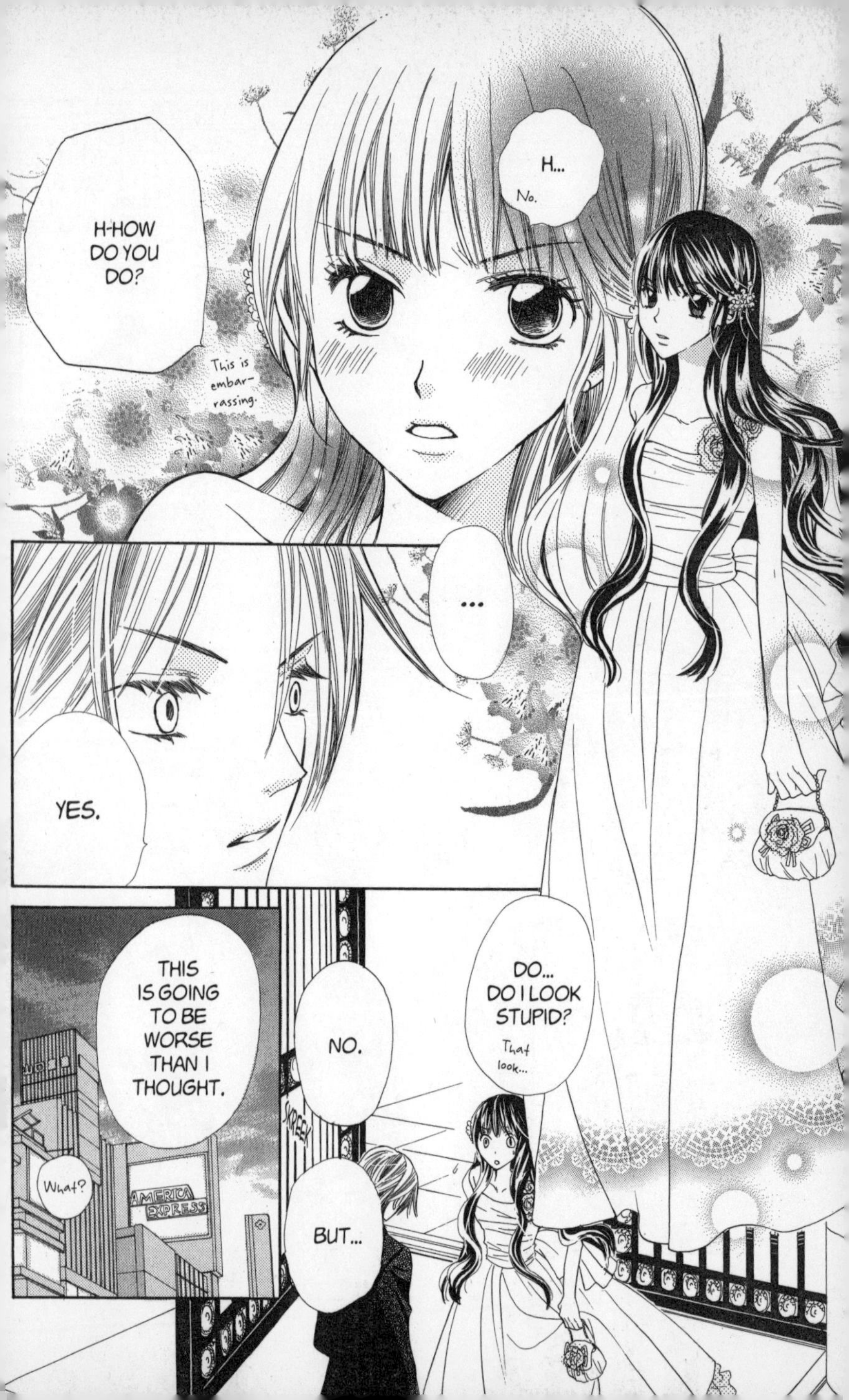
H...
No.
H-HOW DO YOU DO?
This is embarrassing.
...
YES.
DO... DO I LOOK STUPID?
That look...
NO.
SKREEK
BUT...
THIS IS GOING TO BE WORSE THAN I THOUGHT.
What?
AMERICA EXPRESS

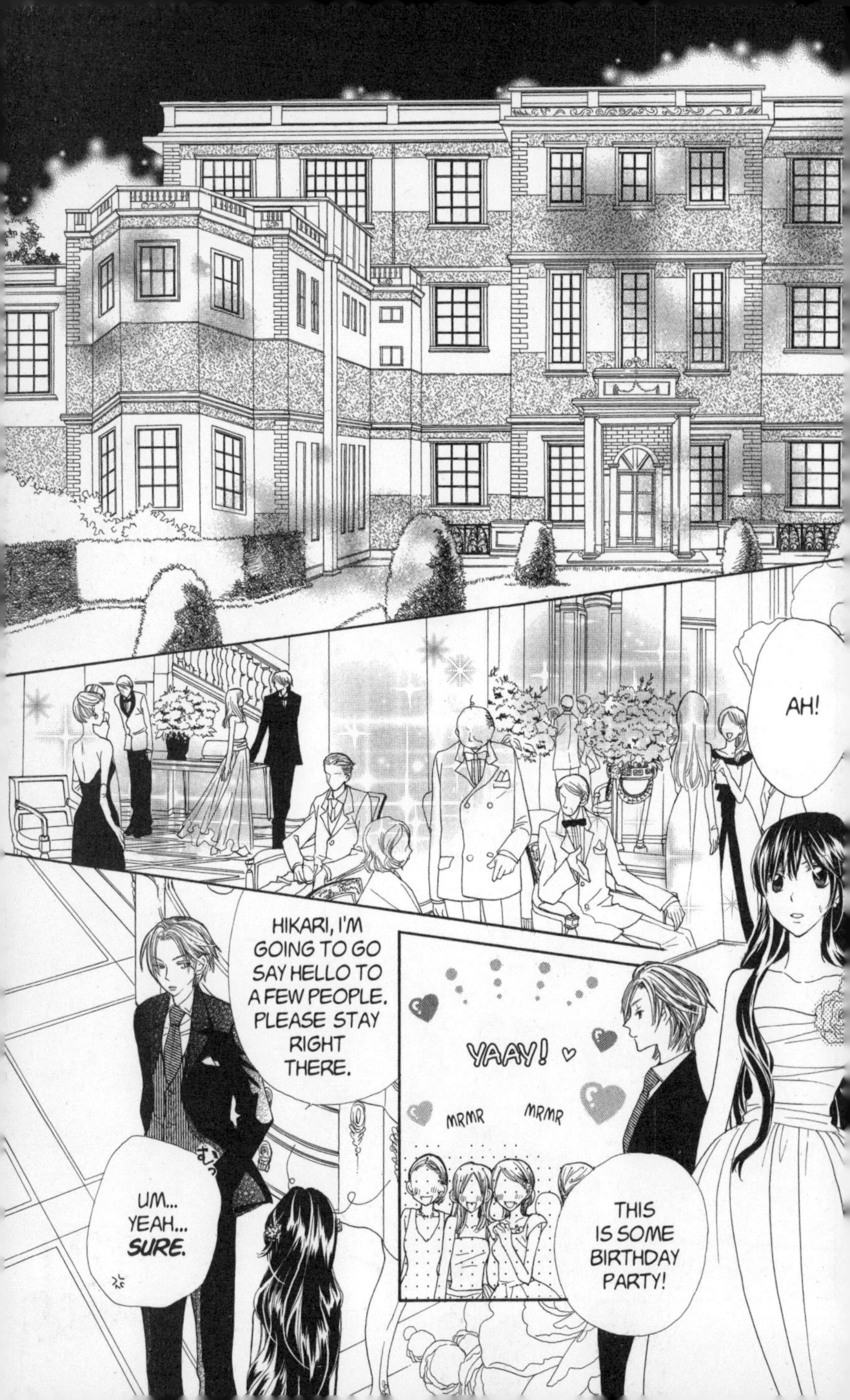
AH!
THIS IS SOME BIRTHDAY PARTY!
YAAY!
MRMR
MRMR
HIKARI, I'M GOING TO GO SAY HELLO TO A FEW PEOPLE. PLEASE STAY RIGHT THERE.
UM... YEAH... **SURE.**

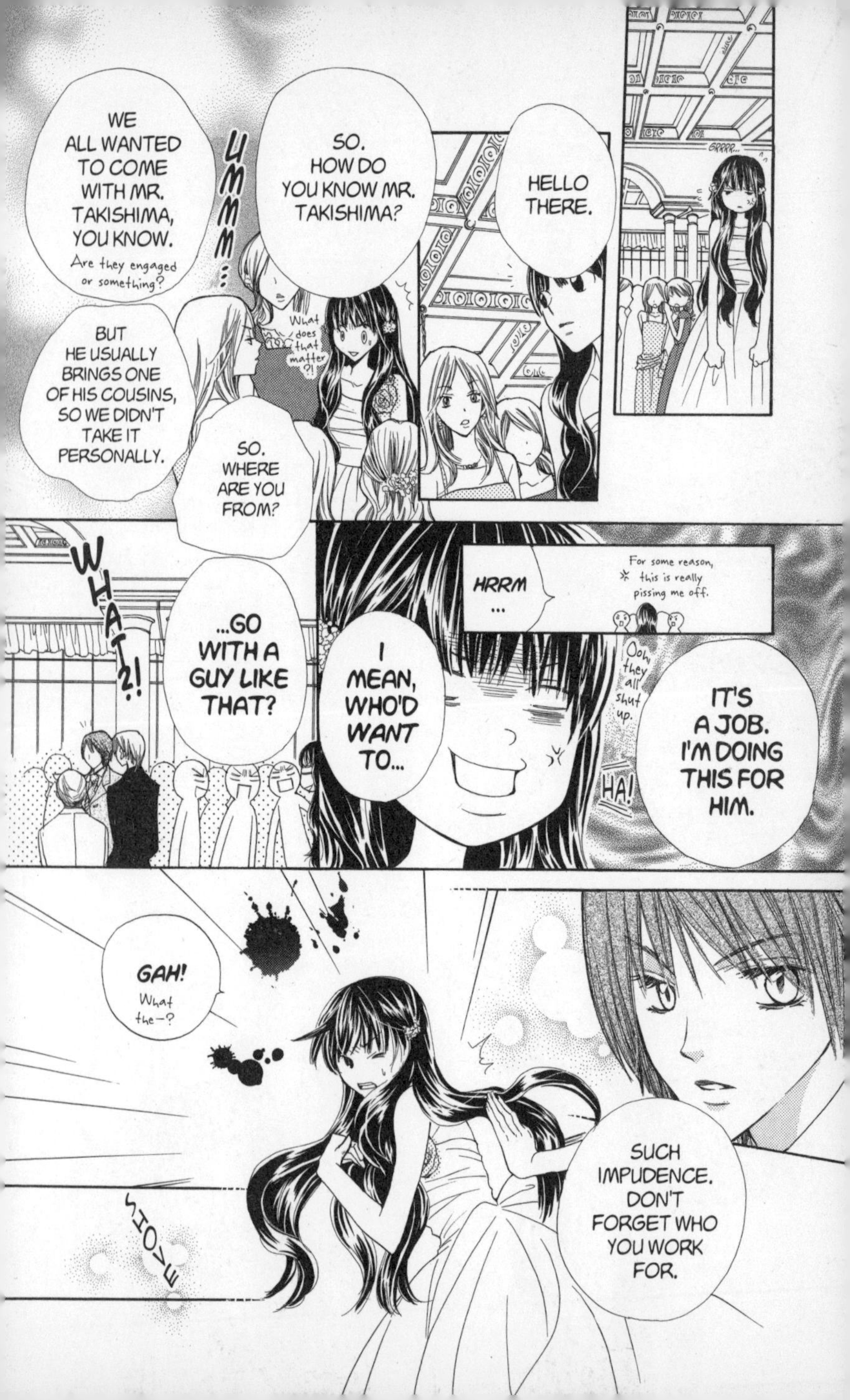
GRRRR...
HELLO THERE.
SO. HOW DO YOU KNOW MR. TAKISHIMA?
What does that matter?!
UMMM...
WE ALL WANTED TO COME WITH MR. TAKISHIMA, YOU KNOW.
Are they engaged or something?
BUT HE USUALLY BRINGS ONE OF HIS COUSINS, SO WE DIDN'T TAKE IT PERSONALLY.
SO. WHERE ARE YOU FROM?
HRRM ...
For some reason, this is really pissing me off.
IT'S A JOB. I'M DOING THIS FOR HIM.
Ooh, they all shut up.
HA!
I MEAN, WHO'D WANT TO...
...GO WITH A GUY LIKE THAT?
WHAT?!
SUCH IMPUDENCE. DON'T FORGET WHO YOU WORK FOR.
GAH! What the-?

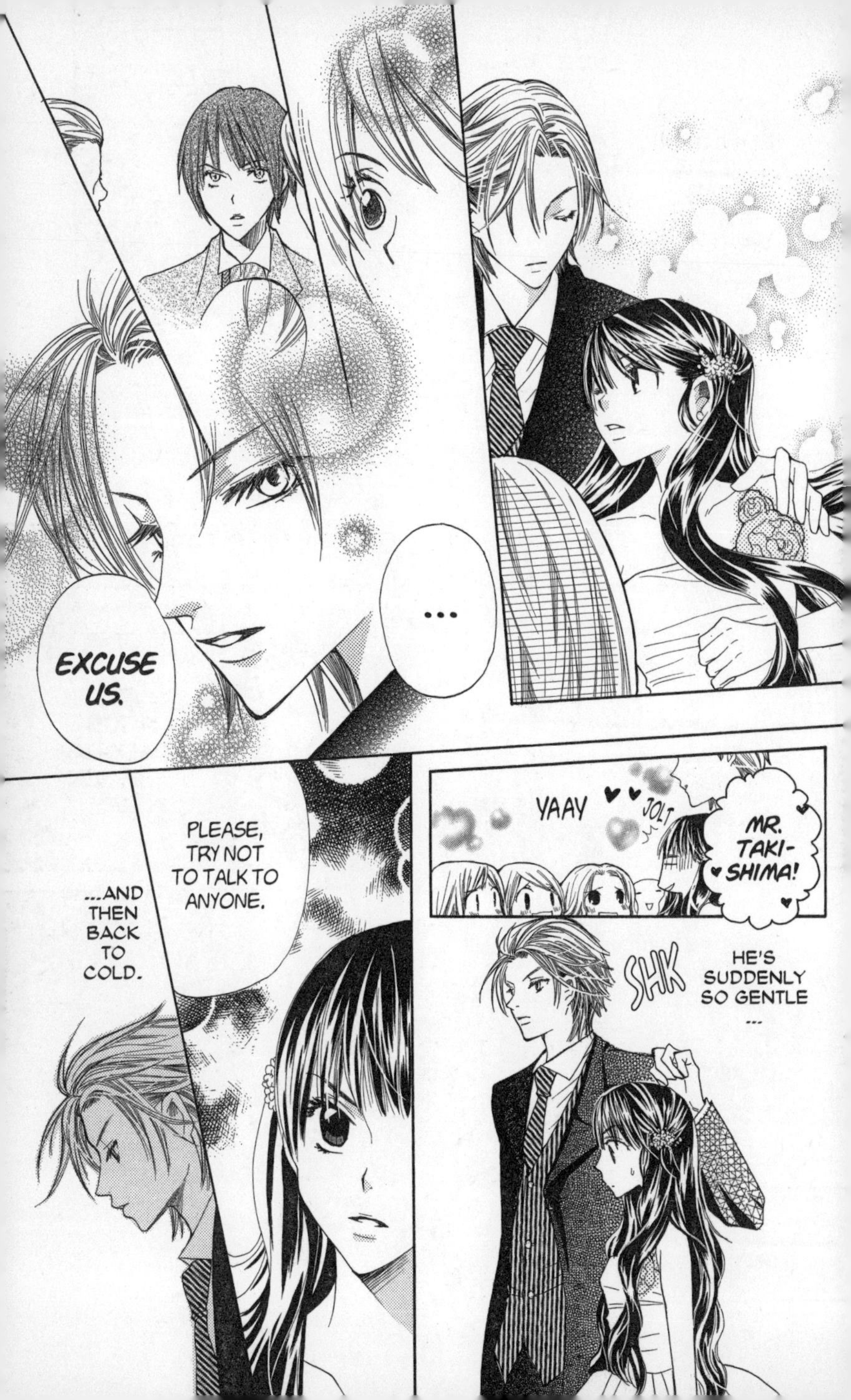
...
EXCUSE US.
MR. TAKI-SHIMA!
JOLT
YAAY
HE'S SUDDENLY SO GENTLE ...
SHK
PLEASE, TRY NOT TO TALK TO ANYONE.
...AND THEN BACK TO COLD.

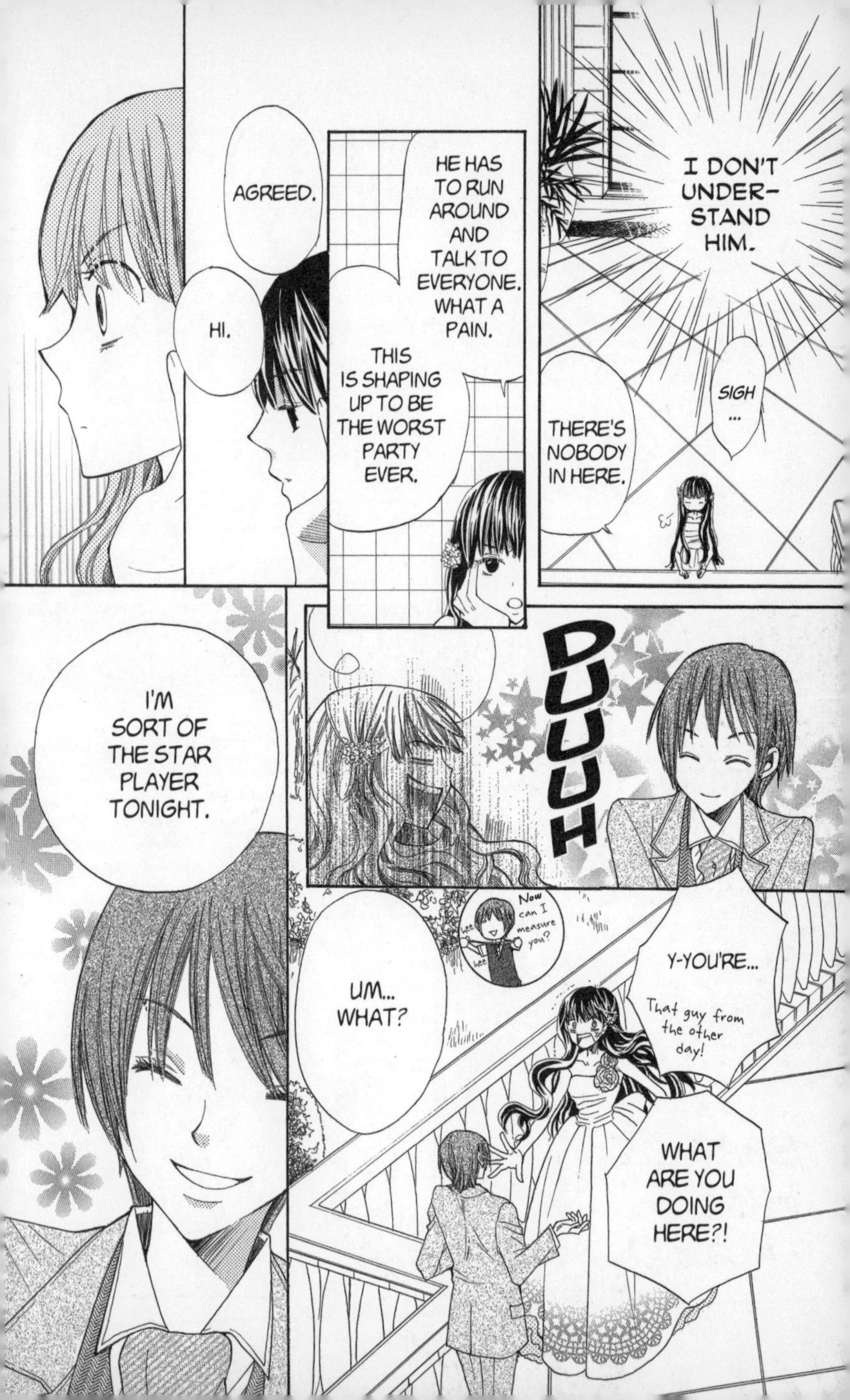
I DON'T UNDER-STAND HIM.
SIGH...
THERE'S NOBODY IN HERE.
HE HAS TO RUN AROUND AND TALK TO EVERYONE. WHAT A PAIN.
THIS IS SHAPING UP TO BE THE WORST PARTY EVER.
AGREED.
HI.
DUUUH
Y-YOU'RE...
That guy from the other day!
WHAT ARE YOU DOING HERE?!
Now can I measure you?
hee hee
UM... WHAT?
I'M SORT OF THE STAR PLAYER TONIGHT.

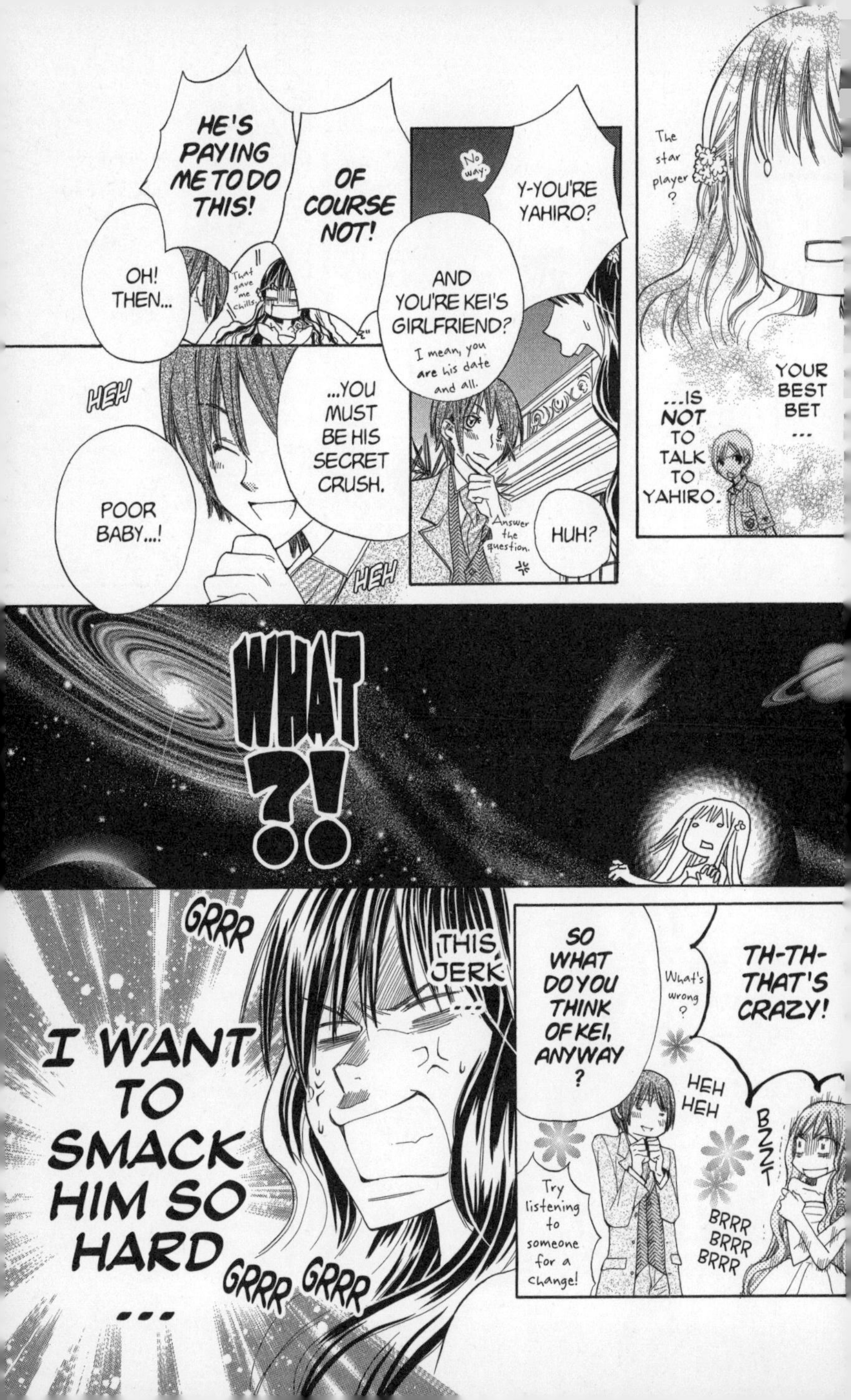
The star player?
YOUR BEST BET...
...IS NOT TO TALK TO YAHIRO.
No way.
Y-YOU'RE YAHIRO?
AND YOU'RE KEI'S GIRLFRIEND?
I mean, you are his date and all.
HUH?
Answer the question.
OF COURSE NOT!
HE'S PAYING ME TO DO THIS!
That gave me chills.
OH! THEN...
...YOU MUST BE HIS SECRET CRUSH.
HEH
POOR BABY...!
HEH
WHAT?!
TH-TH-THAT'S CRAZY!
What's wrong?
SO WHAT DO YOU THINK OF KEI, ANYWAY?
HEH HEH
BZZT
BRRR BRRR BRRR
Try listening to someone for a change!
THIS JERK...
GRRR
I WANT TO SMACK HIM SO HARD...
GRRR GRRR

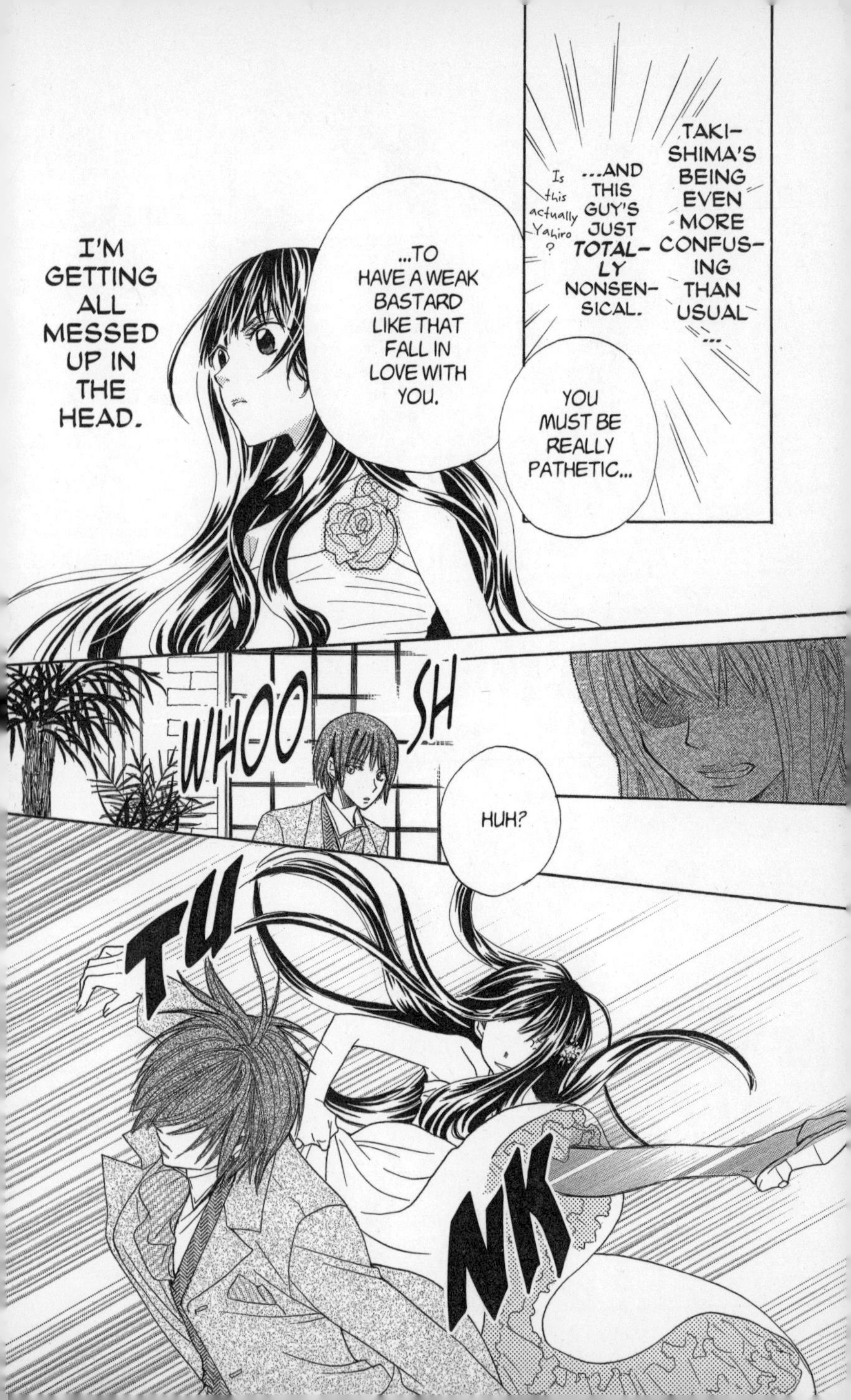
TAKI-SHIMA'S BEING EVEN MORE CONFUSING THAN USUAL...
...AND THIS GUY'S JUST **TOTALLY** NONSENSICAL.
Is this actually Yahiro?
YOU MUST BE REALLY PATHETIC...
...TO HAVE A WEAK BASTARD LIKE THAT FALL IN LOVE WITH YOU.
I'M GETTING ALL MESSED UP IN THE HEAD.
WHOOSH
HUH?
TUNK

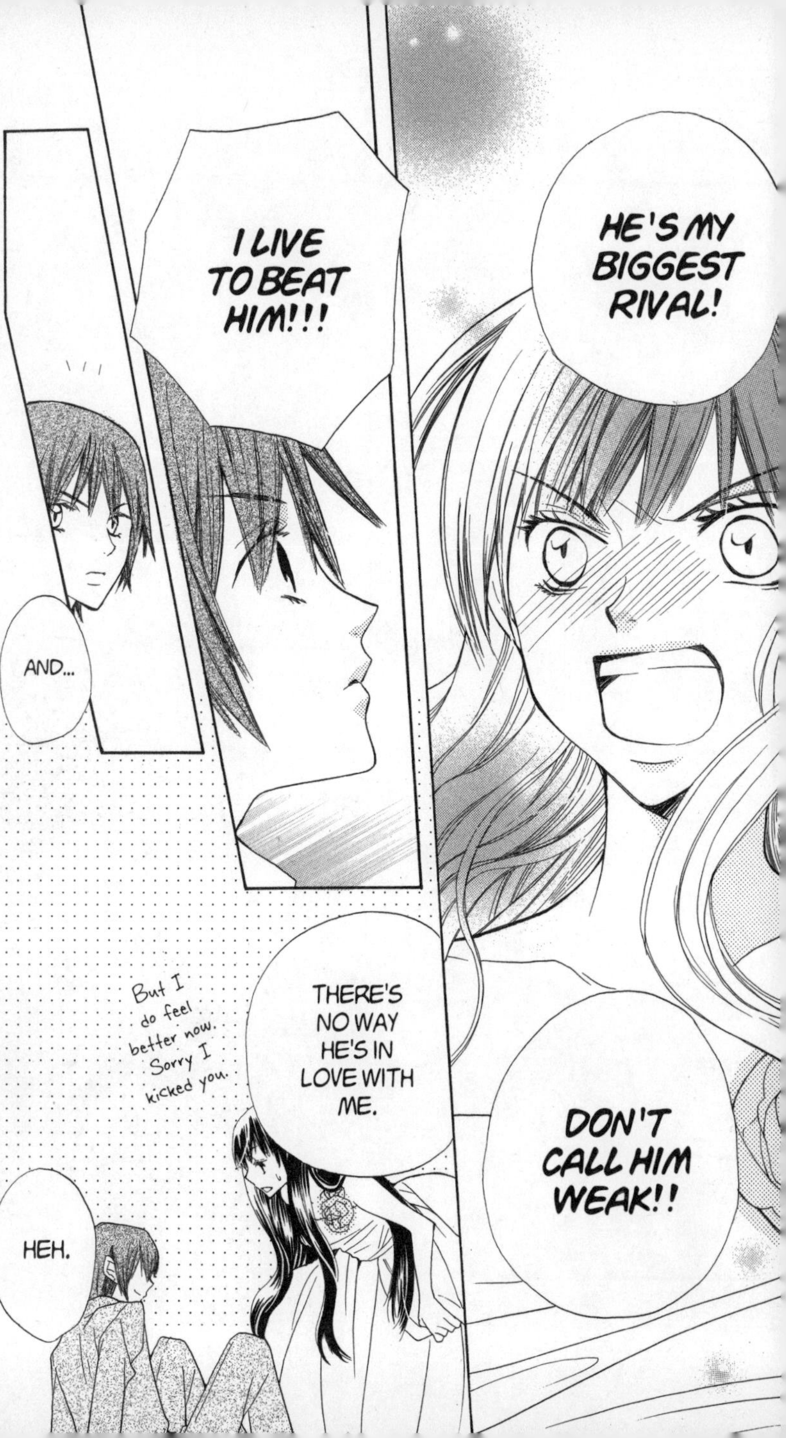
HE'S MY BIGGEST RIVAL!
DON'T CALL HIM WEAK!!
I LIVE TO BEAT HIM!!!
AND...
THERE'S NO WAY HE'S IN LOVE WITH ME.
But I do feel better now. Sorry I kicked you.
HEH.

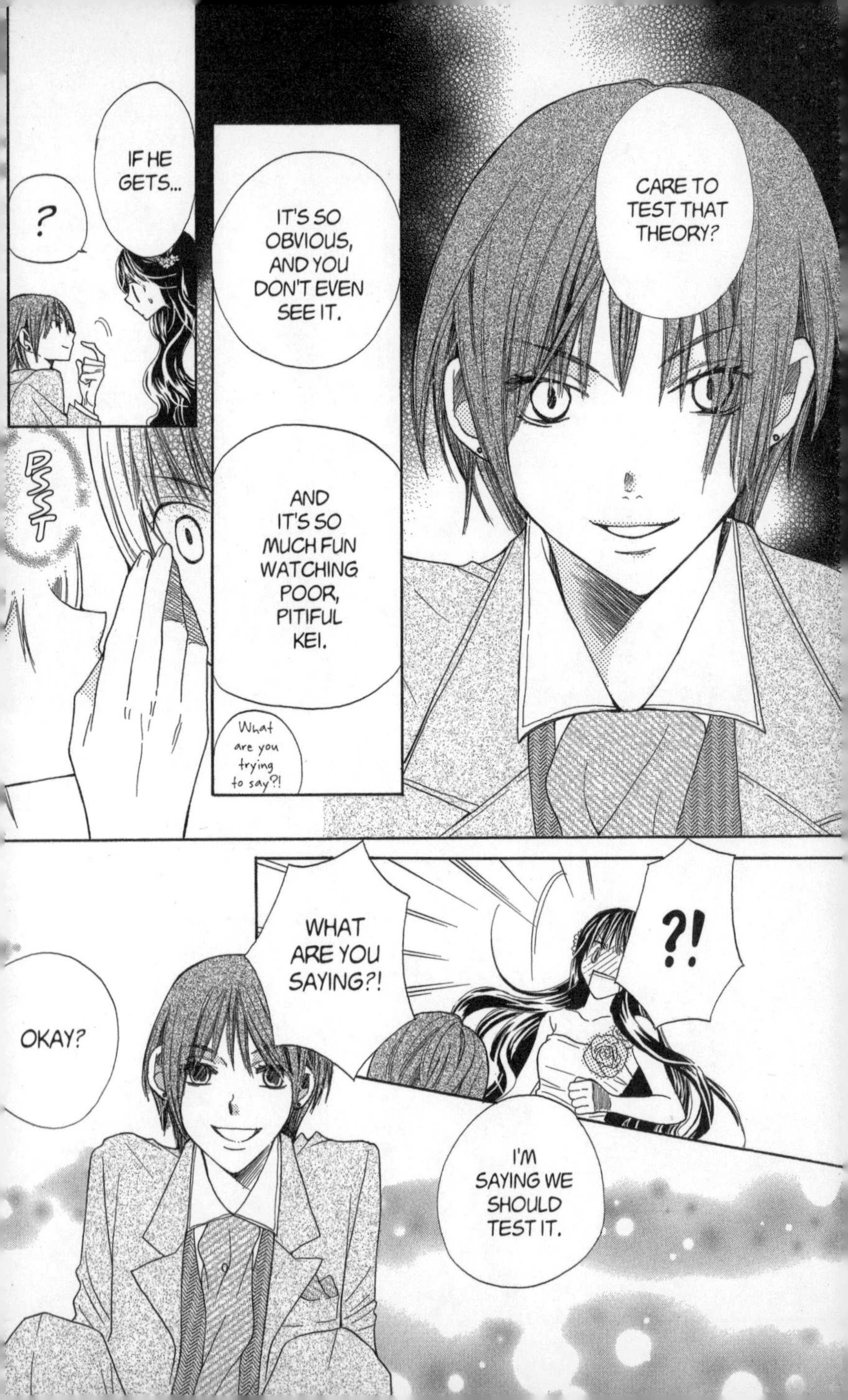
CARE TO TEST THAT THEORY?
IT'S SO OBVIOUS, AND YOU DON'T EVEN SEE IT.
AND IT'S SO MUCH FUN WATCHING POOR, PITIFUL KEI.
What are you trying to say?!
IF HE GETS...
?
PSST
?!
WHAT ARE YOU SAYING?!
I'M SAYING WE SHOULD TEST IT.
OKAY?

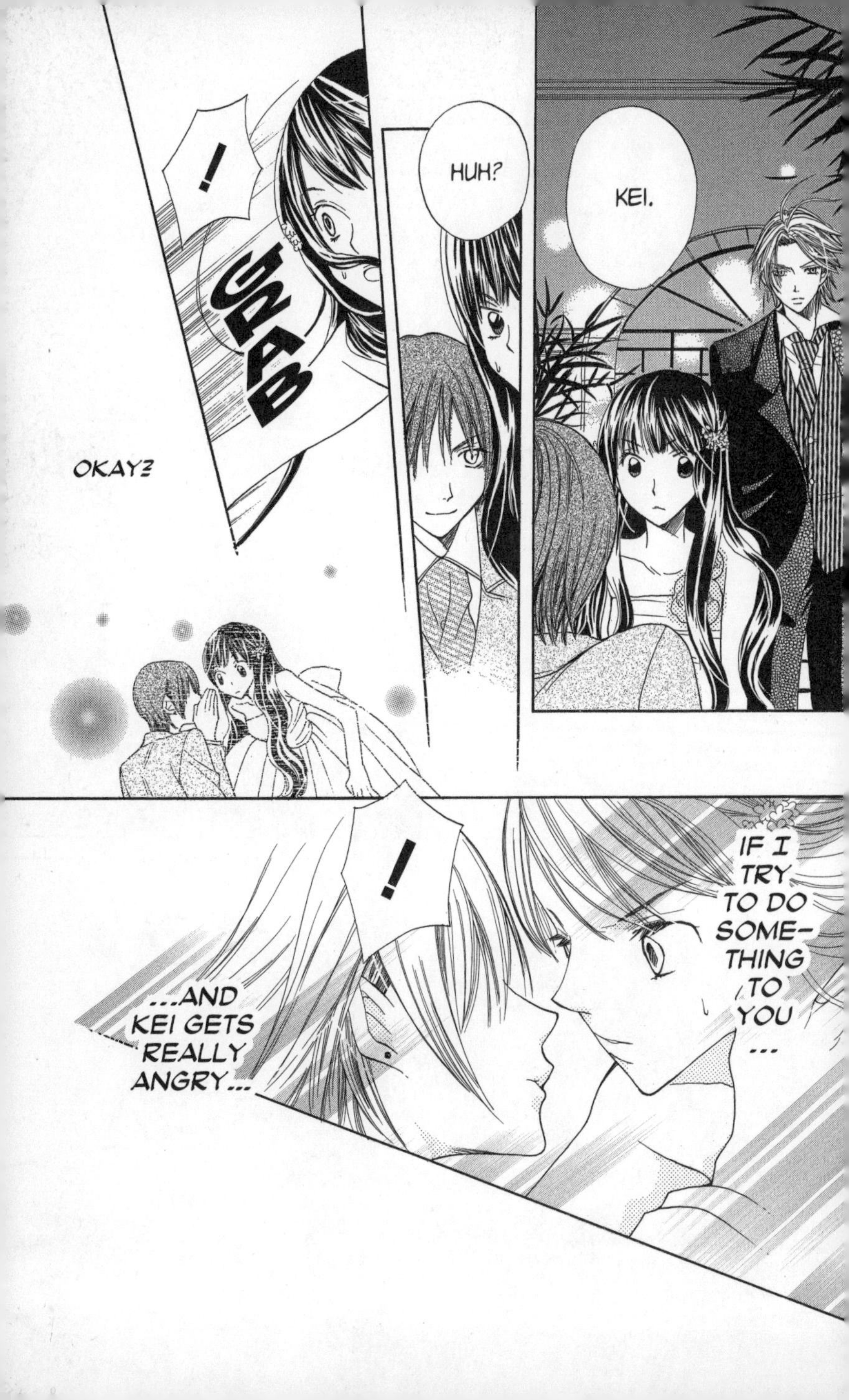
KEI.
HUH?
!
GRAB
OKAY?
IF I TRY TO DO SOME-THING TO YOU...
!
...AND KEI GETS REALLY ANGRY...

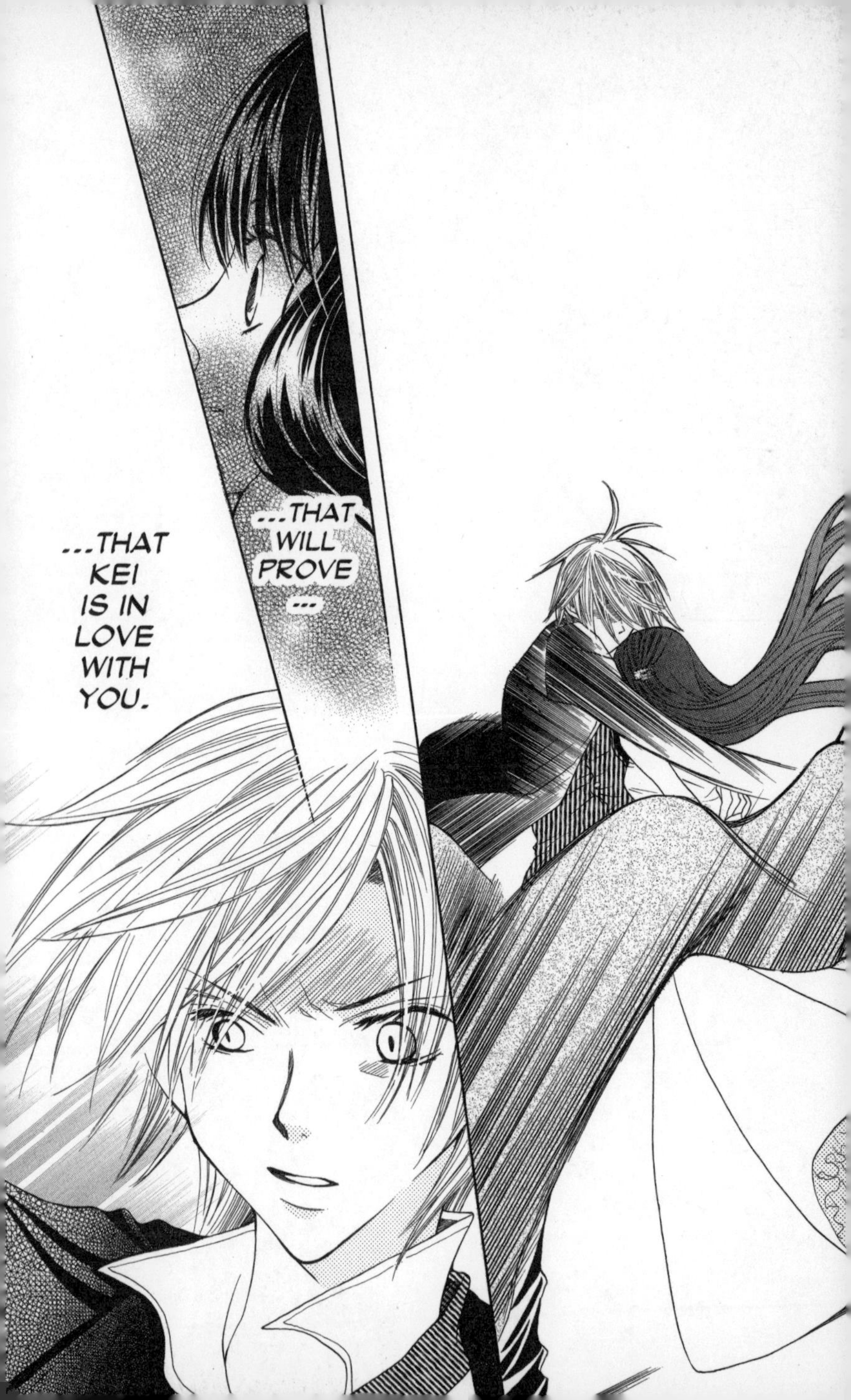
...THAT WILL PROVE ---
...THAT KEI IS IN LOVE WITH YOU.

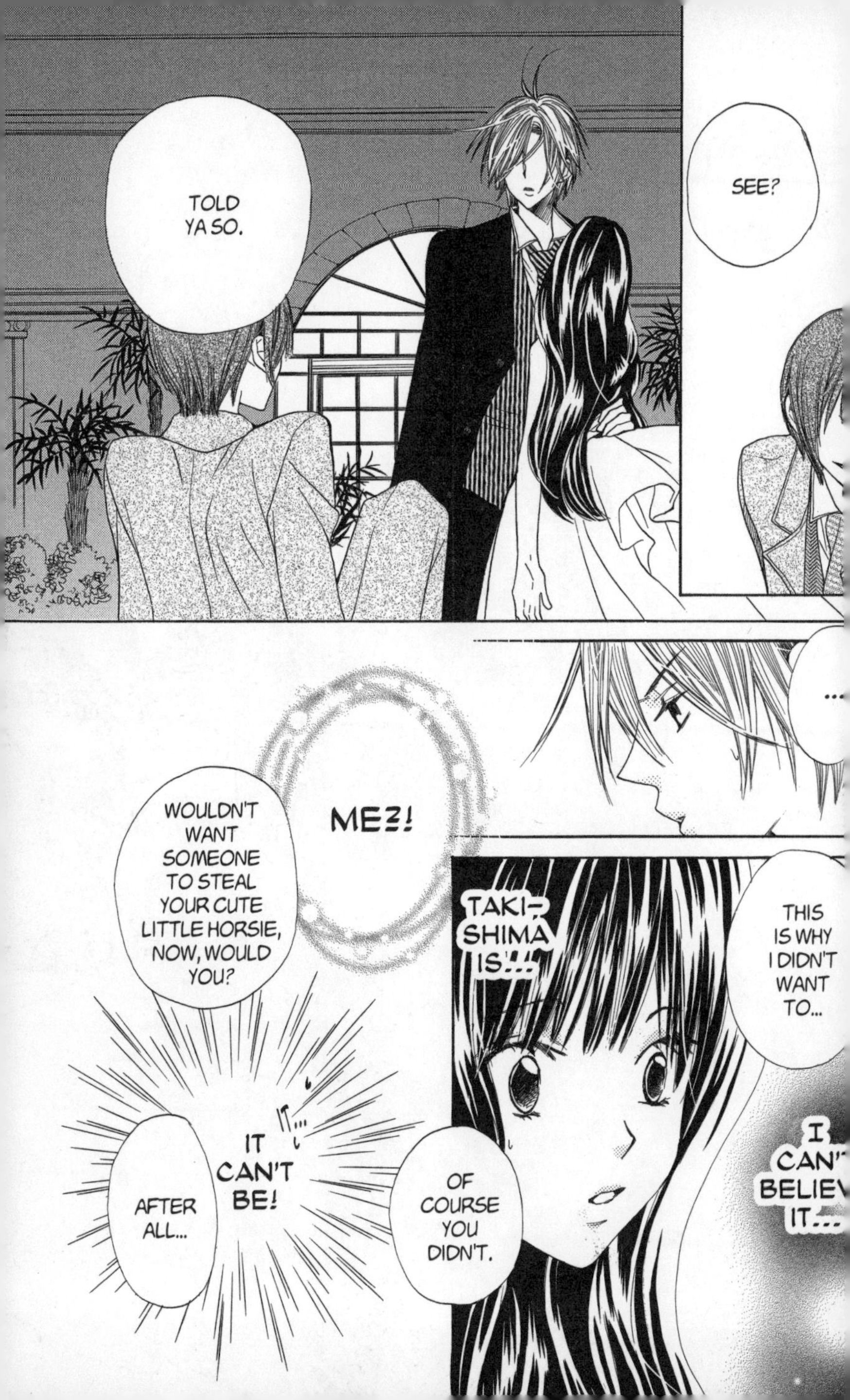
SEE?
TOLD YA SO.
...
ME?!
WOULDN'T WANT SOMEONE TO STEAL YOUR CUTE LITTLE HORSIE, NOW, WOULD YOU?
THIS IS WHY I DIDN'T WANT TO...
TAKI-SHIMA IS...
I CAN'T BELIEVE IT...
OF COURSE YOU DIDN'T.
IT...
IT CAN'T BE!
AFTER ALL...

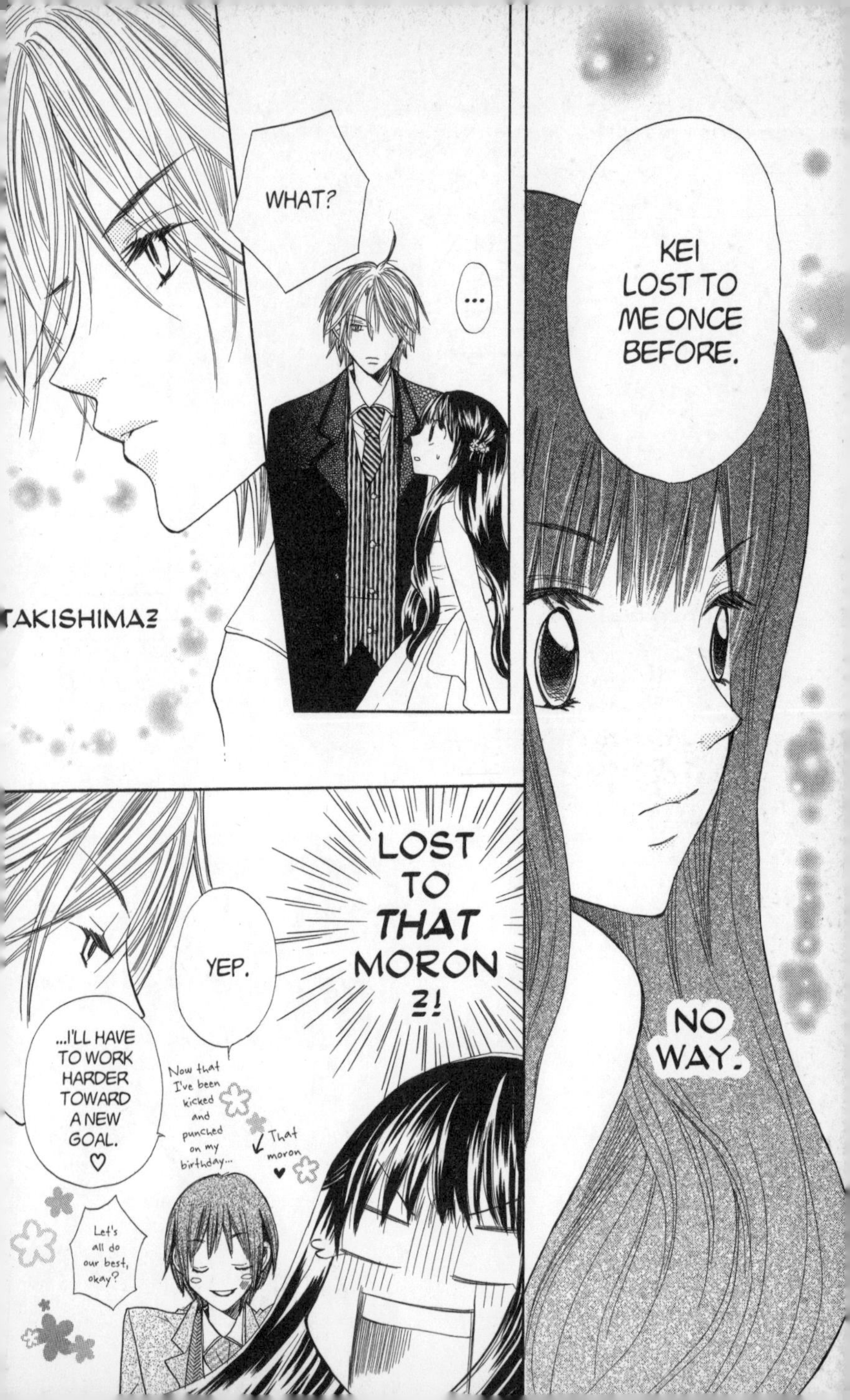
KEI LOST TO ME ONCE BEFORE.
NO WAY.
WHAT?
...
TAKISHIMA?
LOST TO THAT MORON?!
YEP.
...I'LL HAVE TO WORK HARDER TOWARD A NEW GOAL. ♡
Now that I've been kicked and punched on my birthday...
That moron ♥
Let's all do our best, okay?

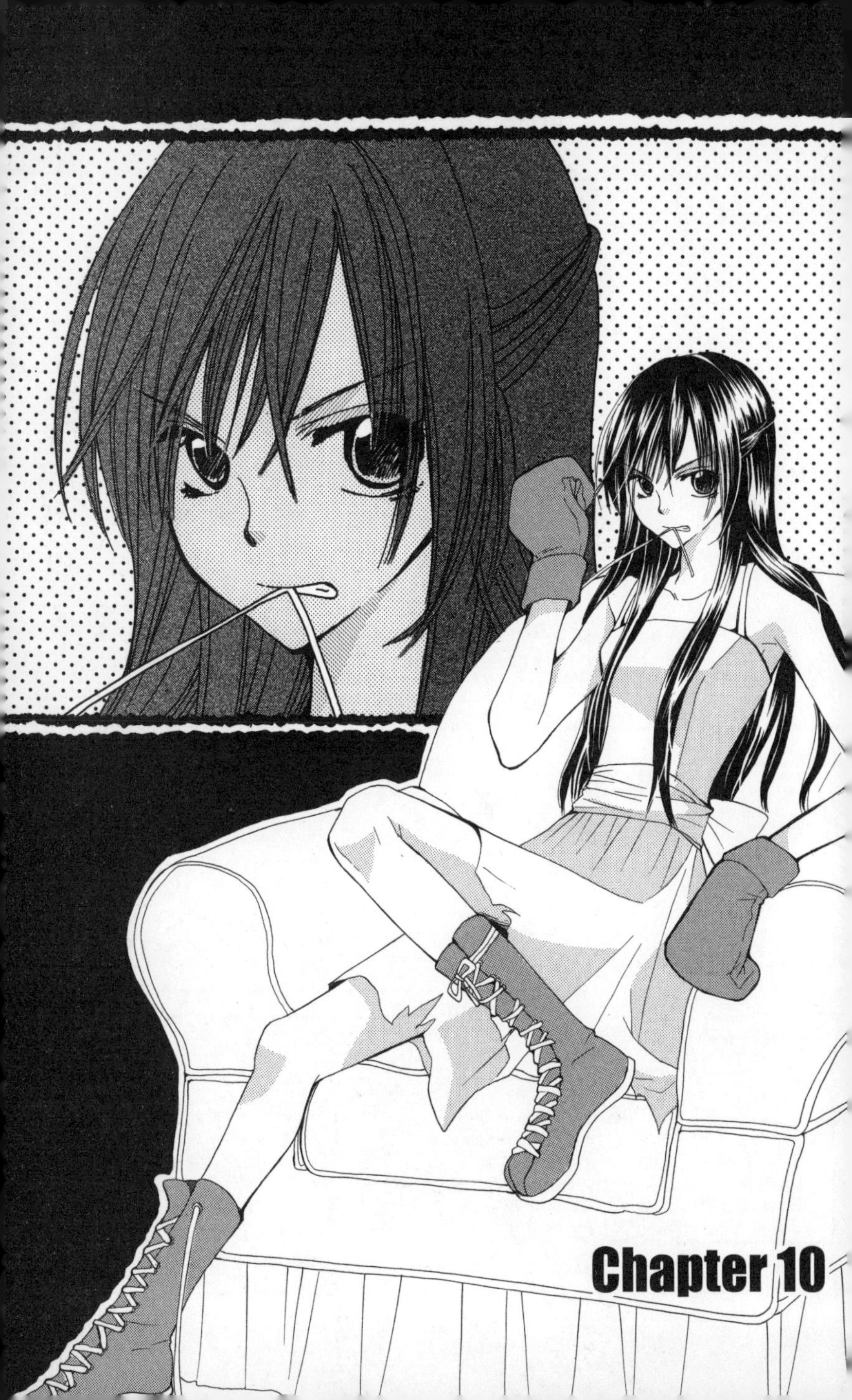
Chapter 10

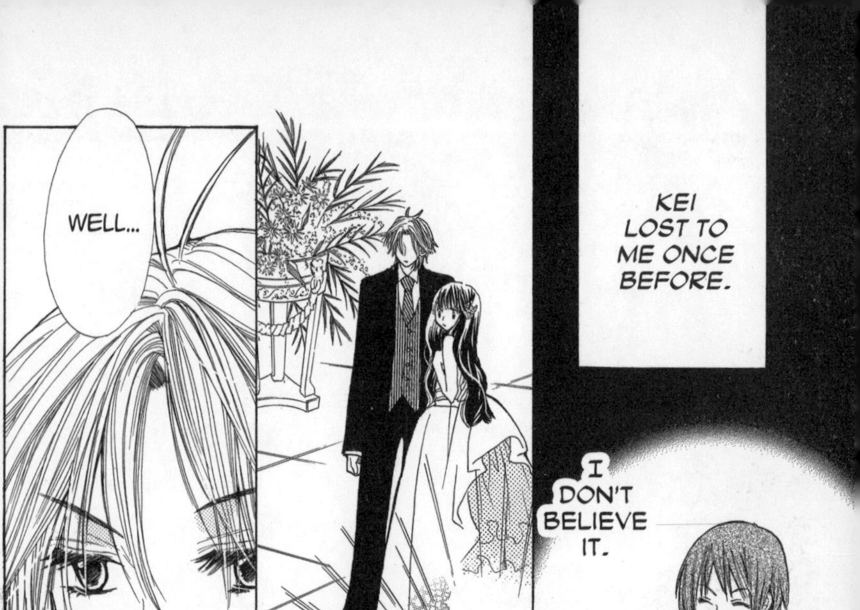
KEI LOST TO ME ONCE BEFORE.
I DON'T BELIEVE IT.
TAKI-SHIMA LOST TO THIS GUY?!
WELL...

• THIS AND THAT •

THANK YOU FOR READING SA!
I WROTE ANOTHER BONUS MANGA FOR THE END OF THIS VOLUME. PLEASE, READ IT IF YOU WANT TO.

Hup!
It's about...well... nonsense. Sorry.

BUT I HOPE YOU LIKE IT AS WELL AS THE MAIN BOOK! BY THE WAY, TADASHI AND AKIRA ARE ON THE COVER OF THIS VOLUME. I LIKE DRAWING THEM. WELL, UNTIL NEXT TIME!

sigh sigh

I HOPE TO SEE YOU AGAIN!!

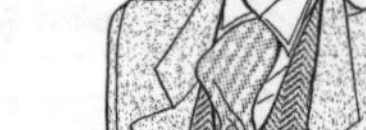
E

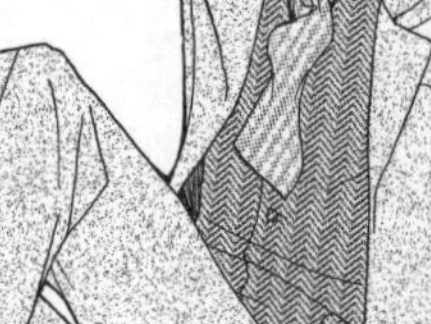
Please feel free to laugh at her.

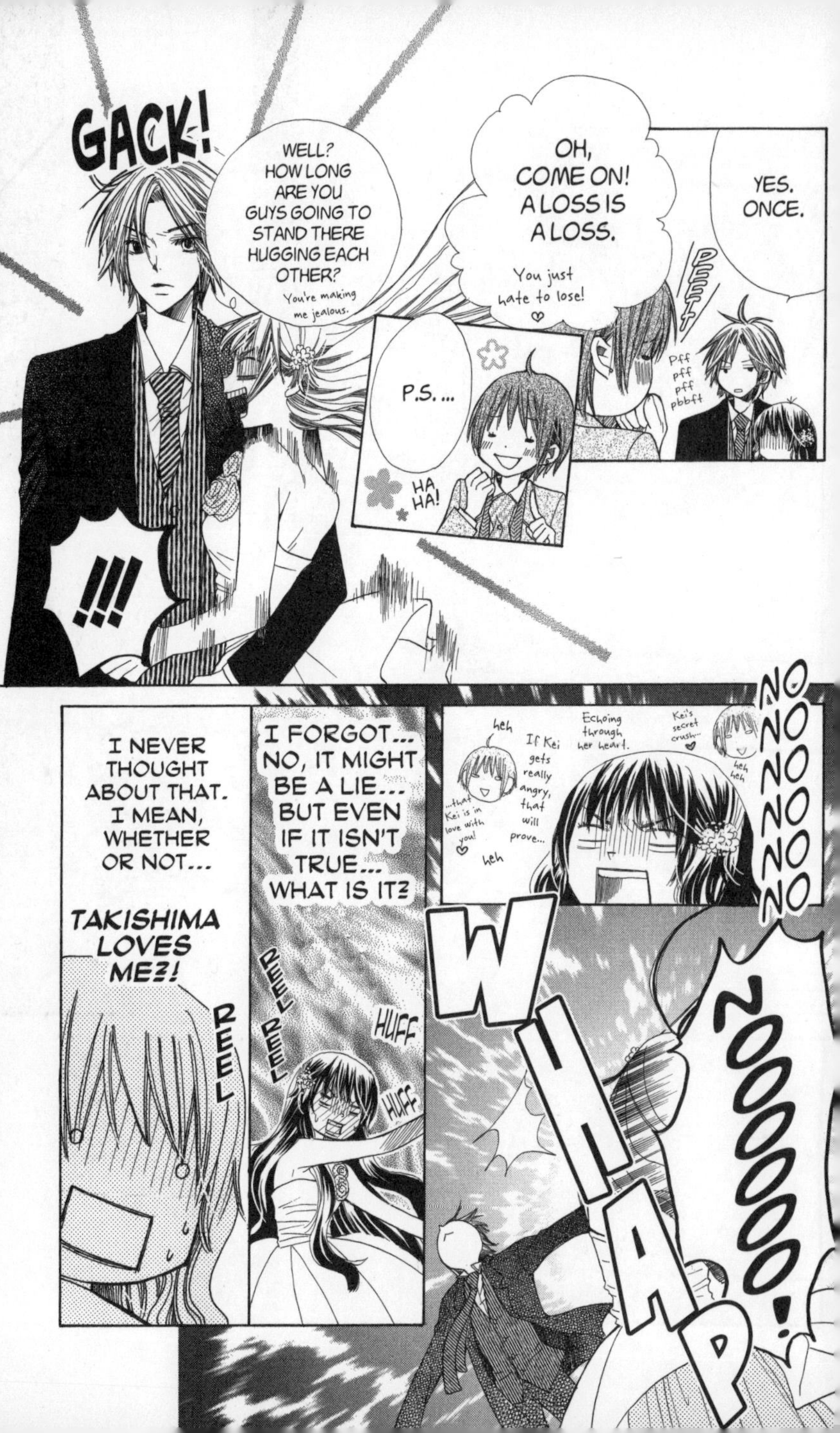
YES. ONCE.
PFFFT
Pff pff pff pbbft
OH, COME ON! A LOSS IS A LOSS.
You just hate to lose! ♥
P.S. ...
HA HA!
GACK!
WELL? HOW LONG ARE YOU GUYS GOING TO STAND THERE HUGGING EACH OTHER?
You're making me jealous.
!!!!
NONONONONONO
Kei's secret crush...
heh heh
Echoing through her heart.
If Kei gets really angry, that will prove...
heh
...that Kei is in love with you! ♥
heh
WHAP
NOOOOOO!
I FORGOT... NO, IT MIGHT BE A LIE... BUT EVEN IF IT ISN'T TRUE... WHAT IS IT?
REEL REEL
HUFF
HUFF
I NEVER THOUGHT ABOUT THAT. I MEAN, WHETHER OR NOT...
TAKISHIMA LOVES ME?!
REEL

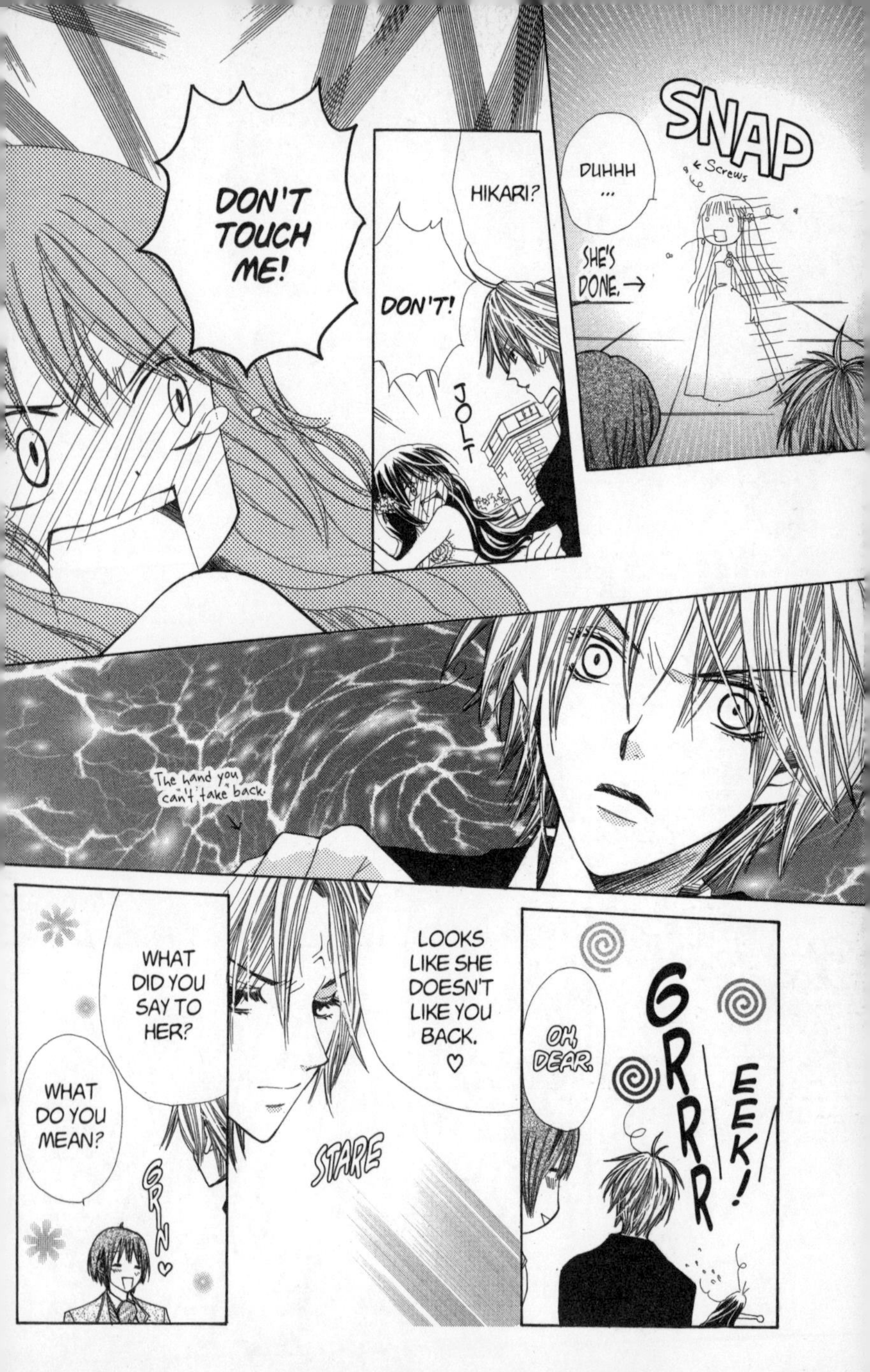
SNAP
← Screws
DUHHH ...
SHE'S DONE. →
HIKARI?
DON'T!
JOLT
DON'T TOUCH ME!
The hand you can't take back.
GRRR
EEK!
OH, DEAR.
LOOKS LIKE SHE DOESN'T LIKE YOU BACK. ♡
STARE
WHAT DID YOU SAY TO HER?
WHAT DO YOU MEAN?
GRIN ♡

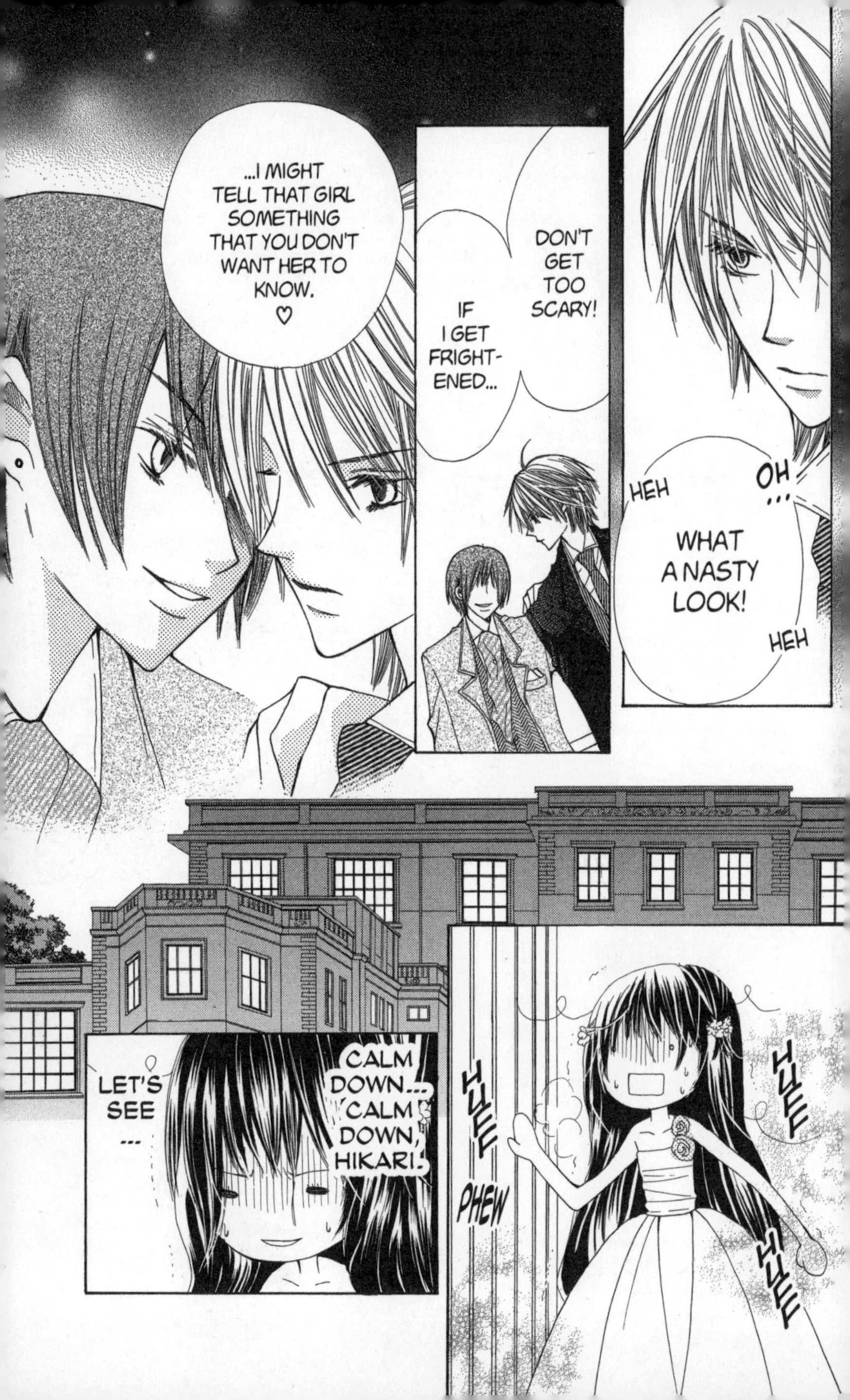
OH...
HEH
WHAT A NASTY LOOK!
HEH
DON'T GET TOO SCARY!
IF I GET FRIGHTENED...
...I MIGHT TELL THAT GIRL SOMETHING THAT YOU DON'T WANT HER TO KNOW. ♡
HUFF
HUFF
HUFF
PHEW
CALM DOWN... CALM DOWN, HIKARI.
LET'S SEE ...

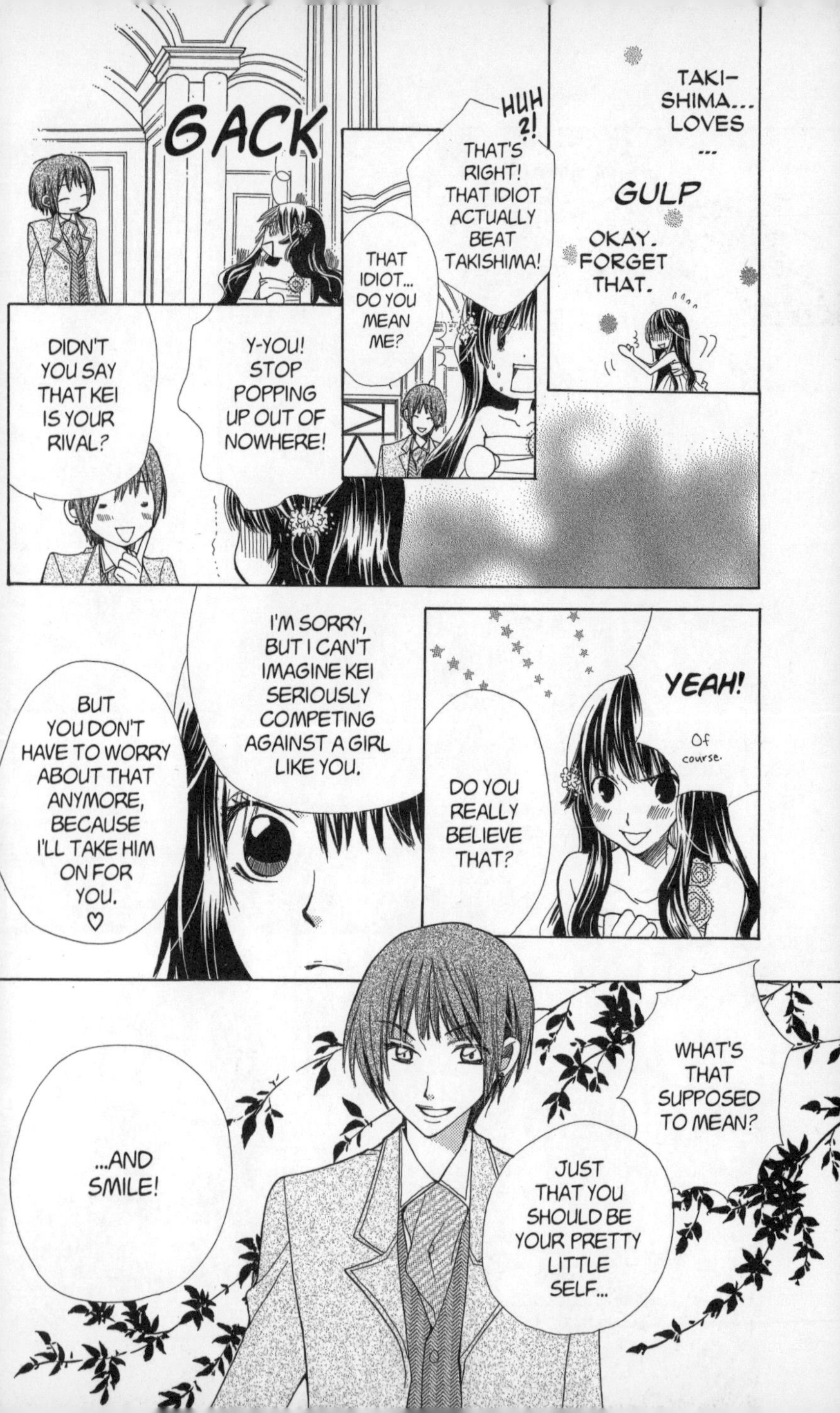
TAKI-SHIMA... LOVES ...
GULP
OKAY. FORGET THAT.
HUH ?!
THAT'S RIGHT! THAT IDIOT ACTUALLY BEAT TAKISHIMA!
THAT IDIOT... DO YOU MEAN ME?
GACK
Y-YOU! STOP POPPING UP OUT OF NOWHERE!
DIDN'T YOU SAY THAT KEI IS YOUR RIVAL?
YEAH!
Of course.
DO YOU REALLY BELIEVE THAT?
I'M SORRY, BUT I CAN'T IMAGINE KEI SERIOUSLY COMPETING AGAINST A GIRL LIKE YOU.
BUT YOU DON'T HAVE TO WORRY ABOUT THAT ANYMORE, BECAUSE I'LL TAKE HIM ON FOR YOU. ♡
WHAT'S THAT SUPPOSED TO MEAN?
JUST THAT YOU SHOULD BE YOUR PRETTY LITTLE SELF...
...AND SMILE!

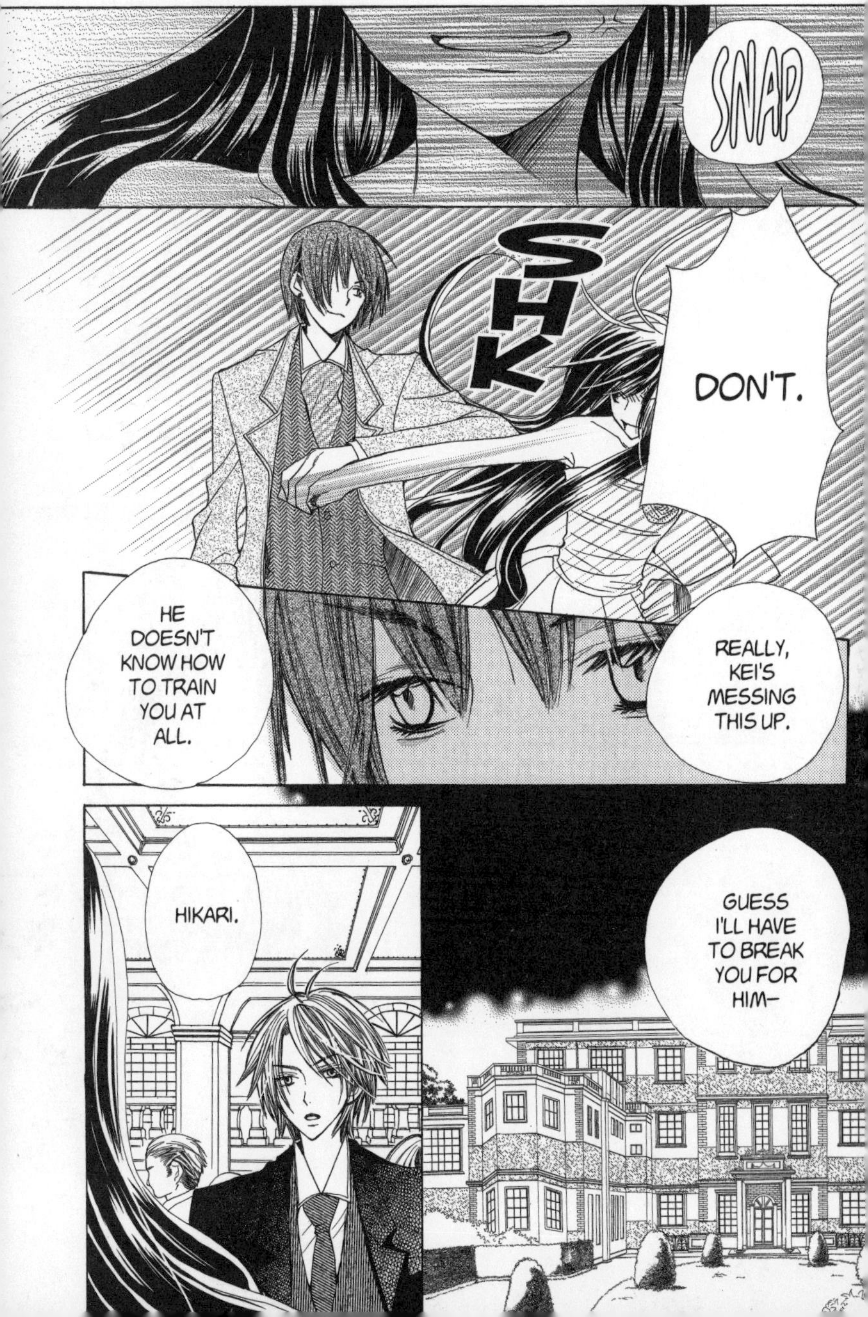
SNAP
DON'T.
SHK
REALLY, KEI'S MESSING THIS UP.
HE DOESN'T KNOW HOW TO TRAIN YOU AT ALL.
GUESS I'LL HAVE TO BREAK YOU FOR HIM—
HIKARI.

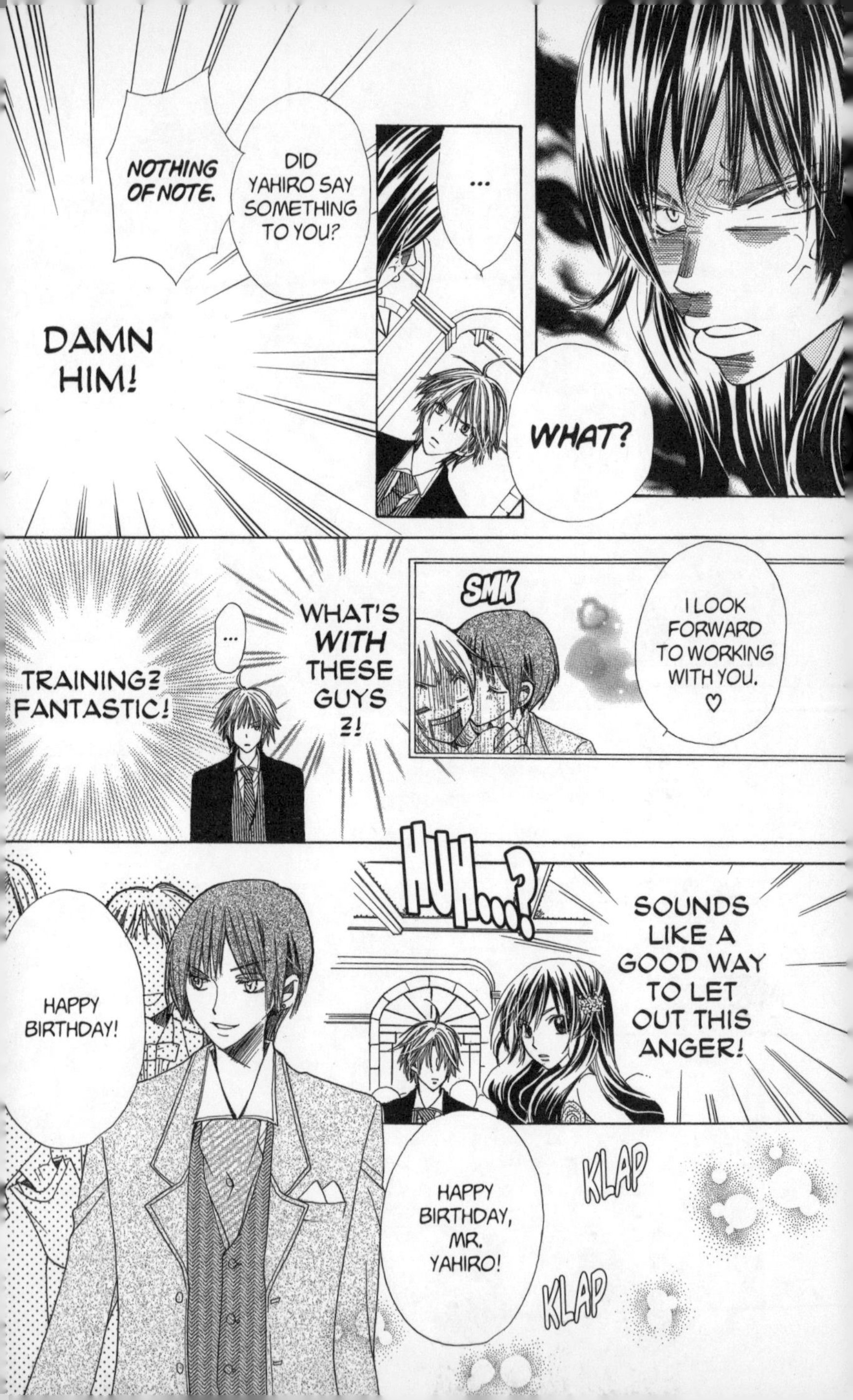
WHAT?
...
DID YAHIRO SAY SOMETHING TO YOU?
NOTHING OF NOTE.
DAMN HIM!
SMK
I LOOK FORWARD TO WORKING WITH YOU. ♡
WHAT'S WITH THESE GUYS?!
...
TRAINING? FANTASTIC!
HUH...?!
SOUNDS LIKE A GOOD WAY TO LET OUT THIS ANGER!
KLAP
KLAP
HAPPY BIRTHDAY, MR. YAHIRO!
HAPPY BIRTHDAY!

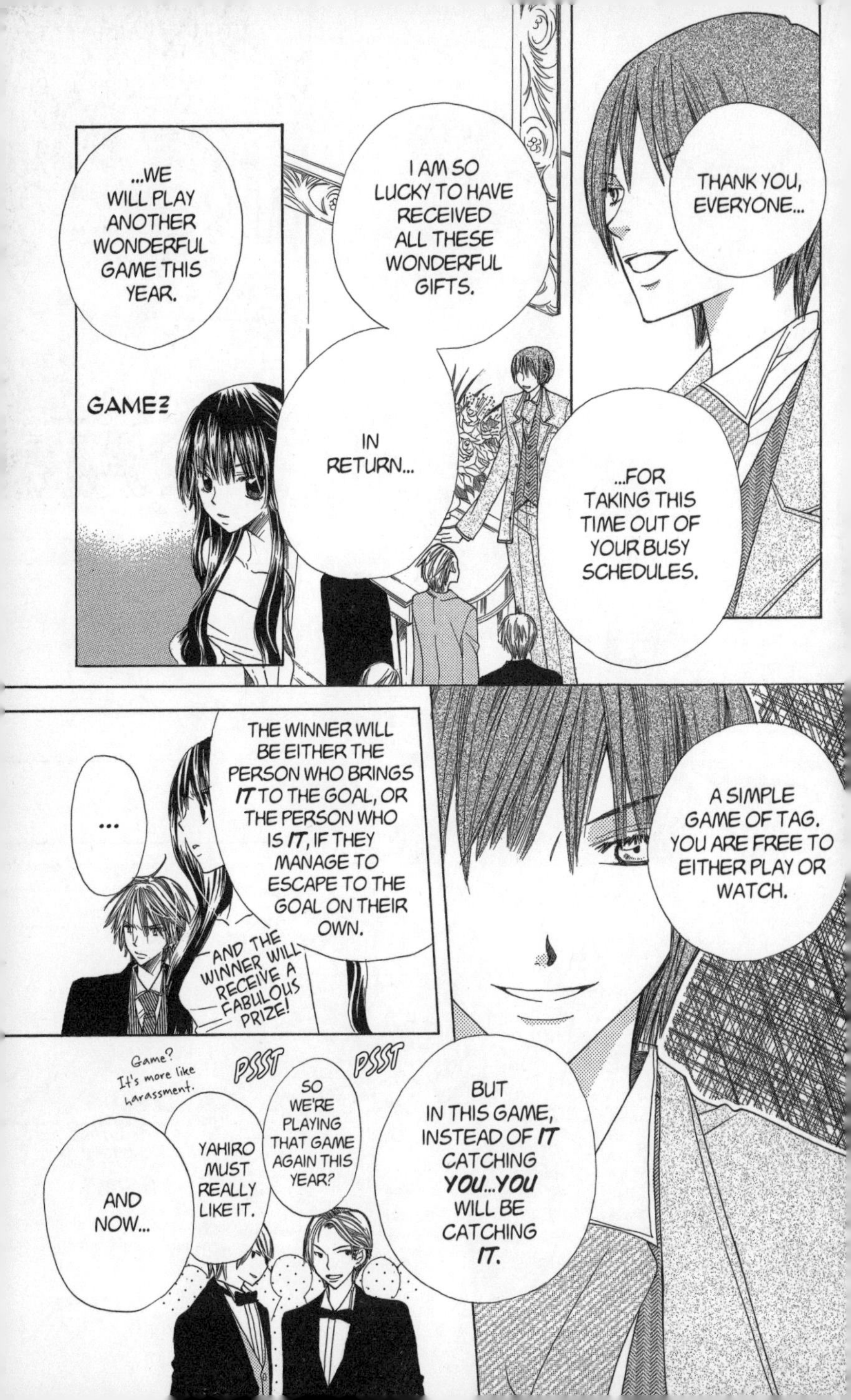
THANK YOU, EVERYONE...
...FOR TAKING THIS TIME OUT OF YOUR BUSY SCHEDULES.
I AM SO LUCKY TO HAVE RECEIVED ALL THESE WONDERFUL GIFTS.
IN RETURN...
...WE WILL PLAY ANOTHER WONDERFUL GAME THIS YEAR.
GAME?
A SIMPLE GAME OF TAG. YOU ARE FREE TO EITHER PLAY OR WATCH.
BUT IN THIS GAME, INSTEAD OF *IT* CATCHING *YOU*...*YOU* WILL BE CATCHING *IT*.
THE WINNER WILL BE EITHER THE PERSON WHO BRINGS *IT* TO THE GOAL, OR THE PERSON WHO IS *IT*, IF THEY MANAGE TO ESCAPE TO THE GOAL ON THEIR OWN.
AND THE WINNER WILL RECEIVE A FABULOUS PRIZE!
...
PSSST
PSSST
SO WE'RE PLAYING THAT GAME AGAIN THIS YEAR?
YAHIRO MUST REALLY LIKE IT.
Game? It's more like harassment.
AND NOW...

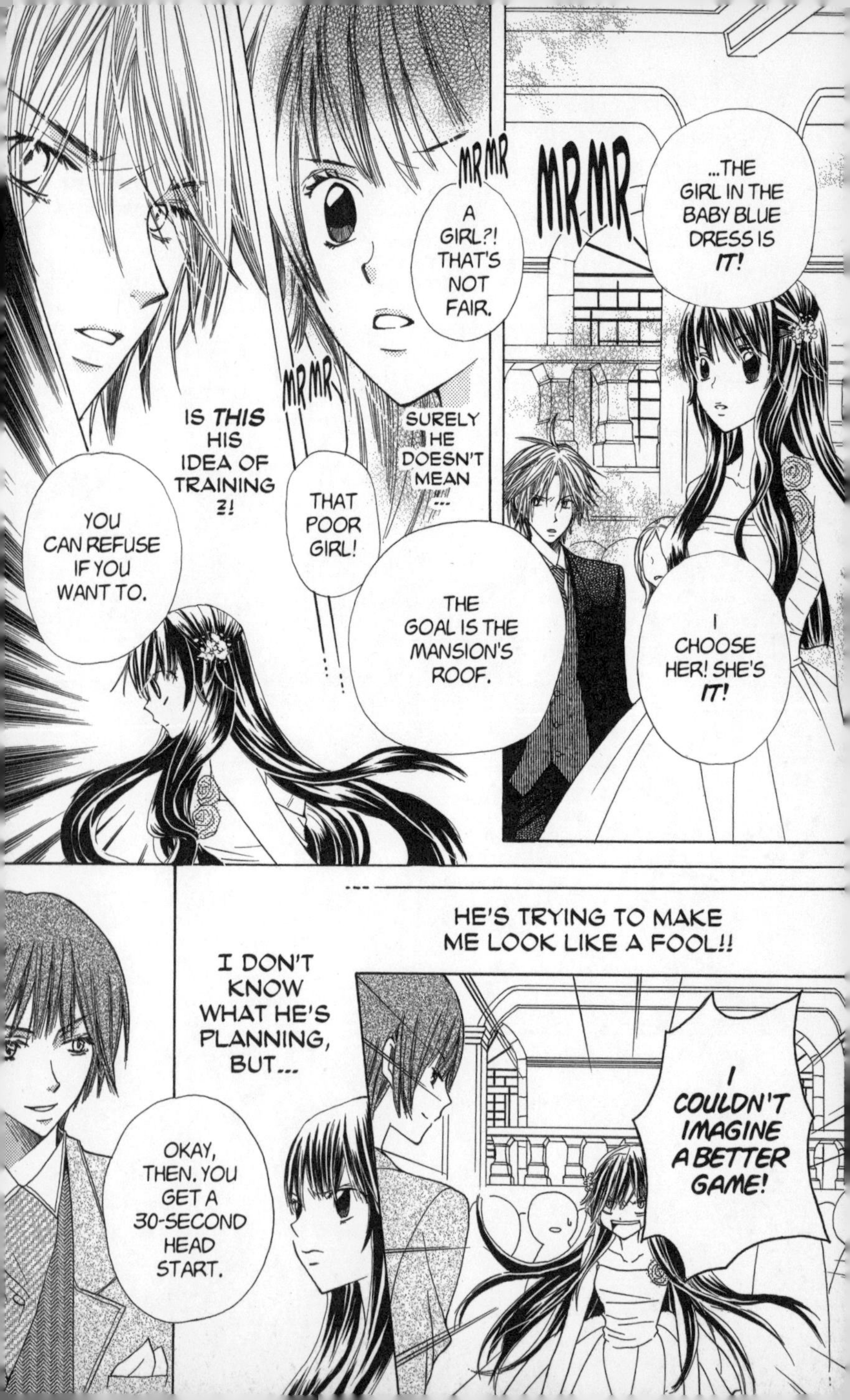
...THE GIRL IN THE BABY BLUE DRESS IS IT!
MRMR
I CHOOSE HER! SHE'S IT!
MRMR
A GIRL?! THAT'S NOT FAIR.
SURELY HE DOESN'T MEAN ---
THE GOAL IS THE MANSION'S ROOF.
MRMR
THAT POOR GIRL!
IS THIS HIS IDEA OF TRAINING ?!
YOU CAN REFUSE IF YOU WANT TO.
--- HE'S TRYING TO MAKE ME LOOK LIKE A FOOL!!
I COULDN'T IMAGINE A BETTER GAME!
I DON'T KNOW WHAT HE'S PLANNING, BUT...
OKAY, THEN. YOU GET A 30-SECOND HEAD START.

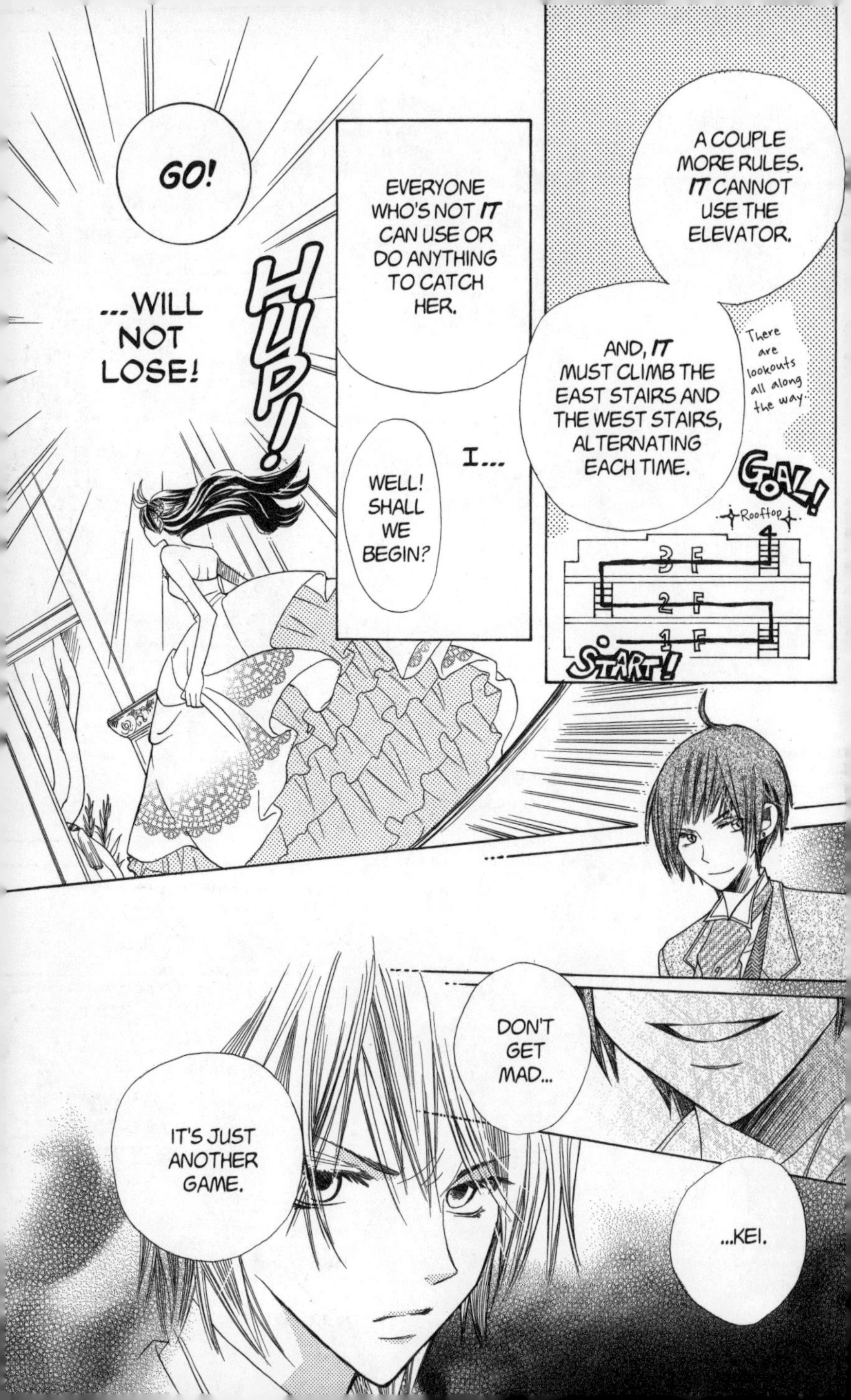
A COUPLE MORE RULES. IT CANNOT USE THE ELEVATOR.
AND, IT MUST CLIMB THE EAST STAIRS AND THE WEST STAIRS, ALTERNATING EACH TIME.
There are lookouts all along the way...
GOAL!
Rooftop
3F
2F
1F
START!
EVERYONE WHO'S NOT IT CAN USE OR DO ANYTHING TO CATCH HER.
I...
WELL! SHALL WE BEGIN?
GO!
HUP!
...WILL NOT LOSE!
...
DON'T GET MAD...
...KEI.
IT'S JUST ANOTHER GAME.

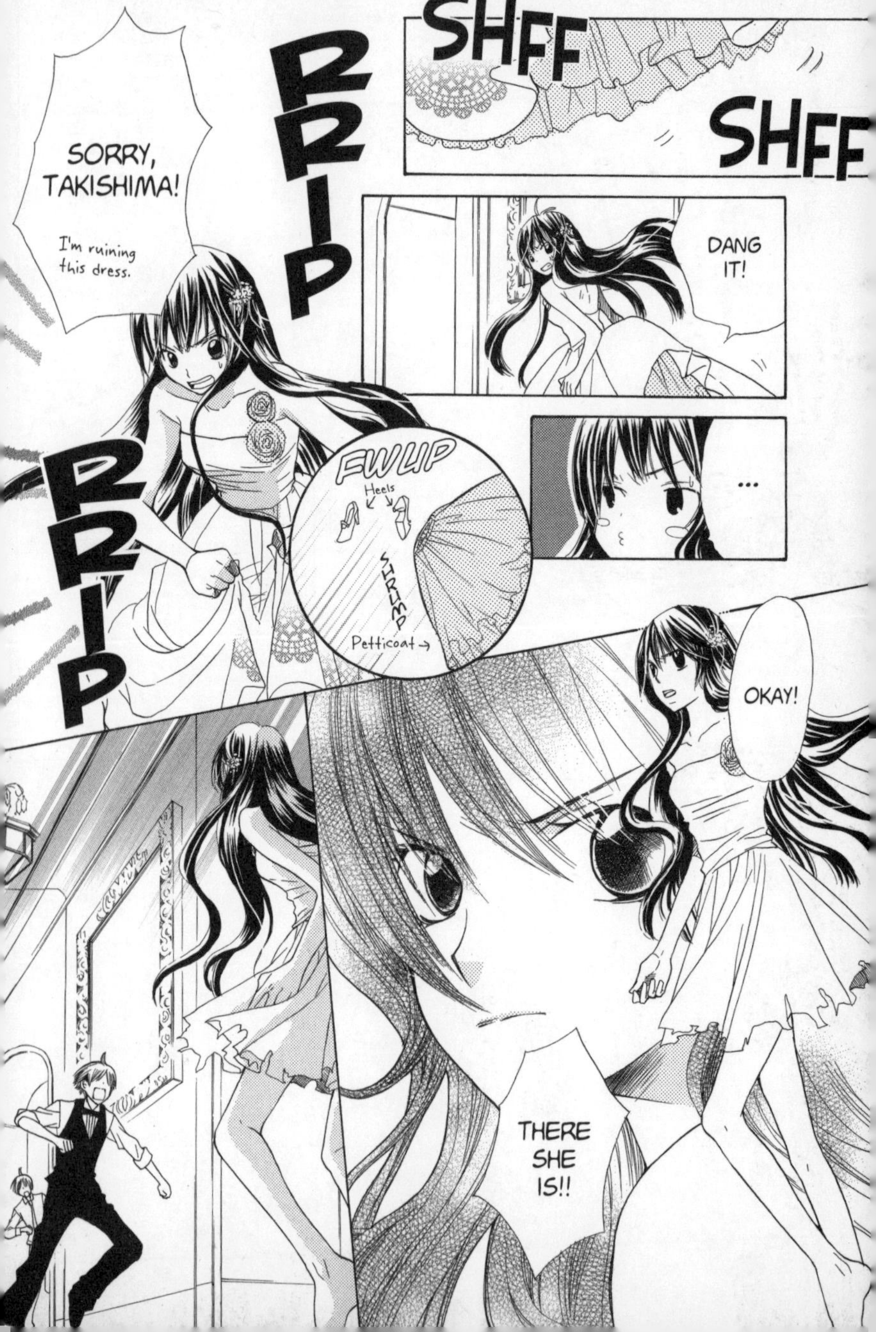
SHFF
SHFF
DANG IT!
...
SORRY, TAKISHIMA!
I'm ruining this dress.
RRIP
RRIP
FWUP
Heels
SHRUMP
Petticoat
OKAY!
THERE SHE IS!!

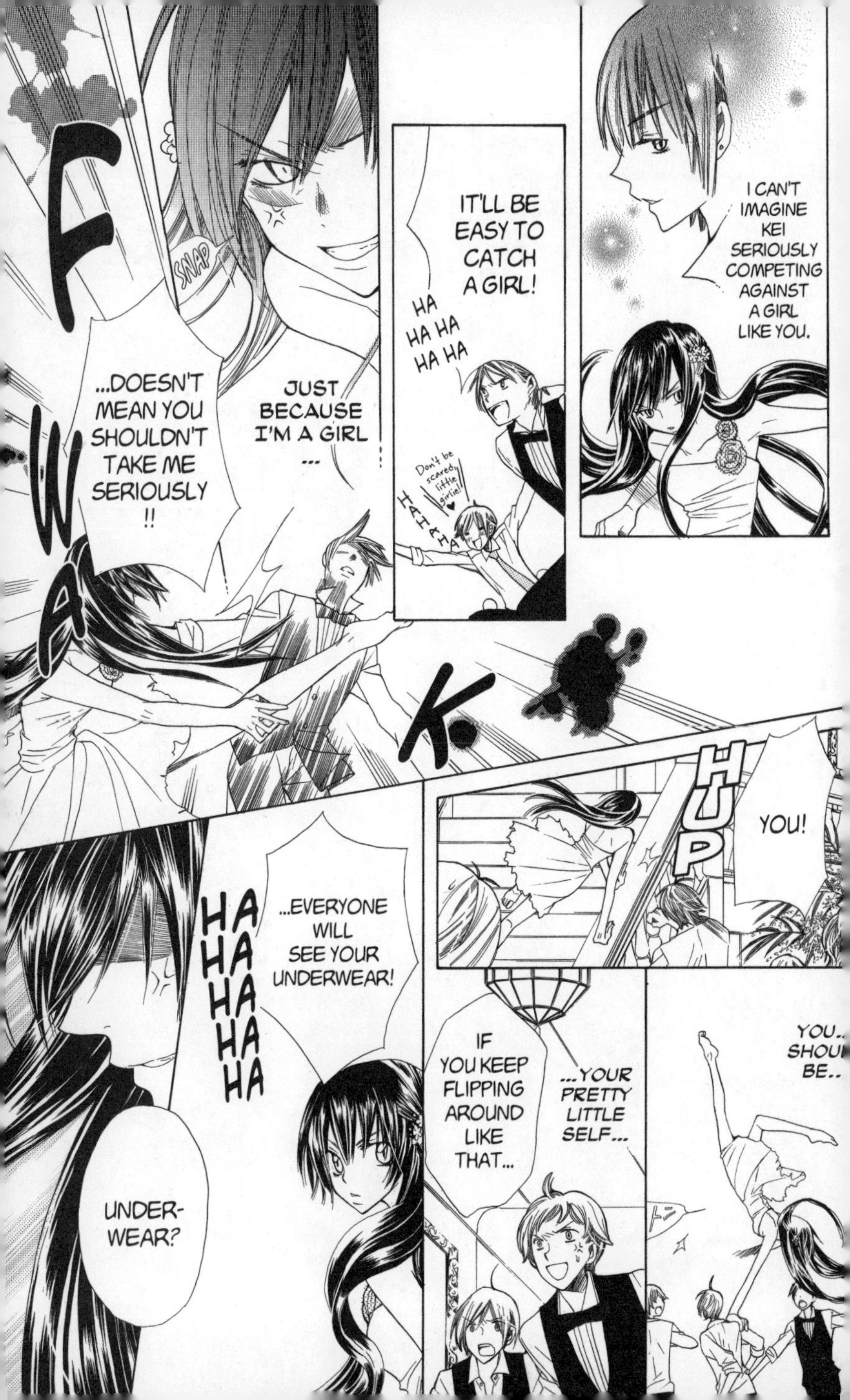
I CAN'T IMAGINE KEI SERIOUSLY COMPETING AGAINST A GIRL LIKE YOU.
IT'LL BE EASY TO CATCH A GIRL!
HA HA HA HA HA
Don't be scared, little girlie!♥
HA HA HA
JUST BECAUSE I'M A GIRL ---
...DOESN'T MEAN YOU SHOULDN'T TAKE ME SERIOUSLY !!
SNAP
FWAK.
YOU!
HUP
YOU.. SHOU BE..
IF YOU KEEP FLIPPING AROUND LIKE THAT...
...YOUR PRETTY LITTLE SELF...
...EVERYONE WILL SEE YOUR UNDERWEAR!
HAHAHAHAHA
HAHAHAHAHA
UNDER-WEAR?

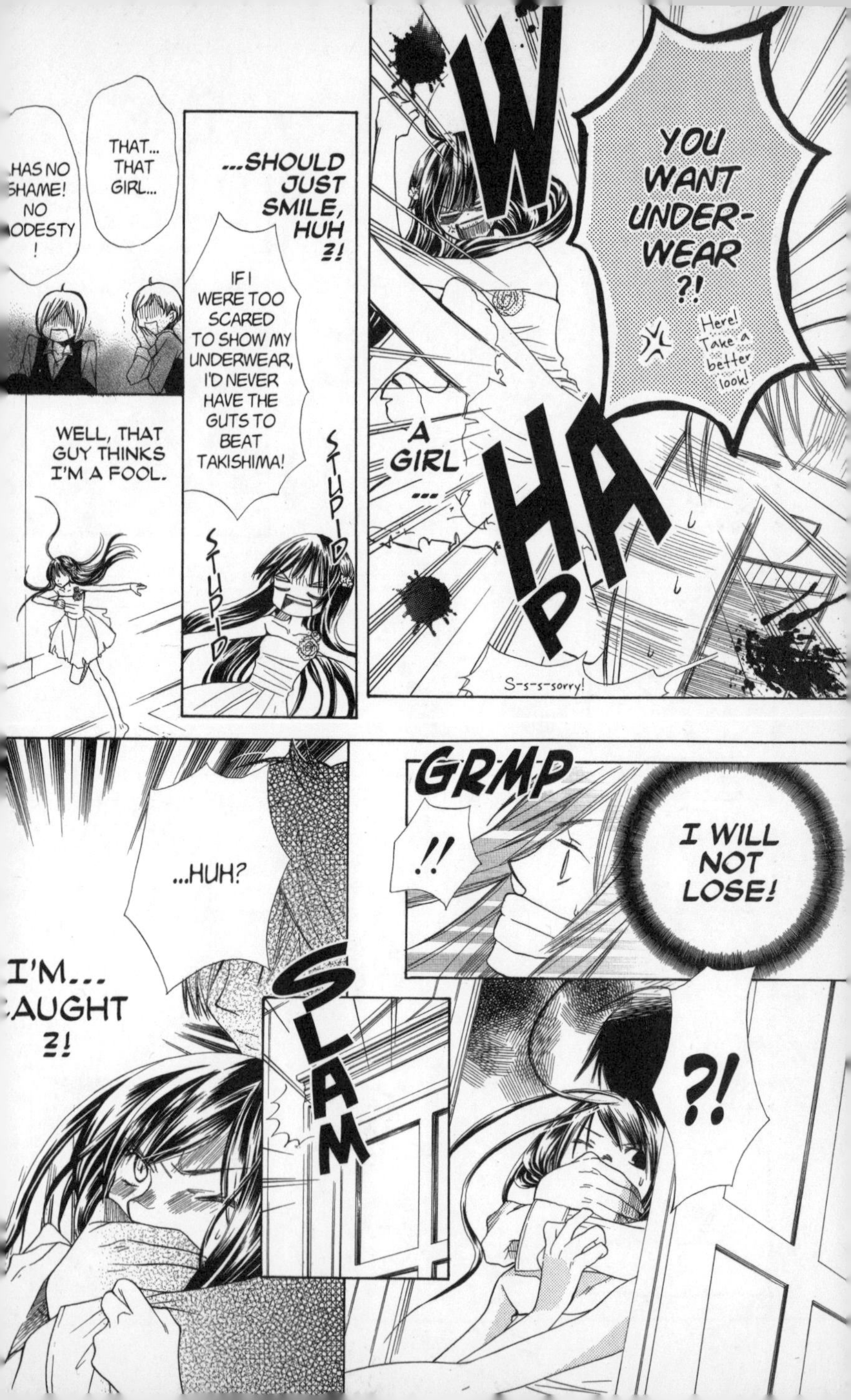
YOU WANT UNDER-WEAR?!
Here! Take a better look!
W
A GIRL...
HA
P
S-s-s-sorry!
...SHOULD JUST SMILE, HUH?!
IF I WERE TOO SCARED TO SHOW MY UNDERWEAR, I'D NEVER HAVE THE GUTS TO BEAT TAKISHIMA!
STUPID
STUPID
THAT... THAT GIRL...
HAS NO SHAME! NO ODESTY!
WELL, THAT GUY THINKS I'M A FOOL.
GRMP
!!
I WILL NOT LOSE!
?!
SLAM
...HUH?
I'M... AUGHT?!

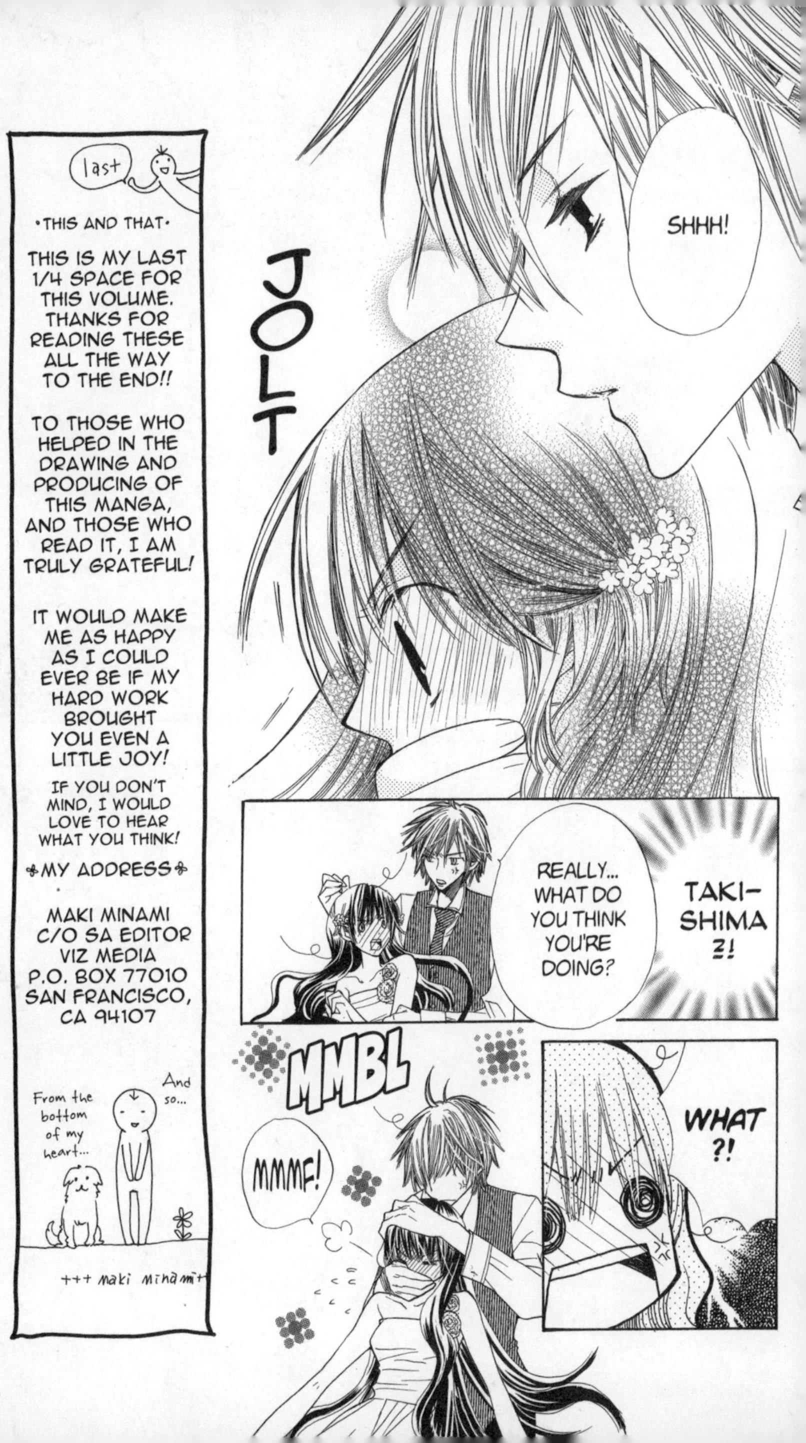
SHHH!
JOLT
TAKI-SHIMA?!
REALLY... WHAT DO YOU THINK YOU'RE DOING?
WHAT?!
MMBL
MMMF!

last

•THIS AND THAT•

THIS IS MY LAST 1/4 SPACE FOR THIS VOLUME. THANKS FOR READING THESE ALL THE WAY TO THE END!!

TO THOSE WHO HELPED IN THE DRAWING AND PRODUCING OF THIS MANGA, AND THOSE WHO READ IT, I AM TRULY GRATEFUL!

IT WOULD MAKE ME AS HAPPY AS I COULD EVER BE IF MY HARD WORK BROUGHT YOU EVEN A LITTLE JOY!

IF YOU DON'T MIND, I WOULD LOVE TO HEAR WHAT YOU THINK!

✤MY ADDRESS✤

MAKI MINAMI
C/O SA EDITOR
VIZ MEDIA
P.O. BOX 77010
SAN FRANCISCO, CA 94107

From the bottom of my heart...

And so...

+++ Maki Minami +++

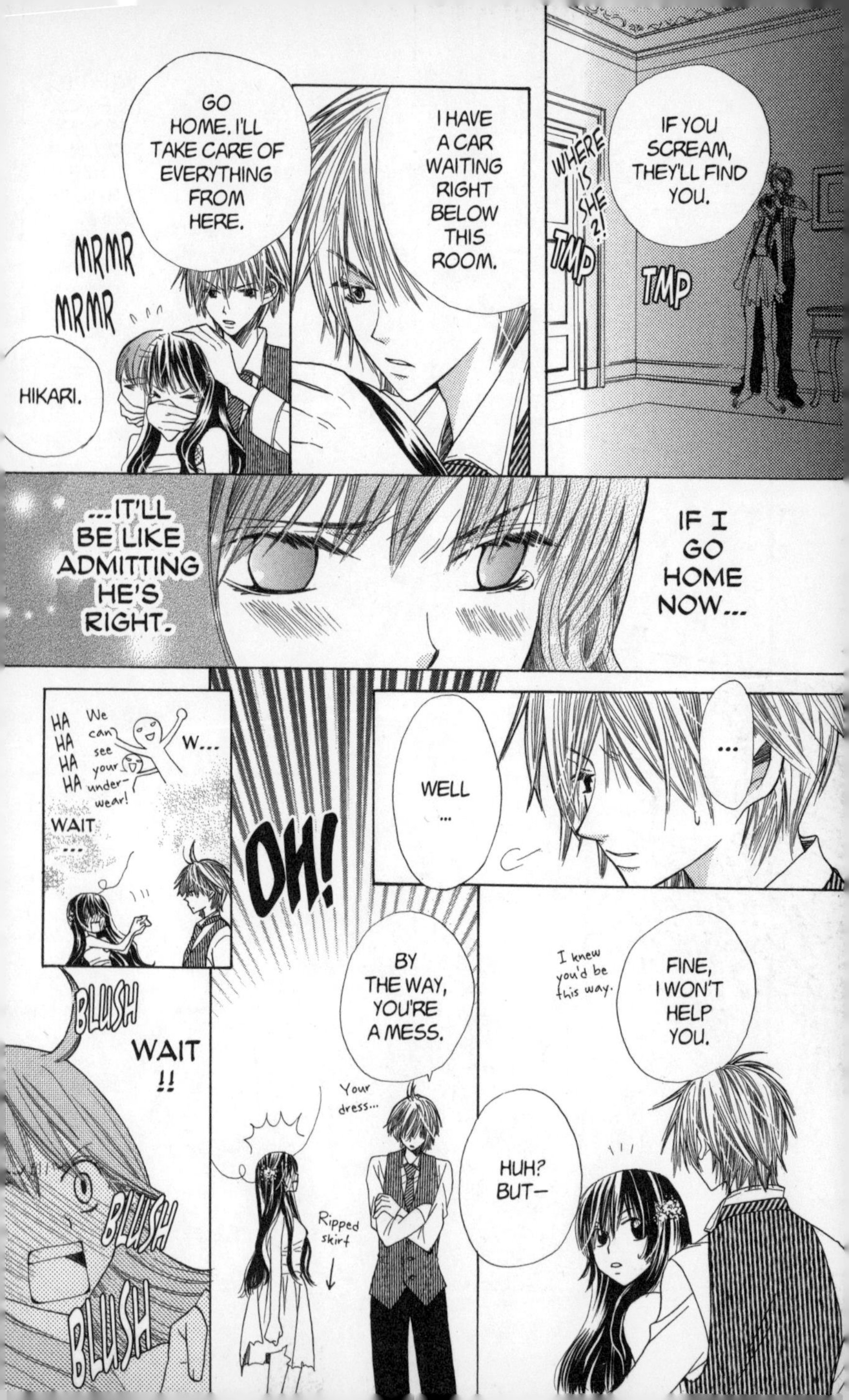
IF YOU SCREAM, THEY'LL FIND YOU.
WHERE IS SHE?!
TMP
TMP
I HAVE A CAR WAITING RIGHT BELOW THIS ROOM.
GO HOME. I'LL TAKE CARE OF EVERYTHING FROM HERE.
MRMR
MRMR
HIKARI.
IF I GO HOME NOW...
...IT'LL BE LIKE ADMITTING HE'S RIGHT.
...
WELL ...
OH!
W...
HA HA HA HA
We can see your under-wear!
WAIT ...
FINE, I WON'T HELP YOU.
I knew you'd be this way.
HUH? BUT—
BY THE WAY, YOU'RE A MESS.
Your dress...
Ripped skirt
BLUSH
WAIT !!
BLUSH
BLUSH

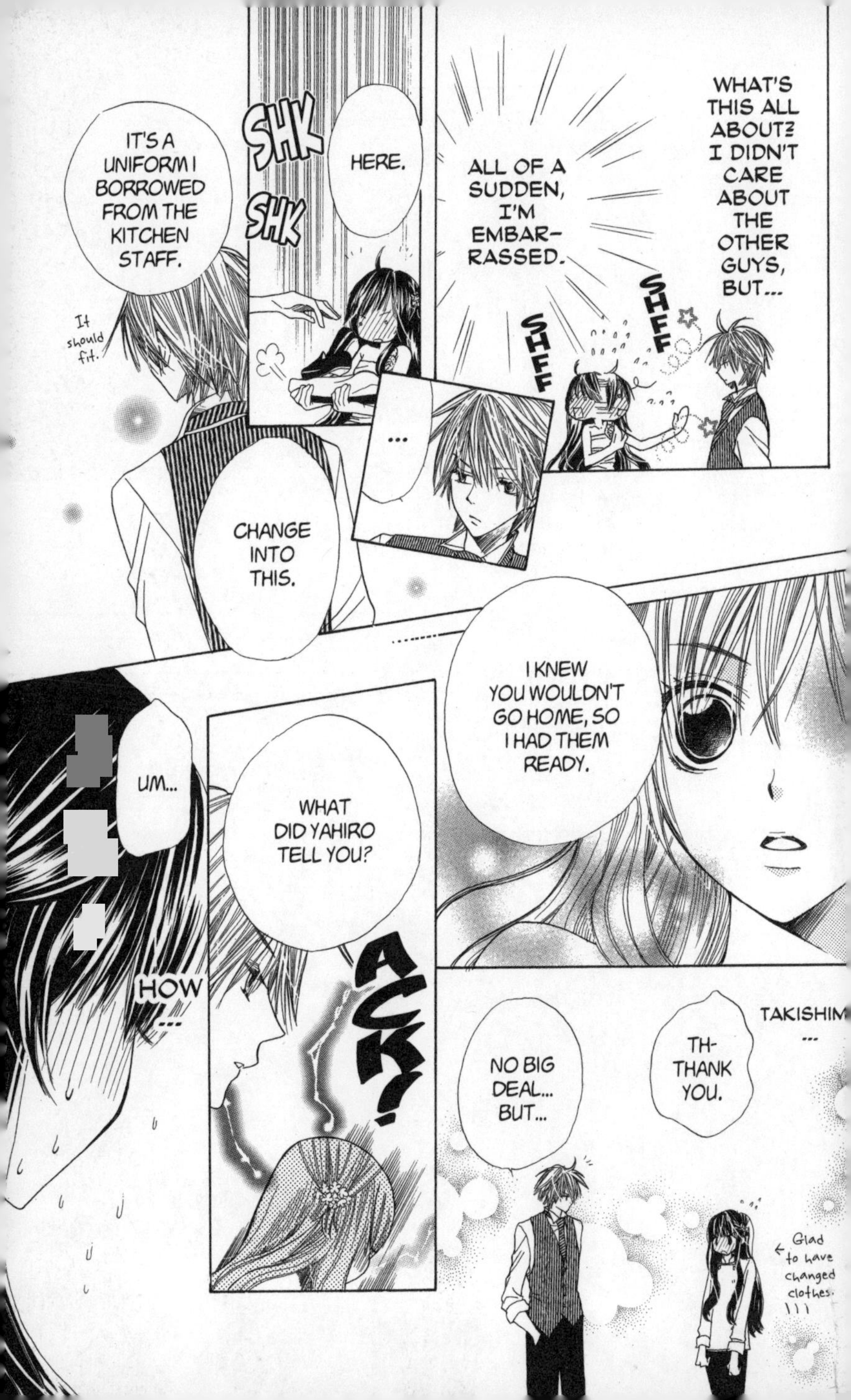
WHAT'S THIS ALL ABOUT? I DIDN'T CARE ABOUT THE OTHER GUYS, BUT...
SHFF
SHFF
ALL OF A SUDDEN, I'M EMBARRASSED.
...
HERE.
SHK
SHK
IT'S A UNIFORM I BORROWED FROM THE KITCHEN STAFF.
It should fit.
CHANGE INTO THIS.
......
I KNEW YOU WOULDN'T GO HOME, SO I HAD THEM READY.
TAKISHIM...
TH-THANK YOU.
NO BIG DEAL... BUT...
Glad to have changed clothes.
WHAT DID YAHIRO TELL YOU?
ACK!?
UM...
HOW...

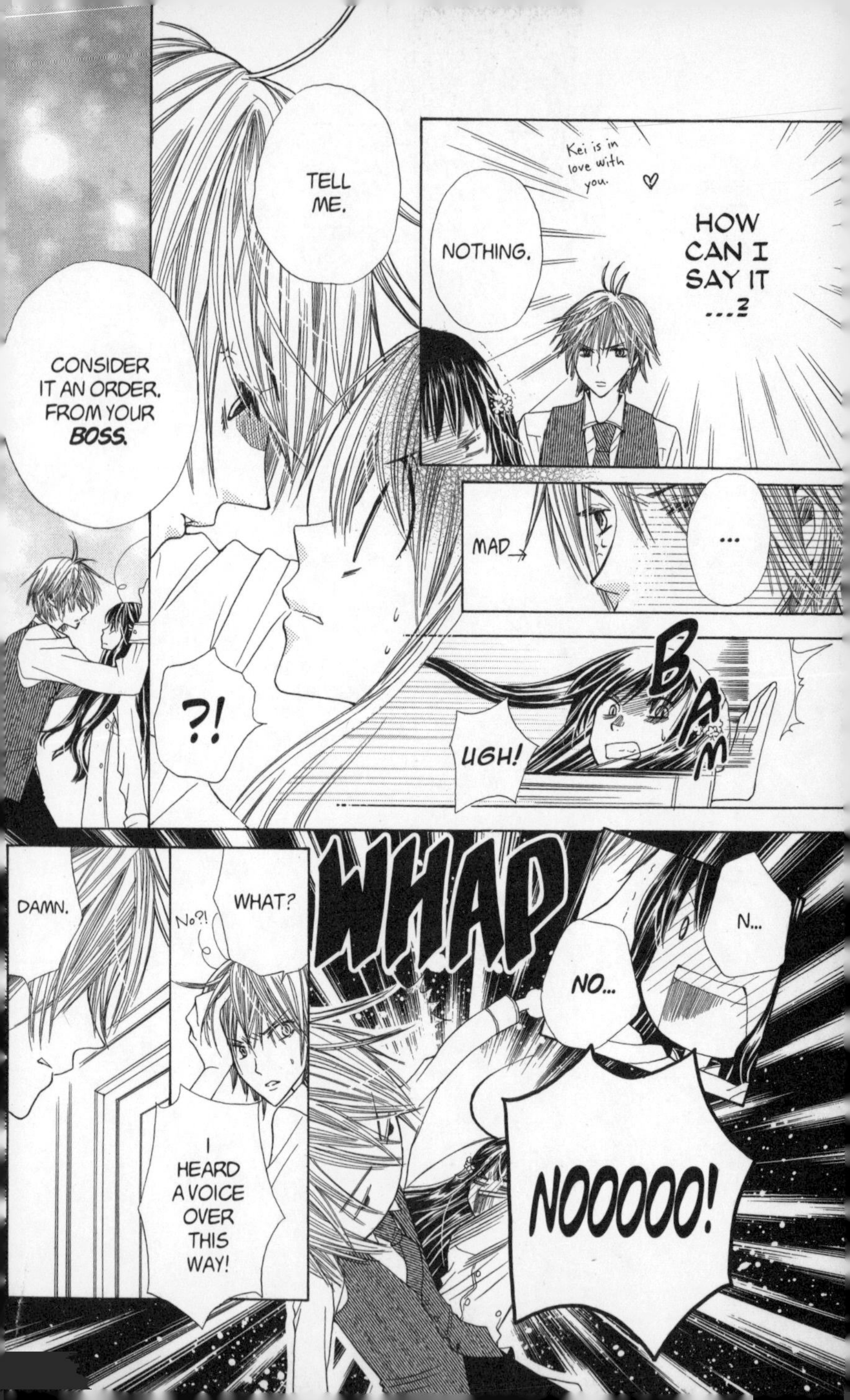
HOW CAN I SAY IT ...?
Kei is in love with you. ♥
NOTHING.
...
MAD
BAM
UGH!
TELL ME.
?!
CONSIDER IT AN ORDER. FROM YOUR BOSS.
N...
NO...
WHAP
NOOOOO!
WHAT?
No?!
I HEARD A VOICE OVER THIS WAY!
DAMN.

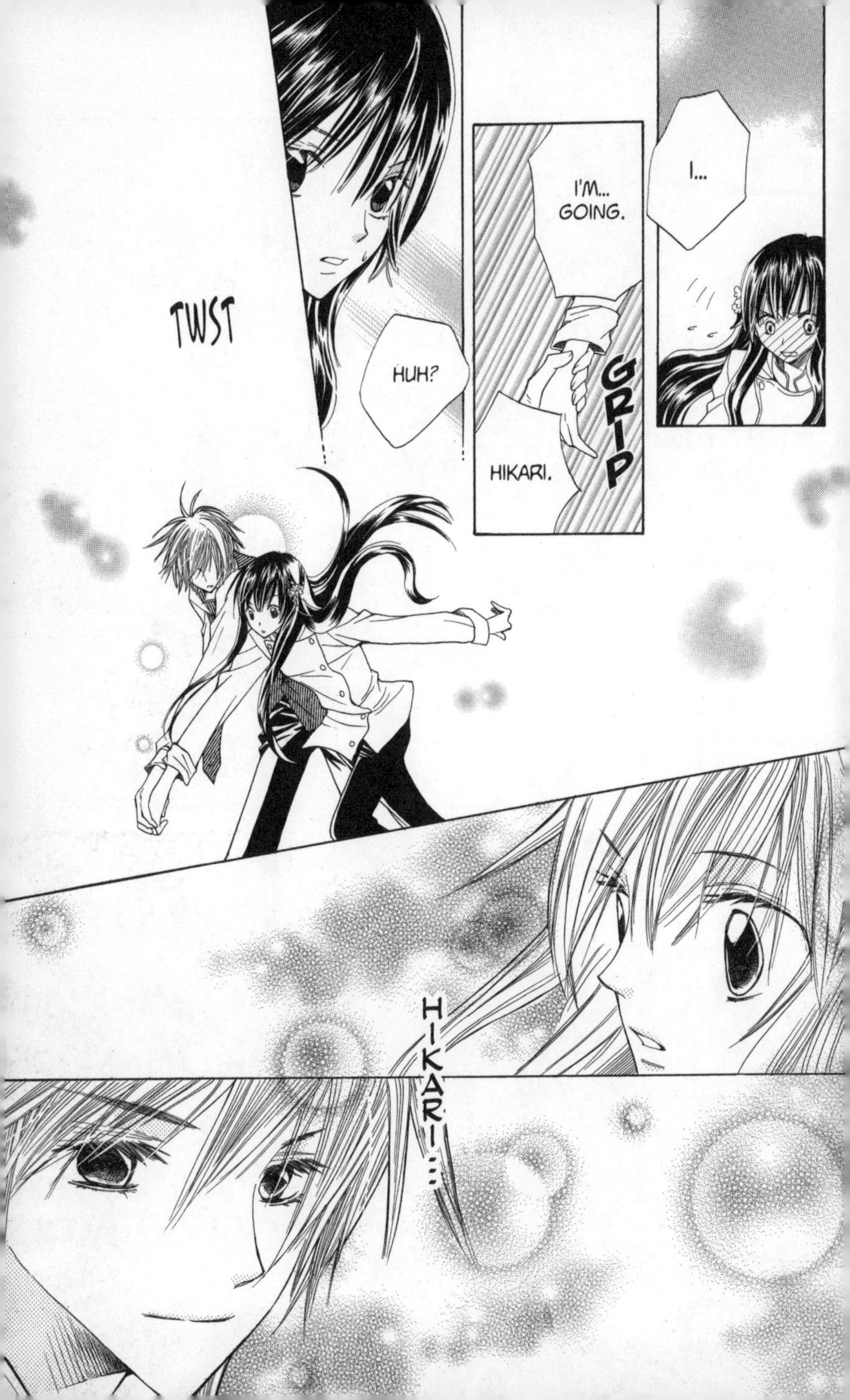
I...
I'M... GOING.
HIKARI.
GRIP
HUH?
TWST
HIKARI...

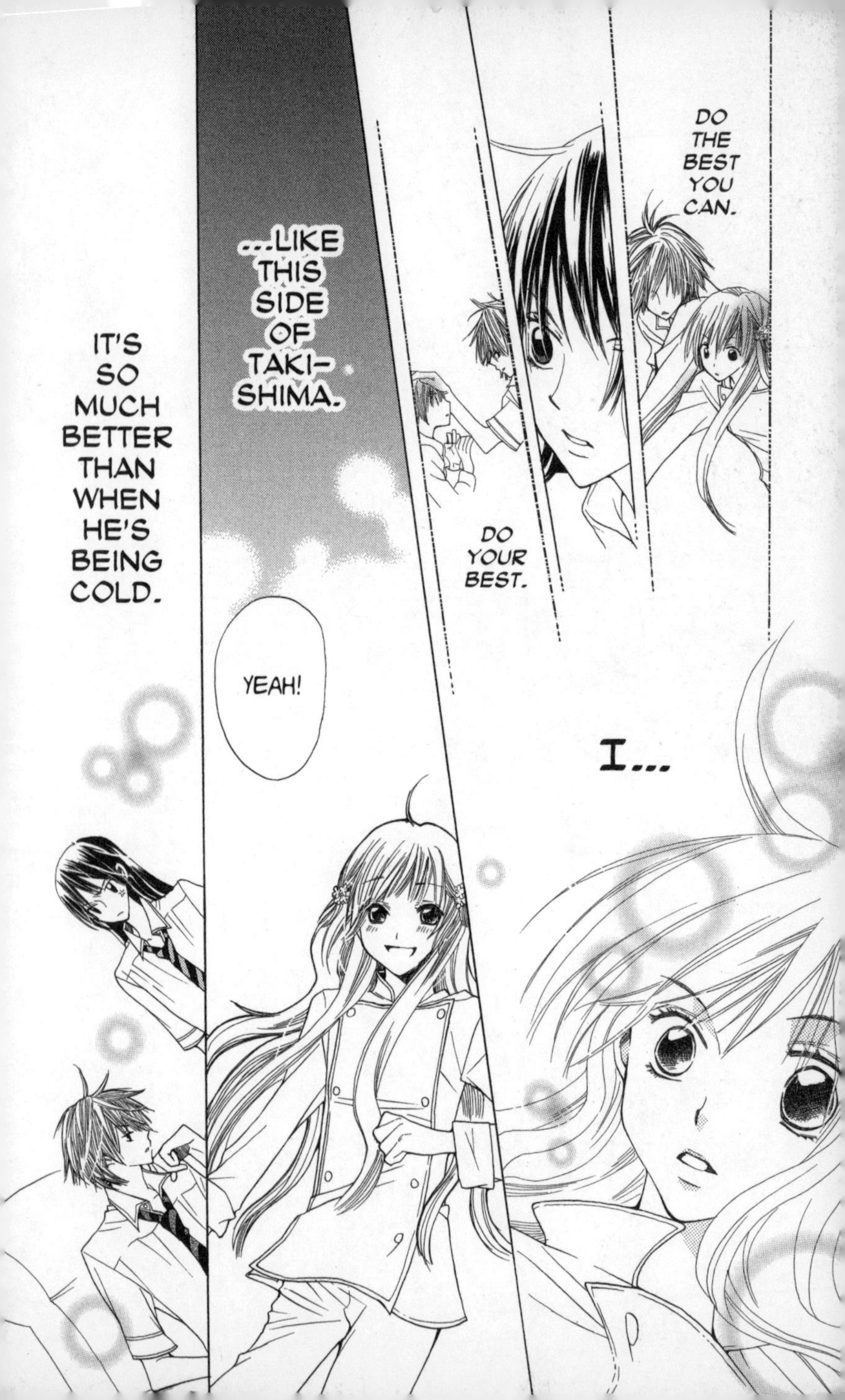
DO THE BEST YOU CAN.
DO YOUR BEST.
I...
...LIKE THIS SIDE OF TAKI-SHIMA.
YEAH!
IT'S SO MUCH BETTER THAN WHEN HE'S BEING COLD.

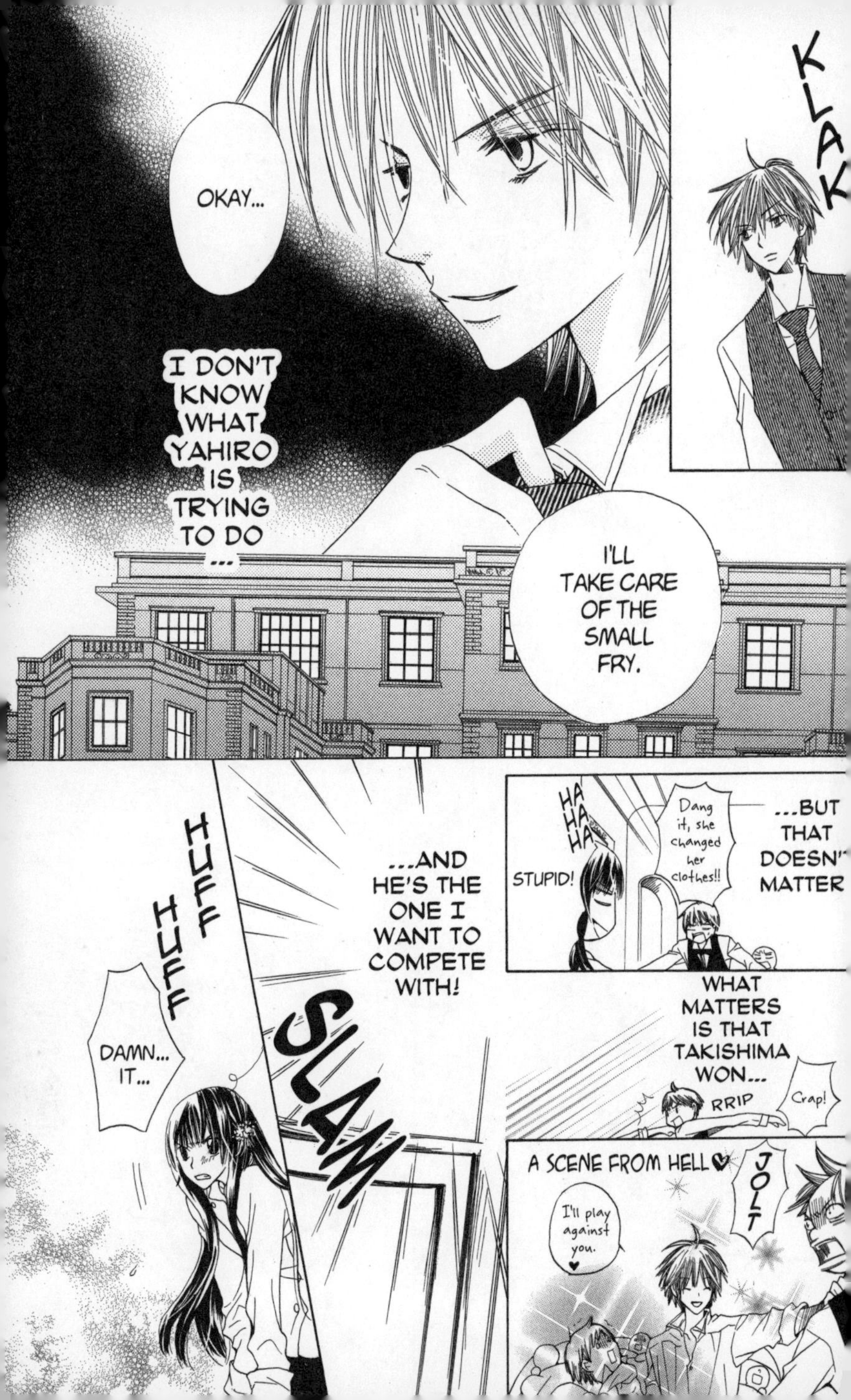
KLAK
OKAY...
I'LL TAKE CARE OF THE SMALL FRY.
I DON'T KNOW WHAT YAHIRO IS TRYING TO DO...
...BUT THAT DOESN'T MATTER
Dang it, she changed her clothes!!
HA HA HA
STUPID!
WHAT MATTERS IS THAT TAKISHIMA WON...
Crap!
RRIP
A SCENE FROM HELL
JOLT
I'll play against you.
...AND HE'S THE ONE I WANT TO COMPETE WITH!
HUFF HUFF
SLAM
DAMN... IT...

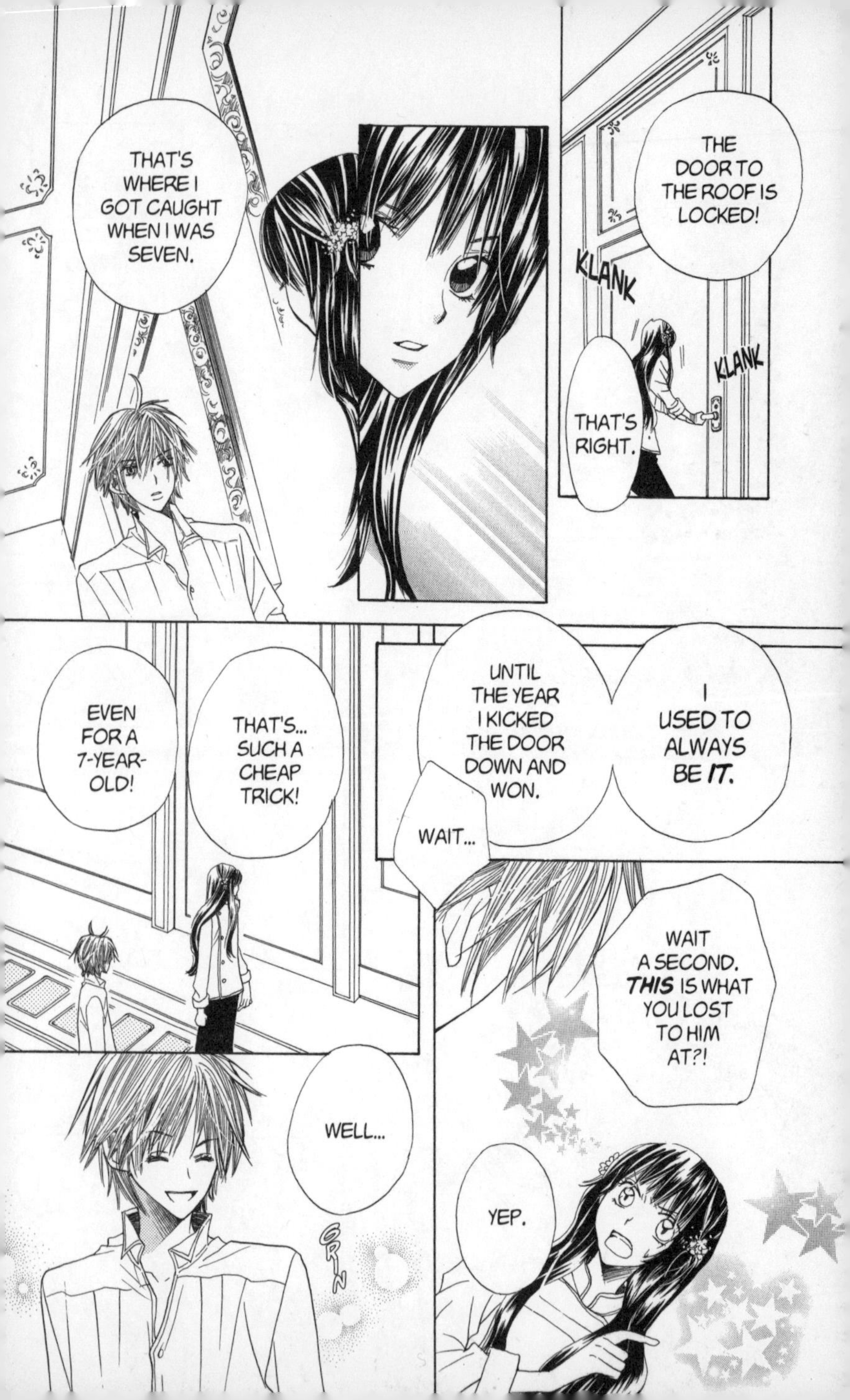
THE DOOR TO THE ROOF IS LOCKED!
KLANK
KLANK
THAT'S RIGHT.
THAT'S WHERE I GOT CAUGHT WHEN I WAS SEVEN.
I USED TO ALWAYS BE IT.
UNTIL THE YEAR I KICKED THE DOOR DOWN AND WON.
WAIT...
THAT'S... SUCH A CHEAP TRICK!
EVEN FOR A 7-YEAR-OLD!
WAIT A SECOND. THIS IS WHAT YOU LOST TO HIM AT?!
YEP.
WELL...
GRIN

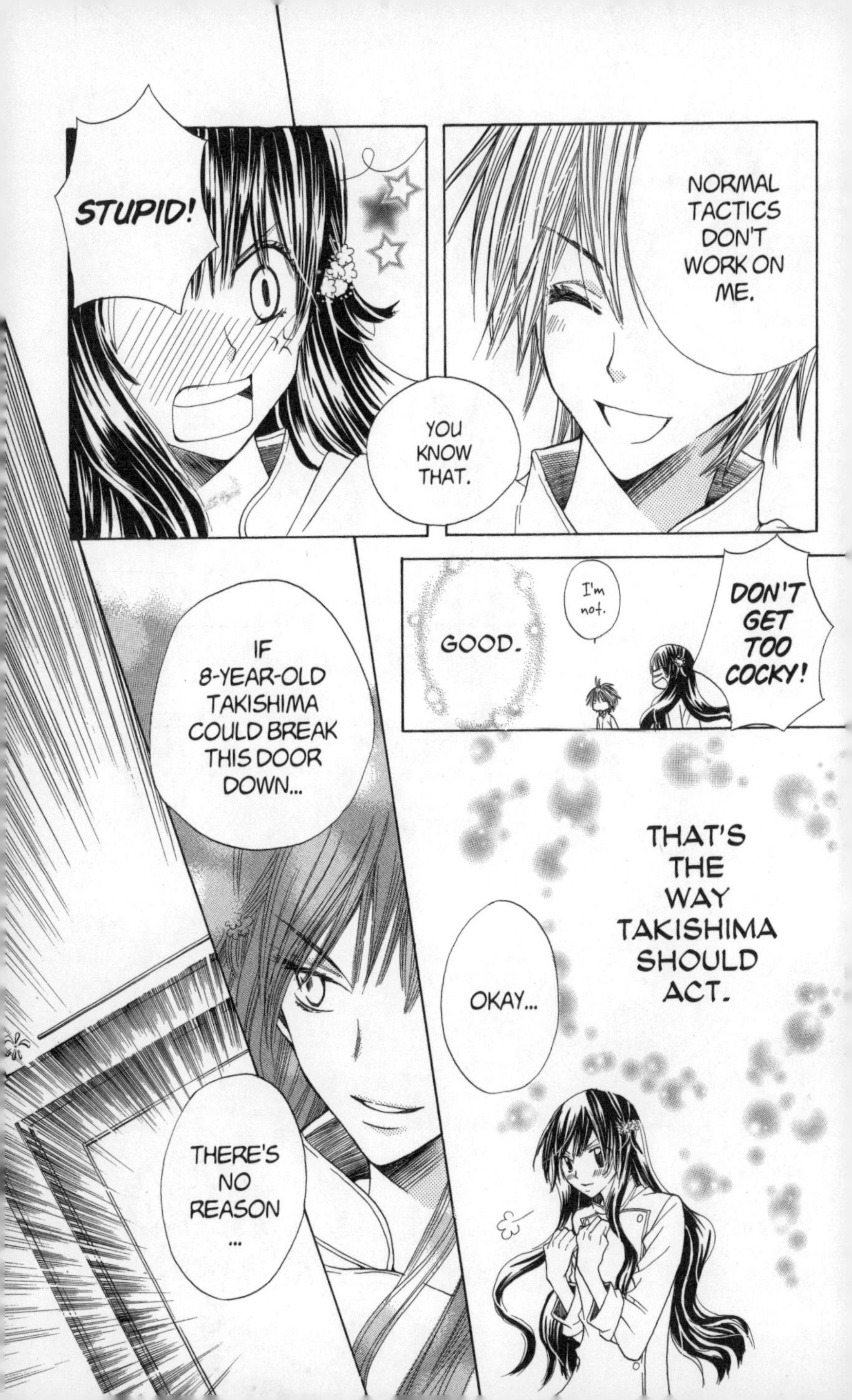
NORMAL TACTICS DON'T WORK ON ME.
YOU KNOW THAT.
STUPID!
DON'T GET TOO COCKY!
I'm not.
GOOD.
THAT'S THE WAY TAKISHIMA SHOULD ACT.
OKAY...
IF 8-YEAR-OLD TAKISHIMA COULD BREAK THIS DOOR DOWN...
THERE'S NO REASON ...

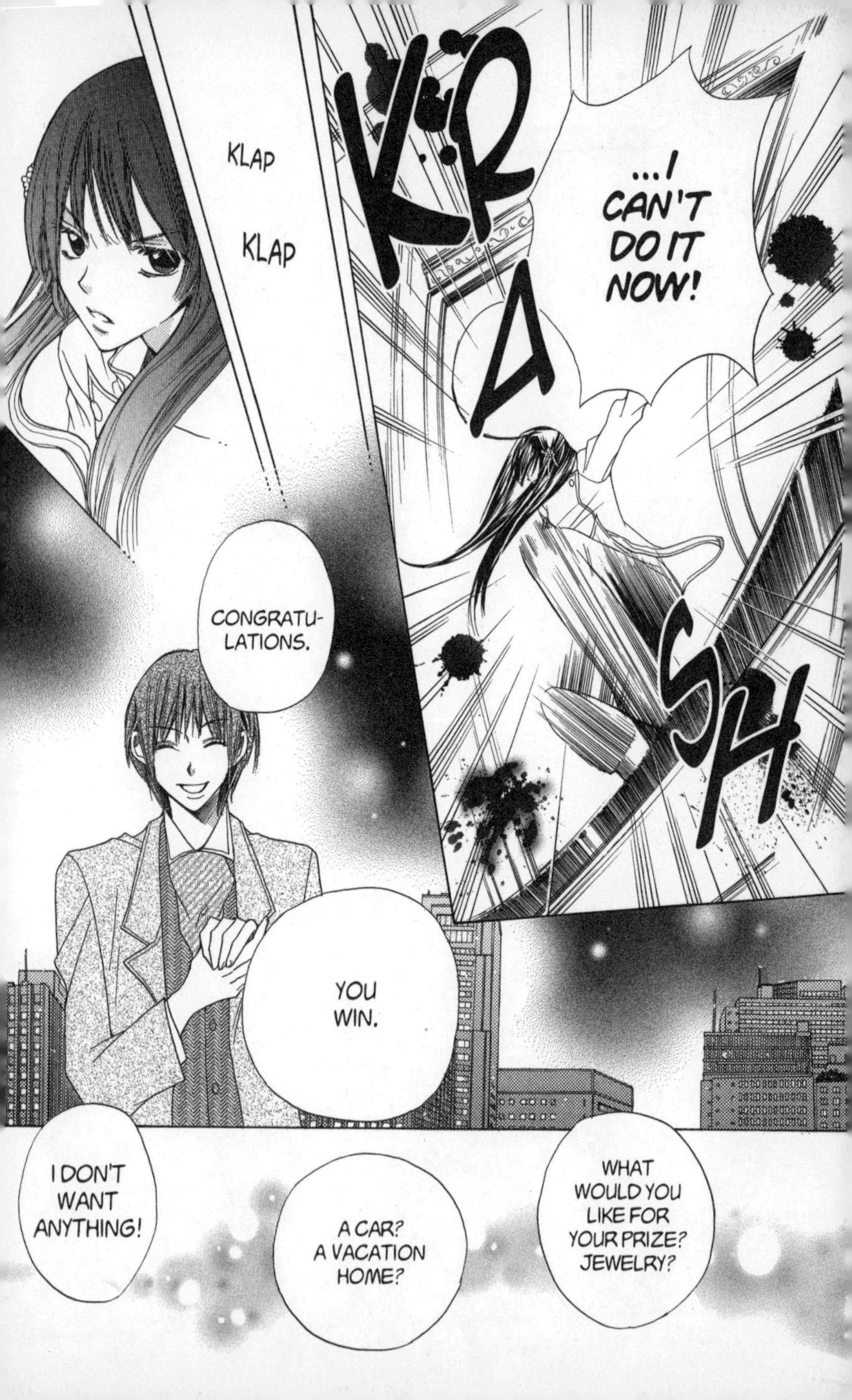
...I CAN'T DO IT NOW!
KRA
SH
KLAP
KLAP
CONGRATU-LATIONS.
YOU WIN.
WHAT WOULD YOU LIKE FOR YOUR PRIZE? JEWELRY?
A CAR? A VACATION HOME?
I DON'T WANT ANYTHING!

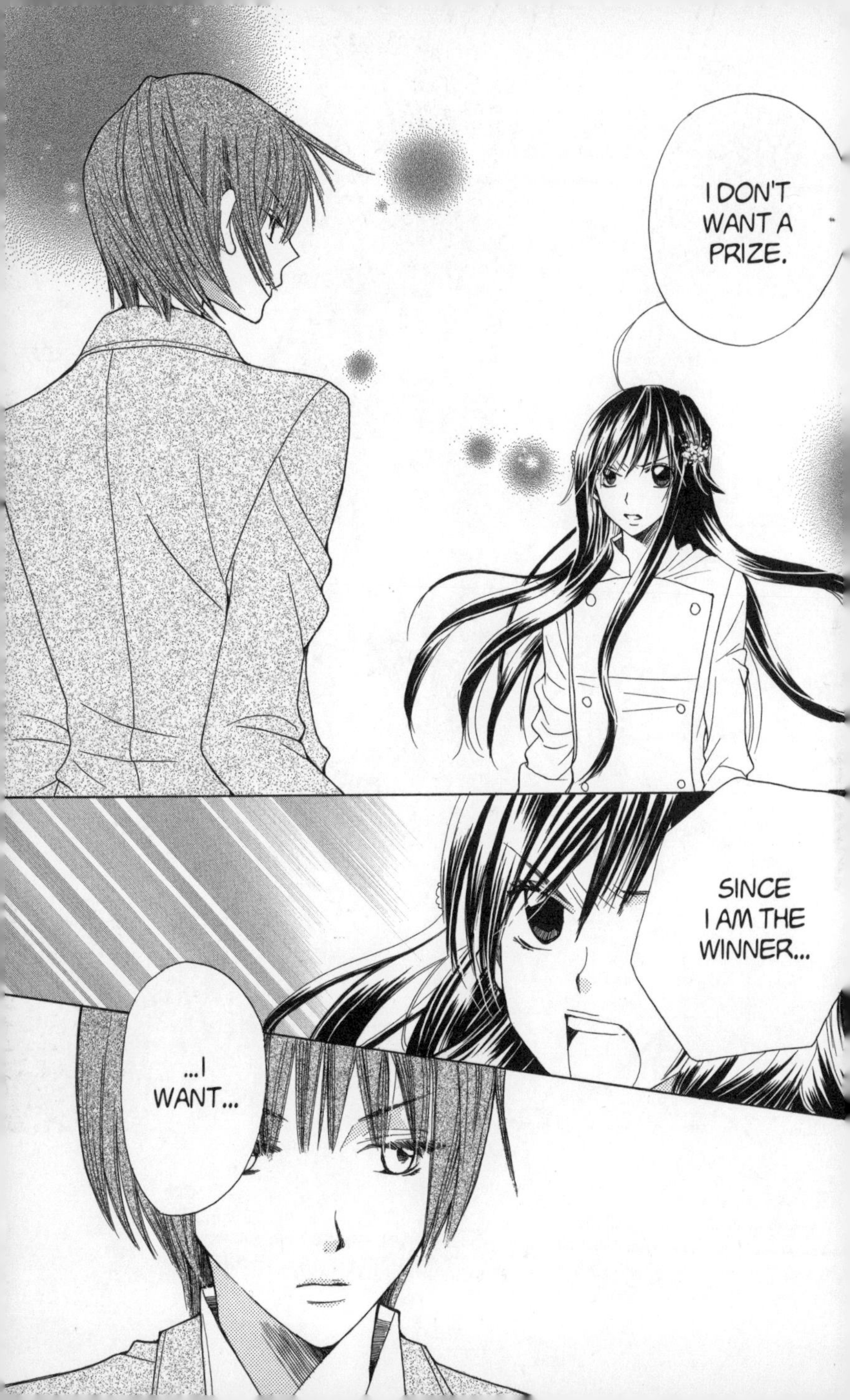
I DON'T WANT A PRIZE.
SINCE I AM THE WINNER...
...I WANT...

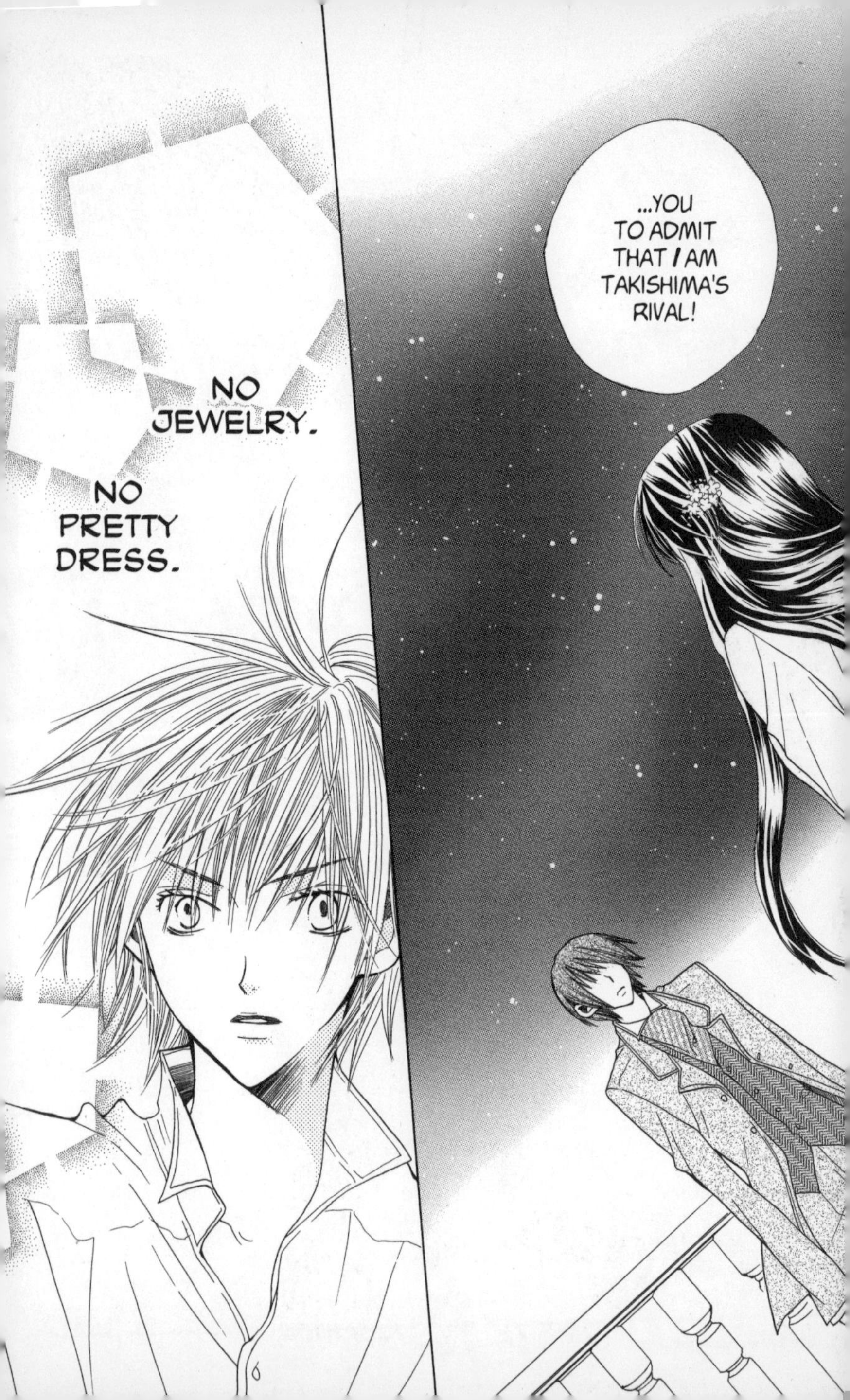
...YOU TO ADMIT THAT I AM TAKISHIMA'S RIVAL!
NO JEWELRY.
NO PRETTY DRESS.

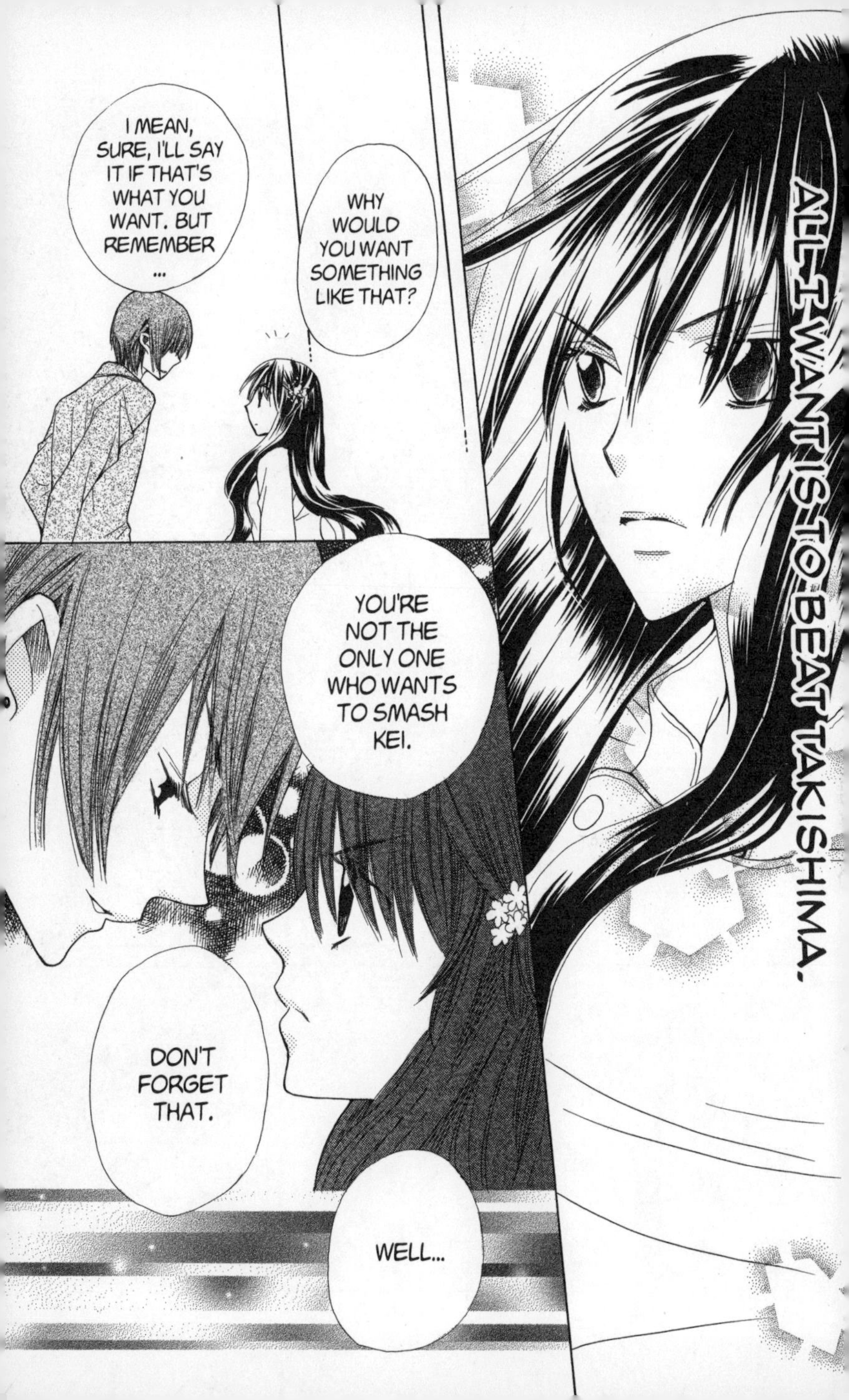
ALL I WANT IS TO BEAT TAKISHIMA.
WHY WOULD YOU WANT SOMETHING LIKE THAT?
I MEAN, SURE, I'LL SAY IT IF THAT'S WHAT YOU WANT. BUT REMEMBER ...
YOU'RE NOT THE ONLY ONE WHO WANTS TO SMASH KEI.
DON'T FORGET THAT.
WELL...

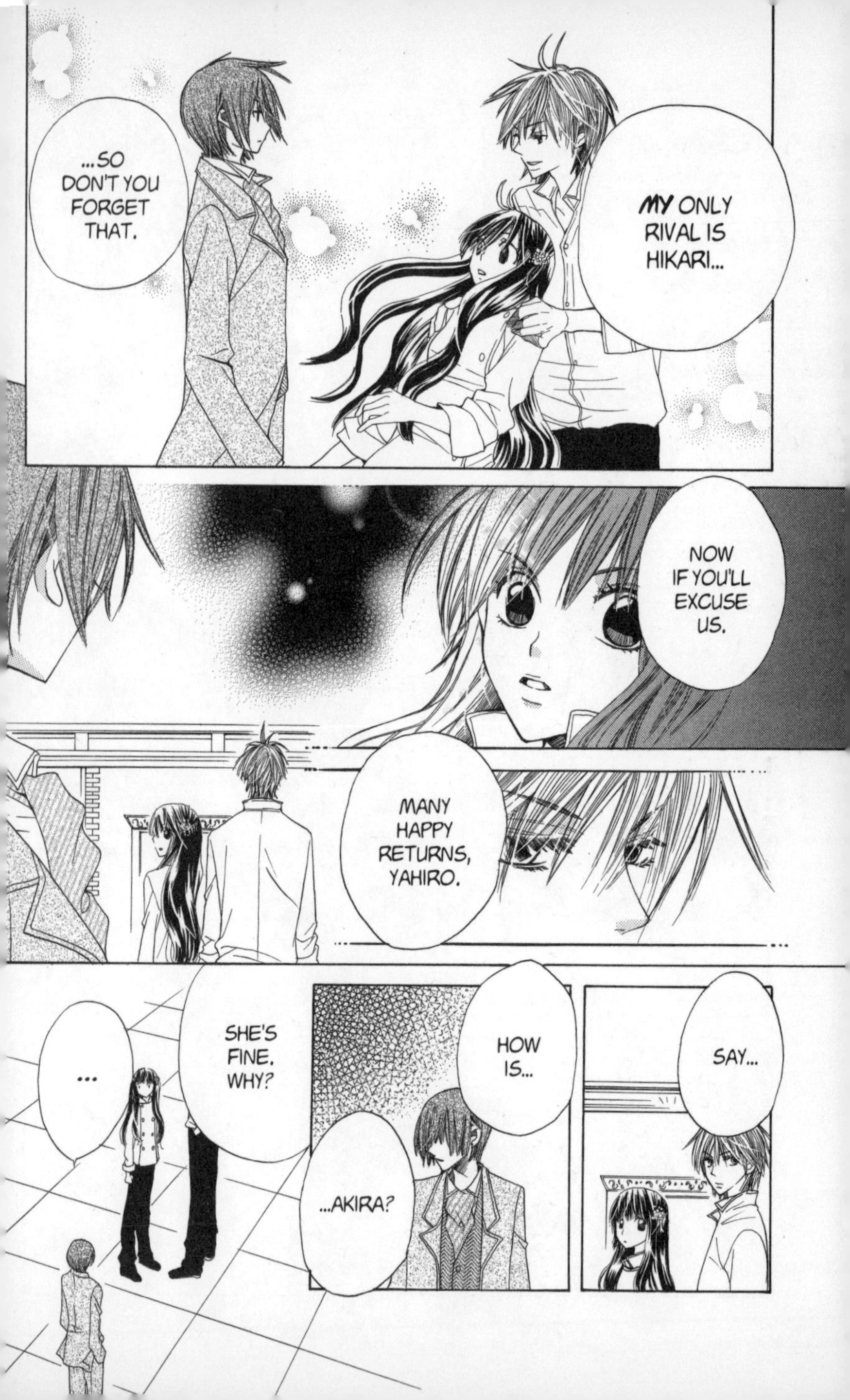
MY ONLY RIVAL IS HIKARI...
...SO DON'T YOU FORGET THAT.
NOW IF YOU'LL EXCUSE US.
MANY HAPPY RETURNS, YAHIRO.
SAY...
HOW IS...
...AKIRA?
SHE'S FINE. WHY?
...

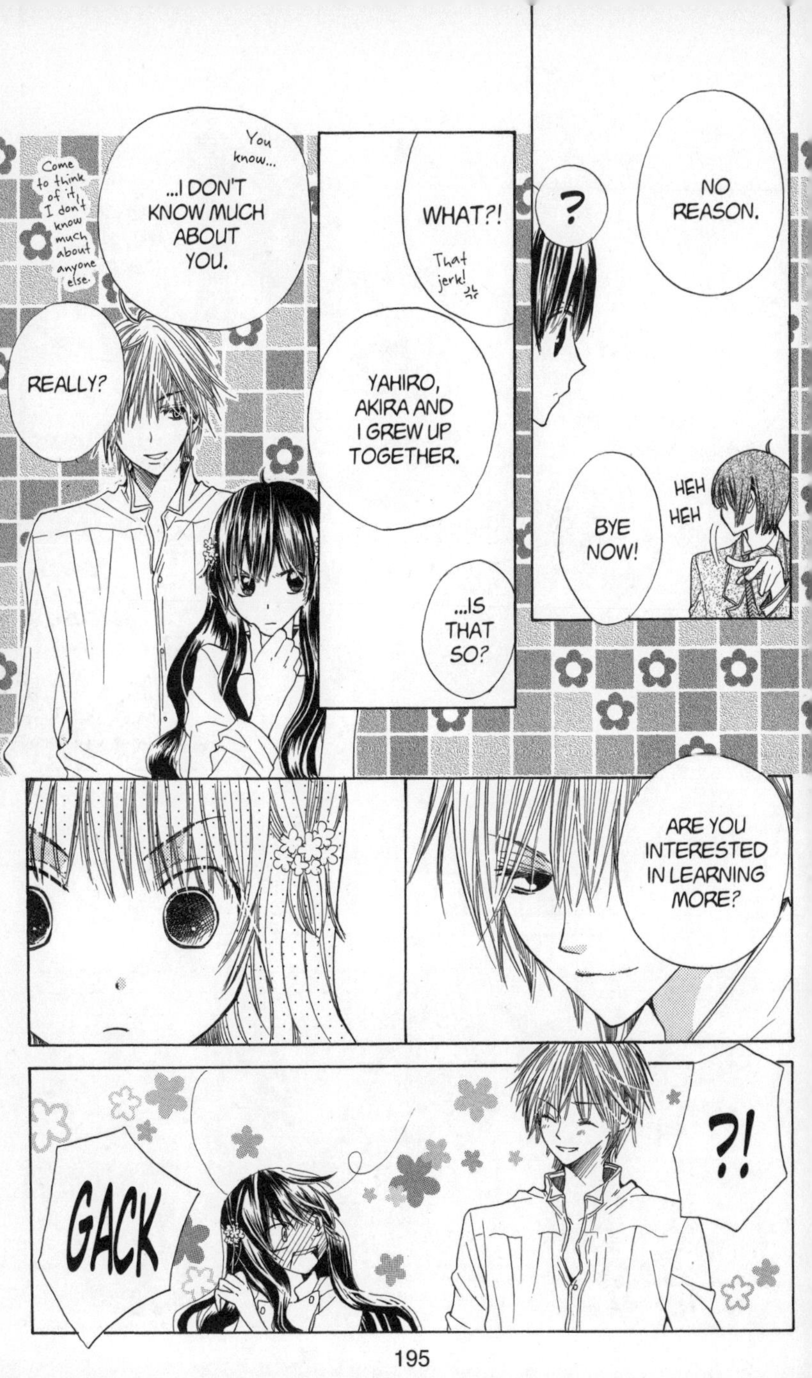
NO REASON.
?
HEH HEH
BYE NOW!
WHAT?!
That jerk!
YAHIRO, AKIRA AND I GREW UP TOGETHER.
...IS THAT SO?
You know...
...I DON'T KNOW MUCH ABOUT YOU.
Come to think of it, I don't know much about anyone else.
REALLY?
ARE YOU INTERESTED IN LEARNING MORE?
?!
GACK

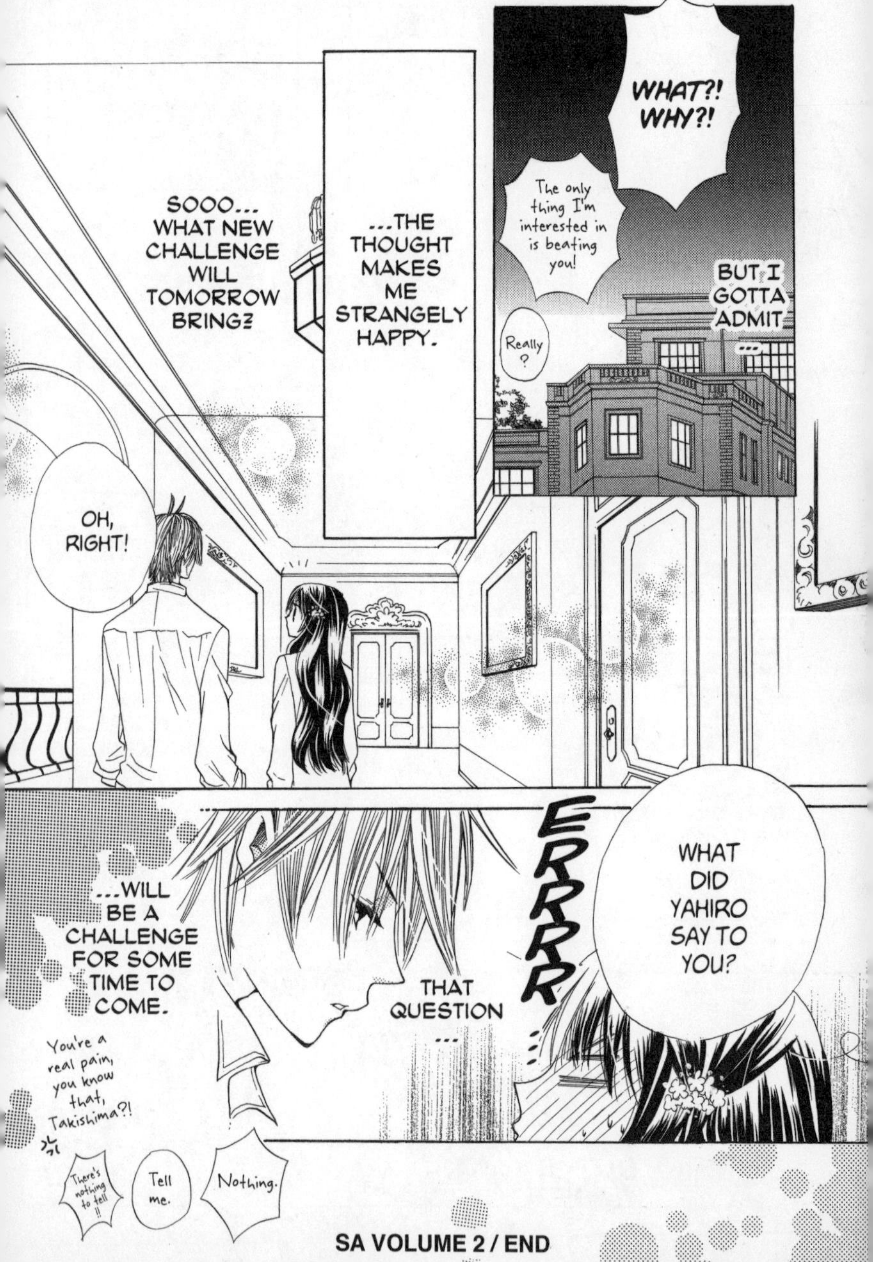

WHAT?! WHY?!
The only thing I'm interested in is beating you!
BUT I GOTTA ADMIT...
Really?
...THE THOUGHT MAKES ME STRANGELY HAPPY.
SOOO... WHAT NEW CHALLENGE WILL TOMORROW BRING?
OH, RIGHT!
WHAT DID YAHIRO SAY TO YOU?
ERRRR
THAT QUESTION...
...WILL BE A CHALLENGE FOR SOME TIME TO COME.
You're a real pain, you know that, Takishima?!
Nothing.
Tell me.
There's nothing to tell!!

SA VOLUME 2 / END

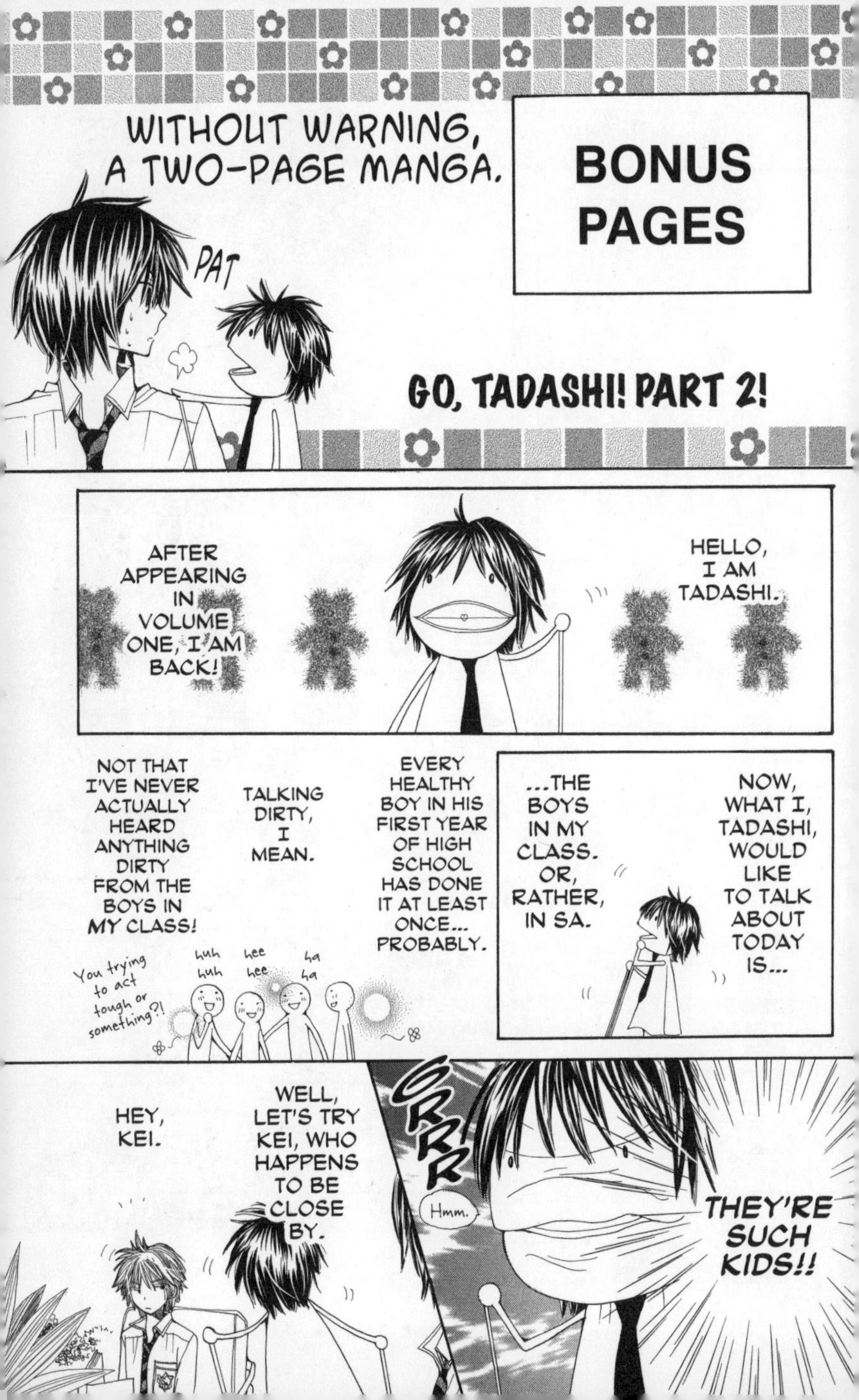
BONUS PAGES
WITHOUT WARNING, A TWO-PAGE MANGA.
PAT
GO, TADASHI! PART 2!
HELLO, I AM TADASHI.
AFTER APPEARING IN VOLUME ONE, I AM BACK!
NOW, WHAT I, TADASHI, WOULD LIKE TO TALK ABOUT TODAY IS...
...THE BOYS IN MY CLASS. OR, RATHER, IN SA.
EVERY HEALTHY BOY IN HIS FIRST YEAR OF HIGH SCHOOL HAS DONE IT AT LEAST ONCE... PROBABLY.
TALKING DIRTY, I MEAN.
NOT THAT I'VE NEVER ACTUALLY HEARD ANYTHING DIRTY FROM THE BOYS IN MY CLASS!
ha ha
hee hee
huh huh
You trying to act tough or something?!
THEY'RE SUCH KIDS!!
Hmm.
GRRR
WELL, LET'S TRY KEI, WHO HAPPENS TO BE CLOSE BY.
HEY, KEI.

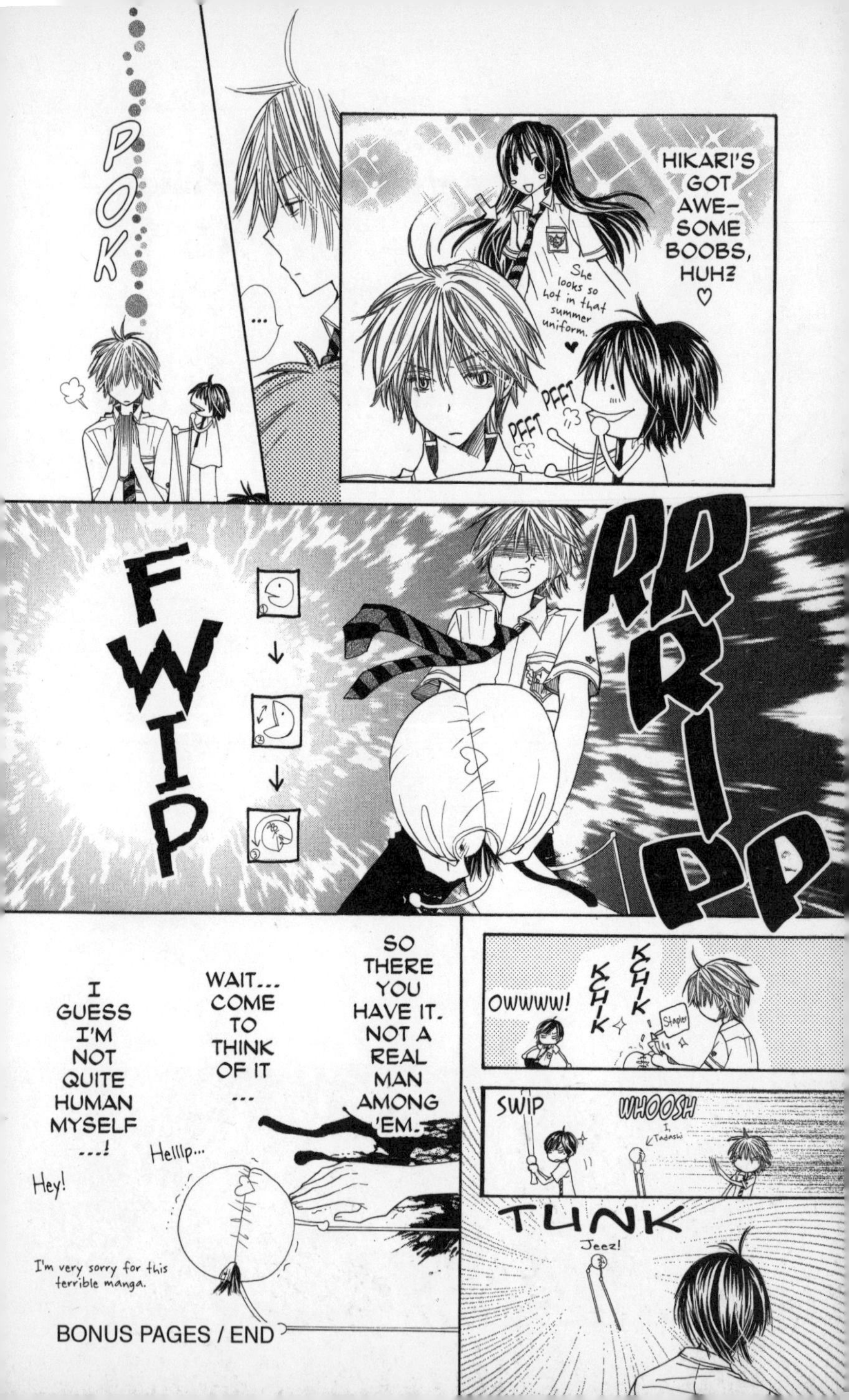
HIKARI'S GOT AWE-SOME BOOBS, HUH? ♡
She looks so hot in that summer uniform. ♥
PFFT
PFFT
...
POK
RRRIPP
FWIP
KCHIK
KCHIK
Stapler
OWWWW!
WHOOSH
I, Tadashi
SWIP
TUNK
Jeez!
SO THERE YOU HAVE IT. NOT A REAL MAN AMONG 'EM.
WAIT... COME TO THINK OF IT ...
I GUESS I'M NOT QUITE HUMAN MYSELF ...!
Helllp...
Hey!
I'm very sorry for this terrible manga.
BONUS PAGES / END

Maki Minami is from Saitama
prefecture in Japan. She debuted
in 2001 with *Kanata no Ao*
(Faraway Blue). Her other works
include *Kimi wa Girlfriend*
(You're My Girlfriend), *Mainichi
ga Takaramono* (Every Day Is a
Treasure) and *Yuki Atataka*
(Warm Winter). *S•A* is her current
series in Japan's *Hana to Yume*
magazine.

S•A

Vol. 2
The Shojo Beat Manga Edition

STORY & ART BY
MAKI MINAMI

English Adaptation/Amanda Hubbard
Translation/JN Productions
Touch-up Art & Lettering/Rina Mapa
Design/Izumi Hirayama
Editor/Carol Fox

Editor in Chief, Books/Alvin Lu
Editor in Chief, Magazines/Marc Weidenbaum
VP, Publishing Licensing/Rika Inouye
VP, Sales & Product Marketing/Gonzalo Ferreyra
VP, Creative/Linda Espinosa
Publisher/Hyoe Narita

Printed in Canada

Published by VIZ Media, LLC
P.O. Box 77010
San Francisco, CA 94107

Shojo Beat Manga Edition
10 9 8 7 6 5 4 3 2
First printing, January 2008
Second printing, September 2008

www.viz.com   store.viz.com

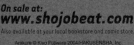

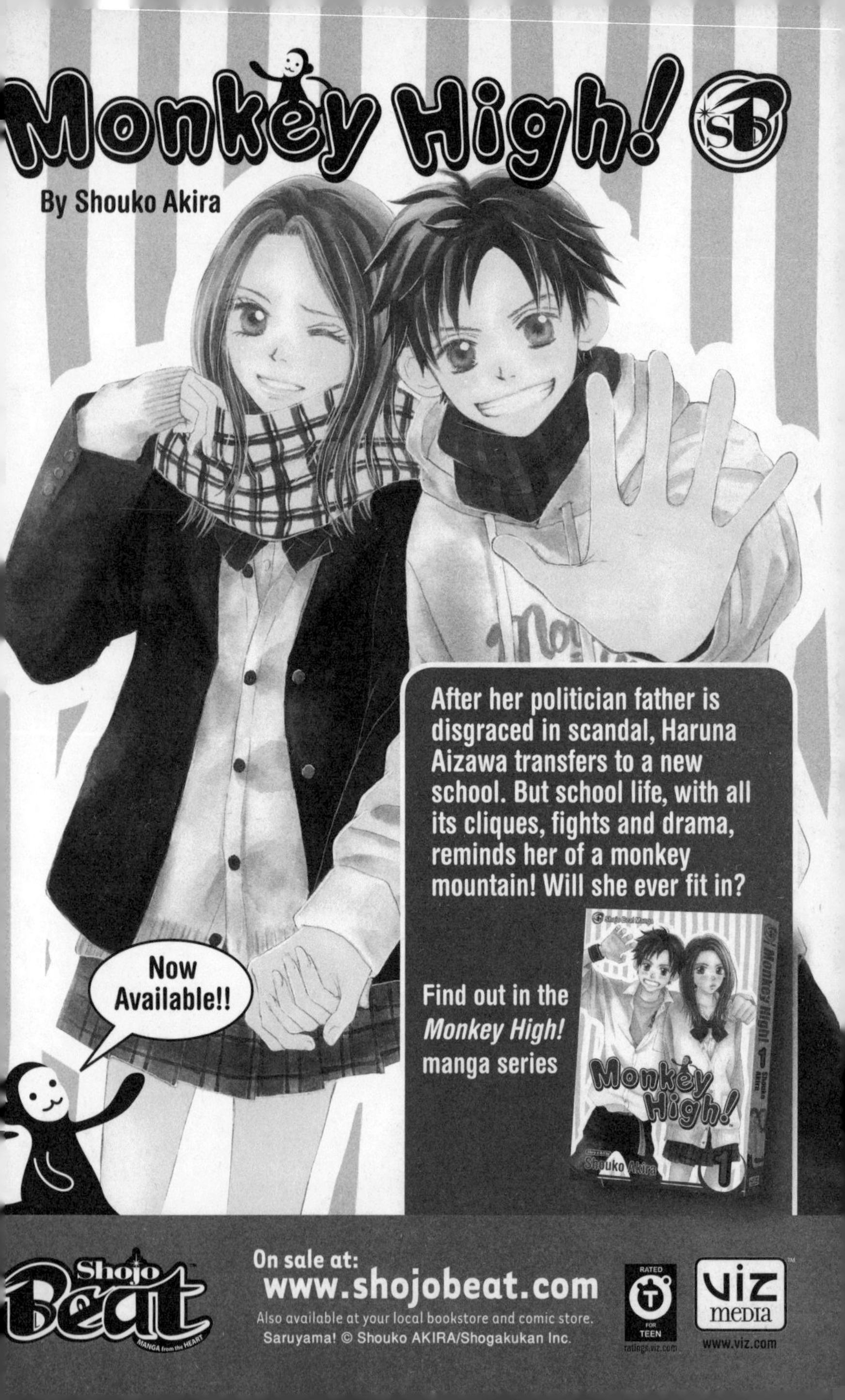
Monkey High!
By Shouko Akira
After her politician father is disgraced in scandal, Haruna Aizawa transfers to a new school. But school life, with all its cliques, fights and drama, reminds her of a monkey mountain! Will she ever fit in?
Now Available!!
Find out in the Monkey High! manga series
Monkey High!
Shouko Akira
1
Shojo Beat
MANGA from the HEART
On sale at:
www.shojobeat.com
Also available at your local bookstore and comic store.
Saruyama! © Shouko AKIRA/Shogakukan Inc.
RATED
T
FOR TEEN
ratings.viz.com
VIZ media
www.viz.com

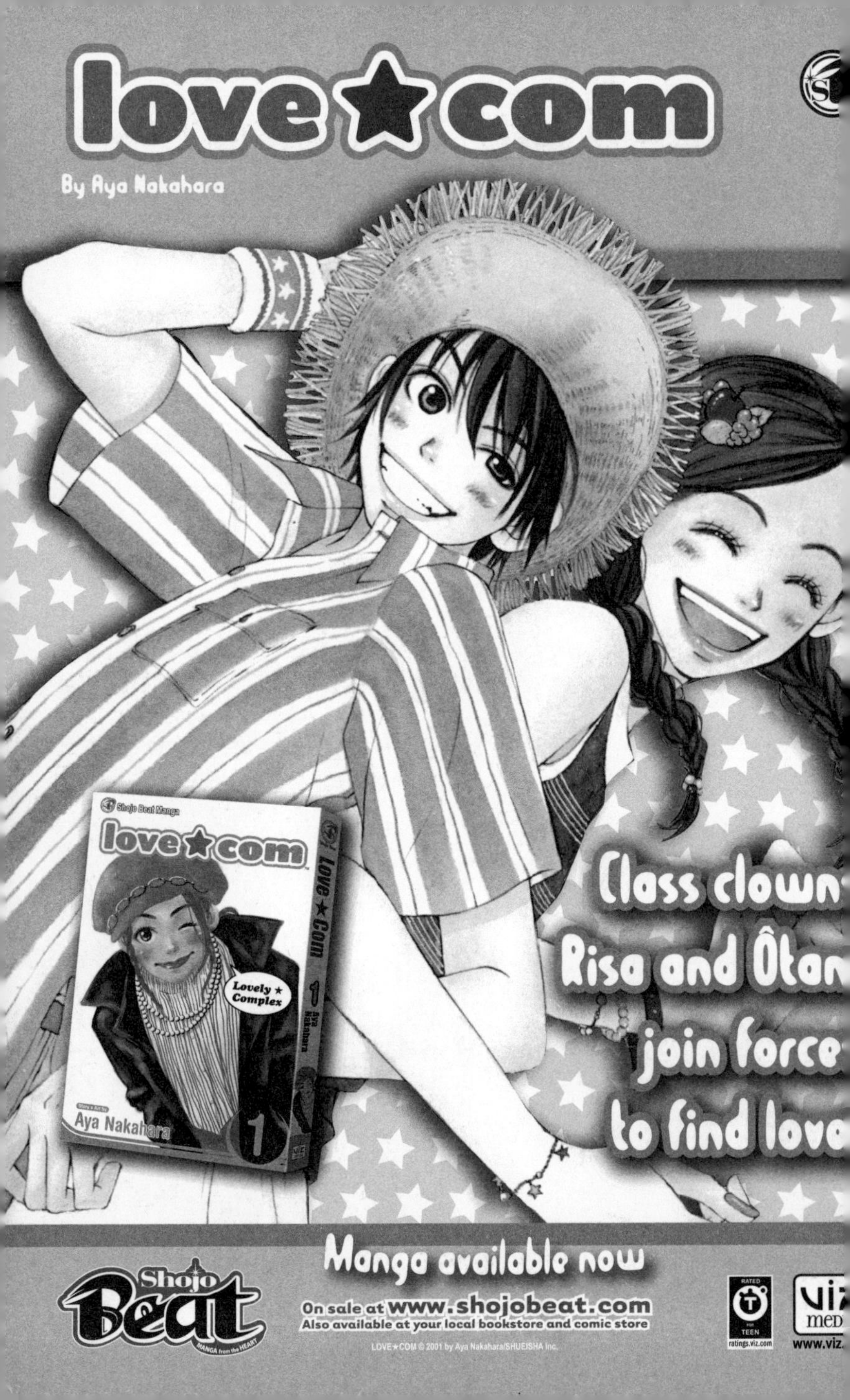

love★com
By Aya Nakahara
Shojo Beat Manga
love★com
Lovely ★ Complex
Story + Art by
Aya Nakahara
1
Class clown
Risa and Ôtan
join force
to find lov
Manga available now
Shojo Beat
MANGA from the HEART
On sale at www.shojobeat.com
Also available at your local bookstore and comic store
LOVE★COM © 2001 by Aya Nakahara/SHUEISHA Inc.
RATED T FOR TEEN
ratings.viz.com

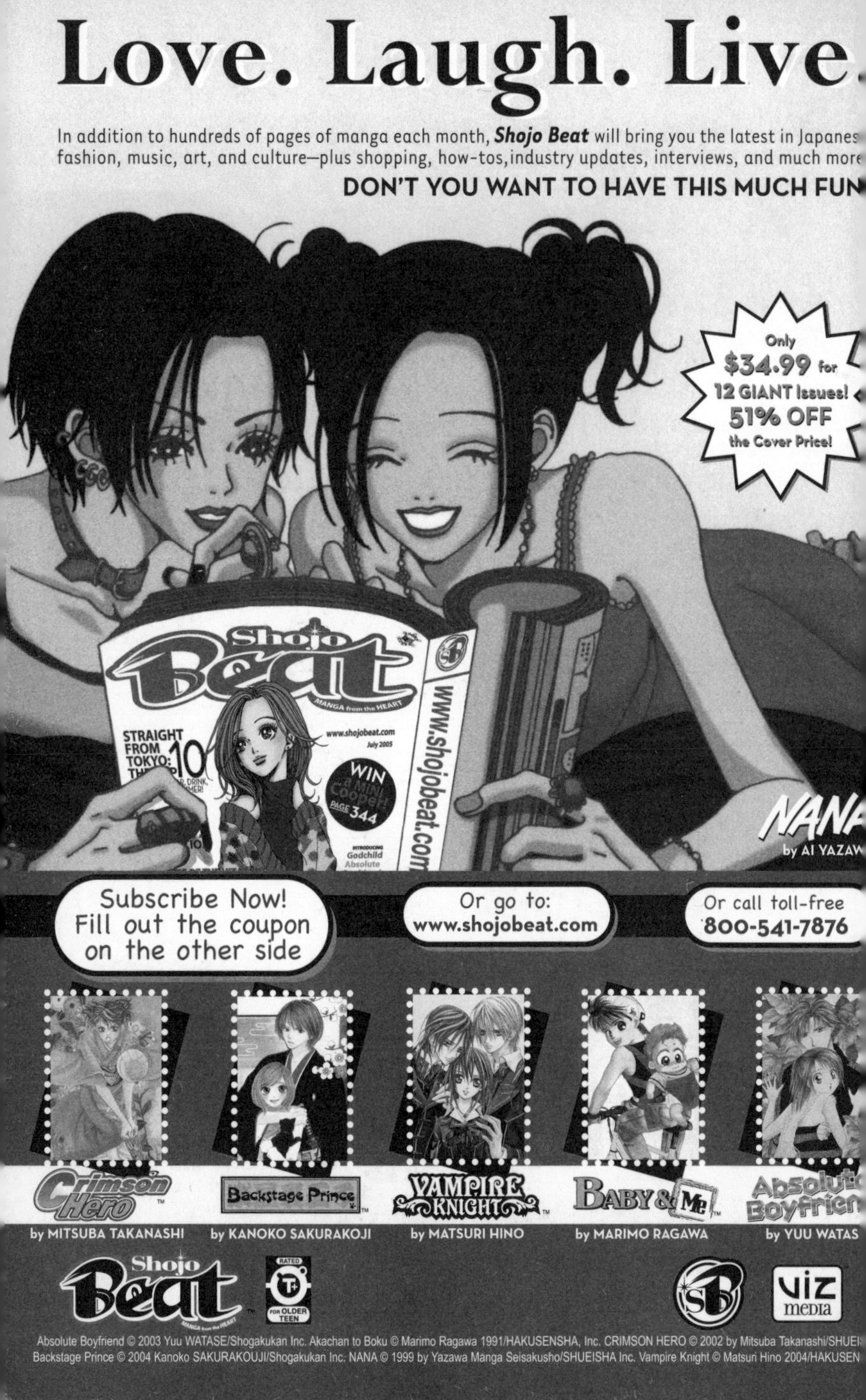
Love. Laugh. Live.
In addition to hundreds of pages of manga each month, Shojo Beat will bring you the latest in Japanes
fashion, music, art, and culture—plus shopping, how-tos, industry updates, interviews, and much more
DON'T YOU WANT TO HAVE THIS MUCH FUN
Only $34.99 for 12 GIANT Issues! 51% OFF the Cover Price!
Shojo Beat
MANGA from the HEART
www.shojobeat.com
July 2005
STRAIGHT FROM TOKYO:
WIN a MINI Cooper! PAGE 344
INTRODUCING Godchild Absolute
www.shojobeat.com
NANA by AI YAZAW
Subscribe Now! Fill out the coupon on the other side
Or go to: www.shojobeat.com
Or call toll-free 800-541-7876
Crimson Hero™ by MITSUBA TAKANASHI
Backstage Prince™ by KANOKO SAKURAKOJI
VAMPIRE KNIGHT™ by MATSURI HINO
BABY & Me™ by MARIMO RAGAWA
Absolute Boyfrien by YUU WATAS
Shojo Beat™ MANGA from the HEART
RATED T+ FOR OLDER TEEN
viz media
Absolute Boyfriend © 2003 Yuu WATASE/Shogakukan Inc. Akachan to Boku © Marimo Ragawa 1991/HAKUSENSHA, Inc. CRIMSON HERO © 2002 by Mitsuba Takanashi/SHUEI
Backstage Prince © 2004 Kanoko SAKURAKOUJI/Shogakukan Inc. NANA © 1999 by Yazawa Manga Seisakusho/SHUEISHA Inc. Vampire Knight © Matsuri Hino 2004/HAKUSEN